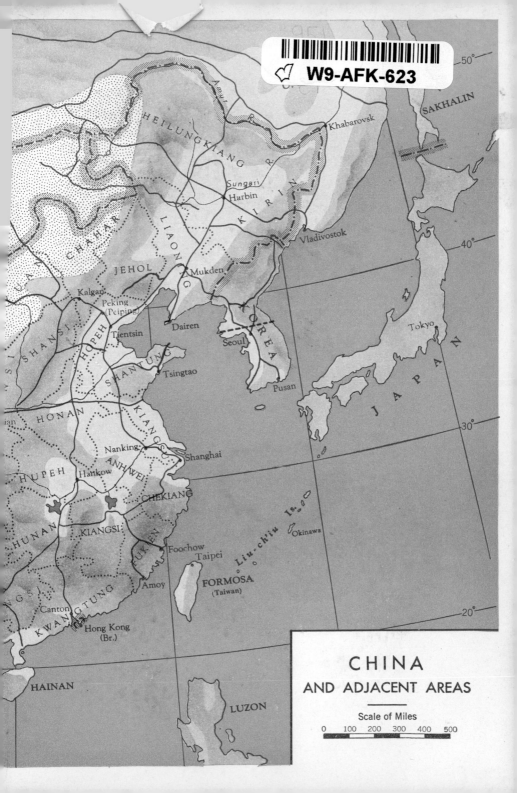

CHINA
AND ADJACENT AREAS

Scale of Miles

0   100   200   300   400   500

The United States and CHINA

The United States and CHINA

NEW EDITION
COMPLETELY REVISED AND ENLARGED

John King Fairbank

HARVARD UNIVERSITY PRESS

Cambridge, Massachusetts

1958

For My Mother
LORENA KING FAIRBANK

Contents

Maps

Introduction
To the New Edition

NO PROBLEM facing American policy-makers in the period since the last war has been so obscured by public emotion and ignorance as that of our relations with China. Characteristically, the very lack of basic knowledge about China — not to speak of the ineffective dissemination in schools and elsewhere of such knowledge as we possessed — has provoked emotional extremism and intolerant certitude to the point where calm and rational views of this question have been rare, difficult, and at times hazardous. Meanwhile the latest Chinese population estimate, revealing a possible population of a billion people before the end of the century, has given a new and troubling dimension to our China problem. It is true that vast difficulties face the Chinese Communists in their attempt to possess themselves of modern technology, but the possibility that they may one day do so could pose problems of staggering implication.

Mr. Fairbank laments our ignorance and our subjectivity. In the 1948 edition of this book he warned: "The Soviet Union and the United States can exert a major influence in Chinese affairs, in the long run, only insofar as they understand the tides of social change in China and work with them." He has himself labored long and effectively to mitigate this ignorance, both as writer and teacher. An impressive group of books on China in the past century by various students of his will be evident in the bibliography at the end of this book to all those who are familiar with his *atelier* at Harvard — which currently includes a coordinated group researching on various problems on recent China.

In its first edition, the present work was greeted by Brooks

Atkinson as "The best book on China in our time," and by a series of eminently competent specialists in the same vein. In this revision, Mr. Fairbank has not only rewritten and expanded earlier portions, but has also widened his subject to include an analysis of the controversial character of the Communist regime in China.

This new regime Mr. Fairbank has sketched in broad lines — wisely, those will agree who are familiar with the inadequate and somewhat random documentation which manages to filter through the bamboo curtain. "Even Mao Tse-tung, lacking statistical services like ours, must often wonder what is actually going on," the author comments. This sprawling new Communist society is pushing on to create — through forced-draft industrialization and the ruthless concomitant collectivization of agriculture — a state hopefully capable of playing an increasingly significant role in the already perilous game of power politics of our day. It is seeking at the same time to find solutions for the complex social problems of an archaic society moving at high speed into the setting of a modern world. We need, however, to see the quest for the achievement of both objectives as severely hampered by the fact that China began her ascent far behind the 1928 per capita production position of the Soviets, and faced with far greater and faster growing population pressures on her food supply.

As an historian of China's past, Mr. Fairbank has examined the present regime steadily in depth — indeed, in the vast depth of three thousand years of history. In this broad-ranging and often brilliant analysis, he has situated the contemporary Communist regime, revealing its persisting and sometimes curious debts to China's past, which he has been careful to contrast with its significant parallel debts to the modern Western world. Mr. Fairbank's analysis has not only depth but width: it reaches out for the helping hand of the anthropologist, the economist, the demographer, the sociologist — unobtrusively and effectively, an encouraging example of the much abused "interpenetration" of the social sciences at its best.

The future of relations between China and the United States, Mr. Fairbank sees studded with intractable difficulties. As in the cycles of the past, the Chinese are once again seeking to use one "barbarian" against another — this time the Soviets against the United States. And, with the full range of Communist controls at their disposal, the Chinese leadership has persistently fostered a massive campaign of anti-Americanism. Unfortunately Americans, with a free press and a nominal opportunity for full discussion of the issues, have responded only too consistently in a similarly uninformed and emotional vein.

Mr. Fairbank is indeed forthright and even devastating in his counsel to his own countrymen to forsake the "fatal flaws" in their response to the Chinese revolution. We have been content to believe that the cause of the Communist revolution in China was a plot in Moscow or treachery in Washington; we have assumed that Chinese values must somehow become the same as ours; in our reliance on material, especially military, means in our foreign policy, we have neglected intellectual, cultural, and psychological means. All these attitudes are only too frustratingly reminiscent of American reactions toward Soviet Russia and toward various of the so-called underdeveloped areas in recent years. At a time when certain of our misconceptions of the Soviets have been subject to the necessary solvent of a kind of national introspection, one might hope that similar doubts about our tenaciously held clichés respecting China might also assail us. There is no better way to begin this process than with a reading of Mr. Fairbank's courageous and penetrating book.

DONALD C. McKAY

May 1958

Introduction
To the First Edition

THE HARVARD UNIVERSITY PRESS can offer the readers of its Foreign Policy Library no more timely or important book than John King Fairbank's *The United States and China.*

During and since the years of the second World War American public opinion has been often confused, and not infrequently altogether baffled, in its effort to understand the course of the developments which are taking place in China and to comprehend the reasons for the innumerable difficulties that have arisen in the conduct of our relations with China.

The American people are being told by a large number of self-proclaimed "experts," only a few of whom have actually lived and worked in China, that the Government of the United States should pursue a policy designed solely to support and strengthen the Nationalist Government of the Kuomintang Party under the leadership of Generalissimo Chiang Kai-shek, and that unless such a policy is vigorously followed China will, within a short time, become a mere satrapy of the Soviet Union.

At the same moment, they are being advised by a smaller, but by no means less vociferous, group that the Communist government which has established itself in Northern China is a purely autonomous regime, by no means subservient to Moscow, and that this government if given the opportunity without foreign interference, can find the means of fashioning purely Chinese solutions for many of the economic and social ills from which the Chinese people have so long suffered.

As so frequently occurs in ideological controversies of this character, both sides to this continuing debate tend to be blinded by their predispositions and by their own individual prejudices. But it can, I think, be safely asserted that those who speak or write as though the 400 millions of the Chinese people could be used today as the servile instrument of the Soviet Union, or of an American policy of containment of the Soviet Union, are offering the people of the United States no objective appraisal of the facts of present international life. The Chinese people are awake. An increasing number are fully aware of their latent power. Nationalism is daily becoming, as it is throughout the Far East, a more potent factor in shaping human destinies.

The fundamental truth which public opinion in the United States should bear in mind in any attempt to grasp the underlying realities in the relations between China and the United States is set forth by Professor Fairbank in this passage of his book:

Chinese society is very different from our own. We cannot hope to succeed in our policy toward China unless we take account of this difference. Consequently, one of our worst enemies is wishful thinking, subjectivism and sentiment. Another is plain ignorance. We court disaster if we let our patriotic defensive measures against Russian expansion, or a purely doctrinaire anti-communism, dictate our China policy. Our policy must take full account of China's own process of social change . . . We cannot remake Chinese society in our own image. We have to go part way in the process of Sino-Western adjustment. Those of us who believe in the American century are not used to this idea. But the Chinese people, when forced to it, will fight for Chinese ideals just as bitterly as we will fight for American ideals.

There can be no doubt that "wishful thinking" and "plain ignorance" have for many generations gravely prejudiced our relations with the greatest nation of the Far East. The concept that we can "remake Chinese society in our own image" has almost always made itself felt in the formulation of American policy toward China. No better example of this could be given than these words spoken to me by an American Secretary of State almost thirty years ago, after the Chinese Empire had been replaced by a Chinese Republic: "Now that the Chinese people are practicing our form of democracy they will, within a quarter of a century, solve all of their difficulties."

Some of us, and I among them, will agree wholeheartedly with Professor Fairbank's assertion that "the Chinese Revolution is fundamentally a matter for the Chinese people to decide." We will also agree with him that the Chinese Communists differ from the Communists of other nationalities in their circumstances rather than in their ideas and that to deal with the Communist problem in China we must pay close attention to the circumstances which lead communism to flourish. For while it is obvious that for reasons of expediency the Soviet system has at times been willing to cooperate with truly democratic parties, and is at times disposed to permit a great measure of independence to local Communist organizations, there is not yet the slightest shred of evidence available which would indicate that any Communist party organization from Brazil to Indonesia, or from Chile to Denmark, is not in the last analysis subservient to the authority centralized in Moscow.

All of these fundamental questions — questions that are of increasingly vital importance to every American citizen — are taken up for full ventilation in Professor Fairbank's book. That is why a volume such as this, which gives the average American an understanding of what Chinese history really is, of what makes the Chinese political, social, and economic machine function, and of the immense contribution that the Chinese people during more than two thousand years have made to civilization, represents a contribution to American thinking that is of almost unique value in these crucial years.

Sumner Welles

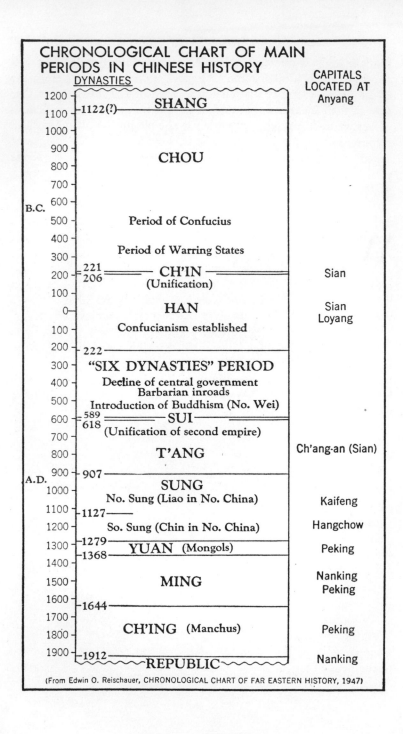

CHRONOLOGICAL CHART OF MAIN PERIODS IN CHINESE HISTORY

DYNASTIES

CAPITALS LOCATED AT

B.C.		
1200	**SHANG**	Anyang
1100	1122(?)	
1000		
900	**CHOU**	
800		
700		
600		
500	Period of Confucius	
400	Period of Warring States	
300		
200	221 — **CH'IN** — 206 (Unification)	Sian
100		
0	**HAN**	Sian Loyang
100	Confucianism established	
200	222	
300	**"SIX DYNASTIES" PERIOD**	
400	Decline of central government	
	Barbarian inroads	
500	Introduction of Buddhism (No. Wei)	
600	589 — **SUI** — 618	
700	(Unification of second empire)	
800	**T'ANG**	Ch'ang-an (Sian)
900	907	
A.D.		
1000	**SUNG**	
	No. Sung (Liao in No. China)	Kaifeng
1100	1127	
1200	So. Sung (Chin in No. China)	Hangchow
1300	1279 **YUAN** (Mongols)	Peking
	1368	
1400		
1500	**MING**	Nanking Peking
1600		
	1644	
1700		
1800	**CH'ING** (Manchus)	Peking
1900	1912 **REPUBLIC**	Nanking

(From Edwin O. Reischauer, CHRONOLOGICAL CHART OF FAR EASTERN HISTORY, 1947)

1

Our China Problem

WHEN THE FIRST EDITION of this book was written ten years ago the American people already faced a tragic but inevitable disaster in their relations with China. The incapacity of the National Government to withstand the Chinese Communists in either war or politics was fully evident by 1948. Disaster ensued. The Communists established control over the mainland by 1950 and for eight years have been trying to remake China in the totalitarian Soviet image. As part of this process they have used the United States as their chief enemy, fought us in Korea, maligned us with elaborately fabricated lies, mistreated American prisoners, and generally tried to turn the traditional friendship between our countries into enmity.

The American response to this disaster has not been to our credit as a people. Under the Communist attack, we have shown ourselves on the whole neither emotionally mature nor politically astute. In spite of our revolutionary tradition, we have proved to be conservatives at heart, satisfied with ourselves in an age of violent change. We have tried to meet the broad challenge of Asian revolutions by generous use of our material resources — arms, economic aid, technology — but not by a serious effort of the mind to understand what is happening to people in Asia.

In avoiding this intellectual effort we have attributed the rise of Communism in China to Kremlin plots, to wrong policies in Washington, to treachery among ourselves, even (or especially, as some view it) to the machinations of professors, paying no attention to the brutal facts of life in China where the Communist take-over actually occurred. Stalemated by narrow loyalties and embalmed in domestic party politics, our China policy since that disaster has been no more creative than our original reaction to it.

We and our allies of the West are already in a numerical minority among mankind. We face the possibility of losing our ascendancy in economic and military power. The menace of this ultimate disaster is now rousing us to serious study.

I use the word "disaster" because the new world of revolutionary Asia, whether Communist or non-Communist, cannot share entirely our Western cultural values, particularly our concern for individual freedom under law and the expression of it, through corporations as well as persons, in a multi-centered pluralistic society. In China especially, a lower political standard of living than ours may be expected to accompany the inevitably lower economic standard as far ahead as we can see. Thus great disparities in values between China and America, reinforced by disparities in the ratio of population to resources, will tend to keep us apart indefinitely.

Our only recourse, I think, is to understand our predicament objectively rather than rebel against it subjectively, to seek to become, as it were, a nation of social scientists with a perspective transcending our feelings, so as to convert political disaster and isolation from all with whom we differ into a basis of strength and cooperation with all with whom we can cooperate.

This requires an unafraid appraisal of revolutionary China on a discriminating basis — discovering the facts (no easy task), evaluating them in the context of history and circumstance and not merely by the standards of our own hearth and home, praising or tolerating what we can, condemning what we must. Only ignorance can persuade us that Communist China is wholly "good" or wholly "bad." Only genuine insight can enable us to defend our proper interests in the face of its massive new nationalism, which is no less strident and unscrupulous than those manipulated by Communists elsewhere.

Unless we ourselves have a practical idea of what is being and can be done to meet the Chinese people's problems of livelihood and political expression, we can hardly criticize Peking in effective terms. The fact is that the American people had no adequate solution for China's problems before 1949, nor have we now. The fact may be that there is no "adequate" solution. Nevertheless, as the earth shrinks and the peoples proliferate, we will soon be living on the same planet with a billion Chinese. We have something to think about.

Unfortunately the extremism of the cold war has made us think with our fears. This will not save us, nor, more important, our institution of freedom of thought. Personally I share the general American aversion to Communism but I do not think feeling should dominate national policy or individual judgment. Yet for all diplomats, journalists, and scholars who write for the American public about Communist China, the extreme anti-Communist approach has been the safe one, as is extreme anti-Americanism in Peking. This being Scylla, one meets Charybdis in the fatuous *pro forma* relativism which tries to get exactly in the middle between the two camps, as though the rising evil of forced labor in China could be neatly balanced by the receding problem of segregation in America, et cetera. The one guide line I can suggest is to try to deal in facts in an historical context and eschew vague generalizations, much as we may like them, about the Chinese Communist sub-continent.

Our need for a brief, comprehensive view of the Chinese people's past experience and recent revolution is greater than ever. This book, in seeking such a view, does not succeed in avoiding broad generalizations. On the contrary, it has them on every page. Yet those of us who work one-eyed in a kingdom of the blind cannot gracefully complain about our myopia, and I will not apologize for dealing with a protean subject in brief compass.

In rewriting this book for this revised edition, however, I have tried to take proper account of the extensive monographic studies of the modern period which have appeared in the past decade. My debts to several score persons are unfortunately too numerous to acknowledge. The appendix of "Suggested Reading" lists certain works by persons mentioned in the text. I am chiefly indebted to colleagues and students at Harvard for the stimuli that come from teaching and research in a community of scholars.

"Our China Problem," Ten Years After. In defining our problems of China policy in 1948, in the early days of the cold war, this book began by asserting that "China . . . fundamentally . . . is a society alien to both Russia and America, which is developing according to its own tradition and circumstances. The greatest error that Americans can make is to look at China but think only of Russian expansion. If we let ourselves become obsessed with power

politics, in our approach to China, we will be disastrously defeated in our policy there."

Writing as a student of history and a regional specialist, I contended that "China has a life of her own. . . . The Chinese people are the most ancient social group in the modern world. Their roots go back continuously for at least three, and more nearly four thousand years, without interruption — their language, their ethical values, their social and political institutions have all had greater continuity than ours, remaining geographically localized and maintaining their own inertia through the centuries in a way that ours have not. It is incredible that Modern China, the greatest and oldest single mass of humanity, could be brought into the orbit of any foreign power — Russian, American, or any other — except insofar as China's own inner development *itself* conduced to such an orientation.

"The Soviet Union and the United States can exert a major influence in Chinese affairs, in the long run, only insofar as they understand the tides of social change in China and work with them. To approach China subjectively, as some of the most vocal Americans are now doing, to seek to use China for American ends, to assume that what is good for us is without question good for the Chinese people, to ignore Chinese public opinion, to accept as our allies in China anyone who will line up with us in power politics, to regard China as a tool and not an end in itself — this way of thought is supremely immoral. Immoral or not, it will lead us to defeat in Asia."

As of 1958 the success or failure of American policy toward Asia still hangs in the balance. In the last ten years we have learned how to assist within certain limits in the economic reconstruction and modernization of many Asian countries. Our record of help to South Korea, South Vietnam, Taiwan, and other areas is impressive, particularly in material matters, even if far from perfect. Only toward the gargantuan problem of mainland China, where we are officially feared and hated, have we remained emotionally stalemated and uncreative in our policy. We still tend to look at China and see only Communism.

Our China problem is fundamentally one of values, and this is what involves our feelings. The fact confronting us is that China's fifth of mankind accepts a degree of political authoritarianism which we will not. The twin revolutions of nationalism and industrialism are creating a powerful Chinese state but not a democratic one in terms that we can accept as democratic. In the new China, as in the old, the individual is given a different evaluation in society and vis-a-vis the state. We may well argue that our evaluation of the individual and the institutions by which we protect him are preferable. But we cannot show how our view can ever be realized within the crowded circumstances of Chinese life.

In order to deal with this difference in values we need an historical understanding of how it came about. We need to perceive the major patterns of thought and conduct, the major political and economic forms, which China's long past has ingrained in Chinese society, and to see their relation to the current Chinese scene. Without an understanding of these traditions, and what produced and maintained them, I see no way for Americans to understand Modern China. To proceed without such understanding is to court disaster.

More broadly, our problem in China is only the forefront of our problem in all of Asia. As a nation we must develop a new understanding and new policies toward the revolutionary process now at work among Asia's peasant masses. The Asian half of mankind is entering upon an era of change which the West has precipitated but which we cannot control. To a large extent the crises and solutions which develop in China — concerning questions of population growth and food supply, of living standards and democratic processes, of industrialization and nationalist chauvinism, of the individual's relation to government — are likely to be common, with variations, for all of Asia. Much of what this book says about China could be said also of Indochina, Indonesia, or India.

One Secret of Communist Success. In the perspective of the half century since 1900, the Chinese Communists have succeeded in achieving certain forms of modernization which preceding regimes failed to achieve. The Manchu dynasty after 1901, the young Republic after the Revolution of 1911, the Kuomintang during the decade of the Nanking Government from 1927 to 1937, even the Japanese in their eight years of puppet rule, all in different degree tried to realize some of the potentialities of modernization which were inherent in the Chinese scene. In the end all were frustrated, though the potentialities steadily accumulated.

To make this more concrete, I tried in 1948 to draw attention to the extreme superficiality of modernization as it had occurred up to that time:

"The Modern China with which we Americans have contact is a thin veneer spread lightly over the surface of an ancient civilization. Beneath it the Old China still endures, in the peasant villages of half a continent. But it is cut off from us by barriers of language, material standards, and social taboos. Americans have no direct contact with the profuse remnants of this old culture. Our knowledge of it must be mediated through Modern China, which includes the educated people, the routes of rail and air communication, the books and newspapers in the modernized language, the new conceptions and interests assimilated from the West, the needs and the techniques of a modern state. All this agglomeration of modern life in China — financiers, students, urban proletariat, ricksha coolies (a new profession), and trained soldiers — are participants in the new society which represents on Chinese soil the new world culture of literacy, telecommunications, world markets, and mass movements in which we too are bound up. But beneath and behind this new China whose life interpenetrates with ours lies the old Chinese society, rooted in an alien cultural tradition. It is this ancient and traditional Chinese society which we Westerners, and often the modern Chinese, fail to understand. It is here that we find the key to China's dissimilarity to the West.

"Our failure in understanding springs partly from our mistaking the modern veneer of China for the whole of Chinese life. This is particularly easy because the modernized top stratum of Chinese society — the moneyed, official, and literate classes — almost monopolize the machinery of power in China today. The government, the banking structure, education and the press, the bureaucracy, are dominated by the new generation, many of whom indeed know English and can the more easily deal with China's foreign problems in a Western way....

"It has been deceptively easy during the past generation for a new class of Chinese scholars, merchants, and officials to use foreign techniques of control — financial, military, and ideological — in order to erect a modern Chinese nation on the ruins of the old Chinese society. Yet how superficial a thing this new nation is may be seen in a few statistics. In mileage of highways, China (78,850 miles in 1943) is about the size of Spain (77,574 miles in 1941). In mileage of steam railroads, China in 1942 (12,036 miles including Manchuria) was smaller than Illinois (12,967 miles) or Italy (14,384 miles). After the ravages of the later war years and the civil war, her railroad tracks are now considerably shorter than those of Spain (10,805 miles in 1941). In cotton spindles China is also about the size of Italy. The telegraph lines at the disposal of an administration governing in China (59,275 miles in 1943) exceed those available in Italy (41,354 miles in 1938) but are less than a third of those in France (229,000 miles in 1937). If we turn to less material matters, the total of 1,163,116 students in secondary schools in China (population say 450 million) hardly exceeds the total of 1,077,000 students in high schools in the two states of Illinois and New York (population roughly 23 million).

"However we look at it, Modern China in its equipment and modern plant is a small show. In industrial production it is smaller than Belgium, in air and sea power negligible, in the gadgets and equipment of American life not as big as a middle western state. Yet this small and relatively insignificant modern state is spread out over the protean body of a vigorous people in a vast and ancient land."

In the ten years since these words were written, the Chinese state under the Communists has mushroomed into a totalitarian monster. As of 1958 its vast hierarchies of millions of administrators and party workers, of mass organizations and peasant cooperatives, have spread over the land and penetrated every village and home. The press and radio, travel and communication, learning and technology, production and consumption are now centrally controlled with unprecedented, albeit imperfect, effectiveness. The inert masses have been given a degree of literacy and activated politically, the village economy reorganized, the army given modern fire-power, the national consciousness aroused. The state has penetrated the traditional society and begun to transform it.

This sudden transformation has been possible precisely because of China's backwardness in 1948, precisely because the modernized layer of Chinese life was so thin, so stunted and embryonic.

The prospect was by no means happy in 1948. Totalitarianism loomed on the Chinese scene as an innate possibility, made feasible there as elsewhere by the combination of a centralized authoritarian political tradition with the growth capacities of the industrial age and long-frustrated nationalism. The twin drives toward industrialism and nationalism had long since been implanted in the minds of all Chinese leaders. To build a strong nation quickly, to industrialize the economy and mobilize the people, these were the overriding imperatives, already apparent to any patriot in the time of the Nationalist Government and Chiang Kai-shek.

We Americans may gain perspective by noting that China in 1948 lacked precisely those essential installations and public services of a modern state that we in the United States could unthinkingly take for granted. The Chinese people needed desperately those things that we already had — peace and order throughout the land, no more fighting; a stable economic process, no more inflation; a strong unified government, no more invasion or special privilege for foreigners. Our political thinking assumes these things. They could not be assumed in pre-Communist China.

The remaking of Chinese life had already begun in pilot-model operations during the years of the Nanking Government and in earlier pioneer efforts of Western missionaries and Chinese educators and reformers. There were programs for land reform, to let the tiller own his land; literacy for the masses, to give the means of self-improvement; public health measures, to check epidemic and chronic diseases; public works, to provide bus, railroad or steamer communication, to control the ravages of flood and famine; and industrialization and technical training, to give employment and build a modern nation. Yet all these things still awaited country-wide realization, mass distribution among the million peasant hamlets.

Americans could see this as plainly as the Communists in China and Russia. These many features of modernity could be made available in the American fashion — gradually, rather expensively, with many institutional prerequisites of legal process and individual and community enterprise still to be developed — or on the Soviet model — quickly, cheaply in capital if not in human suffering, by a bold plan from the top down backed by ruthless force. To say that the Communist regime rose to power by utilizing some of the potentialities of modernization is meant factually, as neither praise nor blame.

What has been done with the opportunity is an entirely different question.

China in our Strategic Thinking. Historical perspective, though pleasureable, is not a luxury but a necessity — to guide our expectations of Chinese performance, to give us insight into Chinese motives and responses. The fragile fabric of international order has been ruptured more than once in the Far East, quite contrary to our crude assumptions.

After World War I the shaky structure of peace cracked first in Manchuria, in 1931. This was precisely the place where the diplomatic frontier of the United States had become unhappily extended beyond our strategic frontier. Through the Open Door policy and the Nine Power Treaty of 1922 we were committed to the support of the territorial integrity of China. Yet through the disarmament agreements at the Washington Conference of 1921-22 we had made ourselves as a nation militarily impotent in the Western Pacific, putting our trust instead in collective action. When Japan seized Manchuria, collective action either outside or through the League of Nations was ineffective. As a result, we were stuck during the uneasy decade that followed 1931 with a Far Eastern policy which sought to maintain China's integrity, as was constantly reiterated on paper, but which was unable to do so in fact. Paper policies that are not backed up invite aggression. It was no accident that we were brought into World War II by Japanese action. The strategic weakness of our own policy toward China had contributed to international instability. For a whole decade, from Mukden to Pearl Harbor, the Japanese, having long since cracked our diplomatic frontier, were never certain where they would strike our military frontier and really provoke us to fight.

The ambiguity of our China policy was not the only stimulus to the Japanese expansionists. They were also misled into defeat by their own assumption that China could be conquered easily. They misjudged the Chinese will to resist.

The first edition of this book in 1948 reached the conclusion that "both Japan and the United States have followed China policies which played them false. Japan's program in China was defeated because she failed to understand and gauge correctly the actual trends of Chinese history. We are in danger of making a similar error today."

Shortly afterward, in 1950, we misjudged the Chinese readiness to intervene in Korea.

Now as of 1958 we hold by force the off-shore islands, Quemoy and Matsu, on the China coast, assuming Peking will not dare to attack them.

Today, if we in America are to discharge the responsibilities which attend our power, we must know not only the conditions in which the Chinese find themselves under Communism but also their traditional patterns of response and aspiration, their mode of action when moved by hope or fear, their channels of expression for ambition, jealousy, pride, or love, their standards of the good life, of duty among friends and to the state, of loyalty to persons and to ideals. We can truly understand Chinese events and relate ourselves to them with wisdom only when we have become sophisticated as to Chinese motives.

In this direction our first step must be the appraisal of Chinese society and culture in all their aspects, through the approaches of history and humanistic learning and of the various social science disciplines.

China's Problem of Social Change. In its historical and social dynamics China's problem is like that of all Asian societies which have suffered the Western impact and been overwhelmed by the power of Western technology organized on a national basis. The nations of the West, expanding abroad simultaneously with their industrial and political revolutions at home, have planted in Asia the seeds both of national consciousness and of scientific know-how. This process began with the expansion of the Portuguese in the sixteenth century. It was greatly stepped up by British commercial imperialism in the nineteenth century and is still accelerating with American and Russian aid today.

The Western impact produced varying reactions among the societies of Asia. Because of her peculiar nature as both an insular and a military society, Japan was able to seize the principles of Western power and use them for her own self-defense and aggrandizement. The kingdoms of Burma, Cochin China, Cambodia, Annam, and Korea, and the sultanates of the Malay world were overwhelmed by the imperialist expansion of modern nations. Siam alone escaped by lying between the jealous spheres of Britain and France. China, on the other hand, was neither subjugated nor roused to a successful self-defense. For a century she remained in limbo, neither an abject colony nor a modern nation, too big to be conquered by the West and yet too different from the West to reorganize herself on modified Western lines as did Japan.

China has been a problem because she was a different type of society, outside the Western scheme of things, a mature state organized on fundamentally different principles. Her enormous size, bigger than all the rest of East Asia together, meant that her culture and way of life could not be obliterated. But essentially her problem was not one of size but of difference. This is still true today. When one-fifth of the human race has developed during a period of four thousand years a way of life which is unique and *sui generis,* and is then brought into instantaneous radio communication and forty-eight hours' flying time from the rest of us, the world community is confronted with a major problem of social adjustment.

The Chinese society which grew up on a self-sufficient basis at the other end of the Eurasian continent was a great peasant-bureaucratic state. It was based on agriculture rather than trade and governed by landlords and bureaucrats rather than merchants and politicians. This oriental peasant society was continental and landlocked, quite unlike the peninsular and seafaring society of Europe. From ancient times the Chinese population has been dense and immobile, tied to the intensive cultivation of small plots of irrigated land by means of the application of large amounts of water and man power. In contrast, the peoples of Europe until recently remained less numerous and have certainly been more mobile, free to exploit the resources of mountain, forest, and sea. In this contrast the geographic environment has obviously played its part. The vast alluvial plains of China lend themselves to public works for drainage, irrigation, canal building, and flood control. Such government works in turn allow the vast mass of the peasantry to live on their fields at the mercy of Heaven and the tax collector. Once this adaptation of man to nature had become institutionalized under a unified central government of China after 221 B.C., it developed a balance and self-sufficiency which preserved it down to our day.

Chinese society rested upon a peasant class, highly cultured in custom and folklore but illiterate and excluded from political life. Their labor in the production of crops, rather than in industry or trade, produced the surplus upon which the higher civilization of China rested. This higher literate culture was the special concern of the landowning-gentry class, whose sons had the leisure necessary to master the Chinese written language and so become scholars from among whom the officials might be selected. Landlords, scholars, and officials together formed an upper stratum with a practical monopoly of learning and therefore of official life and leadership. Military power, though fundamental, was in theory and often in fact subordinate to the civilian bureaucracy.

In this society merchants have been less powerful than officials. Industrial invention and command over machines have been less profitable than official position and command over land and the man power situated on it. Individualism in thought has been less prized than mastery of the great classical tradition. As we shall note below, scientific discoveries were made and technology developed. But they never became socially institutionalized in a systematic and expanding body of knowledge.

In the social context which saw many inventions but no growth of science, there also emerged much trade but no independent capitalism. Investment in large-scale industrial production for a country-wide market never became a major economic force. This was partly because the Emperor and his bureaucracy governed according to the Confucian classical teaching on a basis of ethics, not of law, and of personal relations, not legal procedures. The individual in China thus relied upon his personal relationships in a hierarchy of status such as that maintained in the family system — the filial obedience of son to father, daughter-in-law to mother-in-law, and wife to husband, the loyalty of the subject to his ruler. Nowhere was the individual, in politics or in industry and commerce, protected by a system of law and civil rights. Government being of men, not of laws, was dominated by the bureaucrat and his constituents, the landlords and literati. The entrepreneur could rely only on personal protection and so had no independence.

Another feature of this society was the absence of nationalism as a motivating force in public life. The individual depended so completely upon his family that he hardly functioned as a citizen loyal to the state. On a higher plane than the family, the Emperor was the father of the people but not their representative, nor their leader. He intervened between them and the forces of nature or Heaven. By his virtue, as manifested in his right conduct, he set a correct example and maintained a harmony between the processes of Heaven and of mankind. But the Son of Heaven pursued these cosmic functions upon a universal, not a national, plane. By the barbarians and the lesser countries roundabout he was also recognized as the Son of Heaven. There was no other human authority equal to him. China was thus a world in itself, not a nation among nations. Consequently, down to the nineteenth century, there was little need for the Chinese people to act as a unit in international affairs. They entered the modern age with a cosmopolitan tradition which may still contribute to the world's future but which left them weak and disunited in the current international anarchy.

The problem of China has been therefore how to reorganize an entire society, its institutions and customs, ideas and ideals. The Chinese people have been challenged to think differently and act differently, speak a new national language and read a new written language, and really remake themselves completely. Communism has seemed to provide a way of meeting this challenge, but on an arbitrarily selective basis.

Demography Versus Democracy. In their violent remaking of Chinese life, the Communists are only the latest, though most thorough, in a succession of modernizers. Earlier generations tried to follow Anglo-Saxon or Japanese models, with varying success. The Soviet model followed in Peking today may be expected to become less and less adequate after a certain point of development has been reached.

The central fact is that the Soviet Union was not, like China, densely populated before industrialization really began. Yet the people of Russia have doubled since 1900. Peking's improvement of public health in the thickly inhabited countryside today is producing a population explosion. The Soviet-model industrialization program, stressing heavy industry, promises a vast increase, possibly even a doubling, of the Chinese people with no corresponding betterment of mass living standards. Yet higher living standards appear to be a chief means of lowering the birth rate. Only this lower birth rate can save the Chinese masses from a life continually on the margin of subsistence.

The tragic alternative to a higher living standard and a lower birth rate has been vividly illustrated in the demographic history of British India and Java. In India during the decade from 1891 to 1901 the population increased only 2 per cent, mainly because of the negative check of famine conditions. But extensive public health programs after 1925 were followed during the decade from 1931 to 1941 by an increase of 50 million. In Java under Dutch efforts to increase crop production the population was stimulated to rise as follows: 1816, 5 million; 1860, 13 million; 1905, 30 million; 1930, 41 million. This increase of more than three times from 1860 to 1930 has created a density of population greater than that of Belgium, Britain, or even Japan, with less than one-half acre of agricultural land per capita in a predominantly agricultural country. Meanwhile the Dutch left Java with almost no educational system until after 1900. Population growth far outstripped the rise of living standards. Indonesia suffers today as a result.

The similar multiplication of poverty in China during the next decades of industrialization will be a world calamity.

The importance of the Chinese standard of living lies less in its economic implications for world trade than in its political implications in the struggle between democracy and authoritarianism. Masses of materially insecure people in any country are raw material for authoritarian political organization and the chauvinism which may accompany it. This close connection of authoritarianism with an economy of mass poverty is particularly evident in Chinese history.

Supposing that the Chinese Communist Party had not come to power, the rulers of China today, whoever they were, would confront the same general problem of numbers pressing on subsistence, of dense masses to be mobilized. In their efforts to achieve industrialism and nationalism, their treatment of the individual in China would be very different from our way in America.

This is not said in order to deny the totalitarian evils of Chinese Communism, which are discussed later in this book. On the contrary, the point here is to emphasize our long-term problem, how to live in a shrinking world with a type of tyranny which springs from the brute fact of numbers in the Chinese scene itself and which may well outlast the rule of Communism there. China's historical tradition and social institutions unfortunately lend considerable sanction to this different evaluation of the role of the individual in state and community. In short, the potentialities of our type of individual freedom under law are limited in China. The alternative to Communist tyranny there must be sought by the Chinese people within a narrower range of possibility than we would like. We have to face the implications of this fact.

2

The Chinese Scene

1. THE CONTRAST OF NORTH AND SOUTH

IN THE FINAL DECADE of the century of the Open Door, when American planes flew widely over the territory of an allied power, it was possible to see China as never before. In flying over the face of the land one could almost "see" Chinese society as well. Its many problems, though we think of them in abstract terms, really stood forth from the terrain: the brown eroded hills, the flood plains of muddy rivers, the crowded green fields and hives of simple huts that form the villages, the intricate silver network of terraces and waterways that testify to the back-breaking labor of countless unsung generations — all the overcrowding of too many people upon too little land, and the attendant exhaustion of the land resources and of human ingenuity and fortitude in the effort to maintain life.

To any modern traveler who has flown through the vast gray cloud banks and mists and sunshine of continental China, two pictures will stand out as typical, one of North China and one of the South. On the dry North China plain to the south of Peking where Chinese civilization had its first flowering and established its institutional forms, one sees in summer an endless expanse of dusty green fields over which are scattered clusters of darker green, the trees of tiny earth-walled villages. It is very like the view of our Middle West, where farmsteads and their clumps of trees are dispersed at rough half-mile intervals all over the verdant plain. But where our corn belt has a farm, on the North China plain there is an entire village. When one American farmer's family is established with its barn and sheds among its fields in Iowa or Dakota at a half-mile interval from its neighbors roundabout, in China an entire community of several hundred persons, lives in its tree-studded village, at a half-mile interval from neighbor villages. About seven-tenths of the earth's surface in this region is under human cultivation, mainly by hand, and for each square mile of cultivated land there are at least a thousand human mouths to feed. This is why the American people in spite of their farming background have no appreciation of the population density which subtly conditions every act and thought of a Chinese farmer.

In South China the typical picture is quite different, and like nothing to which we are accustomed. There during much of the year the rice fields are flooded and present a water surface to the air-borne observer. The green terrain is hilly and much less of it is cultivated, but the crescent-shaped rice terraces march up each hill almost to the top and on the other side descend again from near the crest, terrace upon terrace in endless succession, each embankment conforming to the lay of the land like the contour lines of a geographer's chart. In fact the curving pattern of the rice terraces seen from above is a visual index to the slope of the valleys in which they are built — narrow concave strips of paddy field touch the hilltops, and lower terraces grow broader and longer and bulge out as they descend to the valley floor. Gray stone footpaths are built on many of the embankments and the latter form intricate patterns like the product of some giant's doodling. When the sun is out one sees it from the air reflected brilliantly in the water of the rice fields. The sun seems in fact to be shining up through the fields from below, so that the whole ornate network of the embankments and paths and hilltops appears to rush beneath one as though on a great rolling screen, a black lacework moving across the bright silver of shining water.

No one can fly over the rugged green hills of the South without wondering where the 600 millions of China live and what they eat — such vast reaches of mountain and valley seem largely uncultivable and sparsely settled. One's picture of a big empty landscape is mirrored statistically in the estimate that six-sevenths of the population have to concentrate on one-third of the land. The really inhabited part of China, at a rough estimate, is only about half as large as the really inhabited part of the United States, yet it supports almost four times as many people. This is made possible only by crowding almost 1500 human beings onto each square mile of cultivated earth in the valleys and flood plains. Where the United States has some 570,000 square miles under cultivation and could greatly increase this area, China has had perhaps 425,000 square miles of cultivated land (less than one-half acre of food-producing soil per person) with little prospect of increasing this area by more than a small fraction, even if it is used more intensively.

Little is known in statistical terms about the life of the Chinese people upon their crowded land, but sampling studies, in which American investigators have taken a leading part, give us some general indications. The great contrast is between the dry wheat-millet area of North China and the moist rice land of the South. These economic regions divide along a line roughly halfway between the Yellow River and the Yangtze on the thirty-fourth parallel. Let us look at the factors of rainfall, soil, temperature, and human usage which create this striking contrast.

First of all, the rainfall depends upon the continental character of the Chinese climate and the seasonal air flow to which it gives rise. To put it very simply, the Asiatic land mass changes temperature more readily than the Western Pacific and its currents, and the cold dry air which is chilled over the continent in the wintertime tends to flow southeastward to the sea, with minimum precipitation. Conversely, the summer monsoon of moisture-laden sea air is drawn inward and northward over the land mass by the rising of the heated air above it, and precipitation occurs mainly during the summer. This southerly wind of summer crosses the hills of South China first, and they receive a heavy rainfall, which remains relatively dependable with a variation of only about 15 per cent in the amount of precipitation from one year to the next. North China being farther from the South China Sea receives less rainfall and, moreover, the amount of precipitation over the decades has varied as much as 30 per cent from one year to the next. Since the average rainfall of the North China plain is about 20 to 25 inches, like the rainfall of the great American dustbowl, it is hardly more than sufficient to maintain cultivation at the best of times. This high degree of variability from year to year is a most serious problem. North China is normally on the subsistence margin as regards its water supply, and the periodic failure of rainfall means drought and famine. From the point of view of water supply, South China has the better of it.

As regards soil, however, South China suffers by comparison, for

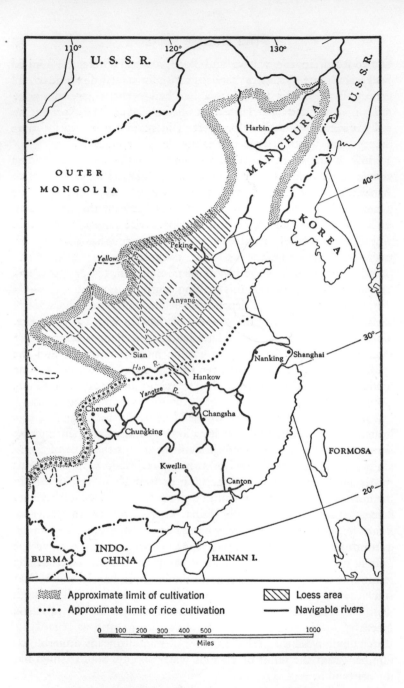

110°	120°	130°

U. S. S. R.

U. S. S. R.

OUTER
MONGOLIA

MANCHURIA

Harbin

KOREA

40°

Yellow

Peking

Anyang

30°

Sian

Han R.

Nanking • Shanghai

Hankow

Yangtze R.

Chengtu

Chungking

Changsha

FORMOSA

Kweilin

Canton

20°

BURMA

INDO-
CHINA

HAINAN I.

▒▒▒ Approximate limit of cultivation   ⧄⧄ Loess area

••••• Approximate limit of rice cultivation   —— Navigable rivers

0   100   200   300   400   500   1000

Miles

the constant seepage of water through its warm earth has dissolved and leached away mineral foods of great importance for plant life. The leached soil resulting is relatively unproductive, and the situation is saved partly by the fact that the constant run-off from the hills brings down new deposits for the cultivated lowlands. Even so, the heavy population centers of the South are to be found mainly on the alluvial flood plains of the Yangtze or on the river deltas, like those inland from Shanghai or around Canton. The soil of North China, on the other hand, thanks to the relative lack of water, remains unleached and richer in minerals. Sometimes, indeed, as in Mongolia, mineral salts are brought to the surface by evaporating water and, in the absence of rainfall to wash them away, form a saline crust which makes cultivation impossible.

Temperature plays its part in preserving the soil of North China, since the severe continental winters, not unlike those of the Middle West, limit the growing season to about half the year. In southernmost China crops are grown the year around and rice is double-cropped. Too easily we forget that Shanghai is in the latitude of New Orleans and Suez, while Canton is in that of Havana and Calcutta, well into the tropics. This helps to explain why the greater part of the Chinese people live in the more fecund rice economy of the South.

Thus the factors of rainfall, soil, and temperature are in a rough balance both North and South, the North having soil which is highly fertile when water is sufficient, but having too often an insufficiency of water and much cold weather; and the South having no lack of water and favorable temperatures but generally infertile soil. In both cases the resources of nature are supplemented by unremitting human endeavor, of which the night-soil (human excrement) industry is but one of the more spectacular forms. Without the redolent returning to the land of human waste or equivalent fertilizers it is safe to say that no region of China could sustain its present population. It is no accident that Chinese cities from the air can be seen surrounded by a belt of dense green crops which fade out at the periphery. Thus each urban center maintains its surrounding truck gardens.

A population map (see p. 20) will show that the Chinese people are packed into four main regions, which include but a small part of the total area of the country. The first region is the North China

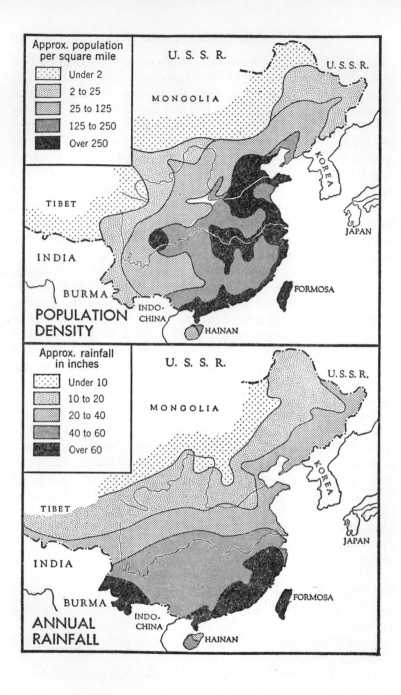

Approx. population
per square mile

- Under 2
- 2 to 25
- 25 to 125
- 125 to 250
- Over 250

U. S. S. R.

U.S.S.R.

MONGOLIA

KOREA

TIBET

JAPAN

INDIA

BURMA

FORMOSA

INDO-
CHINA

POPULATION
DENSITY

HAINAN

Approx. rainfall
in inches

- Under 10
- 10 to 20
- 20 to 40
- 40 to 60
- Over 60

U. S. S. R.

U.S.S.R.

MONGOLIA

KOREA

TIBET

JAPAN

INDIA

BURMA

FORMOSA

INDO-
CHINA

ANNUAL
RAINFALL

HAINAN

plain, the second is the mountain-locked plain of Szechwan in the west, the third is the lower Yangtze valley from Hankow to Shanghai, including the Hunan rice bowl south of Hankow, and the fourth is the Canton delta in the south. Early travelers compared China to Europe, in the variety of dialects and the size of different provinces. To take an example, Germany, before the war, had an area of 182,000 square miles and a population of 70 million; the twin provinces of Hupeh and Hunan, north and south of Hankow in Central China, have about 60 million people, in an area of 155,000 square miles. Szechwan in the west has roughly speaking another 60 million people in practically the same area. Four provinces of the lower Yangtze — Kiangsu, Chekiang, Kiangsi, and Anhwei — have more than 100 million persons in an area of 200,000 square miles. Thus there are three regions comparable in size to Germany along the course of the Yangtze in Central China alone!

Trade and transport routes in South China have followed the waterways, and the great modern cities — Canton, Shanghai, Hankow — have grown up where sea trade can meet the waterborne commerce of the interior. Yet China's foreign trade has never lived up to the foreign merchant's great expectations. We must still think of China as a subcontinent largely sufficient unto herself. As George Washington's contemporary, the great Ch'ien-lung Emperor, put it in his famous edict to King George III, "Our celestial empire possesses all things in prolific abundance and lacks no product within its own borders. There is therefore no need to import the manufactures of outside barbarians."

In spite of the immensity and variety of the Chinese scene, we need not be surprised that this subcontinent has remained a single political unit where Europe has not; for it is held together by a way of life even more deeply rooted than our own, and stretching even farther back uninterruptedly into the past.

2. CULTURAL ORIGINS

The exciting discovery thirty years ago of the bones of Peking man (at Chou-k'ou-tien near Peking) was of tremendous archaeological significance because the excavators found not one but many skeletal remnants of paleolithic man, not isolated but together with the bones of contemporary animals, human tools, and evidence of the use of fire. Finding these cultural evidences together in one place was most unusual. This is still the chief paleolithic find in China. Judged by it, the culture of Peking man appears to have been indigenous and isolated.

In the subsequent ice age, geologists believe that the chill gales blowing from the European ice cap picked up the dust and silt which had been produced by the drying up of the Central Asian plateau and moved it in vast dust storms to the region of Northwest China. Today we know that a blanket of fine, yellow, wind-borne soil lies to a depth of 150 feet or more over an area of some 100,000 square miles in this region. This is the famous loess soil so typical of the area south of the Ordos desert near the great bend of the Yellow River. The period of the deposition of the loess must have seen constant cyclonic gales more fierce than anything North China ever sees today. It can hardly have been a pleasant time to live there and it has been suggested that Peking man, whose paleolithic sites are found below the level of the loess, was forced to withdraw from North China in this period.

After the last glacial period the neolithic culture of North China shows evidence of contact with the West, a tenuous contact across the reaches of Central Asia which has never entirely ceased. Remains of neolithic man in China have been found at several sites in the North. They fall into classes according to the type of pottery. A type of black pottery has been found widely in Northeast China but less in the Northwest, whereas a type of red or painted pottery, which has been found in the Northwest, is very similar to a type of painted pottery found in the Near East. On the other hand the animal-mask (*t'ao-t'ieh*) designs on ancient bronzes, methods of divination by the use of "oracle bones" (scapulomancy), walls of pounded earth, and other early cultural elements all bespeak a connection between prehistoric China and other parts of the Pacific basin.

From this kind of evidence it is deduced that there was an early indigenous culture in China but that neolithic culture traits also entered China over Central Asian routes from the Near East. The painted pottery, for example, marks this trail. In later periods other cultural elements followed — the use of bronze, iron, the chariot, horses, wheat, domestication of animals, and possibly the idea of writing. In short, the culture of the Near East on the basis of present evidence is believed to antedate that of China by many hundred years, if not millennia, and is therefore inferred to have contributed to ancient China.

It is significant that the cultural elements which were diffused into China from the Near East came across the Central Asian land barrier as ideas or methods stripped of all but the essentials and so could more easily be given Chinese garb and assimilated. Chinese society was stimulated across the long Central Asian track but never overwhelmed. Thus the Chinese had the benefit of early Western inventions but were left free to integrate them in their own peculiar society.

In a similar fashion peoples from northern and Central Asia have continually entered the Chinese scene and have sometimes ruled over it but they have never been numerous enough to overwhelm Chinese civilization. The arid steppe land north of the Great Wall has been a breeding ground of nomad invaders but never in such numbers that they could displace the dense population of agrarian China.

In racial stock the Chinese have a deceptive homogeneity which does not stand up under anthropological inspection. It appears that the so-called "Mongoloid" type is made up of very diverse strains in which flat noses and hawk noses, black hair and some red hair, beards and the lack of beards are thoroughly intermixed, and supposedly common denominators such as the Mongolian eye fold are by no means universal.

In this way the indigenous culture of China appears to have been the recipient of continual infusions from the Northwest. One leading American student has called it a "civilization by osmosis."

3. THE HARMONY OF MAN AND NATURE

No matter what elements of civilization — peoples or cultural traits — came into China, they all became integrated in a distinctly Chinese way of life, nourished, conditioned, and limited by the good earth and the use of it. To cite but one example — from neolithic times the people of North China have taken full advantage of the quality of vertical cleavage which is characteristic of the loess and made pit dwellings or cave homes in it. Many hundreds of thousands in the Northwest still live in caves cut into the sides of loess cliffs. They are cool in summer, warm in winter, and secure against everything but earthquakes.

The loess of Northwest China seems never to have supported forests. Where forest land occurred, the Chinese, like other early peoples and recent American pioneers, achieved its deforestation. The consequent erosion through the centuries has changed the face of their country. Erosion today is a major problem. Through its water-borne loess deposits the Yellow River has built up the broad flood plain of North China between Shansi province and the sea, and the process still goes on. Nothing can so vividly convey a feeling of man's impotence in the face of nature as to watch the swirling coffee-colored flood of the Yellow River flowing majestically within its dikes across, and twenty feet above, the crowded plain two hundred miles from the sea; and to realize that this vast yellow torrent is steadily depositing its silt and building its bed higher above the surrounding countryside until the time when human negligence or act of God will allow it again to burst from the dikes and inundate the plain.

Deforestation, erosion, and floods have constantly been met by human efforts at water control. The planting of trees and damming of tributaries in the limitless western watershed of "China's Sorrow" is still a dream to be realized, though efforts now are being made. In all previous periods the rulers of China have been periodically confronted with a *fait accompli* in the debouching of the Yellow River upon the North China plain in full flood, and have lacked the scientific knowledge and the means to get behind this pressing fact. In the earliest period, however, flooding of the plain was no more of a problem than the reclamation of it from its primitive swamp and fen condition; techniques of water control were developed for drainage purposes as well as for irrigation and the prevention of floods. Thus many generations of labor have been spent upon the land to make it what it is today, protected by dikes, crossed by canals and roads worn into the earth, irrigated by streams and wells, divided by paths and parcels of grave land in their groves of trees, and all of it handed down from generation to generation.

This land which Modern China has inherited is used almost entirely for human food production. China cannot afford to raise cattle for food. Of the land which can be used at all, nine-tenths is cultivated for crops and only 2 per cent is pasture for animals. By comparison, in the United States only four-tenths of the land which is used is put into crops, and almost half of it is put into pasture. Some amelioration of this situation might be possible if the Chinese in their great Northwest should become herdsmen, but they are not. Their society and all its mores and institutions have been based from the beginning upon intensive agriculture which will take the fullest advantage of human labor.

The human implications of intensive agriculture can be seen most strikingly in the rice economy which is the backbone of Chinese life everywhere in the Yangzte valley and the South. Rice plants are ordinarily grown for their first month in seed beds, while subsidiary crops are raised and harvested in the dry fields. The fields are then irrigated, fertilized, and plowed (here the water buffalo may supplement man's efforts) in preparation for the transplanting of the rice seedlings. This transplanting is done by human hands, the rows of planters bending from the waist as they move backward step by step through the ankle-high muddy water of each terrace. This goes on in the paddy fields of a whole subcontinent — certainly the greatest expenditure of muscular energy in the world. When the rice is mature, the field is drained and it is harvested, again by hand. Given an unlimited supply of water and of human hands, there is probably no way by which a greater yield could be gained from a given plot of land. Wheat yields an American farmer some 25 bushels per acre; a Chinese farmer, and his children, may harvest some 42 bushels of rice from a similar acre. In this situation land is economically more valuable than labor, or to put it the other way, good muscles are more plentiful than good earth. The Chinese farmer cannot afford to put his labor into extensive agriculture which would yield less per acre. He has lacked both the land and the capital for mechanized or large-scale methods. Obliged to rely on his own family's labor power, he has been obliged to rely on intensive hand gardening in order to feed them.

The contrast between intensive and extensive agriculture is vividly illustrated in the proportion which labor bears to other factors of production in China and the United States. It has been estimated that to grow and harvest one acre of wheat in the United States normally takes an investment of 1.2 days of the time of one man. In China the same operation requires 26 man days. To grow and harvest one acre of cotton in the United States used to require 14 man days and in China 53 man days.

The heavy application of man power to small plots of land has its social repercussions too, for it sets up a vicious interdependence between dense population and intensive use of the soil whereby each makes the other possible. Population density provides both the incentive for intensive land use and the means. Once established, this economy has developed its inertia and set its own human standards, whereby the back-breaking labor of many hands has become the accepted norm and inventive efforts at labor saving have remained the exception. Modernizers of China in their attempts to introduce the machine have constantly run up against the vested interest of Chinese man power, since in the short run the machine appears to be in competition with human hands and backs. Thus railways have been attacked as depriving carters and coolies of their jobs, and there has been no premium upon invention.

This is only one of many ways in which the ecology of the Chinese, their adaptation to physical environment, has influenced their culture. Life on the great river flood plains has always been a hard life, in which man is dependent upon nature more than upon his own initiative. "Heaven nourishes and destroys" is an ancient saying. On the broad stretches of the plain the patient Chinese farmer has been at the mercy of the weather, dependent upon Heaven's gift of sun and rain. He has been forced to accept natural calamity in the traditional forms of drought, flood, pestilence, and famine. This is in striking contrast to the lot of the European who lived in a land of variegated topography. Western man, either on the Mediterranean or on the European continent, was never far from a water supply and could always supplement agriculture by hunting or fishing, provided he exercised initiative. From ancient times seaborne commerce has played an immediate part in Western man's economy. Exploration and invention in the service of commerce have exemplified Western man's struggle against nature, rather than a passive acceptance of it.

A different relation of man to nature in the West and in the East has been one of the salient contrasts between the two civilizations. Man has been in the center of the Western stage. The rest of nature has served as neutral background or as his adversary. Thus Western religion is anthropomorphic and Western painting anthropocentric. We have only to compare Christianity with the relative impersonality of Buddhism, or a Sung landscape and its tiny human figures dwarfed by crags and rivers with an Italian primitive in which nature is an afterthought, to see how great this gulf is.

And yet, paradoxically, Chinese man has been so crowded upon the soil among his fellows that he is also a most socially minded human being, ever conscious of the interplay of personalities and social conventions around him; for he is seldom in all his life beyond earshot of other people.

3

The Nature of Chinese Society

Mao TSE-TUNG'S remaking of Chinese society — his recruiting and indoctrinating an elite, setting it to reorganize the life of the peasantry, and using their labor and product for public works — is not as unprecedented in China as the Communists and some of their critics would have us believe. The Communist opportunity has been due less to wisdom or ingenuity emanating from Moscow than to a favorable local combination of long-term historical factors — namely, the pressure for modernization, and the nature of the traditional society.

1. SOCIAL STRUCTURE

Since ancient times there have been two Chinas — the myriad agricultural communities of the peasantry in the countryside, where each tree-clad village and farm household persists statically upon the soil; and the superstructure of walled towns and cities peopled by the landlords, scholars, merchants, and officials — the families of property and position. There has been no caste system, and the chance to rise from peasant status has not been lacking. Yet China has always remained a country of farmers, four-fifths of the people living on the soil they till. The chief social division has therefore been that between town and countryside, between the 80 per cent or more of the population who have stayed put upon the land and the 10 or 20 per cent of the population who have formed a mobile upper class. This bifurcation still underlies the Chinese political scene and makes it difficult to spread the control of the state from the few to the many.

If we look more closely at this inherited class structure, we note that the upper levels have included really several classes — the land-owning gentry, the scholar-literati, and the officials, as well as the merchants, the militarists and their hangers-on. This composite upper stratum has been the active carrier of Chinese culture in its many aspects. Within this minority segment of the Chinese people have been developed and maintained all the literature and most of the fine arts, all the higher philosophy, ethics, and political ideology of the state, the sanctions of power, and much of the wealth that accompanied them. Culture has filtered down to the masses.

The Peasant: Family and Village. The Chinese people are still mostly peasants tilling the soil, living mainly in villages, in houses of brown sun-dried brick, bamboo, or whitewashed wattle, or sometimes stone, with earth floors, oil lamps, if any, and paper, not glass, in the windows. At least half and sometimes two-thirds to three-quarters of their meager material income is used for food. The other necessaries of life, including rent, heat, light, clothing, and any possible luxuries, come from the tiny remainder. They lack even the luxury of space. Peasant dwellings have usually about four small room-sections for every three persons. Sometimes family members of both sexes and two or three generations must all sleep on the same brick bed. There is little or no meat in the diet, and so simple a thing as iron is scarce for tools or for building. Even today the per capita consumption of steel in the United States is several hundred times that in China. Man power takes the place of the machine for most purposes. In this toilsome, earthbound existence the hazards of life from malnutrition and disease until recently have given the average baby in China, as in India, little more than twenty-six years of life expectancy. Human life compared with the other factors of production is abundant and therefore cheap.

To an American with his higher material standard of living the amazing thing about the Chinese peasantry is their ability to maintain life in these poor conditions.

The answer lies in their social institutions which have carried the individuals of each family through the phases and vicissitudes of human existence according to deeply ingrained patterns of social behavior. These institutions and behavior patterns have been the oldest and most persistent social phenomena in the world. China has been the stronghold of the family system and has derived both strength and inertia from it.

The Chinese family has been a microcosm, the state in miniature.

The family, not the individual, has been the social unit and the responsible element in the political life of its locality. The filial piety and obedience inculcated in family life have been the training ground for loyalty to the ruler and obedience to constituted authority in the state.

This function of the family to raise filial sons who would become loyal subjects can be seen by a glance at the pattern of authority within the traditional family group. The father was a supreme autocrat, with control over the use of all family property and income and a decisive voice in arranging the marriages of the children. The mixed love, fear, and awe of children for their father was strengthened by the great respect paid to age. An old man's loss of vigor was more than offset by his growth in wisdom. As long as he lived in possession of his faculties the patriarch possessed every sanction to enable him to dominate the family scene. He could even sell his children into slavery. In fact, of course, parents were also bound by a reciprocal code of responsibility for their children as family members. But law and custom provided little check on parental tyranny if they chose to exercise it.

The domination of age over youth within the old-style family was matched by the domination of male over female. Chinese baby girls in the old days were more likely than baby boys to suffer infanticide. A girl's marriage was, of course, arranged and not for love. The trembling bride became at once a daughter-in-law under the tyranny of her husband's mother. In a well-to-do family she might see secondary wives or concubines brought into the household, particularly if she did not bear a male heir. She could be repudiated by her husband for various reasons. If he died she could not easily remarry. All this reflected the fact that a woman had no economic independence. Her labor was absorbed in household tasks and brought her no income. Peasant women were universally illiterate. They had few or no property rights. Until the present century their subjection was demonstrated and reinforced by the custom of foot-binding. This crippling practice by which a young girl's feet were tightly wrapped to prevent normal development seems to have begun about the tenth century A.D. The "lily feet" which it produced through the suffering of hundreds of millions of young girls acquired great aesthetic and erotic value. In practice bound feet kept womankind from venturing far abroad.

The inferiority of women imposed upon them by social custom was merely one manifestation of the hierarchic nature of a society of status. It exemplified an entire social code and cosmology. Philosophically, ancient China had seen the world as the product of two interacting complementary elements, *yin* and *yang*. *Yin* was the attribute of all things female, dark, weak, and passive. *Yang* was the attribute of things male, bright, strong, and active. While male and female were both necessary and complementary, one was by nature passive toward the other. Building on such ideological foundations, an endless succession of Chinese male moralists worked out the behavior pattern of obedience and passivity which was to be expected of women. These patterns subordinated girls to boys from their infancy and kept the wife subordinate to her husband and the mother to her son. Forceful women, whom China has never lacked, controlled their families by indirection, not by fiat.

Status within the family was codified in the famous "five relationships," a doctrine emphasized by the Confucian philosophers. These five relationships were those between ruler and subject (prince and minister), father and son, elder brother and younger brother, husband and wife, and friend and friend. To an egalitarian Westerner the most striking thing about this doctrine is that three of the five relations were within the family, and four of the five were between superior and subordinate. The relationship of mother and son, which in Western life often allows matriarchal domination, was not stressed in theory, though naturally important in fact.

Within the family every child from birth was involved in a highly ordered system of kinship relations with elder brothers, sisters, maternal elder brother's wives, and other kinds of aunts, uncles, and cousins, grandparents, and in-laws too numerous for a Westerner to keep in mind. These relationships were not only more clearly named and differentiated than in the West but also carried with them more compelling rights and duties dependent upon status. A first son, for example, could not long remain unaware of the Confucian teaching as to his duties toward the family line and his precedence over his younger brothers and his sisters.

Chinese well habituated to the family system have been prepared to accept similar patterns of status in other institutions, including the official hierarchy of the government. One advantage of a system of status (as opposed to our individualist system of contractual relations) is that a man knows automatically where he stands in his family or society. He can have security in the knowledge that if he does his prescribed part he may expect reciprocal action from others in the system. It has often been observed that a Chinese community overseas tends to organize its activities and meet new situations in a hierarchic fashion.

The life cycle of the individual in a peasant family is inextricably interwoven with the seasonal cycle of intensive agriculture upon the land. The life and death of the people follow a rhythm which inter-penetrates the growing and harvesting of the crops. The peasant village which still forms the bedrock of Chinese society is built out of family units; village, family, and individual follow the rhythm of seasons and crops, of birth, marriage, and death.

Socially, the Chinese in the village are organized primarily in their kinship system and only secondarily as a neighborhood community. The village has ordinarily consisted of a group of family or kinship units (clans) which are permanently settled from one generation to the next and continuously dependent upon the use of certain land-holdings. Each family household is both a social and an economic unit. Its members derive their sustenance from working its fields and their social status from membership in it.

The Chinese kinship system is patrilineal, the family headship passing in the male line from father to eldest son. Thus the men stay in the family while the girls marry outside of it into other family households, in neither case following the life pattern which Western individuals take as a matter of course. Until recently a Chinese boy and girl did not choose each other as life mates, nor did they set up an independent household together after marriage. Instead, they entered the husband's father's household and assumed responsibil-ities for its maintenance, subordinating married life to family life in a way that modern Americans would consider insupportable.

From the time of the first imperial unification, before Christ, the Chinese abandoned the institution of primogeniture by which the eldest son would have retained all the father's property while the younger sons sought their fortunes elsewhere. The enormous sig-nificance of this institutional change can be seen by comparison with a country like England or Japan where younger sons who have not shared their father's estate have provided the personnel for govern-ment, business, and empire. By the abolition of primogeniture the

Chinese created a system of equal division of the land among the sons of the family. They left the eldest son only certain ceremonial duties, to acknowledge his position, and sometimes an extra share of property; otherwise the land was divided. This constant parcelization of the land has tended to destroy the continuity of family land-holding, forestall the growth of landed particularism among great officials, and keep peasant families on the margin of subsistence. Under this system the prime duty of each married couple has been to produce a son who can maintain the family line, and yet the birth of more than one son may mean impoverishment.

Contrary to a common myth, a large family with several children has not been the peasant norm. The scarcity of land, as well as disease and famine, has set a limit to the number of people likely to survive in each family unit. The large joint family of several married sons with many children all within one compound, which has usually been regarded as typical of China, appears to have been the ideal exception, a luxury which only the well-to-do could afford. The average peasant family was limited to four, five, or six persons. Division of the land among the sons has constantly checked the accumulation of property and savings and the typical family has had little opportunity to rise in the social scale. The peasantry have been bound to the soil not by law and custom so much as by their own numbers.

2. THE GENTRY CLASS

This group dominated Chinese life, so much so that sociologists have called China a "gentry state" and even ordinary people may speak of the "scholar gentry" as a class. But do not let yourself be reminded of the landed gentry with their roast beef and fox hunts in merry England, for "gentry" in the case of China is a technical term with two principal meanings and an inner ambiguity. It requires special handling.

Non-Marxists generally agree, first of all, that the gentry were not a mere "feudal landlord" class, because Chinese society was not organized in any system that can be called "feudalism," except possibly before 221 B.C. While "feudal" may still be a useful swear word, it has little value as a Western term applied to China. For instance, an essential characteristic of feudalism, as the word has been used with reference to medieval Europe and Japan, has been the inalienability of the land. The medieval serf was bound to the land and could not himself either leave it or dispose of it, whereas the Chinese peasant both in law and in fact has been free to sell and, if he had the means, to purchase land. His bondage has resulted from a press of many circumstances but not from a legal institution similar to European feudalism. Nor has it been maintained by the domination of a professional warrior caste. Avoidance of the term feudal to describe the Chinese peasant's situation in life by no means signifies that it has been less miserable. But if the word feudal is to retain a valid meaning for European and other institutions to which it was originally applied, it cannot be very meaningful in a general Chinese context.

The Chinese gentry can be understood only in a dual, economic-and-political sense, as connected both with landholding and with office holding. The narrow definition, following the traditional Chinese term *shen-shih,* confines gentry status to those *individuals* who held official degrees gained normally by passing examinations, or sometimes by recommendation or purchase. This has the merit of being concrete and even quantifiable — the gentry in this narrow sense were degree-holders, as officially listed, and not dependent for their status on economic resources, particularly landowning, which is so hard to quantify from the historical record.

Yet in an agrarian society one can hardly ignore the importance of landholding as one source of upper-class strength, much as one may wish to avoid the Marxist exaggeration of the role of economic relations. The main point about the gentry as individuals was that they were public functionaries, playing political and administrative roles, in addition to any connection with the landlord class. Yet, being Chinese, they were also enmeshed in family relations, on which they could rely for material sustenance. This political-economic dualism has led many writers to define the term gentry more broadly, as a group of *families* rather than of individual degree-holders only. Both the narrow and the broad definitions must be kept in mind.

Looked at descriptively, the gentry families lived chiefly in the walled towns rather than in the villages. They constituted a stratum of families based on landed property which intervened between the earth-bound masses of the peasantry, on the one hand, and the officials and merchants who formed a fluid matrix of overall administrative and commercial activity, on the other. They were the local elite, who carried on certain functions connected with the peasantry below and certain others connected with the officials above.

For the peasant community they included the big landowners, the lowest economic rung of the great ruling class. Their big high-walled compounds enclosing many courtyards, replete with servants and hoarded supplies and proof against bandits, still dominate the old market towns. This is the type of "big house" celebrated in both Chinese and Western novels of China. As a local ruling class the gentry managed the system of customary and legal rights to the use of the land. These ordinarily were so incredibly diverse and complicated that decided managerial ability was required to keep them straight. The varied tenant relationships, loans, mortgages, customary payments and obligations on both sides formed such a complex within the community that many peasants could hardly say whether they were themselves mainly small landowners or mainly tenants. In general, a peasant's loss of title to his land was more likely to make him a tenant and decrease his share of its product than to make him a displaced and homeless wanderer. Peasant poverty was reflected sometimes in the increase of landless laborers in the villages, but it was marked chiefly by the increased payment of land rent.

In the 1930's it was estimated that perhaps three-fifths (or possibly only half) of the Chinese peasants owned their own land, about one-fifth were part owners and part tenants, and one-fifth outright tenants. Tenantry was more frequent in South China and was increasing. Tenants paid between half and two-thirds (sometimes three-fourths) of their crop in rent. If a farmer owned his land, he still had to pay the land tax.

More significant than the proportion of tenants was the high proportion of land and capital in landlord hands. As in all farming, the seasonal need of capital permitted usurious interest on loans, which ran as high as 12 per cent a month, depending on what the traffic would bear. Since capital was accumulated from the surplus product of the land, landowners were moneylenders. The gentry families thus rested in part upon property rights and money power, as well as social prestige. In the early twentieth century, they still dominated the back country in most provinces. Modern developments like absentee landlordism strengthened rather than weakened their position, by stressing economic claims untempered by personal relations.

For the officials of the old China the gentry families were one medium through whom tax collections were effected. By this same token they were for the peasantry intermediaries who could palliate official oppression. They influenced official policy in the process of carrying it out. Conditions of flood or famine or incipient rebellion and the multitude of minor criminal cases and projects for public works were dealt with by the local officials through the help of the gentry community. It was the buffer between populace and officialdom.

The economic role of the gentry families was no more than half the story, for they had very important political-administrative functions in the Chinese state which made them unlike any group in Western history. Here we meet a problem of historical interpretation, created by the ambivalence of the term "gentry," which in the present literature on China may refer either to landowning families or to degree-holding individuals. Unfortunately for the clarity of the term, the latter group was not entirely included within the former. Peasants without landlord-family backing could and did rise through the examination system to become degree-holders and officials. Thus a poor man, by his educational qualifications alone, could become a member of the gentry in the narrow sense used above, even though he was not connected with a gentry family in the broad sense used above. This fact makes the term "gentry" ambiguous and therefore subject to dispute.

The view taken here is that the degree-holding individuals were in most cases connected with landowning families, and the latter in most cases had degree-holding members. Until the subject is clarified by further research we can only proceed on the assumption that, in general and for the most part, the gentry families were the out-of-office reservoir of the degree-holders and the bureaucracy. The big families were the seedbed in which officeholders were nurtured and the haven to which dismissed or worn-out bureaucrats could return.

If we turn to the narrower and more concrete, political-administrative definition of the gentry, we find that in each local community the gentry as individuals, in the basic sense of literati or degree-holders, had many important public functions. They raised funds for and supervised public works — the building and upkeep of irrigation and communication facilities such as canals, dikes, dams, roads, bridges, ferries. They supported Confucian institutions and morals — establishing and maintaining schools, shrines and local temples of Confucius, publishing books, especially local histories or gazetteers, and issuing moral homilies and exhortations to the populace. In time of peace they set the tone of public life. In time of disorder they organized and commanded militia defense forces. From day to day they arbitrated disputes informally, in place of the continual litigation which goes on in any American town. The gentry also set up charities and handled trust funds to help the community, and made contributions at official request to help the state, especially in time of war, flood, or famine. So useful were these contributions that most dynasties got revenue by selling the lowest literary degrees, thus admitting many persons to degree-holding status without examination. While this abused the system, it also let men of wealth rise for a price into the upper class and share the gentry privileges, such as contact with the officials and immunity from corporal punishment.

The position of the gentry families as the reservoir from which most of the individual scholar-officials emerged may explain why officialdom did not penetrate lower down into Chinese society. The imperial government remained a superstructure which did not directly enter the villages because it rested upon the gentry as its foundation. The many public functions of the local degree-holders made a platform under the imperial bureaucracy and let the officials move about with remarkable fluidity and seeming independence of local roots. Actually, the Emperor's appointee to any magistracy could administer it only with the cooperation of the gentry in that area. All in all, in a country of over 400 million people, a century ago, there were less than 20,000 regular imperial officials but roughly one and a quarter million scholarly degree-holders.

Continued domination of the gentry families over the peasantry was assured not only by landowning but also by the fact that the gentry mainly produced the scholar class from which officials were chosen. This near-monopoly of scholarship was made possible in turn by the nature of the Chinese language.

3. THE CHINESE WRITTEN LANGUAGE—THE SCHOLAR

Chinese writing is not only different to look at, it is based on utterly different principles from the phonetically written tongues of western Asia and Europe, many of which look to us just as baffling as Chinese but are in fact closely similar to our own language. Even Siamese children, for example, when they study Thai in school go through a process very similar to American children, learning the sounds to associate with a number of otherwise meaningless symbols, or alphabet. As far as their mode of thought and study is concerned, they could just as well learn the English alphabet (with various adjustments to convey Thai sounds) and then proceed to write down words heard in everyday life and develop their vocabularies and powers of self-expression. With a Chinese child it is different. He learns symbols which have meaning because of their appearance, and which exist like pictures or like the figure 5, apart from any sounds.

The earliest Chinese characters have been found at the archaeological site of the ancient Shang dynasty capital of Anyang, which is in Honan province north of the Yellow River. It appears that the ancient kings' diviners took the auspices by applying a hot point to flat slips of bone, producing cracks which could be interpreted as the advice of the ancestors. Characters were scratched on these "oracle bones" and the results were recorded there. This written language was both pictographic and symbolic, in either case ideographic rather than phonetic.

The Chinese language today consists of well over forty thousand characters in the biggest dictionary. But these boil down to about seven thousand necessary for a newspaper font, including about three thousand that one needs to know in order to be really literate. The form of these characters has hardly changed since the early Christian era. Until a generation ago the Chinese were still getting along with a written language comparable in age to ancient Greek and Latin, so terse that it usually had to be seen to be understood — the sound alone being inadequate. This was one factor helping to keep China, down to the twentieth century, in its archaic Confucian mold. The language inhibited easy contact with alien societies, whose students of Chinese found it even harder then than now.

A Note on Chinese Writing. Chinese characters began as pictures or symbols. The ancient character ☉ (later written 日) was the sun, and ☽ (later 月) the moon. Sun and moon together 明 meant bright, illustrious, clear. 木 meant a tree, two trees 林 meant a forest, and three 森 a dense growth. The symbols 一 二 三 are certainly easier than "one, two, three." 囗 indicates an enclosure or "to surround," while a smaller square 口 is the sign for the mouth and by extension means a hole, a pass, a harbor, and the like.

In its early growth the Chinese written language could not expand on a purely pictographic basis (like the joining of "sun" and "moon" to make "bright," noted above). A phonetic element crept into it. As a result most Chinese characters are combinations of other simple characters. One part of the combination usually indicates the root meaning, while the other part indicates something about the sound.

For example, take the character for east, 東, which in the Peking dialect has had the sound "tung" (pronounced like "doong," as in Mao Tse-tung's name). Since a Chinese character is read aloud as a single syllable and since spoken Chinese is also rather short of sounds (there are only about four hundred different syllables in the whole language), it has been plagued with homophones, words that sound like other words, like "soul" and "sole" or "all" and "awl" in English. It happened that the spoken word meaning freeze had the sound "tung." So did a spoken word meaning a roof beam. When the Chinese went to write down the character for freeze, they took the character for east and put beside it the symbol for ice 冫, which makes the character 凍 ("tung," to freeze). To write down the word sounding "tung" which meant roof beam, they wrote the character east and put before it the symbol for wood 木 making 棟 ("tung," a roof beam).

These are simple examples. Indeed any part of the Chinese language is simple in itself. It becomes difficult because there is so much of it, so many meanings and allusions, to be remembered. When the lexicographers wanted to arrange thousands of Chinese characters in a dictionary, for instance, the best they could do in the absence of an alphabet was to work out a list of 214 classifiers, one of which was sure to be in each character in the language. These 214 classifiers, for dictionary purposes, correspond to the 26 letters of our alphabet, but are more ambiguous and less efficient.

In spite of its cumbersomeness the Chinese written language was used to produce a greater volume of recorded literature than any other language before modern times. One sober estimate is that until 1750 there had been more books published in Chinese than in all the other languages in the world put together.

Perhaps enough has been said to indicate why written Chinese became a monopoly of the scribes. The Chinese language had the character of an institution, rather than a tool, of society. Men worshipped it, and devoted long lives to mastering even parts of its literature, which was a world of its own, into which one might gain admittance only by strenuous effort. The Chinese writing system was not a convenient device lying ready at hand for every schoolboy to pick up and use as he prepared to meet life's problems. It was itself one of life's problems. If little Lao-san could not find the time for long-continued study of it, he was forever debarred from social advancement. Thus the Chinese written language, rather than an open door through which China's peasantry could find truth and light, was a heavy barrier pressing against any upward advance and requiring real effort to overcome — a hindrance, not a help to learning.

Consequently much of Chinese learning stopped with the language and the classical literature. Students were exhausted merely by the mastery of them. In the old days a boy needed ten years of leisure in which to master the myriad literary allusions to be found in the classics. Only a gentry family could normally afford it.

The Scholar. The scholar class produced by mastery of the characters was closely integrated with both the gentry families beneath it and the official system above. When successful as a degree-holder and perhaps an official, the scholar found his channel of expression and achievement through the established structure of government. He could become an official, however, only by mastering the official ideology of the state as set down in the canonical works of the Chinese classics. These texts were part of a system of ideas and ritual practices in which the scholar-official learned and applied the Confucian rules and attitudes on the plane of verbal conduct while participating in the personal relationships, political cliques, organized perquisites, and systematic squeeze which distinguished the official class on the plane of practical action.

For the scholar who did not rise into official life there was always the alternative of the family system from which he had sprung. His status as a degree-holder gave him contact with the lower fringes of official power and through this personal contact he could serve his family by representing its interests. This function again called for the use of Confucian ideas in verbal and literary expression. In this way the scholar, whether in official life or out of it, was wedded to the established order of family and state. His living depended upon them and in practice he served them both. As a cultivated gentleman incapable of manual labor or trade and trained to be the bearer of the family-state ideology, he had no alternative.

It was the security of the individual boy in the gentry family which made it possible for him to take the risk involved in the investment of his time in scholarship. His preparation for the examinations and for official life required many years of study. Yet the examinations were a gamble and talented youths could be fed into the system only from sources which had means. The risk and mobility of official life contrasted with the security and stability of the landed gentry. The point of balance between them was the examination system. In a society which seems to us remarkable for its emphasis upon personal relations, the Chinese examinations appear to have been amazingly impersonal and universalistic. When the system was functioning effectively at the height of a dynasty, every effort was made to eliminate personal favoritism. Candidates were locked in their cubicles, several thousand of which in long rows covered a broad area at each provincial capital. Papers were marked with the writer's number only. Such precautions were, of course, necessary for the maintenance of any rational and objective standards in the selection of candidates for office. They expressed the Chinese ruler's genuine need of talented personnel to maintain an efficient administration. Once the best talent of the land had been chosen by this impersonal institution, however, it was then perfectly consistent that the officials should conduct a highly personal administration of the government, following a "virtue ethic" which attached importance to the qualities of individual personality rather than a "command ethic" which laid emphasis upon an impersonal and higher law.

The fact and the myth of social mobility in the Chinese state are still matters of debate. Most dynasties which supported the examination system as a mechanism for the selection of talent gave extensive lip service to the myth that all might enter high position, depending only upon ability. Western writers for long assumed that the Chinese examinations were a really democratic institution, providing opportunity for the intelligent peasant to rise in the world. In fact, however, this seems to have happened rather seldom. The many years of assiduous study required for the examinations were a barrier which no ordinary peasant could surmount. The legend of the villagers who clubbed together to support the studies of the local peasant genius has been an inspiring tradition. But it was not an every day occurrence.

Of the various avenues open to the common peasant, advancement could not be sought through the use of new land or founding of new enterprises, nor, except rarely, through increased agricultural production and the accumulation of profits and savings. This fact has given Chinese life a character far different from our own and makes the American doctrine of individualism and free enterprise, when transplanted to China, an almost incomprehensible and rather dubious jumble of slogans. In Chinese circumstances, advancement for the common man has lain in the direction of connections with the bureaucracy. Entrance into the official class or into the penumbra of money handlers and fixers which surrounded it was a goal to be achieved through personal contacts and personal services. But this route on the whole led through the gentry and not around them.

Thus landlords, scholars, and officials were all parts of a composite ruling class. Landowning families, having some agricultural surplus, could give their sons leisure for study to become scholars. Scholars, with a mastery of classical learning, could pass examinations and become officials. Officials, with the perquisites and profits of bureaucratic government, could protect and increase their family landholdings. The structure was flexible, automatically self-perpetuating and very stable.

4. NONDEVELOPMENT OF CAPITALISM — THE MERCHANT

In all of Chinese history one of the most urgent questions which a Westerner will ask is the reason why the Chinese merchant class failed to break away from its dependence upon officialdom and create an independent industrial and entrepreneurial power. The answer is not simple but it can be attempted.

First of all, the Chinese merchant had an attitude of mind quite different from that of the Western entrepreneur extolled by our classical economists of the last century. According to the doctrine of the latter, the economic man can prosper most by producing, and securing from his increased production the profit which the market will give him. In the Chinese tradition, however, the economic man will do best not by increasing production but by increasing his own share of what has already been produced. He will rise by competing against his fellows directly rather than by creating new wealth through the conquest of nature, or the increased exploitation of her resources, or the applications of improved technologies. This bespeaks the fact that the Chinese economy has had from early times a maximum of people competing for a minimum of natural resources, instead of great continents and new industries to develop.

This Chinese view can be more easily understood by looking at the trend toward monopoly in the modern West. The capitalists who organized large-scale industry, and by its efficiency and increased production made their early fortunes, have often been succeeded by capital manipulators who have found that the organization of industrial monopolies will yield increased profits without any increase in production. The tradition in China has been not to build a better mousetrap but to get the official mouse monopoly.

The ideal gentleman in China was, therefore, the man who had risen above the necessity to produce and was able to devote himself to leisure and the scholarly pursuits which symbolized it. The person most esteemed was he who had achieved leisure, not he who (like the modern big-time operator with his telecommunications and office staffs working day and night) outdid his fellows in setting the pace of frenzied business activity. This leisurely ideal could be seen only recently in the Chinese village where a leisure class appeared at the top level of the peasantry although at an amazingly low level of income. The relatively well-to-do peasant, though still bone poor by our standards, would seize the first opportunity to change his status from that of a laborer who uses his back and hands in the fields to that of a gentleman who wears a long gown and affects some literate interest. The long fingernails of old China were certainly the cheapest badge of leisure ever invented.

From the earliest period official position was the key to wealth and leisure, for the official had the greatest opportunity to increase his share of the things already produced. With his official status went the power to settle human affairs and profit thereby. More specifically, the official represented the Emperor's power to conscript *corvée* labor, to levy taxes, to dispense justice, and to regulate the economic and social activities of the people.

Coming from the local gentry, Chinese officials usually brought to their careers the attitude of a *rentier* class. They sought perquisites rather than opportunities for enterprise. It is this aspect of the "bureaucratic spirit" which most irks modern exponents of the "entrepreneurial spirit."

Now the merchant was a competitor of the official, since he also was occupied not in agricultural production but in manipulations and exchanges which would secure a greater share of the goods already available. In theory the merchant from ancient times had been regarded by the scholar-official as nonproductive and parasitic. His activities in transporting produce from place to place were given no credit in the classical literature. He was placed at the bottom of the social scale.

In actual fact, however, the merchant was kept in check by the official as a minor ally whose activities could be used and milked in the interest of the official class or of the state. Commercial transactions were always subject to the superintendence and taxation of the officials. Government monopolies of staple articles, like salt and iron in ancient times, or like tea, silk, opium, tobacco, salt, and matches more recently, have been an expression of the overriding economic prerogatives of the state. No merchant class was allowed to rise independently and encroach upon these prerogatives.

On the other hand, it was always possible to work out a close community of interest between the merchant and the official, for official patronage and support were necessary for any big commercial undertaking. Both could profit where neither could succeed alone. Merchants, bankers, brokers, and traders of all sorts were therefore a class attached as subordinates to the bureaucracy. As handlers and manipulators of goods and capital, they assisted the officials not only in extracting the surplus from commerce but also in extracting the surplus from agriculture.

Merchants indeed could move with some ease into the gentry class through purchase of land and literary degrees and intermarriage. The fact that farmers were free to sell their land gave the merchant class an opportunity to buy it and gain both steady income and social prestige. Unlike Europe, China had little foreign trade in which a merchant could invest. Land remained the great object of his investment, and so the merchant class produced landlords more readily than independent commercial capitalists.

Chinese guild organization, though capable of great feats of passive resistance in the form of strikes or non-cooperation, bears out the subservience of merchants to officials. The strength of the guild institution has lain in the craft guild which the artisans of a certain handicraft have used to preserve their monopoly of technical processes and productive rights. Merchant guilds such as led the way in early European trade have been notably weak in China. The Canton Cohong, one of the main examples, was notoriously a tool of court officials.

China's premodern financial system has offered another body of evidence. Savings which represent accumulated capital have ordinarily been invested in moneylending because of the high interest rates obtainable. The usurious rates have been an index of the farmer's high seasonal demand for money, both to pay his taxes and for subsistence until the next harvest. Short-term credits to farmers have paid higher interest than long-term industrial loans. As a result there has been less incentive in China than in America for investment of savings in industrial production.

One sign of the predominance of agriculture in the Chinese economy has been the restricted use of money. Creation of credit among the villages has been retarded by the relative self-sufficiency of the peasant household and its dependence upon short-term purchases from sources close at hand. Similarly the government used to rely heavily upon taxation in kind and the payments of stipends in grain. The capital at Peking, for example, was fed by grain shipments from the provinces via the Grand Canal. In addition the government had at its command resources of *corvée* labor which received no money wages.

The old currency system itself was extremely complex and inefficient. The unit of account (under the Manchus, the ounce or *tael*) varied from place to place and also as between trades and agencies of government. Twenty different units of account might be in common use in one city at one time. It was not possible to maintain a minted currency of fixed value. Reliance had to be placed upon the clumsy circulation of pure silver, each ingot of which had to be weighed and also assayed for its purity. Few governments could refrain from debasing the copper coinage. The resulting confusion of currency units, and exchange arrangements among them, was in itself a serious handicap to any merchant. It represented the domination of the money manipulator, who profited by this complexity, over the investor who wanted to put his money into planned productive enterprises. One may surmise that this inefficiency of the money system was tolerated because it helped the ruling class's money operations more than it hindered them, just as the scholars tolerated an ideographic language the difficulty of which preserved their semi-monopoly over it. In any case this inefficient money system bespoke a loose decentralized economy in which commercial activity was mainly limited to local trade.

In this context it is possible to find an explanation of the non-development of capitalism in China in the fact that the merchant was never able to become established outside the control of the gentry and their representatives in the bureaucracy. In feudal Europe the merchant class was able to develop in the towns. Since the landed ruling class in Europe were settled in their manors upon the land, the European towns could grow up outside the feudal system instead of being integrated in it. Medieval burghers gained their independence by having a separate habitat in these new towns, and a new political authority to protect them, in the persons of the kings of national states.

In China these conditions were lacking. The early abolition of feudalism and the dependence of the Emperor and his officials upon the local gentry left no political power outside the established order to which the merchant could turn for special protection. In addition the gentry families of China early became the dominant class in the towns, which grew up primarily as administrative centers. The essential connection of the gentry with officialdom drew them into these centers. The gentry family's best security, in short, lay not in a sole reliance upon landowning but in a union of landowning with official prerogatives. Family property in itself was no security but officials who were family members could give it protection.

Thus the gentry class, as an elite stratum over the peasant economy, inevitably congregated in the towns. The villages depended upon the towns economically as centers of handicraft production and of exchange. They depended upon the towns also politically as centers of administration and of the authority necessary to maintain peace and order. Finally, the towns were cultural centers as well as walled havens of protection against bandits or irate peasants, and for all these reasons they were the seat of the gentry. But the latter found their security in land and office, not in trade and industry. Between them, the gentry and officials saw to it that the merchant remained under control and contributed to their coffers instead of setting up a separate economy.

5. CHINA AS AN "ORIENTAL" SOCIETY

If we put together all the foregoing elements — peasant villages, landlord gentry families, merchants, scholars, and officials — we have a structure of social classes different from anything in Europe or America, with a different type of economic organization and political control. Following the lead of a pioneer social historian in this field, Dr. K. A. Wittfogel, we can classify traditional China as a representative of an ancient "oriental" type of society, fundamentally distinct from the more recent modern society of Europe and America. This is not to say that China is somehow exotic and tangential to the norm of social organization. Quite the contrary, in this view China may be an exemplar of the norm while America is a freak.

Traditional China is classed by Wittfogel with other ancient empires of Egypt, Mesopotamia, and India and also with the empires of the Incas, the Aztecs, or the Maya in pre-Columbian America. All these ancient societies were organized under centralized monolithic governments in which the bureaucracy was dominant in almost all aspects of large-scale activity — administrative, military, religious, and economic — so that no sanction for private enterprise ever became established. An imperial monopoly of administrative activities in the collection of taxes, maintenance of local order, dispensing of justice, or management of the civil service may not seem unusual to us. Centralized control over the military also may not seem unexpected, nor even efforts to control religious life and thought. But these governments' customary monopoly of large-scale economic activity will seem to modern Americans most different and "unnatural."

To understand this difference we must recall that the Greco-Roman world and the European Middle Ages both saw the growth of dominant social classes which were originally outside the framework of government and were based on private property. The Greek city-state, for instance, was dominated by a propertied class which manipulated the government and made every effort to prevent the growth of an independent bureaucracy. In this Greek society of private property, taxes were collected by tax farmers, the mines and customs were likewise farmed out to private individuals, slaves were used as scribes, and the citizens who took office were rotated so rapidly that no one official could accumulate personal power based on official position. Under the Roman Republic the taxes and customs were collected by tax farmers. Public works were made the responsibility of private persons. In feudal Europe the enlargement of the sphere of private activity was of course even more striking, in the military and administrative sectors as well as in the economic. It is no accident that the modern West found the roots of individualism in Greek philosophy and Roman law as well as in the medieval town.

Without attempting hard and fast generalizations, we may note certain characteristics of the economic life of China and other politically centralized oriental countries which distinguish them from our own. In the first place these societies have been based upon agricultural production. Their governments have performed the function of controlling the economic ingredients of this production. This has involved control in varying degrees over the land, the man power, and the water supply. In ancient times the ruler's claim to the disposal of the land and of the people on it was seldom questioned, although it was usually found through experience that private landowning was a useful incentive to peasant production and did not impede the collection of taxes. The institution of compulsory *corvée* labor by the people at the behest of the government usually became well established. This made possible the construction of enormous public works which still amaze us, like the pyramids of Egypt or the Great Wall of China.

Control of the water supply for agricultural production was a strategic factor in the growth of the government's economic function. It was typical of these societies that, unlike Western Europe, they were in regions of semi-aridity where the water supply of great rivers, if properly used, would supplement the insufficiency of rainfall. But irrigation to be effective must be centrally controlled. In like manner its cognate principle, flood prevention, requires centralized direction. Both irrigation ditches and river dikes must be maintained throughout their length on a basis of over-all direction — in short, by the government and its bureaucracy.

Once established, a government of this type found itself dependent upon the extension of the same principle of economic control. The building and maintenance of canals for transportation purposes and of highways for transport and communication were parelleled by the growth of the civil service. Scribes and administrators were essential to collect the agricultural surplus and superintend the public works. The concentration of population in enormous capital cities at the imperial administrative center went hand in hand with an increased density of man power upon the land. When urban handicraft industry stimulated exchange between town and countryside, there was no opportunity for the new industrial and merchant class to escape the overshadowing domination of government. The idea never occurred to them.

In effect this meant that heavy industry, which in these early societies was represented by such things as the Great Wall or the Grand Canal and other heavy waterworks, was from the first in the hands of the government. Private enterprise might develop freely in small-scale agricultural production within the grip of government taxation, but this was not a capitalist type of private enterprise. From the peasants' more assiduous cultivation of their privately owned land, the bureaucracy would garner a greater surplus by taxation. By the same principle they also stood ready to collect from the merchant or industrial producer any surplus which he might accumulate. Merchants appear in the records of ancient China but never as a class having political power. Early Emperors specifically barred them from taking the examinations for entrance into official life. The growth of commerce was less important to the rulers of a politically centralized oriental state than the continued supervision of the agricultural economy. The state depended upon land taxes rather than trade taxes.

Behind this disesteem of commerce lay the fact that the agrarian economy of China has always been decentralized, fragmented, and unintegrated. Given the relative self-sufficiency of each farming locality, trade and a money economy have remained at a minimum in spite of the centralization of political power for tax collections and public works.

More fundamentally, the establishment of these institutions of agriculture, public works, and bureaucracy was accompanied by a persistent pattern of assumptions and expectations in the minds of the people, expressed in the evaluations of the classical literature, which placed the official high and the merchant low in public esteem, and was perpetuated by the educational system based on the classics. Instead of a philosophy of individual initiative and enterprise, or the limitless possibilities of invention and personal acquisitiveness, these oriental societies subscribed to a philosophy of hierarchic status with an emphasis upon individual conformity.

Chinese Militarism. The pattern of an oriental society is also visible in China's treatment of the soldier. The standard dogma perpetuated by Chinese scholars and civilian chroniclers has been that "good iron is not used to make a nail nor a good man to make a soldier." This expresses the idea of the literatus who governs by moral sanctions and uses every opportunity to disparage the warrior who takes power by force. Disparagement of the soldier is deeply ingrained in the old Chinese system of values. Yet few empires in history have had a more impressive military record. In periods of strong government as under the Han, the T'ang, the early Ming, or the early Ch'ing (see Chart on p. 2), powerful military expeditions have gone beyond China's borders into Annam or Korea, or across the wastes of Mongolia and Central Asia. Meanwhile every dynasty has been founded by the sword. Decades at a time have seen an endless succession of rebel hordes, imperial armies, and alien invaders marching across the face of the land. The nomad dynasties of conquest have actually been supported by a professional military caste.

Nevertheless the Chinese military tradition is of a different type from the European or the Japanese. Once an imperial regime has been instituted, civilian government has been esteemed over military. It took a soldier to found a dynasty but he and his descendants invariably found it easier to rule as sages, through civilian officials. This is undobtedly because power over the Chinese economy invariably settled in the hands of administrators, bureaucrats who got wealth in the form of revenues, not warriors who got it in the form of loot. Chinese history has had no counterpart to the Elizabethan or Japanese institutions of maritime adventure and piracy whereby the central power waxed strong on its overseas takings. No doubt one factor was the early disappearance of feudalism. In China the fighting man gave place to the administrator some two thousand years before he did so in Japan. Just as the commercial society of the United States prefers civilian to military government, so the bureaucratic polity of China sought constantly to avoid domination by any independent military power.

In practice this meant that the problem of force in China was essentially a police problem, how to maintain surveillance over an unarmed and settled population and muster enough strength to suppress those who might turn bandit. Once a dynasty had become well established, armies for the attack and destruction of enemies were not needed within the Wall. This created the constant problem of reconciling the police institutions of China proper with the type of warfare required on the Chinese frontier against the professional fighting men of the steppe. Unlike the Mongols or the Manchus, Chinese farmers could never become a nation in arms in which each individual had a stake in the national cause. Chinese armies have been much more a form of public works, created at times of crisis by the same conscription of cheap man power which has provided the *corvée* labor gangs for building a Great Wall, a Burma Road, or a Huai River dike.

4

The Confucian Pattern

CONFUCIUS and Karl Marx had even less in common than the ideologies which bear their names, and the differences between Confucianism and Marx-Leninism-Maoism are as great as the similarities. Yet both traditional China and Communist China have stressed the role of ideology, and no one can understand Chiang Kai-shek or even Mao Tse-tung without knowing something of the Confucian tradition.

Superficial Western observers, looking only at the texts of the Confucian classics, have been impressed with their agnostic this-worldliness and their ethical emphasis upon proper conduct in personal relations. In its larger sense as a philosophy of life, we have generally associated with Confucianism those quiet virtues so artfully described in Lin Yutang's *My Country and My People* — patience, pacifism and compromise, the golden mean, conservatism and contentment, reverence for the ancestors, the aged, and the learned, and, above all, a mellow humanism — taking man, not God, as the center of the universe.

All this need not be denied. But if we take this Confucian view of life in its social and political context, we will see that its esteem for age over youth, for the past over the present, for established authority over innovation, has in fact provided one of the great historic answers to the problem of social stability. It has been the most successful of all systems of conservatism. For most of two thousand years the Confucian ideology was made the chief subject of study in the world's largest state. Nowhere else have the sanctions of government power been based for so many centuries upon a single consistent pattern of ideas attributed to one ancient sage.

Naturally, in the course of two thousand years many changes have occurred within the broad limits of what we call Confucianism — periods of decline and revival, repeated movements for reform, new emphases and even innovations within the inherited tradition. The range of variety may be less broad than among the multiple facets of Christianity but it is certainly comparable. Consequently the term Confucianism means many things and must be used with care.

As a code of personal conduct Confucianism tried to make each individual a moral being, ready to act on ideal grounds, to uphold virtue against human error, especially against evil rulers. There were many Confucian scholars of moral grandeur, uncompromising foes of tyranny. But their reforming zeal, the dynamics of their creed, aimed to reaffirm and conserve the traditional polity, not to change its fundamental premises.

That Confucian ideas persist in the minds of Chinese politicians today should not surprise us. Confucianism began as a means of bringing social order out of the chaos of a period of warring states. It has been a philosophy of status and obedience according to status, and consequently a ready tool for autocracy and bureaucracy whenever they have flourished. Unifiers of China have been irresistibly attracted to it, for reasons that are not hard to see.

When Chiang Kai-shek on Christmas day 1936 was released by the mutinous subordinates who had forcibly held him at Sian, he returned to Nanking amid unprecedented national rejoicing. Yet four days later he submitted his resignation.

Since I am leading the military forces of the country, I should set a good example for my fellow servicemen. It is apparent that my work failed to command the obedience of my followers; for otherwise the mutiny . . . would not have occurred . . . I sincerely hope that the central executive committee will censure me for my negligence of duties. After the Sian incident, it is no longer fit for me to continue in office.

Nine years later in his famous wartime book, *China's Destiny,* Chiang Kai-shek said:

To cultivate the moral qualities necessary to our national salvation . . . we must revive and extend our traditional ethical principles. The most important task is to develop our people's sense of propriety, righteousness, integrity, and honor. These qualities are based upon the Four

Cardinal Principles and the Eight Virtues, which in turn are based on
Loyalty and Filial Piety . . .

These two examples could be multiplied. They demonstrate the
degree to which China down to recent decades remained a Confucian state. In the first case no one wanted Chiang to resign, nor
did he intend to do so, and his resignation was elaborately declined.
In the second case no one expected that China's national salvation
in the midst of Japanese aggression, blockade, and inflation could
be achieved through moral qualities alone, nor did Chiang think so.
But in both cases his words delineated the traditional Confucian way.

Countless Chinese leaders before Chiang Kai-shek have quoted
Confucius while fighting off rivals or alien invaders, who, like
the Japanese, have invoked the Sage on their part while trying to
take over China. Peking today sings a different tune, but there are
Confucian overtones in the Marxist orchestration. The crucial role
of ideology under communism lends particular interest to China's
ideological past.

1. CONFUCIAN PRINCIPLES

The principles of Confucian government, which still lie somewhere
below the surface of Chinese politics, were worked out before the
time of Christ. Modifications made in later centuries, though extensive, have not been fundamental.

First of all, from the beginning of Chinese history in the Shang
and Chou periods (from prehistoric times before 1400 B.C. to the
third century B.C.) there was a marked stratification into the
classes of the officials and nobility on the one hand, and the common
people on the other. Thus the term "hundred names" (*pai-hsing*)
referred originally to the clans of the officials who were in a category
quite different from the common people (*min*). It was not until
much later that the modern term "old hundred names" (*lao-pai-
hsing*) became transferred to the populace. This difference between
the ancient ruling class and the common people gave rise to a
particular type of aristocratic tradition which has been preserved
and transmitted through Confucianism down to the present. The
Confucian aristocrat has been the scholar-official.

In the second place, Confucianism has been the idealogy of the
bureaucrat. The bureaucratic ruling class came into its own after

the decentralized feudalism of ancient China gave way to an imperial government. The unification of 221 B.C., in which one of the warring states (Ch'in) swallowed the others, required violent dictatorial methods and a philosophy of absolutism (that of the so-called "Legalist" philosophers). But after the short-lived Ch'in dynasty was succeeded by the Han in 202 B.C., a less tyrannical system of administration evolved. The Emperors came to rely upon a new class of administrators who superintended the great public works — dikes and ditches, walls, palaces, and granaries — and who drafted peasant labor and collected the land tax to support them. These administrators supplanted the hereditary nobility of feudal times and became the backbone of the imperial regime.

In the two centuries before Christ the early Han rulers firmly established certain principles. First, that the political authority in the state was centralized in the one man at the top who ruled as Emperor. Second, the Emperor's authority in the conduct of the administration was exercised on his behalf by his chief ministers, who stood at the top of a graded bureaucracy and who were responsible to him for the success or failure of their administration. Third, this bureaucracy was centralized in the vast palace at the capital where the Emperor exercised the power of appointment to office. His chief task became the selection of civil servants, with an eye to the maintenance of his power and his dynasty. For this reason the appointment of relatives, particularly from the maternal side, became an early practice. (Maternal relatives were the one group of persons completely dependent upon the ruler's favor as well as tied to him by family bonds, in contrast to paternal relatives who might compete for the succession.) Fourth, the early Han rulers developed the institution of inspection which later became the censorate, whereby an official in the provinces was checked upon by another official of lower rank, who was sent independently and was not responsible for the acts of his superior. In this and in many other ways the central problem of the imperial administration became that of selecting and controlling bureaucrats. It was here that Confucianism played its central role.

This ideology did not, of course, begin with Confucius (551–479? B.C.). The interesting concept of the Mandate of Heaven, for example, went back to the early Chou period (ca. 1000–771 B.C.). According to the classic *Book of History*, the wickedness of the last ruler of the preceding dynasty of Shang, who was a tyrant, caused Heaven to give a mandate to the Chou to destroy him and supplant his dynasty, inasmuch as the Shang people themselves had failed to overthrow the tyrant. As later amplified this ancient idea became the famous "right of rebellion," the last resort of the populace against tyrannical government. It emphasized the good conduct or virtue of the ruler as the ethical sanction for preserving his dynasty. Bad conduct on his part destroyed the sanction, Heaven withdrew its Mandate, and the people were justified in deposing the dynasty, if they could. Consequently any successful rebellion was justified and a new rule sanctioned, by the very fact of its success. · "Heaven decides as the people decide." The Chinese literati have censored bad government and rebels have risen against it in terms of this theory. It has also reinforced the belief that the ruler should be advised by learned men in order to ensure his right conduct.

Government by Moral Prestige. Confucius and his fellow philosophers achieved their position by being teachers who advised rulers as to their right conduct, in an age when feudal princes were competing for hegemony. Confucius was an aristocrat and maintained at his home a school for the elucidation and transmission of the moral principles of conduct and princely rule. Here he taught the upper class how to behave. He emphasized court etiquette, state ceremonies, and proper conduct * towards one's ancestors and in the famous five degrees of relationship. One of the central principles of this code was expressed in the idea of "proper behavior according to status" (*li*). The Confucian gentleman or *chün-tzu* ("the superior man," "the princely man") was guided by *li*, the precepts of which were written in the classics.

It is important to note that this code which came to guide the conduct of the scholar-official did not originally apply to the common people, whose conduct was to be regulated by rewards and punishments rather than moral principles.

---

* "When he (Confucius) was in his native village, he bore himself with simplicity, as if he had no gifts of speech. But when in the ancestral temple or at court, he expressed himself readily and clearly, yet with a measure of reserve . . . At court, when conversing with the higher great officials, he spoke respectfully. When conversing with the lower great officials, he spoke out boldly . . . When he entered the palace gate, he appeared to stoop . . . When he hastened forward, it was with a respectful appearance . . . When the prince summoned him to receive a visitor, his expression seemed to change . . . When his prince commanded his presence, he did not wait for the carriage to be yoked, but went off on foot . . . He would not sit on his mat unless it was straight." Translated by D. Bodde from *Shih Chi*.

This complex system of abstruse rules which the Confucians became experts at applying stemmed from the relationship of Chinese man to nature, which has already been mentioned. This relation had early been expressed in a primitive animism in which the spirits of land, wind, and water were thought to play an active part in human affairs. The idea is still prevalent in the practice of Chinese geomancy or *feng-shui* (lit., "wind and water"), which sees to it that buildings in China are properly placed in their natural surroundings. Temples, for example, commonly face south with protecting hills behind them and a water course nearby. In its more rationalized form this idea of the close relation between human and natural phenomena led to the conception that human conduct is reflected in acts of nature. To put it another way, man is so much a part of the natural order that improper conduct on his part will throw the whole of nature out of joint. Therefore man's conduct must be made to harmonize with the unseen forces of nature, lest calamity ensue.

This was the rationale of the Confucian emphasis on right conduct on the part of the ruler, for the ruler was thought to intervene between mankind and the forces of nature. As the Son of Heaven he stood between Heaven above and the people below. He maintained the universal harmony of man and nature by doing the right thing at the right time. It was, therefore, logical to assume that when natural calamity came, it was the ruler's fault. It was for this reason that the Confucian scholar became so important. Only he, by his knowledge of the rules of right conduct, could properly advise the ruler in his cosmic role.

The main point of this theory of "government by goodness," by which Confucianism achieved an emphasis so different from anything in the West, was the idea of the virtue which was attached to right conduct. To conduct oneself according to the rules of propriety or *li* in itself gave one a moral status or prestige. This moral prestige in turn gave one influence over the people. "The people (are) like grass, the ruler like the wind"; as the wind blew, so the grass was inclined. Right conduct gave the ruler power.*

* In the *Analects* Confucius said: "When a prince's personal conduct is correct, his government is effective without the issuing of orders. If his personal conduct is not correct, he may issue orders but they will not be followed." (See Chiang Kai-shek's statement at the beginning of this chapter.) In the *Great Learning* it was said: " . . . the ruler will first take pains about his own virtue. Possessing virtue will give him the people. Possessing the people will give him the territory. Possessing

On this basis the Confucian scholars established themselves as an essential part of the government, specially competent to maintain its moral nature and so retain the Mandate of Heaven. Where the Legalist philosophers of the Ch'in unification had had ruthlessly efficient methods of government but no moral justification for them, the Confucianists offered an ideological basis. They finally eclipsed the many other ancient schools of philosophy. As interpreters of the *li*, they became technical experts, whose explanations of natural portents and calamities and of the implications of the rulers' actions could be denied or rejected only on the basis of the classical doctrines of which they were themselves the masters. This gave them a strategic position from which to influence government policy. In return they provided the regime with a rational and ethical sanction for the exercise of its authority, at a time when most rulers of empires relied mainly upon religious sanctions. This was a great political invention.

2. THE CLASSICAL ORTHODOXY

The Confucian doctrines were transmitted through the Chinese classics. As might be expected, these ancient books have formed a canon, the texts of which have been interpreted and reinterpreted through the centuries. In this process later texts, sometimes written for the purpose, have become canonized as more ancient, and books of early importance have fallen into obscurity. In the early Han period the classics usually mentioned are the *Book of Changes* (for divination), the *Book of History,* the *Odes* (ancient folk poems), the *Book of Ceremonies and Proper Conduct,* and the *Spring and Autumn Annals* (chronicles of Confucius' own state of Lu, in Shantung province) with their commentaries. It was not until much later, in the T'ang dynasty (618–907 A.D.) that the ancient book of the philosopher Mencius (fl. 324–314 B.C.) was elevated to the position of a classic. By degrees there was accumu-

the territory will give him its wealth. Possessing the wealth, he will have resources for expenditure. Virtue is the root, wealth is the result." Cp. Chiang Kai-shek in *China's Destiny:* "So long as we have a few men who will set an example, the people in a village, in a district, or in the whole country will unconsciously act likewise. As the grass is bent by the wind, so the social tone is influenced by the example of such men."

lated a canon of thirteen classics, which with their commentaries today fill some 120 volumes. In order to simplify this unwieldy corpus of ancient texts, scholars of the Sung (960–1279 A.D.) selected the famous Four Books (the *Analects of Confucius*, the *Book of Mencius*, the *Doctrine of the Mean*, and the *Great Learning*), which were so brief that any gentleman could master them.

The apothegms and aphorisms of the Four Books depict paternal government as the key to social order and the defense of the state. "If your Majesty," says Mencius to King Hui, "will indeed dispense a benevolent government to the people, being sparing in the use of punishments and fines, and making the taxes and levies light, so causing that the fields shall be plowed deep, and the weeding of them be carefully attended to, and that the strong-bodied during their days of leisure shall cultivate their filial piety, fraternal respectfulness, sincerity, and truthfulness, serving thereby at home their fathers and elder brothers and, abroad, their elders and superiors — you will then have a people who can be employed, with sticks which they have prepared, to oppose the strong mail and sharp weapons of the troops of Ch'in and Ch'u." *

Though eminently rational in form, this official doctrine had its religious side, expressed in the official rites at the Confucian temples, the pantheon of sages and their tablets, and the ritual veneration of them — all forming a state cult closely allied to the veneration of ancestors in the people's homes below and the Emperor's ritual acts above. While not anthropomorphic, this was a religious cult. One might call it a cult of state humanism, based on faith in the power of virtuous conduct to capture men's hearts and so lead them in the path of order under wise and benevolent authority.

The vicissitudes of the Confucian creed, like those of Catholicism, are a most instructive study and show how deeply it has penetrated Chinese life. In the third to sixth centuries A.D., during the decline of central authority which followed the Han Empire, Confucianism

---

* As Chiang Kai-shek put it 2250 years later in his book *Chinese Economic Theory*, "the government's duties are to support the people on the one hand and to protect them on the other. National plans for the support of the people are plans for the people's livelihood. But since this livelihood must also be protected, plans for livelihood become plans for the national defense . . . From the Chinese standpoint, therefore, Western economics is merely the study of private enterprise or of market transactions, whereas Chinese economic theory is a combination of the people's livelihood and national defense."

was all but eclipsed by Buddhism. But in the second great imperial period of China's long history, under the T'ang and Sung dynasties of the seventh to thirteenth centuries, the Confucian system was re-established and remolded into a form more stable, enduring, and unchangeable than ever.

Neo-Confucianism. The revival of Confucian government under the T'ang was part of a general revival of Chinese society in politics, administration, literature and art as well as thought. The T'ang rulers in the seventh century and until the middle of the eighth century extended their control in all directions, into Korea and Annam and over the nomad tribes and the settled oases of Central Asia. Meanwhile the T'ang capital at Ch'ang-an (modern Sian) became a metropolitan center of almost two million persons and a focus of travel and trade from Byzantium and all the Middle East.

It is interesting to note that in the early period of T'ang strength, when the state and the economy were expanding and both the legal system and the examinations were functioning vigorously, the revived Confucian bureaucracy was remarkably tolerant of foreign creeds. Foreign visitors brought with them all the variety of medieval religions — Judaism, the fifth century Christian heresy known as Nestorian Christianity, and Manichaeism and Zoroastrianism from Persia. But when the first great rebellion threatened the dynasty in the middle of the eighth century, and its problems of revenue and military control continued to grow more pressing, the self-confidence of Chinese power was evidently shaken, and the cosmopolitan spirit declined with it.

After the collapse of the T'ang and the successive incursions of barbarian rulers on the northern frontier, the Sung dynasty failed to recapture the international position which the early T'ang had achieved. Chinese rulers throughout the Sung were on the defensive against the peoples of the steppe. Handicraft production and domestic and overseas trade brought financial well-being to the government, but they were offset by military weakness. The later Sung became a great commercial empire whose exports of copper cash, silks, and porcelain reached all of Eastern Asia and spread into Indonesia, India, the Middle East, and Africa. The Sung period saw the development of a highly sophisticated urban life, the perfection of landscape painting, and the use and abuse of paper money long before its introduction in Europe. But through all this period

China's reaction to the invaders from Inner Asia remained rather unwarlike. Chinese influence abroad was based on commerce and culture rather than on military power.

This experience of foreign aggression in the Sung period of the eleventh and twelfth centuries (and the Mongol conquest which followed it in the thirteenth century) strengthened in Chinese society an ethnocentricity which has remained one of its chief characteristics. Of course many other factors also influenced the thought of this period, but during it the Confucian orthodoxy was reinforced and never lost its grip thereafter.

This new orthodoxy was an all-embracing system of thought which has been known to the West as Neo-Confucianism. It was more systematic and more complete than the ancient classics and by a reinterpretation of them gave Confucianism more metaphysical content than it had had before. The subject has not been widely studied, but scholars seem to agree that in its new form Confucianism was rounded out to provide more of the answers which man asks of life. The absorption of definitely idealistic elements, mainly from Buddhism, undoubtedly made Confucianism more satisfactory to Chinese intellectuals and so offered Christianity, when it came to China by sea in the sixteenth century, a good deal less of a spiritual vacuum to fill. By that time there was more to Confucianism than met the missionary's eye when he perused the religiously arid Chinese classics.

The greatest of the Neo-Confucian synthesizers was the twelfth-century philosopher, Chu Hsi (1130–1200), whose historic role in China has sometimes been compared with that of St. Thomas Aquinas (d. 1274) in the West. As would be expected, his work was the culmination of the efforts of several generations of Confucian writers reaching back to the T'ang dynasty, who had had large numbers of disciples and whose writings had established a number of philosophical elements which Chu Hsi was able to combine.

The Neo-Confucian system of the Sung which became orthodox for seven hundred years thereafter, had its basis in an absolute first principle called the Supreme Ultimate, subsisting beyond time and space. The Supreme Ultimate in turn was manifest in an infinitude of *li* (not the old Confucian term) which may be translated here as laws or principles of form. Each separate type or category of thing has its *li* and each *li* is a manifestation of the Supreme

Ultimate. Physical matter, on the other hand, consists of the primordial ether or first substance (*ch'i*), the stuff of the physical universe. In each thing, therefore, the *li* and *ch'i*, or law and matter, are mutually essential and complementary. A house, for example, must be made of bricks (*ch'i*), but they must be put together according to a plan (*li*). The comparability of this system to the Platonic ideas is plain.

In dealing with the ethical problem of evil, Chu Hsi asserted that the nature of any living creature is the *li* of that creature as found combined with the *ch'i*. The *li* in itself is perfectly good but in the physical world it is always found in combination with *ch'i*. Evil consists in the obscuring of the *li* by the *ch'i*. Thus there is no active principle of evil. It results from situations which arise. Man's instincts are fundamentally good. The highest Confucian virtue therefore became an unswerving determination and honesty expressed in the term *ch'eng*, "complete sincerity." By means of complete sincerity of heart the *li* or principles can be cleansed of the *ch'i* or physical obstructions which obscure them. This remains today one of the fundamental Chinese ideals, and explains why Japanese and Chinese diplomats, or Nationalist and Communist negotiators, can hurl no verbal thunderbolt more devastating than the charge of "insincerity." *

This doctrine of original goodness was expressed in the opening lines of the famous *Three Character Classic* studied first by every schoolboy for generation after generation: "At men's beginning their nature is fundamentally good, by nature they are similar but in practice they grow apart." It is not surprising that the Western missionary's somber conception of original sin has always had difficulty in overcoming this happier Confucian view.

In politics the Neo-Confucianists believed that the ruler must gain understanding in the true principles of government and be-

* Cp. the *Doctrine of the Mean:* "Sincerity is the way of Heaven . . . He who possesses sincerity is he who, without an effort, hits what is right, and apprehends, without the exercise of thought — he is the sage who naturally and easily embodies the right way . . . It is only he who is possessed of the most complete sincerity . . . who can transform others."

Cp. Chiang Kai-shek (*China's Destiny*): "Sincerity is the moving spirit of real action. With sincerity, a man concerns himself with public, not personal, interests. With sincerity, a man works for a just cause in perfect self-possession, pushing steadfastly and calmly onwards, unheedful of difficulties and dangers, until he finally succeeds."

come a sage by moral self-discipline. In practice the new Confucian orthodoxy put its primary stress upon the moral development of man. It became an ever more effective mechanism for the inculcation, through the study of the classics and the examination system, of the Confucian doctrines of loyalty and social responsibility and conformity. For the individual this philosophy was essentially monistic rather than dualistic, the *li* and *ch'i* being complementary and harmonious. Hell, heaven, and personal immortality were not conceived of, nor was a personal deity.

After the expulsion of the Mongols and the re-establishment of Chinese control over China under the Ming dynasty (1368–1644), the Sung Neo-Confucianism, because of its very inclusiveness, became a strait jacket on the Chinese mind. The Ming rulers used it as a tool of government. Chu Hsi's system became a dogma. Mencius became the greatest sage after Confucius. The Four Books and Five Classics became the intellectual fare of all ambitious men, as though Chinese society could find refuge by turning back into its own cultural heritage and could protect itself by staying within an established framework of ideas. This age saw the introduction of the famous "eight-legged essay," a style which put a premium upon balanced and antithetic forms of writing. Its influence can be seen in the habit of alternating sentences of six and four characters and of presenting no idea without balancing it against an opposite, which characterizes the traditional essay style.

Lest the above suggest that old misconception of the ignorant West that China was "unchanging," we should note the development of the rather metaphysical school of Ming philosophy which culminated in Wang Yang-ming (1472–1529). Revolting against the Neo-Confucian orthodoxy, Wang asserted that man has intuitive moral knowledge within his own mind and through self-cultivation can develop it and even reach a subjective enlightenment. For this he must achieve a disciplined unity between knowledge and conduct — an idea we will find echoed in modern times, even today under Communism.

Again, at the end of the seventeenth century under the Manchu dynasty (1644–1911) certain Confucian scholars began to develop a more pragmatic and critical view of the classics and their doctrines. This was called the "Han learning," as opposed to the "Sung learning." It was part of a general movement of critical scholarship manifest in historical, geographical, and textual studies. But for all their obvious intellectual vigor, these later scholars clearly remained within the Confucian strait jacket. Their enormous and exhaustive compendia (the largest was in 36,300 chapters!) stand today as a monument to the vitality of Chinese scholarship in carrying on and developing a great tradition, but not to its creative originality in meeting the new and unprecedented problems which have confronted the Chinese people.

3. THE NONDEVELOPMENT OF SCIENCE

In this atmosphere of orthodoxy there was little incentive for the development of scientific method. It was during this Neo-Confucian period from the thirteenth to the nineteenth century that China certainly fell behind the West in technology. The brilliant early developments of paper and printing, gunpowder and the compass, the Chinese mathematical discoveries and their perfection of bronze-casting, porcelain and other handicrafts, were not followed by the growth of an organized technology and the formulation of a body of scientific principles. In short, science failed to develop as a persisting social *institution,* a system of theory and practice socially transmitted, though meanwhile there was no lack of inventiveness. During the first thirteen centuries of the Christian era, according to the historian of Chinese science, Joseph Needham, a continuous series of technological inventions came to Europe from China. In addition to the more famous items mentioned above, the wheelbarrow and sailing-carriage, the cross-bow, the kite, deep drilling techniques, cast iron, iron-chain suspension bridges, canal lock-gates, the fore-and-aft rig, water-tight compartments, and the sternpost rudder, among other things, all seem to have been known in China much earlier than elsewhere. Why did science not result?

The answer, of course, will be complex. In the realm of thought, Chu Hsi had taught that sincerity of heart was to be approached by a study of external objects, "the investigation of things," after which one might proceed to the understanding of one's self. This phrase, "the investigation of things," however, was interpreted to mean not scientific observation but rather the study of human affairs. Human society and personal relationships continued to be the focus of Chinese learning, not the conquest of man over nature.

The lack of scientific development is connected with the Chinese failure to work out a fuller system of logic whereby ideas could be tested by ideas, by confronting one statement systematically with another. Philosophers assumed that their principles were self-evident when stated. They made less distinction than the Greeks between grammar and rhetoric, and therefore between abstract and concrete or general and particular. Chinese writers relied more heavily on general ideas of proportion, the balance of opposites, and the harmony of the natural order. Their famous method of chain-reasoning, which was a clincher for Chinese scholars of twenty centuries, was from the Greek point of view a fancy series of non sequiturs.*

Underlying this weakness in logic was the physical nature of the Chinese written language. The use of an ideographic script for the transmission of the cultural inheritance from one generation to the next gave the characters themselves an independent status. They seemed to be enduring entities, not mere tools for the expression of ideas. For example, the virtues of which Confucius and Chu Hsi and their millions of disciples have thought and written, have been represented in writing by specific symbols to which extensive philosophical connotations have become attached. It is not in the nature of the Chinese language to express these ideas in other terms which are interchangeable or synonymous. The five Confucian virtues of *jen, i, li, chih,* and *hsin* 仁 義 禮 智 信 (roughly equivalent to benevolent love, righteousness, propriety, wisdom, and faith-fulness) are not easily expressed by other characters or by circumlocu-

---

* Take the following key passage from the *Great Learning:*

"The ancients who wished to be illustriously virtuous throughout the kingdom, first ordered well their own states. Wishing to order well their states, they first regulated their families. Wishing to regulate their families, they first cultivated their persons. Wishing to cultivate their persons, they first rectified their hearts. Wishing to rectify their hearts, they first sought to be sincere in their thoughts. Wishing to be sincere in their thoughts, they first extended to the utmost their knowledge. Such extension of knowledge lay in the investigation of things.

"Things being investigated, knowledge became complete. Their knowledge being complete, their thoughts were sincere. Their thoughts being sincere, their hearts were then rectified. Their hearts being rectified, their persons were cultivated. Their persons being cultivated, their families were regulated. Their families being regulated, their states were rightly governed. Their states being rightly governed, the whole kingdom was made tranquil and happy. From the Son of Heaven down to the mass of the people, all must consider the cultivation of the person the root of everything besides."

tions. The tyranny of terms is greater in Chinese than in an alphabetic language. The Chinese have been less able to escape from it than Western thinkers. To question the Confucian virtues would have been to deny the existence of the written characters which expressed them.

This tyranny of language was reinforced by an educational method in which the Chinese student traditionally memorized the classics before he understood them. Only after the characters were firmly established in the eye and ear, and in the muscular coordination of the hand in writing them, was their meaning studied and discussed. The enormous weight of the classic texts which had to be mastered put a premium upon memory, which already played an inordinate part in the learning of Chinese characters. The linguistic system of China was a natural matrix for authoritarian thinking.

One concomitant of the tyranny of language and its emphasis upon memory was the nonuse of the hands in connection with intellectual work. To be sure, the scholar sought to develop his calligraphy into a fine art. But once he put on his long gown he gave up manual work, which was a sign of a different social level. Chinese life pressed so closely upon subsistence, and learning was so clearly established as a path to economic security, that the scholar set great store upon the badge of learning, his long gown, and the ritual observances of the scholarly life, in which there was no time or occasion for manual labor. People who worked with their hands were not scholars. Scholars therefore did not meet the artisan in his workshop and the craftsman who needed new techniques. This separation of hand and brain stands in marked contrast to the example of the early European pioneers of science from Leonardo on down, who often came from the tradition of craftsmanship and, although scholars, were not debarred by the mores of their society from setting up their own laboratories. In early modern Europe the heritage of learning and the manual skills of technology might be focused in one man of genius. This seldom if ever happened in China.

Behind these shortcomings in thought and action may be seen economic and social circumstances which acted as a check upon the development of science. The state monopoly over large-scale economic organization and production was inimical to private enterprise whenever it threatened to assume large-scale proportions by the use of inventions and machinery. Again, the abundance of man power militated against the introduction of laborsaving mechanical devices. The dominant position of the official class and their power to tax without check by law made it difficult for new projects to develop except under their wing. In short, the nondevelopment of science was an aspect of the nondevelopment of an industrial economy. This in turn went back to the essentially agrarian and bureaucratic nature of the Confucian state.

Traditional China was not unchanging nor static nor inert. On the contrary there were continual change and great variety, but always within the limits of a distinctive cultural and institutional pattern. This over-all pattern persisted so strongly because, within their geographic confines, Chinese institutions — economic, political, social, cultural — over the centuries had developed great self-sufficiency, balance, and stability. Continuity, in short, had created inertia in the sense of momentum, persistence in established channels, not inertness.

The deep-laid inertia of the Confucian pattern in Chinese political life during two millennia explains why China's modern revolution against it has been so grievously long-drawn-out. Yet we can really appreciate the persistent vigor of this pattern only if we realize how foreign conquest of China, far from destroying, served to reinforce it.

5

Alien Rule and Dynastic Cycles

THE UNFOLDING of Chinese-Russian relations in the next decades must have overtones of China's past relations with invaders from the north. We should look at the historical record not as a portent of the future but as a source of insight and perspective.

During the last thousand years North China has been ruled more than half the time by alien invaders. This is one of the facts of history which inspired Japanese militarists in their schemes for conquest and rule through Chinese puppets. Alas for the Tanakas and Doiharas — they studied Chinese history all too well, but did not bring it down to date! Modern Chinese nationalism is a new force in history and the past glories of the Mongol and Manchu conquests cannot be revived today.

Yet the record must be kept in mind, not with the thought that Russia can do today what Japan could not do yesterday, but in order to understand the complex problems of the Russo-Chinese relationship. For the twentieth-century nationalism of Modern China must find its boundaries and achieve expression on a geographical and cultural frontier, between China and Russia, where the centuries have produced distinctive institutions and remarkable patterns.

1. NOMAD CONQUEST

The great continuing contrast in the life of Eastern Asia has been that between the steppe and the sown, between the pastoral nomads of the plateaus of inner Asia and the settled villages based on the intensive agriculture of China. This contrast is a striking one in nearly every respect.

On the steppe, population is thinly scattered and there are today perhaps two million Mongols and hardly more than that number of Tibetans in the arid plateau regions which more than equal the area occupied by some 600 million Chinese. The thinness of population in Central Asia in itself makes the life of the steppe nomad vastly different from the crowded life of China. "Nomadism" of course does not mean aimless wandering over the grasslands so much as the seasonal removal of camps and flocks from one known place to another, to the hills in summer and the lowlands in winter, as climate and rainfall make necessary, in search of pasture. Just as intensive agriculture has molded China, so the sheep economy of Central Asia has conditioned the nomad. From his flocks he secures food, sheepskins for clothing, shelter in the form of felt for his yurt, and fuel in the form of sheep dung. Cultivation of the soil being unreliable, he relies upon the management of his animals for a livelihood and upon his horses for a mobility which will save him from the aridity of the steppe. He must therefore be constantly resourceful and ready for new ventures. Custom does not tie him to the land, but he remains inevitably dependent upon a certain minimum of trade with settled regions. He is often more free than the Chinese farmer and at the same time more poor than the Chinese landlord, since he cannot accumulate immobile wealth from generation to generation. He is also a trained hunter and horseman, and so a potential warrior.

During the centuries a series of nomad peoples have appeared on the frontier of Chinese history. The Mongols are only the most famous of these groups. The ancient Hsiung-nu, who threatened Han China and later perhaps appeared in European history as the Huns, the Iranian people known to the Chinese as the Yüeh-chih who later formed an empire in northern India and Russian Turkestan, and half a dozen other succeeding tribes and peoples, including the Uigur Turks who in medieval times accepted Nestorian Christianity, have marched across the centuries in the steppe region. The Manchus who conquered China in the seventeenth century were the last of this series. For reasons unknown these peoples have drifted mainly from east to west. With some exceptions their languages have belonged to that group known as Altaic, which includes Turkish, Mongol, and Manchu. In early times these peoples who appeared on the Chinese frontier were mainly of Turkish stock but in more recent times Mongolian.

Early in the settled history of China the greater military striking power of the mounted barbarian archer became a constant problem to the farming peoples of the plain. So powerful have been the barbarian invasions of North China that a succession of Chinese states and dynasties has been of barbarian origin: the Northern Wei dynasty (386–534 A.D.) in the interregnum after the Han, and the Liao dynasty (907–1127 A.D.) of the Khitan Mongols, are almost as well known as the Yuan dynasty of the Mongols (1279–1368) and the recent Ch'ing dynasty of the Manchus (1644–1911).

Chinese defensive efforts in the third century B.C., when the First Emperor of Ch'in joined together existing local walls to make the original Great Wall of China, to keep out the nomads, were followed by constant later efforts to achieve security, either through defensive attack or through diplomacy and negotiation. In some cases, like that of the Han, the T'ang, or the Ming, native Chinese dynasties have conducted great military campaigns into the steppe. In the process of invasion and counter-invasion during the centuries there has been a great mixing of population. There has also grown up in Chinese society a vast body of lore and tradition concerning the barbarians and how to deal with them. The steppe nomads, in fact, gave China her background in foreign and international relations before the advent of the modern West.

Thus the relations of the Chinese with the nomads of Central Asia have significance not only for China but for us, for in modern times the West has taken the place of the barbarian menace. The modern invasion of China by the Western world, from the point of view of the Confucian way of life, is only the most recent in a long series of invasions of alien cultures carried by alien peoples. There is of course no comparison between the impact of the nomads upon Chinese life and the impact of the West. But the Chinese response to the West has been conditioned by Chinese experience in meeting the nomads.

The fact that China's agrarian way of life could not expand into the steppe and that the nomad herdsman could never permanently dominate the life of China led to a see-saw of Chinese-barbarian relations in the frontier region beyond the Great Wall. In these border areas, so aptly termed by Owen Lattimore "the Inner Asian Frontiers of China," a mixed economy of marginal agriculture and pastoralism formed the background for mixed political relations. Nomad leaders at times became settled territorial rulers. Chinese officialdom at other times exercised its sway over border tribes.

Lattimore suggests that the alternation of Chinese advance and retreat and barbarian submission and domination on the frontier was a product of interaction between two cycles: the cycle of dynastic change within China and the cycle of unification and dispersion among the tribes of the steppe. When a nomad leader, drawn by the trade at the border region, extended his power over it, he was obliged to take on settled ways. While this might lead the barbarians further toward domination of China south of the Wall, sedentary life would also in the end lead to a weakening of barbarian vigor and a decline of their new and transitory power over the sown.

Nomad invaders found that it was possible to rule China only in the Chinese way. Usually they achieved power by taking the advice of border statesmen who understood the Confucian system and could operate it in their behalf. One of its merits was that it could maintain an organized state no matter who might have inherited the Mandate of Heaven, so long as the inheritors would abide by Confucian principles.

In Chinese politics this experience of alien rule seems to have confirmed rather than weakened the Confucian tradition because it put it on a universal rather than a regional plane. The fact that an alien Emperor followed Confucianism confirmed the fact that it was, as it claimed to be, an all-embracing and universal philosophy of government, to which there was no civilized alternative. The Chinese way in politics, like the rice economy of the paddy fields, appeared to be more fundamental than dynasties or races.

Undoubtedly this is one reason why culture (the way of life) has been more fundamental in China than nationalism. The early Chinese Emperors began by asserting that they ruled over all mankind without distinction of race or language. Barbarian invaders who succeeded them found it expedient to continue and reinforce this tradition. To any Confucian ruler, Chinese or alien, the important thing was the loyalty of his administrators and their right conduct according to the Confucian code. Color and speech were of little account as long as a man understood the classics and could act accordingly. The successful barbarian rulers were those who acknowledged this fact by becoming assiduous classical scholars, calligraphers, and connoisseurs. They proved their legitimacy by quoting Confucius, conducting the rites, granting amnesties, maintaining the examination system, appointing officials, and issuing edicts in the manner of preceding Sons of Heaven. So long as they did so, they wrought no revolution in the Chinese political system and were accepted.

This ability to persist under alien rule was also a measure of the extent to which Confucian government was a benevolent despotism. It mattered little who was the despot as long as he fitted "benevolently" into the system.

In Western eyes one blot on the history of Modern China has been the institution of puppetry, or cooperation with a foreign invader. How could the handsome patriot Wang Ching-wei, a leading disciple of Sun Yat-sen, who himself had written down the leader's last will that every schoolboy under the Kuomintang government recited on Monday mornings and who had been second only to Chiang Kai-shek in the Nanking Government, go over to the Japanese late in 1938 and become until his death the leader of a puppet "Kuomintang" in a puppet Nanking? How often have Chinese patriots become traitors? Has "patriot" a different meaning in Chinese? How many Chinese today are ready to accept veiled Russian domination? Or American? How far may the Chinese Communists subordinate the interests of the new Chinese nation to those of international Communism?

Such questions cannot be answered by reference to the political experience of national states in the West. In trying to answer them in Chinese terms we must note the background of alien dynastic rule. Specifically, let us look at the example of the alien dynasties set up in China by non-Chinese invaders.

2. THE FIRST SINO-FOREIGN EMPIRES

The Khitan Mongols, from whom North China got the name "Cathay," maintained an empire for over two centuries (907–1127) on both sides of the Great Wall, including parts of North China, Manchuria, and Mongolia. Their original way of life had been only semi-nomadic, for they appear to have relied on agricultural crops, especially millet, as well as on sheep, horses, and pigs. Indeed, they rose to power by the very fact that they straddled the frontier between steppe and sown and could thus combine the military force of nomad cavalry with the economic sustenance of peasant tillage. The federation of tribes which founded the empire was led by the imperial Yeh-lü clan, who prolonged their rule by adopting the Chinese institution of hereditary monarchy and many of the forms of Confucian government. The result was a dual state, Chinese in the south, barbarian in the north, the southern half governed through institutions of civil bureaucracy inherited from the T'ang, the northern half by men on horseback. Thus while the Emperor's officials for one area were being recruited through the classical examination system, the mounted archers of the north were being mobilized and trained to serve in his elite guard, the *ordo* (from which derives our term "horde"). Eventually a dozen *ordos* were set up in separate areas, totalling perhaps 60,000 horsemen, a mobile shock force held in reserve.

Aside from this interesting dualism of government, the Liao Empire contributed little to Chinese culture. Its population was only about four million, less than one tenth, perhaps one-twentieth, the size of the Sung Empire to the south, yet the Liao cavalry had such striking power that the Sung finally paid them annual subsidies to keep peace on the border. When the Liao state was taken over by the Jurchen tribes of northern Manchuria, who called their dynasty Chin or "golden" (1127–1234), the same pattern continued — the Sino-barbarian Chin Empire could combine the horses of the steppe and the grain of North China to mount military assaults and force the Sung southward. (The Northern Sung, 960–1127, had their capital at Kaifeng, on the Yellow River; the Southern Sung, 1127–1279, at Hangchow, south of the Yangtze.) But these Sino-barbarian achievements were in the realm of power, not of culture, and had historical significance mainly as a fore-taste of the disaster to come.

The Mongol conquest and the Yuan dynasty set up by it in China (1279–1368) have been viewed by succeeding generations of Chinese scholars as an unhappy interlude during which the Chinese people were under a foreign tyranny. It is true that the Yuan dynasty lasted less than a century and the Mongol power generated by Chingis Khan (ca. 1167–1227) and spread over China by the great Khubilai (1214–1292) withered and disintegrated with unusual rapidity after the Mongols became rulers of China. But this egregious failure of the Mongols to maintain themselves in China stands out in such marked contrast to the later success of the Manchus that it deserves more than passing analysis.

The Mongols finally succeeded in imposing themselves over all China by the sword in 1279 after two generations of fighting and maneuvering, only to be expelled in 1368. The Manchus came to the throne with relative ease in 1644 and maintained a regime which the Chinese literati of the nineteenth century still stood ready to defend with their lives and fortunes. The key to this contrast lies in the failure of the Mongols and the success of the Manchus in strengthening the Confucian system and using it for their own ends.

Of the factors which operated to prevent the Mongols from ruling China in Chinese fashion, the most immediate was probably their inability to assimilate Chinese culture and make it their own: they were full nomads, unaccustomed to agriculture or settled life. Their background was illiterate, their language different, their daily food and costume outlandish, their moral and legal codes at variance with Chinese tradition. This difficulty was reinforced by the fact that the Mongols in China were but one part of the great Mongol Empire which was the product of the organizing genius of the Great Khan, Chingis (Genghis, lit., "Emperor within the Seas," the title he took in 1206), and his sons and grandsons.

It is startling to note that Chingis in early middle age was still a vassal of a minor Mongol chieftain, among a tribal steppe people who did not yet recognize the common linguistic bond later expressed in the name Mongol. His achievement in unifying and inspiring these tribes of the steppe to embark upon the greatest course of territorial conquest in early history can be understood only by reference to the propitious circumstances of the time in Central Asia.

About the year 1200 there stretched across that region from east to west a belt of settled communities founded on agriculture and connected with one another by trade. China was divided between the Chinese Sung dynasty in the south at Hangchow and the alien Chin dynasty in the north at Peking. In Northwest China was a kingdom founded by a Tibetan people. Westward in Chinese Turkestan were the Uigur Turks and west of them in Russian Turkestan were Turkish Moslem sultanates such as Bokhara and Samarkand. Finally in Persia there was the Abbassid caliphate with its capital at Bagdad. Commerce among these settled states gave them wealth but none of them was warlike nor strong enough to dominate its neighbor. They were a tempting prize for invaders from the steppe.

Another east to west belt of peoples stretched across Central Asia on the north. These were the nomad tribes of the arid plateau country. They were Turkish, Mongolian, and Tungusic in various mixtures and lived by an extensive pastoral economy. They had the nomad's mobility and comparative self-sufficiency; their patriarchal clan organization made them amenable to strong leadership.

Chingis rose through adversity from the lower nobility and built his power on personal loyalty. He asserted his mission to rule the world as the delegate of the eternal blue sky. He gave his tribal name, Mongol, to all the tribes that joined him. He codified their customary law, borrowing the Uigur script for the purpose, and declared it supreme and universal. He organized his warriors on a family principle under clans, tribes, and divisions of the empire. In all these ways he created a nation in arms. His carefully selected personal bodyguard or *ordo* formed an elite corps from which he drew his generals. The war machine thus created depended upon flying columns of Mongol cavalry, disciplined, hard-riding, and ruthless, who lived always for the loot which lay ahead and which gave them a constant incentive to expansion. Their compound bows and armor-piercing arrows and their sudden and deceptive battle tactics made them an irresistible force and the scourge of Asia. The descendants of Chingis set up their khanates in southern Russia, in Persia, and in Russian Turkestan, as well as in China.

This international scope of the Mongol Empire makes it comparable to the expansion of Europe as a cause of cultural and institutional mixing. In both cases the representatives of one kind of society invaded several others. Mongol conquerors who overran settled agricultural states in South Russia, Persia, and China met a bewildering variety of languages, religions and local customs, yet in each case faced certain general problems — how to maintain order, conduct a civil administration through a bureaucracy and secure tax collections, how to retain the Mongol grip on power, and therefore in the final analysis how to maintain their own identity, unity, and vigor. It is truly amazing how far these illiterate warriors succeeded in these exacting tasks. The Mongols of the Golden Horde ruled in South Russia for 200 years and those in Persia for a century. In both countries, as in China, they seem to have built up the political institution of centralized despotism. During the thirteenth century contact among these far-flung domains was kept up by the famous Mongol post routes across the grasslands and oases of Central Asia, the strategic inner core of the empire. This made possible Europe's first direct contact with Cathay.

Unfortunately for the Mongols, their grip proved less strong than their striking power. In China they faced the problem of ruling in a Chinese fashion and yet retaining political control in Mongol hands. To do this it was essential not only that they have force in reserve and that they maintain order which would bring prosperity, but that they also give opportunity for the exercise of Chinese talent in the official system.

Early in their career of conquest the Mongols had learned the necessity of employing experienced civil administrators who knew how to levy taxes, manage finance, and recruit a bureaucracy. For this work in China they relied mainly upon Chinese but they also used in their administration other semi-nomads of the border region and many foreigners. Marco Polo (in China 1275–1292) was such a person. There were also others from Europe and a great number of Moslems, both Persian and Turkish, as well as Uigur administrators drawn from the states of Central Asia. The Mongols revived the examination system as a means of recruiting Chinese but it never worked well enough to get the best Chinese talent into the government.

The splendors of the reign of Khubilai, his new capital built at Peking, his extension of the imperial post roads and of the Grand Canal from Hangchow to Peking, and the great commercial development of such centers as Hangchow and Canton, described by Polo, demonstrated the vigor of Mongol rule in its heyday. But Mongol leadership after Khubilai soon deteriorated. The early fourteenth century saw a succession of weak rulers and finally internal dissensions among the Mongol clans. Lamaism, the type of Buddhism developed in Tibet, spread its superstitious practices among the Mongol tribes. Lamaist excesses in China outraged the Confucian literati and stigmatized the Mongols as a people of primitive culture. Yellow River floods, financial difficulties and at the last an inflation of paper currency undermined the regime, rebels arose in several southern provinces to compete for the succession, and the strong man who succeeded among them expelled the Mongols and founded the Chinese Ming dynasty in 1368.

From the moment of its establishment one of the chief preoccupations of the Ming was to defend itself against the Mongol power.

The first Emperor sent big expeditions into the steppe against the Mongols. He recovered Manchuria, secured the allegiance of a new dynasty in Korea, and was finally able to engineer the Mongols' collapse and disintegration into eastern and western kingdoms on the steppe. The second Ming Emperor led four expeditions personally against them. He assisted the western Mongols to crush the eastern Mongols and later helped the eastern Mongols to fight the western. Even so, the Chinese were not able to wipe out the Mongol threat, for they could not destroy nor could they Sinify the steppe society across the Gobi. They were therefore forced to fall back on the age-old expedient of using one barbarian tribe against another and preserving the forms of a suzerain-vassal relationship with them all. In the end this led to their undoing, for they could not keep under control the Manchu state which grew up as a vassal on their north-eastern frontier.

3. THE MANCHU ACHIEVEMENT

The Manchus who ruled China from 1644 to 1911 were a non-Chinese people of different habitat, language, and culture. Yet they succeeded in maintaining their power by traditional Confucian means for as long a period as any Chinese dynasty. The secret of this achievement may lie in the fact that, while they governed in a Chinese fashion, their alien origin and background helped them to retain political vigor within the ruling group. Some understanding of their success may help us to account for the tardy development of Chinese nationalism in modern times.

The essential point about the Manchu conquest of 1644 is that the Manchus by the time they came to power in China had already mastered the Confucian art of government and reconciled their own political institutions with it. Their development to this stage of political sophistication had been made possible by the fact that they were a border people on the frontier of the Chinese state where tribalism and bureacracy could be synthesized.

Modern Western students of the Chinese frontier under Latti-more's inspiration have worked out an interpretation of the way in which the Chinese and barbarian societies interacted. In China, intensive agriculture was the basis for a bureaucratic government, in a region where land was scarce in relation to manpower and the state depended upon revenue derived from the land. On the steppe, nomad pastoralism was the basis for a tribal form of government, in a region where man power was more scarce than land and the power of a chieftain consisted in his ability to command the personal loyalty of the warriors. The Chinese populace had to be governed through an officialdom. The non-Chinese barbarians could be controlled only through personal vassal relations. The Manchus were fortunate in coming from a region where these two systems met and intermixed.

Manchuria in the sixteenth century had been brought under the Chinese type of intensive agriculture only in the southernmost region below Mukden on either side of the Liao River. Northwestern Manchuria was still a nomad steppe country. The northeast, the original home of the Manchus, was a partly forested region suitable for hunting and fishing and the use of horses as well as some agriculture. The Ming had recognized the frontier nature of South Manchuria by organizing it in military districts rather than under a civil administration only. By establishing hereditary and registered military units at strategic points, separate from the civil administration of this agricultural area, the Ming Chinese sought to maintain both a military buffer against barbarian inroads and a check upon any separatist tendencies of local Chinese officials; for they could not overlook the fact that South Manchuria was a hostage to fortune which could be cut off from North China at the bottleneck of Shanhaikuan, where the Great Wall escarpment comes to the sea.

In their rise to power the Manchus took full advantage of their strategic position on a frontier where they could learn Chinese ways and yet not be entirely subjected to Chinese rule. The founder of the Manchu state, Nurhachi (1559–1626), began as a minor chieftain on the eastern border of the agricultural basin of South Manchuria. Like Chingis among the Mongols, he brought adjoining tribes under his personal rule and early in the seventeenth century set up his capital at Mukden. His successor subjugated Korea on the east and made alliances with the Mongol tribes on the west in Inner Mongolia. In 1636 he gave the name Manchu to his people and proclaimed the Ch'ing ("Pure") dynasty.

The Manchus by this time had made several incursions into North China but had not yet been able to defeat the Ming. The Ming regime in China, however, had grown progressively weaker. Rebellion was already endemic. The leading figure in the disorder of the time was a Chinese rebel (named Li Tzu-ch'eng) whose banditti had raided widely in Northwest China and even into Szechwan and the Yangtze valley. This leader had finally secured literate advisers and begun to set up a framework of dynastic government. In 1644 he succeeded in capturing Peking and had the dynastic succession within his grasp. But he was unable to consolidate institutionally the position that he had won by force. Chinese officialdom and the scholar-gentry class who provided the personnel of government were not drawn to him. Meanwhile a loyal Ming official in charge at Shanhaikuan mistakenly invited the Manchus inside the Wall. They came at his bidding, destroyed the rebel Li, and stayed. Within twenty years they had all but completed the conquest of China and their government of the empire remained stable for two centuries thereafter. Their success where a Chinese rebel had failed was essentially an achievement in the creation of political institutions.

The Manchus' first problem (as studied by Franz Michael) had been to develop beyond the state of tribal politics. This they did by creating a territorial administration over their lands, paralleled by a military organization of all the Manchu fighting men in eight divisions, each with a different flag or "banner." The Manchu bannermen had lands assigned to them but these lands were kept scattered and the banners did not become territorial units. Mongols and Chinese who came over to the Manchus were taken into the system and organized in their own banner units. Nurhachi appointed his sons to head the banners but their power was brought under central control in a state council. In this way the originally personal relations between the head of the state and his loyal tribal chieftains were put into an impersonal institutional form.

Finally, the early Manchu rulers, like the Liao, Chin, and Yuan Emperors before them, took over the terminology, forms, and ideas of Confucianism and used them, as they were meant to be used, for the support and maintenance of political authority. They promoted the study of the classics and the veneration of the ancestors, set up the state cult of Confucius, talked and wrote of the "way of the ruler" (like the Japanese in "Manchukuo" three centuries later), extolled the Confucian virtues, and accepted the idea that the ruler rules by virtue of his moral goodness. More than a decade before their entrance into China, they had created in Mukden a miniature civil administration in imitation of Peking. The Six Ministries and other elements of Ming government were formally established and staffed by a bureaucracy in which Manchus, Mongols, and Chinese were represented. When they entered North China and assumed the Mandate of Heaven they were fully prepared to solve their fundamental problem, how to rule in the Chinese way but maintain their identity as Manchus.

Several circumstances aided them in this achievement. For one thing, unlike the Mongols, they had no vast empire to the west to distract them from the all-important problem of China. Having come from the frontier region of South Manchuria, rather than from the Mongolian steppe itself, they did not have to leap the great cultural gap between the steppe and the sown. The unusually long and vigorous reigns of the early emperors also provided a strong executive leadership: the K'ang-hsi Emperor (reg. 1662–1723) and the Ch'ien-lung Emperor (reg. 1736–1796) were both hard-working and conscientious sovereigns who commonly saw their ministers every day at dawn, studied the classics assiduously, traveled widely over the empire, and maintained a vigorous personal rule.

The various devices by which the Manchus sought to preserve their dynastic vitality are an interesting study. In order to preserve their identity as a racial group they closed their homeland to Chinese immigration and maintained North Manchuria as a hunting land outside the Chinese agricultural economy. To check Chinese immigration from South Manchuria northward, they built a willow palisade several hundred miles long (a big ditch with willows planted along it) to mark the boundary beyond which the Chinese should not expand. They organized Manchuria under a Manchu military government. In spite of a periodic overflow of Chinese settlers in time of famine, they succeeded on the whole in checking further Chinese settlement. North of the Chinese basin in the south, Manchuria remained a sparsely populated vacuum down to the late nineteenth century — a tempting prize for Russian and Japanese imperialists.

In addition to this geographical basis the Manchus sought to preserve themselves by maintaining their racial purity. They banned intermarriage between Chinese and Manchus and fostered differences of custom between the two groups. Manchu women, for example, were not supposed to have bound feet. Manchus were not supposed to engage in trade or labor. The Manchu clan organization was preserved by their shamanistic religious system.

Manchu military control of China was maintained by the establishment of banner garrisons at strategic points. There was a military cordon of twenty-five garrisoned cities around Peking, to preserve the capital as a symbol of imperial power. There was a northern belt of garrisons to defend North China against Mongol inroads. Finally, there were garrisons of Manchu bannermen in the bigger provincial capitals, Nanking, Hangchow, Chengtu, Foochow, and Canton. These garrisons in a separate Manchu military quarter in the big cities symbolized force held in reserve. The only Chinese troops given a recognized existence were provincial forces who were used mainly as a constabulary on the post routes and against bandits but lacked any training as a striking force.

In order to preserve strong leadership, the early Manchu Emperors arranged that the imperial princes should be pensioned and given wealth but not allowed to become territorial lords. They were kept at Peking out of power. Every effort was made to avoid the historic curse of government by women and by eunuchs, which had resulted so often in palace intrigue.

In the civil administration of China the Manchus used a system of dual appointments, whereby both Chinese and Manchus were placed in charge of important functions. At first they needed a capable Chinese to do the work and a loyal Manchu to check upon him. At the capital Manchus outnumbered Chinese, but in the provinces Chinese officials predominated. In order to draw into their service the most able and promising Chinese, the Manchus saw to it that the examination system continued to function with the highest prestige and efficiency.

Further to absorb the energies of Chinese scholars produced by the examination system, the Manchu emperors became great patrons of literature and sponsored enormous projects of criticism and compilation. The K'ang-hsi Emperor at the turn of the eighteenth century, like Dr. Johnson and the Encyclopedists in the contemporary West, presided over the production of a famous dictionary and of a vast encyclopedia in 5020 chapters. His great successor, the Ch'ien-lung Emperor, sponsored an edition of the twenty-four dynastic histories and a collection of all Chinese literature in "The

Complete Library of the Four Treasuries." This compilation included 3462 works. It was too large to print and only seven copies were made by hand. The printed catalogue alone ran to 92 chapters.

By means of this vast project the Manchu court in fact conducted a literary inquisition, one of their objects being to suppress all works that reflected on alien rulers. In searching out rare books and complete texts for inclusion in this master library, the compilers were able at the same time to search out all heterodox works which should be banned or destroyed. They paid high prices for rare works and even conducted house-to-house canvasses. The works proscribed included studies of military or frontier affairs, criticisms anti-barbarian in tone, and chiefly items which extolled the preceding Chinese dynasty of the Ming. Altogether, some 2320 works were suppressed. This was thought control on the largest scale.

By these various expedients and devices the alien rulers of China under the Ch'ing dynasty maintained their racial and social identity, preserved their military and administrative control, and yet gave prestige and opportunity to Chinese of talent. The Manchu possession of temporal power in the Chinese state turned Chinese men of genius to literary and cultural activity. It also preserved in early Modern China the non-nationalistic tradition that it makes little difference who governs as long as he governs in the proper fashion.

4. THE DYNASTIC CYCLE

One basic approach to China's history of the early twentieth century is to regard it as a dynastic interregnum. Viewed in the light of the famous twenty-four histories of Chinese dynastic periods, the efforts of Sun Yat-sen, Chiang Kai-shek and Mao Tse-tung to seize and organize central power are variations on an ancient theme. China's two thousand years of recorded politics have produced apparent rhythms and pulsations. Always, even though the current struggle might ravage the Middle Kingdom, most Chinese have had utter faith that unity would come again.

Anyone who seeks historical uniformities, or who makes societies and civilizations his units of study, will find the Chinese chronicles inexhaustible. Nowhere else are there so many recorded facts of imperial administration, waiting to be selected, ordered, and generalized about by philosophers of history or by Marxist and anti-Marxist system-makers or by ordinary political pundits and historians in off moments. Here if anywhere one might hope to catch History in the act of repeating herself. Only the unimaginative can resist the idea that, if we can read correctly the story of China's last two millennia, we can foresee her next two decades — a vain hope but an entrancing one.

Students of several generations have been impressed by the peculiarly parallel sequences in ancient China and in the Greco-Roman world: an age of philosophers and warring states, an age of unification and empire, and an age of disintegration and collapse of central power. Thus Confucius and his disciples are noted to have been roughly contemporary with Plato and Aristotle, Alexander the Great precedes the First Emperor of the Ch'in by only a century, and the imperial systems of Rome and Han flourished contemporaneously.

Similarly the barbarians on the northern frontier grew more dangerous as each of these empires declined and the economic and political disintegration within the "universal state," in Toynbee's phrase, was marked by the spread of foreign religions to which the distressed people turned for solace. The entrance of the northern nomads into China and the spread of Buddhism in the period from the third to the sixth centuries A.D. were actually contemporary with the inroads of the Goths and Vandals and the spread of Christianity in the West. To all who seek intellectual security in the formulation of laws which govern human affairs, these parallels have been a starting point both for generalization and for further research.

Within Chinese history the most interesting uniformity which strikes the superficial observer is the sequence of phases centering about the Han and T'ang dynasties respectively. Preceding each of these imperial periods was a time of intellectual ferment marked, respectively, by the philosophers of the late-Chou period, and the flourishing of Taoism and Buddhism after the Han. Each phase of imperial greatness was inaugurated by a short-lived powerful dynasty which unified the state, the Ch'in (221–206 B.C.) and Sui (589–618 A.D.) respectively. Both the Han and the T'ang, once established on the basis of a new unity, achieved an expansion of Chinese political power in neighboring regions, especially Central Asia, and a corresponding development of foreign contact.

Stimulated by this parallelism between two major dynasties,

students have attempted numerous formulations of cycles. Underlying all these attempts is the fundamental phenomenon observed by Chinese historians and recorded by them so assiduously, namely, the dynastic cycle. In the twenty-four dynastic histories there is naturally a certain recurrence of ideas, since the chroniclers in each case were recording the life history of a ruling family which came to power, had its heyday, and shuffled from the scene. Toward the close of each regime, for example, natural calamities, comets, eclipses, and other heavenly portents become more numerous in the record, evidence that the improper conduct of the ruler is losing him the Mandate of Heaven.

Autosuggestion, indeed, on the plane of public morale and social psychology may have played its part in the dynastic cycle. For so great was the dynasty's dependence on its moral prestige that its loss of "face" in certain instances might set in motion a process in which the ideology, as it were, turned against the regime and hastened its downfall. Once the literati who set the tone of public opinion became convinced that a dynasty had lost its moral claim to the throne, little could save it. This is a factor in Chinese politics today.

Time after time dynastic decline went hand in hand with the increasing inefficiency of the ruling house. The family in power accumulated over the generations a heavy load of dead wood and dead weight, fastened upon it by the family system. This was most flagrantly visible in the peculations and profligacy of maternal relatives who became entrenched in the imperial household. Wine, women, and song at the court led to increasing personal weakness of the rulers. This danger attended the Sinification of barbarian conquerors. The Mongol khans, for example, became effete and were undone by their own excesses.

The economic interpretation of Chinese history has been used even more extensively to explain the dynastic cycle. This approach concentrates particularly upon the land tax, which in the agrarian economy of China has been the chief source of government revenue and power. One process which seems to have appeared in each dynasty was the progressive withdrawal of land from taxation, for the benefit of the ruling official class and to the detriment of the imperial revenues. At the beginning of a dynasty the land and the population were usually estimated and recorded in a rough sort of "census." New tax registers could be used as a firm basis for revenue collection. As time went on there ensued a struggle between the interest of the imperial government and of the individuals who dominatd it. Gradually the ruling class were able to increase their landholdings and to remove them from taxation by various expedients such as the destruction of tax registers, official connivance, or legal falsification. This created a vicious circle in which a greater burden was placed upon the land of the peasantry which still paid taxes, at the same time that the demands of the government for revenue were likely to increase. In this way a progressively smaller proportion of the land was expected to pay a progressively larger amount of revenue. Peasant disorders eventually resulted.

In some cases the final collapse of a dynasty came through peasant rebellion under fanatical religious leadership. Since no dynasty has tolerated an organized opposition, its opponents have had recourse to secret societies. For example, as the Mongol administration lost its efficiency and morale in the middle of the fourteenth century, revolt became endemic in many provinces. Some of these revolts were led by secret groups like the White Lotus Society which had a symbolic ritual, esoteric signs and passwords, oaths sealed in blood, and an underground organization. Other revolts were led by religious leaders, usually Buddhist, who might proclaim the imminent advent of the bodhisattva Maitreya. Some rebels claimed to be legitimate successors to the preceding Sung dynasty. Others were content to be mere bandit chiefs who became local warlords and competed in the struggle for the survival of the fittest to receive the Mandate of Heaven. A bandit chieftain in Hupeh got control of much of the central Yangtze region, another chieftain seized part of Honan, another rose at the same time in the lower Yangtze, and finally a pirate leader arose in Fukien. Each of them assumed a dynastic title. The eventual founder of the Ming dynasty got himself established in the richest area of the country, around Nanking, and knew how to combine clever politics with the forcible seizure of power. He was himself the son of a laborer and had been a Buddhist monk before seeking his fortune in rebellion. He conciliated the common people, maintained discipline among his forces, and prevented plundering. By 1368 he had conquered or absorbed his rivals and was able to seize Peking, where his last successor was not dispossessed until 1644, almost three centuries later.

It is an interesting coincidence that the Ming Emperors reigned for 276 years and their successors, the Manchus, for 267 years — a span which attests the stability of their political institutions, no matter whether Chinese or non-Chinese were on the throne.

6

The Political Tradition

THE IMPERIAL SYSTEM survived until 1912, the year Woodrow Wilson was elected President of the United States. The leaders of Modern China grew up under it. Even the generation who dominate the Chinese scene today need think back only fifty years to recall the imperial splendor of the old Empress Dowager, the lavish trappings of despotism, the eunuchs, concubines, and court attendants, palace guards and palanquins, formal audiences, kowtow and lesser rituals within the high red walls and gold-tiled roofs of the palace at Peking. These things have barely passed away. To look at Modern China, as we usually do, without seeing them in the background makes no more sense than to look at the United States without any recollection of Washington and Jefferson, Dan Boone and Abe Lincoln, manifest destiny, or the rise of the common man and John D. Rockefeller.

1. BUREAUCRACY

One key to the understanding of the Communist administration in China is the fact that the old imperial government was a bureaucracy of the most thoroughly developed and sophisticated sort. To the American who has confronted the problems of bureaucracy only recently, the effort of modern Chinese to escape from the evils and capitalize upon the good points of their own bureaucratic tradition is a matter of absorbing interest.

The Capital. The old government centered in the capital. Without question the vast symmetrical plan of Peking makes it the most magnificent of all capital cities. Paris and London, Washington and

Moscow are creations of yesterday and do not attest, in the balance of gate against gate and avenue against avenue, the omnipotence of oriental despots who created their capital city as an outer cover to their palace. Peking centers upon the moats and red walls of the Forbidden City. Within it the yellow-roofed throne halls rising from their marble platforms form the main axis of the whole metropolis. Behind them a great man-made hill of earth protects them from the north. Before them, broad avenues and today the Red Square lead south to the Front Gate of the city. No Western capital is so plainly a symbol of centralized and absolute monarchy.

At Peking, for the greater part of thirteen centuries the civil administration of China was divided among the famous Six Ministries (or Boards), namely those of civil office (appointment of officials), revenue, ceremonies, war, punishments, and public works (such as flood control). This structure, adumbrated in the first imperial system of the Ch'in and Han, had been formally established under the T'ang. In addition to the Six Ministries there were two other independent hierarchies of administration — the military establishment and the Censorate, as well as a number of minor offices — the imperial academy of literature, a court to review criminal cases, a historiographer's office, the imperial stud, and offices in charge of banquets and sacrificial worship. At the apex of everything the Ming had created the Grand Secretariat, in which high officials assisted the Emperor in his personal administration of affairs. One of the few Manchu innovations was to add in 1729 a less formal body, the Grand Council, which handled military and other important matters and so became the real top of the administration.

The Provinces. Spread out over the eighteen provinces of China under the Manchu dynasty was a network of territorial divisions. Each province was divided into several circuits (*tao*) and below them into prefectures, departments, and *hsien* (districts or counties) in descending order. The mandarins in charge of these divisions with their ubiquitous assistants and subordinates formed the main body of the territorial magistracy. Like civil servants trained in the classics at Oxford, they were supposedly omnicompetent, responsible for the collection of revenue, maintenance of order, dispensing of justice, conduct of literary examinations, superintendence of the postal service, and in general for all public events within their areas. Theoretically, they stood *in loco parentis* to the people and were called, or rather called themselves, the "father and mother officials."

The imperial civil service was divided into nine ranks, each of which was divided into upper and lower grades. Each rank was entitled to a particular and very fine costume, including a colored button on the cap and insignia such as "mandarin squares" embroidered on the front and back of the gown. Prerogatives, titles, and dignities were minutely set forth in the statutes. High officials might be rewarded with the right to wear a peacock feather or bear the title of "Junior Guardian of the Heir Apparent."

Intervening between the hierarchy of local officials and the government at the capital stood the higher administration in each province. This consisted of a governor-general who was in most cases responsible for two provinces and, as his junior colleague, a governor responsible for a single province. These two officials were of course so placed as to check each other, for they were expected to act and report jointly on important matters. Under the Ch'ing (Manchu) dynasty, frequently the governor-general was a Manchu and the governor Chinese. Beneath them were four provincial officers who exercised province-wide functions — a treasurer, judge, salt comptroller, and grain intendant (who supervised the collection of grain for the capital).

Official business over the far-flung Chinese empire was conducted as in all bureaucracies by a flow of documents of many kinds. In their special forms and designations these multifarious communications mirrored the elaborate proliferation of red tape. A governor addressed his imperial master in certain prescribed forms and addressed his subordinates in others. Every communication began with a clear indication of its nature as a document to a superior, an equal, or a subordinate. Similarly there were special forms for memorials submitted to the Emperor and edicts issued from him. Each document also went through a certain procedure of preparation, transmission, and reception. Hundreds of thousands of brush-wielding scriveners were kept busy year in and year out transcribing, recording, and processing official communications. In the imperial archives in the Peking palace are more than one hundred different types of documents which were in common use.

The flow of paper work was maintained by an official post which reached to all corners of the empire but was limited to the transportation of official mail, official shipments (as of funds), and persons traveling on official business. This postal system was made up of some two thousand stations stretched out along five main and many subsidiary routes which ran into Manchuria, across Mongolia, westward to Turkestan and Tibet, southeastward through the coastal provinces, and southward through the interior of Central China. Couriers and travelers on these routes were provided with official tallies entitling them to the use of the transportation facilities, which in different areas might be horses, camels, donkeys, chairs (palanquins), or boats. In time of crisis couriers could cover 250 miles a day. (See map, p. 121.)

Such speed was achieved by the use of horses in relays, a system which the Mongols had developed to cover the distances of Central Asia. In the early nineteenth century this pony express regularly transmitted messages from Canton to Peking in less than three weeks and from Shanghai to Peking in one week.

Central Controls. Given this network of officials, connected by a flow of documents and persons along the postal routes, it was the problem of the capital to stimulate the local bureaucrats to perform their functions and yet prevent them from getting out of hand. This control was achieved by the application of techniques common to bureaucracies everywhere, in addition to the special measures (noted above) whereby the Manchus sought to preserve their dynasty.

Among these techniques the first was the appointment of all officers down to the rank of district magistrate by the Emperor himself. This made them all aware of their dependence upon the Son of Heaven and their duty of personal loyalty to him. Circulation in office was another device. No official was left in one post for more than three years or at most six years. Ordinarily when moving from one post to another the official passed through the capital and participated in an imperial audience to renew his contact with the ruler.

Thus Chinese officialdom was a mobile body which circulated through all parts of the empire without taking root in any one place. In this it was aided by its reliance upon the Mandarin (Peking) dialect as a lingua franca of universal currency in official circles. Frequently an official would arrive at his new post to find himself quite incapable of understanding the local dialect and therefore the more closely confined to his official level.

One means to prevent officials taking local root was the "law of avoidance" according to which no mandarin could be appointed to office in his native province, where the claims of family loyalty might impair devotion to the imperial regime.

Another custom, which interrupted an official's rise to power, was the rule of three years' mourning (actually some twenty-five months) after the death of his father, during which an official retired to a life of quiet abstention from worldly activities. As Arthur Waley says, this was "a sort of 'sabbatical' occurring as a rule toward the middle of a man's official career. It gave him a period for study and reflection, for writing at last the book that he had planned . . . , for repairing a life ravaged by official banqueting, a constitution exhausted by the joint claims of concubinage and matrimony."

In general the bureaucratic principle was to set one official to check upon another. This was done particularly through the system of joint responsibility. The Six Ministries each had two presidents, one Manchu and one Chinese, who watched each other. It was common to appoint one man after he had gained prominence to several offices so that he was not able to master any one of them, and at the same time to appoint many men to perform one job so that no one of them could completely control it. Indeed many offices were sometimes created to carry on the same function, checking each other through their duplication of activity. The result of this duplication of offices and mutual responsibility was to hedge each official about with a multiplicity of commitments in each of which others were concerned. It was something like the unlimited liability of a partnership in which there were dozens of partners. Over and above all these immediate checks created by the involvement of many officials in a common responsibility, there was the system of the Censorate. Under it some fifty-six censors selected for their loyalty and uprightness were stationed in fifteen circuits through the provinces with the duty of keeping the Emperor informed upon all matters concerning the welfare of the people and the dynasty.

The evils inherent in bureaucracy were all too evident. All business was in form originated at the bottom and passed upward to the Emperor for decision at the top, memorials from the provinces being addressed to the Emperor at the capital. The higher authority was thus left to choose alternatives of action proposed, and yet the proposal of novel or unprecedented action was both difficult and dangerous for the lower official. The greater safety of conformity tended to kill initiative at the bottom. On the other hand the efficiency of the one man at the top was constantly impaired by his becoming a bottleneck. All business of importance was expected to receive his approval. All legislation and precedent were established by his edict. Modern China still suffers from this tradition.

In view of the complete and arbitrary power which the imperial bureaucracy asserted over the whole of Chinese life, it is amazing how few and how scattered the officials were in number. The total of civil officials for whom posts were statutorily available, both at the capital and in the provinces, was hardly more than 9000. The military officials were supposed to number only about 7500. It is true, of course, that there were a great many supernumerary or "expectant" officials who might be assigned to various functions without receiving substantive appointments. There was also the vast body of clerks and factota necessary for the copying, recording, negotiating, and going and coming in each Chinese official's establishment or "yamen." Down to the gatemen, runners, and chairbearers, these human elements in the official machine no doubt totaled millions. But if we look for the men of genuine official status who could take official action and report it in the hierarchy as representatives of his imperial majesty, we find them few and thinly spread, totaling at a rough estimate hardly more than 30 or 40 thousand "officials" at most, ruling over a country of about 200 million which grew to perhaps 400 million by the middle of the nineteenth century. Of the nine ranks, for example, the seventh rank near the bottom of the scale began with the district magistrate who was responsible for a population on the order of 250,000 persons. This relative smallness of the imperial administration no doubt reflects the fact that it depended upon the gentry class to lead and dominate the peasantry in the villages, as indicated in Chapter 3 above.

Government as Organized "Corruption." Another anomaly of the bureaucracy was its low salaries. According to the official redbook, a governor-general in charge of two provinces as big as European countries received from his imperial master a salary equivalent in our terms to only $300 a year. To this nominal sum was added a larger payment drawn from the provincial rather than the imperial treasury. For the governor-general in question this supplementary salary (*yang-lien,* lit. "to nourish honesty"), would be equivalent to some $41,000 a year. But still, when added together from all sources, such salaries could not begin to meet the needs of an officer who had to employ a great retinue of private secretaries and special assistants.

The imperial officials were held responsible for all public events within their jurisdiction but not for all public funds. Budgeting and accounting procedures were rudimentary. The bureaucracy lived by what we today would call systematized corruption which sometimes became extortion. This was a necessary concomitant of the system of intricate personal realtionships that each official had to maintain with his superiors, colleagues, and subordinates.

Among the bureaucracies of history, the Chinese has been distinguished by the way in which the twin institutions of "squeeze" and nepotism reinforced each other. The former operated through forms of politeness rather than secrecy. Junior officials in the course of their duties gave their superiors customary "gifts." But like all prices in old China, the amount of such a gift resulted from the working out of a personal relationship. The "squeeze" system was no more cut and dried than any other part of the man-to-man bargaining which pervaded Chinese life. The extralegal sums which passed between officials were larger but no different in kind from the small commissions extracted until only recently from every money transaction by underpaid houseboys.

Nepotism supported the "squeeze" or "leakage" system by giving an added sanction for personal arrangements contrary to the public interest. Even classic texts extolled duty to family, and particularly filial piety, as superior to any duty to the state. Thus the interest of the imperial administration at the capital, which needed the sustenance of revenue from the provinces, was constantly in conflict with the multifarious private interests of all the officials, each of whom had to provide for his relatives and his further career. High office commonly meant riches. The favorite minister of the Ch'ien-lung Emperor, when tried for corruption and other crimes by that Emperor's successor in 1799, was found to have an estate worth in our terms of that period more than one billion dollars — probably an all-time record. Another high Manchu, who fell into disfavor at the time of the Opium War in 1841, was found to have an estate of some 425,000 acres of land, $30,000,000 worth of gold, silver, and precious stones, and shares in 90 banks and pawnshops. I would not suggest that Westerners have been backward or less adept in the art of graft. But in China corruption remained longer into modern times an accepted institution, unashamed and unafraid.

Communist China's vast new bureaucratism must be seen against the tradition sketched above. Today's totalitarianism, though utterly unprecedented in its total effect, has certain ancient foundations to build on. It also faces the age-old problem — how to keep the bureaucrats energetic, efficient, and honest.

2. LAW

In the Western tradition bureaucracy has been tempered by law. Against the tyranny of officialdom the individual has had recourse to legal protection. Our civil liberties rest upon this. But the law in Chinese life has not been similarly developed to protect the individual either in his political rights or in his economic position. The early use of law by the Legalist school of the third century B.C. was as a tool of absolutism to aid in administrative unification. Later the imperial government under the Han continued to use certain Legalist practices, like that of mutual responsibility among family members. Thus the "Confucian state," for all its exaltation of the name and teachings of Confucius, came to incorporate elements of the Legalist tradition as well. This tradition has lingered on and been reasserted from time to time ever since.

Modern students of legal history have as yet hardly glanced at the enormous and ramified documentation of Chinese law. The great T'ang code of the eighth century and its successors in the Sung, Yuan, Ming, and Ch'ing periods, still await analysis by Western scholars. But it is plain that by any pre-modern standard the Chinese codes were monuments of their kind. As with so many other aspects of Chinese society, the old legal system was "unmodern" yet in the context of its times we should be slow to call it "backward."

Nevertheless the Chinese concept of law was fundamentally different from legal conceptions in the West. It began with the ancient Chinese idea of the order of nature, the necessity of human actions harmonizing with it, and the ruler's function of maintaining this harmony. Since the ruler swayed the people by his virtuous conduct and moral example, not by law, it was felt that enlightened and civilized persons would be guided by such an example without the need of regulations. Punishment was necessary in this theory only for barbarous and uncivilized persons who could not appreciate the ruler's example and must be intimidated. Rewards and punishments were useful in order to make clear the activities proper to each person according to his status. But they were always considered in theory a secondary means of securing people's right conduct. The object was to "punish only to be able to stop punishing."

Certain generalizations can be attempted about this Chinese legal system. First of all, the law was not regarded as an external and categorical element in society; there was no "higher law" given to mankind through divine revelation. Moses received his golden tablets on a mountain top, but Confucius reasoned from daily life without the aid of any deity. For his rules of propriety, he did not claim any metaphysical sanction. Rather disingenuously, he merely said they came from the moral character of the natural universe itself, from this world, not from another world beyond man's ken. It followed that legal rules were but one expression of this morality — models or examples to be followed, or working rules of administration or ritual observance. So the breaking of such rules was a matter of practical expedience rather than of religious principle. Law was subordinate to morality. Its sanction lay in reason or the common social experience which underlay morals. This avoided the unhappy dualism which grew up in the West between the letter of the law and the dictates of common sense morality.*

In practice the Chinese imperial code was chiefly penal, a corrective for the untutored. It was also administrative, and prescribed the details of the rites. In other words, the code was nearly all public law, referring to administration, marriage, inheritance, and other matters relative to and important in government administration. Very little of it could be called private law. Business deals, private contracts, and the like were generally arranged according to old custom and usage, not by formal law or lawsuits.

Another characteristic of Chinese law was the fact that it was made only by the ruler, as a tool for his purposes of administration, and not by judges in court decisions. The Emperor established the

* Chiang Kai-shek in a commentary on Sun Yat-sen's *Three Principles* quotes Hsün-tzu, who said, "Law does not operate of itself." By this is meant, says Chiang, that "a state cannot be governed without law, but the enforcement of the law still rests with men." *China's Destiny*, Wang ed., p. 204.

code. Cases were collected, but relatively little generalization was attempted concerning them. There was little development of legal doctrines and principles. The experience gathered together in successive editions of the collected statutes was multifarious and sometimes contradictory.

The law was seldom strictly applied. This was partly because the law, being in general terms to serve as a model for conduct, was not always directly applicable. Thus the editor of the collected statutes of the Ming dynasty about the year 1509 wrote, "we have also written down laws that are good in themselves, even though they are not to be applied."

The strict application of the law was also tempered by the feeling that to appeal to the letter of the law, like Shylock, was to disregard true morality or to admit the moral weakness of one's case. The law had to be tempered by circumstance in order to achieve justice. Legality was an inferior substitute for morality. As the traditional saying put it, "when a state is about to perish, the regulations increase in number." *

This nondevelopment of Chinese law along lines familiar to the West was plainly related to the nondevelopment of capitalism and an independent business class in the old China. There was no idea

---

* A modern scholar (Dr. C. H. Peake) makes this brief characterization: ". . . Harmony, not abstract justice, was the ideal which [the Chinese] sought to establish in all relations. This harmony was to rest upon mutual self-respect, adherence to a policy of live and let live in conformity with the natural moral order. Due consideration was given to altered and changing circumstances beyond individual or group control and responsibility, which left the way ever open to the arts of diplomacy, arbitration and compromise for the alteration or annulment of agreements previously entered upon. The Chinese saw no inconsistency in the simultaneous recognition of the doctrines of *rebus sic stantibus* and *pacta sunt servanda* as both were interpreted in a relativistic sense and were subordinated to a higher principle which stressed the desirability, if not the necessity, of maintaining harmonious relations. Rights and obligations stipulated in a signed treaty or contract were subject to alteration in the light of larger duties arising from the necessity for preserving the natural or moral order.

"Likewise the characteristics of Chinese customary law with its emphasis on human rights over property rights, on duty over right, on individual and group responsibility for the social consequences of all acts, stand in marked contrast to the significant characteristics of Western law. The skill of the Chinese in the arts of compromise and conciliation born of a deep-seated distaste for litigation, and of distrust of the courts, has placed striking and definite limitations upon the sphere in which law operates in their society in contrast with the ever widening sphere through which law operates in Western societies" (*Political Science Quarterly,* March 1937, p. 137).

of the corporation as a legal individual. Big firms were family affairs. Business relations were not cold impersonal matters governed by the general principles of the law and of contract in a world apart from home and family. Business was a segment of the whole web of human friendship, kinship obligations, and personal relations which supported Chinese life. In old China the law, sanctity of contract, and free private enterprise never became a sacred trinity.

3. RELIGION

Another part of China's heritage from her past, which lies behind modern authoritarianism, was the peculiarly passive attitude of non-officials toward government, the apparent irresponsibility of the individual citizen toward affairs of state. Sun Yat-sen complained that his people were like "a heap of loose sand." Many writers used to deplore the selfish opportunism, competitive jealousy, and disregard for others which they discerned in individual conduct outside the bond of family, clan, and personal relations. It is a perennially fascinating paradox — this contrast, to the Western way of thinking, between loyalty to family and friends and disregard of the public interest, between the most meticulous sense of responsibility, when responsibility was customarily expected and clearly undertaken, and a callous irresponsibility regarding the suffering of strangers or public evils that concerned no one in particular.

Obviously this unwestern ideal of conduct springs partly from the fact that the family has outweighed the community both as an object of loyalty and a source of benefits. But the secret of this paradox undoubtedly lies also in the passive and individualistic aspects of China's religions. This passivity complements, and also conduces to, authoritarian government. To understand it we should look briefly at the religious alternatives to the Confucian doctrine.

Taoism. Taoism (*tao* means "the path," "the way") has expressed the common people's naturalistic cosmology and belief in certain traditional superstitions. It has also provided an escape from Confucianism, profiting by each revulsion of scholars against the overnice ritualism and detailed prescriptions of the classics. It has been a refuge from the world of affairs. It is aptly said that the Chinese scholar has been a Confucian when in office and a Taoist when out of office.

Traditionally Taoism stems from Lao-tzu (lit. "The Old Master") who was claimed by his followers to have been an elder contemporary of Confucius. The school of thought ascribed to him became a repository for a variety of beliefs and practices which Confucianism had refused, including early popular animism, alchemy, ancient magic, the search for the elixir of immortality and the Isles of the Blest, early Chinese medicine, and mysticism generally, both native and imported from India. Finally the Taoist church as an organization in China was influenced profoundly by Buddhism.

In general the Taoist philosophical writers who followed the brilliant literary example of Chuang-tzu (fl. 339–329 B.C.) raised their doubting questions from what we would now call a relativistic point of view. It was Chuang-tzu who delighted succeeding generations by writing that he had dreamt he was a butterfly playing in the sunshine; and after he awoke he could not be sure whether he was still Chuang-tzu who had dreamt that he was a butterfly, or actually a butterfly dreaming that it was the philosopher Chuang-tzu. The early Taoists were bright people. Applying the idea of the unity of opposites, they argued that human moral ideas are the reflection of human depravity, that the idea of filial piety springs from the fact of impiety, that the Confucian statement of the rules of propriety is really a reflection of the world's moral disorder. Following this line of thought, the typical Taoist took refuge in a philosophy of passivity expressed in the term *wu-wei,* meaning "action by inaction" or "effortlessness." This took the form of *laissez faire,* of following one's unrationalized inner nature and accepting without struggle the experience of life. This was plainly the philosophy of those who condemned government meddling and moral crusading and who sought to be resigned to the burdens of life since they could not be avoided. The famous "Seven Sages of the Bamboo Grove" got a great reputation for bibulous irresponsibility in pursuit of the elixir of life and a good time. One practical Taoist contribution came from their protoscientific experiments. Their search for elixirs and herbs built up the great Chinese pharmacopoeia, on which the world is still drawing, and also contributed to the technology of porcelain, dyes, alloys, and other Chinese inventions like the compass and gunpowder.

The Taoist church, as distinct from the philosophers, reached the masses with an imposing pantheon and many sects but failed to build up a worldly organization or appeal to the literati. Monasteries

and temples remained disconnected units, catering to popular super-
stition. By its nature Taoism could not become a vigorous organized
force in Chinese politics. It expressed an alternative to Confucianism but left the field of practical action to the Confucians.

Buddhism. The Buddhist element in Chinese life is difficult for
Westerners to assess because of our ignorance of Buddhism. Its
influence in setting the tone of oriental life is familiar to us through
Buddhist art, but its ideas are little studied.

In retrospect we can see that the Buddhist age, roughly from the
fourth to the ninth centuries A.D., when a foreign religion with a
new system of values and institutions became dominant in Chinese
life, is the chief prototype of the modern invasion of China by the
West. What example does China's experience of this foreign religion set before us? Neither Christianity nor Marxism form exact
parallels. Yet China's acceptance of foreign faiths today has overtones of the past. Religious enthusiasm among Chinese rebel movements is an ancient thing. In the case of Buddhism the new faith was
taken up first by the barbarian invaders who were entering China
from the north. But it was never a political tool of a foreign power.

To understand the appeal of Buddhism in China, we must note
its major conceptions. One of the most ancient tenets of Buddhism
is that life is painful and that it is not limited to the mortal span with
which we are familiar; this is the concept of transmigration.

The Buddha, who lived probably during the sixth century B.C.
in Nepal, was born of a noble family and began life as an aristocrat.
After renouncing his palace and its harem and luxuries he achieved
through meditation an illumination in which he realized the great
principle of the wheel of the law or the wheel of the Buddha.

This may be defined as a theory of the "dependent origination"
of life: that everything is conditioned by something else in a closed
sequence, so that in effect the misery of life is dependent upon certain conditions, and by eliminating these conditions it is possible
to eliminate the misery itself. Thus desire originates in dependence
upon sensation, which in turn originates in dependence upon contact and the six senses, and so on. The Buddhist objective therefore
becomes to cut the chain of conditions which bind one into this
sequence of passions, desires, and attachments. From this premise
that misery is conditioned and that the conditions can be destroyed,
the early Buddhists developed many theories.

One central idea of peculiar interest today is that of the dharmas.

This is actually a theory of elements or atoms, according to which an entity does not exist in itself but is made up of its parts. The old Buddhist monks believed that man himself is composed merely of these many parts or dharmas; he has no personality, soul, or self. The dharmas are of several types. Some relate to form and substance, others to sensation, and others to mental activity. Taken together they make a very neat explanation of experience and form a basis for the denial of the existence of self. This is just what the Buddhist sought, as a way of escaping life's misery. Since all the elements of experience could be analyzed to be disparate, unconnected, and atomic, both in space and in time, it was held that a proper realization of this truth could lead to elimination of the self and a release from the wheel of the law. This sort of escape or enlightenment, as you prefer, has been sought by mystics the world over and was eagerly pursued in medieval China.

Early Buddhism was institutionalized in a monastic order that developed its rule on lines which may be compared and contrasted with the monasticism of Christianity at a later date. By these early Buddhist monks the sutras (traditional sermons and teachings of the Buddha) were finally written down.

Buddhism in China. By the time of its expansion to the Far East the Buddhist school of the Mahayana (the "greater vehicle") had wrought profound changes in the ancient doctrines and made them more likely to appeal to the masses of the population. One of these developments was the idea of salvation, which became possible through the intercession of the bodhisattva (or "enlightened ones") who had attained to the enlightenment of the Buddha but continued their existence in this world in order to rescue others. Probably the most famous of these deities has been the so-called Chinese Goddess of Mercy or Kuan-yin, who is an abstraction of the principle of compassion.

Another is the Buddha of Endless Light, Amitabha (in Chinese O-mi-t'o-fo). Salvation of others through the efforts of these enlightened ones was made possible on the theory that merit could be transferred. Along with this went the concept of charity, which supplemented the original Buddhist faith and has made it in China and Japan a more positive social force.

The Mahayana school also developed a positive doctrine of nirvana, the state which it was the object of Buddhist effort to attain but which the Buddha himself had regarded as so completely indescribable that he had said nothing about it. The Buddhist teachings were set forth in the great Buddhist canon or tripitaka. Translation of sutras from this canon became the chief work of the first Buddhist monks in China. They and their followers faced enormously complex linguistic as well as intellectual problems — how to translate from Sanskrit, which was highly inflected and alphabetic like English and other Indo-European languages, into the uninflected, ideographic script of China; how to convey, in that rather terse and concrete medium, the highly imaginative and metaphysical abstractions of Indian mysticism. No wonder that the Buddhist impact on Chinese culture went through successive phases during several hundred years.

Barbarian invaders of North China, in the third century A.D. and after, accepted Buddhism partly because, like themselves, it came from outside the old order which they were taking over. Buddhist priests could be allies in securing, as Arthur Wright puts it, "submission and docility among the masses." * For the Chinese upper class who had fled to the south, Buddhism also offered an explanation and solace, intellectually sophisticated and aesthetically satisfying, for the collapse of their old society. Emperors and commoners alike sought religious salvation in an age of social disaster. When the rulers of the brief Sui dynasty (589–618) and of the early T'ang (618–907) revived a strong central government, they patronized Buddhism as a state religion. Great works of art, statues and rock-cut temples, have come down from this period. Fruitful comparisons and contrasts can be made between the roles of clergy and monasticism, the growth of sects and relations of church and state, during this age of faith in China and its later counterpart in Medieval Europe. Buddhist monasteries, for example, served as hostels for travelers, havens of refuge and sources of charity. They also became great landowners and assumed quasi-official positions in the administration.

The early period of borrowing and domestication had been followed by one of acceptance and independent growth. This native Buddhism was influenced extensively by Taoism, and influenced it in return. New sects arose in China, catering to Chinese needs.

* *Journal of Asian Studies,* November 1957.

Best known to us today through its influence on Oriental art was the school which sought enlightenment through practices of meditation (called in Chinese Ch'an, or in the Japanese pronunciation, Zen).

The Buddhist contribution to Chinese culture still awaits thorough appraisal but perhaps enough has been said to indicate the very complex interaction between such elements as Indian Buddhism, the barbarian invaders, native Taoism and the eventual growth, flowering, and decay of Chinese Buddhism. The latter's profound influence on Neo-Confucianism has been briefly noted in Chapter 4.

A comparison of Buddhism's role in China with that of Christianity in Europe should show one striking difference on the political plane. After the revival of strong government in the T'ang, the imperial bureaucracy eventually sought to bring the Buddhist church under firm control. Under Buddhist influence, Confucianism was gradually reinvigorated in the form of Neo-Confucianism. But so little had Buddhism disrupted the political tradition that the government had relatively little difficulty in reducing the economic power of the Buddhist monasteries. The several persecutions of Buddhism were in part a struggle to keep land out of the hands of the church and more easily amenable to taxation. No struggle between church and state developed in medievel China comparable to that in the West. The church was quite unable to achieve independence of the temporal power. Neither Buddhism nor Taoism was able to do this. Their priesthood and temples in recent centuries have remained loosely decentralized, dependent on local support but without organized lay congregations or any nation-wide administration, and passive in matters of politics. Meanwhile by its persistent proscription of religious organization, Confucianism more easily succeeded in dominating both the field of ethics and the major aspects of religious life, notably the family cult of ancestor reverence.

As a result of all this, in modern times China's resistance to Christianity has been not only ideological but also institutional — against any organized church independent of official control.

4. CHINESE HUMANISM

The preceding pages have stressed certain political and social institutions which on the whole tended toward authoritarian government in traditional China. Since most imperial governments, East and West, have been authoritarian down to recent times, this should be neither a surprise nor a stigma. The pertinent question today is whether China's political tradition can offer inspiration for democracy as well as for totalitarianism.

The answer must be yes, but within certain limits. There was a strong and indeed inspiring tradition that the Confucian scholar had a moral responsibility to speak out against misgovernment. The famous maxim (Buddhist-tinged, to be sure) was handed down from a Sung reformer: "A scholar should be the first to become concerned with the world's troubles and the last to rejoice in its happiness." Scholar-officials in disfavor at the late Ming court were publicly beaten with the bamboo; no laws protected them. Nevertheless those of the Tung-lin ("Eastern forest") Academy inveighed against the misrule of the eunuchs, suffering torture and death accordingly. Chinese history has not lacked heroes who attacked evil in terms of principle — only the principles have been a bit different from our own. If we speak of a Chinese tradition of humanism, we must note the difference in values which sets it apart from our Western tradition.

These different values can be perceived in the rich heritage of China's art and literature. T'ang poetry and Sung landscape painting represent a society which in its day outshone that of Europe, an aesthetic level which the West has not surpassed. But even a superficial glance at the status of the individual in Chinese art and literature will disclose that his place is less prominent than in the West. The Chinese tradition was humanistic, in short, in its concern for man-in-society, in its preoccupation with human relations in this world, especially the problem of conduct.

China's long experience of crowded community and family life produced a body of accepted norms of conduct. The individual farmer had first of all to accept the austerity of a bamboo-and-vegetable (as opposed to our iron-and-meat) standard of material wealth. This fostered in him the virtue of frugality. As in most peasant societies, he esteemed personal honesty, industry, and thrift. His life was particularly marked, however, by an emphasis upon propriety. He acknowledged the strength of social conventions and subordinated himself to them. He paid special respect to the old, he revered past generations, he yielded to family. In all these social forms there was a heavy discipline.

The Chinese type of humanism included a concern for the dignity of the individual, but from a social point of view. "Face" has been a social matter. Personal dignity has been derived from right conduct and the social approval it has secured. "Loss of face" came from failure to observe the rules of conduct so that others saw one at a disadvantage. Personal worth was not considered innate within each human soul, as in the West, but had to be acquired. Chinese humanism recognized that some persons had more gifts than others — human beings, though by nature good, were not equal in their capacities; there was no theory that each had an immortal soul.

On the contrary, right conduct was attuned to a hierarchic society in which some people dominated others because of their status. The center of Confucian moral life, *jen* or "benevolent love," was a distinctly unchristian though logical doctrine which called for loving others in a graded fashion, beginning with one's own father, family, and friends. Chinese humanism, indeed, was something of an upper-class luxury. The niceties of right conduct in social relations were less to be expected from the unlettered.

All this meant that the acts of a person were to be judged mainly by their contribution to social stability. The individual as such was not exalted. He was neither unique, immortal, nor the center of the universe. The proper study of mankind was mankind. Emphasis upon individual self-expression tended too often toward license and anarchy, and so the Chinese tradition emphasized social conduct. Compromise and tolerance, perspective and sense of humor, wisdom concerning human nature, character achieved through self-discipline were all parts of a structure of goals and sanctions which gave each individual his motivation within his community.

Certainly this code may be called humanistic, in its concern for human affairs, yet it fostered paternalism in government and permitted a high degree of authoritarianism. The Emperor and his officials had sweeping prerogatives over the goods and persons of the economy. They created at will state monopolies of salt and iron, controlled production or distribution of various goods, conscripted labor gangs and soldiery on a vast and merciless scale, forbade social gatherings and all unlicensed organizations, and generally ruled without fear of any higher law. Yet this absolutism was tempered by an all-pervading concern with human relations and social stability. In spite of the theories and devices of autocracy, the Chinese tradition distinctly did not put the state above mankind. It was not *étatism*. But the main reason for this, less a matter of theory than of circumstance, was that the government remained superficial, merely the top layer of the whole society.

Recent generations have seen this ancient structure collapse. Nationalism, science, democracy, and other dynamic elements of a world-wide civilization have shattered the old scheme of things. Today under Communism it is being refashioned with emphasis upon the authoritarian elements in the great tradition. But the latter is rich and various. Tomorrow other elements may emerge from it.

The foregoing pages should indicate the continuing vigor of the Chinese heritage. One stimulus to China's adaptation to modern life has been her tradition of superiority. This cultural pride forms a more than adequate basis for national cohesion. Another stimulus has been the poverty of the people. Between the pride bequeathed from a long past and the poverty presented in everyday life, there has been no lack of incentive for change and growth.

7

The Western Impact

POWERFUL INVADERS are nothing new to the Middle
Kingdom. It is the barbarians' possession of an allegedly superior
culture that forms the unprecedented novelty of modern times.
China's tragedy has been, not that she has come up against a more
powerful civilization from overseas, but that the alien West has
been culturally so different from the old China. Whether Western
ways are really and truly "superior" to Chinese is unimportant;
during the past century they have seemed so to the West. Now they
seem so even to Chinese, for the influx of Communism, whether we
like it or not, must be viewed as the latest phase of a process stimulated by Western contact.

China's modernization has been profoundly influenced by the
way in which she came into contact with the West. The American
role in China has had exotic nuances which came not from American life but from the precedents established by our European
predecessors in the East. Sino-American relations developed within
the shadow of older Sino-European relations.

1. EUROPEAN VERSUS CHINESE EXPANSION

The expansion of Europe which brought Western civilization into
direct contact with China can be described in general terms under
the headings of capitalism, nationalism, and Christianity. These
headings may serve to remind us of the characteristics of Western
society. The growth of capitalism can be traced from the time when
the crusades aided in the revival of trade between Western Europe
and the Eastern Mediterranean through waters which had been

closed off by Arab domination. This revival was accompanied by the development of commercial techniques and eventually the rise of towns with their urban classes, stimulation of industrial production, the accumulation of investment capital and its use through new techniques of banking and finance. This economic development during the later Middle Ages was paralleled by the gradual rise of the national states.

Except by hindsight it cannot be said that either of these phenomena, capitalism or nationalism, was inevitable. Neither of them followed patterns that were familiar to the ancient world. Older societies, for example, had been organized in city states or else in universal empires. The nation state was something new. It appears to have had many roots — in the self-consciousness and the kingship institution of the Germanic tribes, in the economic needs of new enterprises growing beyond the limits of the city-state type of economy, in the growth of representative institutions as a means of bringing people into larger political groupings than had been possible in the direct assemblies of the ancient world.

Once the national states for these and other reasons had become self-conscious units, the rivalry and warfare among them encouraged economic expansion and technological innovation. Capitalism and nationalism, which are of course no more than convenient over-all abstractions for descriptive purposes, thus appear to have interacted upon each other as aspects of a single expansive process. In doing so they stimulated learning, science, and invention. None of these developments had equal counterparts in China.

The expansive energy of Christian evangelism, particularly that of the Jesuits and other orders in the time of the Counter Reformation, may no doubt be compared more easily with Chinese experience in the time of the Buddhist expansion. But the crusading zeal of the Spanish against the infidel Moors in Spain and later overseas in the New World represents a type of religious enthusiasm foreign to the traditional Confucian mind. Taken with the other factors mentioned above, the proselytizing energy of early modern Europe must be viewed as still another manifestation of a social growth quite different in its nature and processes from the traditional society of China.

The West approached China in modern times through the medium of China's foreign trade. The Western impact can be understood only against this commercial background. The six-teenth-century Portuguese and the seventeenth-century British ad-venturers and merchants who opened the China trade discovered unknown regions, just as their colleagues of the same generations were opening up the New World. The all-important difference was that Eastern Asia, far from being a virgin continent, was already the center of an enormous and ramified commercial life of its own. The early Western ventures of exploration and trade were but small increments in channels of commerce already centuries old. It is a striking fact that British trade was opened at Canton in 1637 within a very few years of the founding of New England. Yet British trade with China was not able to expand outside of Canton until the nineteenth century, when New England had long since been settled and become part of a new and independent nation ready itself to aid in expanding the Canton trade.

The contrast between European expansion in America and its retardation in China must be understood from an Asian as well as a European point of view. It was not solely that European expan-sionist hopes and rivalries became more easily focused upon the New World. From the Chinese side, as also from the Japanese, this contrast between European expansion in Asia and in America was a tribute to the effectiveness of the Asian defense against foreign encroachment. This in turn rested upon the Asian achievement in controlling foreign trade.

The Arab Role. Except for brief intervals the trade between medi-eval China and the West down to the modern period was mediated through the Arabs.

It is not always remembered that the Arab expansion of the seventh and eighth centuries across North Africa and into Spain, which made the Mediterranean a "Moslem lake," was paralleled by a similar expansion to the east. The battle of Tours (738) at which the Arabs were turned back in France may be compared with the battle of Talas (751) at which Arab forces in Central Asia north of the Pamirs defeated a Chinese army of the T'ang dynasty. The spread of Islam into Chinese Turkestan, and the accession of Moslem dynasties in India in the twelfth century and later, were part of a continuing expansion toward the east which carried Arab merchants all the way to China and eventually set up Moslem sul-tanates on the Malay Peninsula and the islands of Indonesia.

Further research should indicate that the Indian Ocean in late medieval times was equally a "Moslem lake" in which the spice trade from the East Indies to the Levant formed but one of the staples. China was an outpost in this Arab trading world.

It was in keeping with the nature of the Chinese state as a land-based power that its maritime commercial expansion should begin only after foreign merchants had come to it and established the channels of trade. The records show early "tribute missions," by which we may understand traders, arriving from the Roman East in the Han period, but do not tell of Chinese trading expeditions to the south or west. When the Sung dynasty in the twelfth century was forced by the barbarian invasions to withdraw to South China, there was an increased concern for the foreign trade which already had a history of a thousand years and yet had not to that time become a major focus of Chinese energies. Under the Sung, trade was already confined to certain ports and foreign traders to a certain quarter of the city.

At what point Chinese merchants in large numbers began to go abroad in search of trade is still uncertain. In asserting his claim to rule all mankind, Khubilai Khan sent a dozen expeditions to Southeast Asia to secure the vassalage of the native rulers. While these costly efforts led to no permanent results for the Mongols, they acknowledged the existence of a well-established Chinese commercial interest.

By the beginning of the Ming period in 1368 we know from contemporary records that Chinese traders were well aware of the routes to the Southern Ocean (*nan-yang*), that is, the coasts and islands of Southeast Asia. This commercial background makes sense of the otherwise startling and inexplicable Ming expeditions into and across the Indian Ocean in the early fifteenth century.

The Ming Explorations. These famous expeditions were first studied from the Chinese texts chiefly by Western scholars. Coming a generation or, more before the Portuguese efforts to reach the East by sea, this Chinese achievement in geographical exploration is an amazing phenomenon and has yet to be fully understood. But it is already quite plain that it had little significance in the Chinese scheme of things. Perhaps there is no more telling point of contrast between the China and Europe of the fifteenth century than their respective attitudes toward maritime exploration.

The expeditions were under the superintendency of the chief court eunuch of the time, named Cheng Ho. There were seven separate ventures in the period between 1403 and 1433. The first expedition, for example, was composed of 62 ships carrying 28,000 men. The third voyage sent ships as far west as the terminus of navigation in the Persian Gulf and to Aden. Seven Chinese reached Mecca. Chinese vessels touched on the coast of Africa as well as Arabia. So-called tribute missions came to China from these places — from Bengal eleven times in this period and from a score of other states. The King of Malacca and his family came to the Chinese court four times in person.

The motive of the Ming court in supporting these vast undertakings is by no means clear. It is true that the eunuchs were able to use the tribute missions and strange gifts from far-away potentates as a means of flattery and ingratiation at court. Elephants and ostriches, strange products and stranger tales could be used to gain imperial favor. Giraffes brought from Arabia were touted as unicorns — in Chinese mythology a symbol of imperial virtue and an occasion for flowery congratulations to the ruler.

A traditional Chinese explanation of these voyages, that they were intended to seek out a deposed Emperor who still claimed the throne, hardly seems like the full story. Perhaps their motivation will be found in a combination of political and commercial interests. Possibly their political sanction lay in the desire on the part of the Ming court to perfect its claim to rule all men by bringing the maritime trading nations of the world into the traditional suzerain-vassal relationship which was demanded by Confucian theory as an alternative to the direct rule of the Son of Heaven. Ming sovereignty was vigorously asserted over the tribes of Central Asia in the early fifteenth century. It remains to be seen from further study whether the Cheng Ho expeditions were not equally an effort to assert Chinese suzerainty over rulers accessible by sea.

In any case the comparison between these Ming expeditions through the Indian Ocean and the contemporary Portuguese expeditions down the coast of Africa is both spectacular and instructive. Portuguese exploration of the African coast had begun as early as 1270. From 1418 Prince Henry the Navigator sent out expeditions almost every year. Cape Verde was not reached until 1445, by which

time the Ming court had already ceased its activity. In size the
Chinese fleets were uniformly larger than the Portuguese, they
sailed farther, and were undoubtedly comparable in technical abilities of sailing and navigation. Yet the Chinese fleets, for all their
competence, lacked any incentive to reach Europe around Africa
or even to establish trading posts. The similar abilities of the
Chinese and Portuguese voyagers in this period makes the contrast
between their motivations all the greater. The Chinese simply lacked
the expansive urge which the Europeans had, and this fact made
all the difference.

Early Maritime Contact. After the Portuguese entered the channels of China's maritime commerce, from 1514, they began a
process of trade and evangelism which was to culminate three
centuries later in the unequal treaty system of our own day. The
chief focus of the new Sino-European relationship was trade. The
Portuguese carried the silks of China to Japan as well as the spices
of the Indies to Europe. Their commercial empire was built on a
far-flung network of fortified trading posts, in India, at Malacca,
at Nagasaki and after 1557 at Macao near Canton. Development of
bigger ships and guns and of skill in navigating by compass,
astrolabe and written sailing directions gave the Portuguese their
century of supremacy in the eastern seas. They were eclipsed in the
seventeenth century by the Dutch and British, whose East India
Companies were better organized and financed, but the same network of trading posts continued to facilitate European penetration
of the Far East. Each one was an outpost containing the seeds of
empire — claims to national sovereignty, zeal for Christian evangelism, demands for Western legal practices, fluid capital funds and
superior military technology — all planted on Oriental shores and
ready to sprout when conditions permitted.

The Spanish from Manila and the Dutch from Batavia soon
expanded over the adjacent territories to create colonial domains.
But Japan and China, being centralized empires already, were able
to keep the Europeans quarantined for the time being at designated
ports like Nagasaki, Macao, and Canton, which became the predecessors of the nineteenth-century treaty ports.

The striking contrast between the Japanese and Chinese responses
to Western contact was one of timing as well as degree: Japan re-
acted more rapidly and extremely, though China eventually fol-

lowed a somewhat similar pattern. Within forty years after the first Portuguese reached Japan in 1542, the Jesuits had 75 priests at work there and some 150,000 converts. After a century, however, by 1640, Japan was closed to Western intercourse and Christianity was proscribed. In China the process went more slowly. St. Francis Xavier, one of the founders of the Jesuit order, had entered Japan in 1549 but he died off the coast of China in 1552. During the next two centuries he was followed in the effort to Christianize China by some 463 selected and highly trained evangelists whose devotion and pertinacity have seldom been surpassed. The great Jesuit pioneer, Matteo Ricci (1552–1610), took twenty years to work his way step by step from the Portuguese community at Macao to the court at Peking.

Ricci was one of the greatest proponents of boring from within. He became Chinese in name, dress, and language, published a score of works in classical style, and represented Christianity as a system of wisdom and ethics compatible with Confucianism. Through Western mathematics, astronomy, and geography he and his successors at Peking made themselves indispensable. They revised the imperial calendar, mapped the empire, and gained princes and ministers as converts to their faith. After the Manchu conquest in 1644 the Jesuits at Peking continued in charge of astronomy and the calendar, until in the eighteenth century an altercation (the Rites Controversy) between the Pope and the Son of Heaven, neither of whom would renounce his prerogatives, led to the eventual end of the mission, more than a century after Japan had closed her doors.

Through this early contact the elite of Chinese scholarship at Peking had been made acquainted with the best of Western learning. With what result? One of the greatest seventeenth-century literati (Ku Yen-wu) could only repeat the old wives' tale recorded in the official Ming History: "Portugal is south of Java . . . She sent an envoy for the purpose of buying small children to cook and eat." The imperial encyclopedia of 1747 called Ricci a liar: "His description of the five continents is nothing more than a wild fabulous story." After all, Cheng Ho had sailed west seven times in the Ming dynasty and never come across Italy, Portugal, or Europe! The early knowledge of the West in China had little influence, and although trade continued, it was kept under control at Canton, on the southern edge of the empire.

Meanwhile the early Russian contact by land across Siberia was slower to develop, though in the end more permanent. Cossack bands penetrated North Manchuria in the middle of the seventeenth century, but the power they could muster there, across the barren continental reaches of Siberia, could not yet compare with that of European warships on the China coast. After the treaty of Nertchinsk in 1689 the Manchus obliged the Russians to remain outside the Amur watershed for a century and a half. A trade treaty in 1727 let Russia maintain a non-diplomatic ecclesiastical mission — a few priests and language students — at Peking. Thus Russian commercial relations were controlled like those of all other foreigners, but from the first the Russian political contact by land was different from that of the Europeans by sea. Russia gradually became a territorial neighbor, something like the Mongol tribes of Inner Asia.

2. CHINA'S IMPACT ON EUROPE

Europe was the aggressor in opening relations with China. The impact of the new relations was therefore felt first in Europe. This is really no paradox, for the responsiveness to stimuli which led Europeans overseas, made them sensitive to what they found there. Until a century ago, China played a greater part in Western life than the West did in China. American understanding of Chinese society today is still colored and a bit befuddled by this inheritance from our own past.

The Europeans' discovery of Asia by sea in the sixteenth and seventeenth centuries revolutionized their view of the world. Before the great sea voyages, and except for the brief contact with Cathay in the time of Marco Polo, the only other society known to Europe contemporaneously had been that of the Moslems and Turks, the infidel on the border of the known world against whom medieval Christendom had struggled. Even in the sixteenth century in Europe there were still more books published on the Turks than on the New World. But the discovery of mighty kingdoms and ancient societies in Asia which were non-Christian and had actually survived for centuries without benefit of Christianity eventually had a profound effect on Western thought.

The implication of these new facts was fully developed only in the eighteenth-century Enlightenment. In it the conflict between natural morality and revealed religion came to a head. And China was taken as evidence to support the argument that the deity could be found through the natural order without revelation. The favorable picture of Cathay so brilliantly sketched by the Jesuit letters of the seventeenth century from Peking tended to show that virtuous conduct, in many ways adequate to Christian standards, could be achieved without revealed religion. This afforded a basis for the separation of morality and religion as sought by the Enlightenment. The translation of the Confucian classics into Latin at Paris in 1687 provided textual evidence. Writers like Leibnitz, who had already been profoundly influenced by China, asserted that the Chinese were actually superior in the practical organization of their society and the administration of its affairs, even though Europe remained superior in theoretical studies. For a generation which sought to show how the natural law underlay human institutions even in the absence of religion, China provided a perfect answer. In the China portrayed in the classics, a philosopher-king indeed appeared to be the benevolent father of his people.

Among the writers of the Enlightenment, Voltaire gave enormous prestige to Chinese civilization by his discussion of it in the first two chapters of his *Essay on Morals* published in 1756. He stated that the highest achievement of China was "morality and law." The Chinese officials were benevolent guardians of the people, the whole kingdom a family, and the public weal the first duty of government. As evidence of this he pointed to the Chinese officials' concern for public works, roads, and canals, and other activities fostering economic prosperity. He pointed out that the laws not only punished crime but also recompensed virtue, as when the Emperor honored virtuous persons on the suggestion of his ministers.

Finally, the physiocrats in seeking the reform of administration in France and other countries also got inspiration from China. As prophets of the industrial revolution and the rise of the modern middle class, the physiocrats stressed the inviolability of private property. In their reaction against mercantilism they argued that the private individual should be able to accumulate wealth without government supervision. In their view the state should foster and protect the natural right of private property. The leader of the physiocrats, Dr. Quesnay, who was known as the "Confucius of the West," published his book, *The Despotism of China*, in 1767.

In it he argued that the Emperor of China was a despot in a good sense, ruling over a government founded on wise laws which the ruler himself also observed. The Chinese despot, in short, although an absolute monarch, ruled within the framework of natural law.

Chinese society approached Quesnay's idea of perfection. There was no hereditary nobility. The son succeeded to the goods of his father but could succeed to his father's dignity only by study and self-improvement. China seemed to him a deistic society which worshiped the Supreme Being. Property rights were well assured. Taxes were regulated by the Emperor and no lands except temples were exempt. Quesnay did observe that commerce was not sufficiently encouraged and that corruption among the officials and the despotism of the ruler were only partly tempered by fear of rebellion. But on the whole his estimate was favorable and had wide influence.

Even Rousseau, who inveighed against the slave mentality of Manchu China, was at one with Mencius in his belief in the essential goodness of ordinary human nature.

China's impact on early modern Europe was thus highly selective, mediated through thinkers who found in the example of China certain things that they wanted to find. This set a style that still persists among travelers who take to China, prefabricated, their later impressions of the place.

In the nineteenth century this second-hand idealized view of the Enlightenment was rudely shattered by the maledictions of treaty-port merchants and consuls not interested in philosophy.

3. THE TRIBUTE SYSTEM

In the past century, from 1842 to 1943 to be exact, China has labored under the handicap of the unequal treaties by which she was opened to Western commercial and religious enterprise. Although the unequal treaty system was finally abolished before the Communist victory, it still meets their need for a focus of patriotic resentment in retrospect. National disasters in the United States, like the Civil War or the Great Depression, have commonly been utilized in the appeals of domestic politics; so the leaders of Modern China have found the treaty system a valuable symbol of national humiliation. Chiang Kai-shek, in *China's Destiny,* attributed to it all

Modern China's ills — economic, political, social, psychological, and moral — and the Communist denunciations are even more violent and comprehensive.

To understand the one-sidedness and inequality of the unequal treaties which the Western powers imposed upon the Chinese empire, one must look at the ancient tribute system which China first imposed upon Western visitors. This old Chinese system was in some ways just as unequal as the treaty system which supplanted it.

The tribute system was an application to foreign affairs of the Confucian doctrines by which Chinese rulers gained an ethical sanction for their exercise of political authority. Just as the virtuous ruler by his moral example had prestige and influence among the people of the Middle Kingdom, so he irresistibly attracted the barbarians who were outside the pale of Chinese culture. To a Confucian scholar it was inconceivable that the rude tribes of the frontier should not appreciate China's cultural superiority and therefore seek the benefits of Chinese civilization. Since the Emperor exercised the Mandate of Heaven to rule all mankind, it was his function to be compassionate and generous to all "men from afar." The imperial benevolence should be reciprocated, it was felt, by the humble submission of the foreigner.

Once the latter, however, had recognized the unique position of the Son of Heaven it was unavoidable that these reciprocal relations of compassionate benevolence and humble submission should be demonstrated in ritual form, by the ceremonial bestowal of gifts and of tribute respectively. Tribute thus became one of the rites of the Chinese court. It betokened the admission of a barbarian to the civilization of the Middle Kingdom. It was a boon and privilege, and not ignominious. As the original Chinese culture-island spread through the centuries to absorb barbarian tribes, the formalities of tribute relations were developed into a mechanism by which barbarous regions outside the empire might be given their place in the all-embracing Sinocentric cosmos.

When Europeans first came to China by sea these formalities were naturally expected of them. According to the collected statutes of the Manchu dynasty, a tributary ruler of a foreign state should receive an imperial patent of appointment which acknowledged his tributary status. There should also be conferred upon him a noble rank and an imperial seal for use in signing his memorials, which should be dated by the Chinese calendar. When his tribute missions came, they should be limited in size to one hundred men, of whom only twenty might proceed to the capital, by the imperial post. At the capital the mission was lodged, carefully protected and entertained. Eventually it was received in audience by the Emperor. This was the time of all others when the tribute envoys performed the kowtow.

Early European envoys, like the unhappy Hollanders who presented tribute at the Manchu court in 1795, were inclined to feel that this calisthenic ceremony more than offset the imperial benevolence which filtered down to them through the sticky hands of the officials who had them in charge. The full kowtow was no mere prostration of the body but a prolonged series of three separate kneelings, each one leading to three successive prostrations, nose upon the floor. The "three kneelings and nine prostrations" left no doubt in anyone's mind, least of all in the performer's, as to who was inferior and who superior. Egalitarian Westerners usually failed to appreciate that this abasement of the individual who kowtowed was a normal aspect of the ceremonial life in a society of status. The Emperor kowtowed to Heaven and his parents, the highest grandees kowtowed to the Emperor. In a less formal way friends might kowtow to each other, as polite Japanese almost do today. From a tribute bearer it was therefore no more than good manners.

The secret of the tribute system was the fact that it had become a vehicle for trade. The Ming chroniclers, by including the long defunct Roman East, fictitious principalities, and border tribes, had listed more than 120 tributaries. The Manchus put the border tribes under a special office and reduced their list of genuine tributaries to less than a dozen including the still shadowy countries of the "Western Ocean" whose merchants had already appeared at Canton. Because the Manchu empire chiefly sought stability in its foreign relations, it dealt only with neighboring countries or with those who came to China. If foreign merchants came and their ruler wanted to promote their trade, he could present tribute. It was as simple as that.

The trading states of East Asia presented tribute to the Chinese court in order to maintain their trade and friendly relations and were duly enrolled as tributaries. Certain ports and markets were designated for them. Thus tribute and trade from Korea came by land through Shanhaikuan, from the Liu-ch'iu Islands through Foochow, from Siam through Canton. When the first Europeans reached Canton, they were similarly enrolled and almost without realizing it became part of China's tributary firmament. Until the nineteenth century the diplomatic missions sent from Western powers to China, although they totaled more than a score, did little or nothing to shatter the Chinese institution of tribute and the conviction of superiority which it signified. It was still possible for the Ch'ien-lung Emperor, in his famous mandate of 1793 to King George III, to compliment the barbarian ruler on his "respectful humility" while at the same time refusing to permit any exchange of diplomatic representatives or expansion of British trade outside Canton.

The old Canton trade in its heyday (c. 1760–1840) was carried on under a working compromise between the Chinese system of tributary trade and European mercantilism. During the Napoleonic wars one of the great survivors of the mercantilist era, the British East India Company, based on India, beat out its Continental competitors and brought the growing tea exports of Canton into a profitable triangular trade between England, India, and China. Fleets of East Indiamen voyaged annually from London to Canton, where the Company by its charter monopolized all British trade and dealt with a comparable monopoly on the Chinese side — a licensed guild of about a dozen firms, or "hongs." These hong merchants were responsible to the imperial officials for the foreign trade and traders. The latter in turn were restricted by various regulations which, for example, confined them largely to their factories and kept them outside the walls of Canton. Thus by mutual agreement during the greater part of the century, in spite of continual disputes, the old Canton trade proved mutually profitable within the limits imposed by two, Chinese and foreign, systems of trade regulation.

Western expansion, and free trade in particular, disrupted the Canton system after the East India Company lost its monopoly of Britain's China trade in 1833. Unfortunately for the repute of private enterprise in the Orient, it reached the China coast at this time chiefly in the form of the opium trade conducted by private traders. This historical circumstance has poisoned Sino-Western relations ever since.

The opium was grown and taxed chiefly in areas under E.I.C. jurisdiction in India. Opium was carried to China by private British and Indian traders, as well as by Americans who competed as best they could by buying opium in Turkey. They usually found Chinese merchants and mandarins eager to flout the Emperor's prohibitions of smoking and importation. The result was an illegal trade openly connived at by British, American, Chinese, and other merchants and officials — too valuable to the British Indian exchequer to be refrained from, too necessary to the balancing of the tea export trade to be given up by the merchants, and too profitable to them and to venal Chinese officials to be easily suppressed.

In the retrospect of Chinese patriots today it makes little difference that the opium traffic was a fully bilateral activity, or that its evils hardly equalled those of the contemporary smuggling of Africans for sale in U.S.A. In China the opium trade remains a classic symbol of Western commercial imperialism — foreign greed and violence demoralizing and exploiting an inoffensive people. British humanitarians denounced it as such at the time.* A century later we can see it as part of an unavoidable conflict, Western expansion clashing head-on with China's traditional order. Conflict was bound to come. Opium provided the first occasion, though not the last. Similarly, the West was bound to win. (Whether that was a good thing depends on what you think of modern life.)

In the Chinese view, the Western barbarians have always been outlandish in their physical characteristics, generally uncouth and smelling of mutton fat. In slang even today they are not inappropriately called "foreign devils" (*fan-kuei* or *yang-kuei-tzu*), "big noses" (*ta-pi-tzu*), or simply "hairy ones" (*mao-tzu*). The official history of the Ming had described in some detail the Portuguese method of boiling and eating little Chinese children. Nineteenth-century mission orphanages were thought to make medicine out of children's eyes and hearts. Foreign diplomats seemed to the mandarins wily and inscrutable, unpredictable "as dogs and sheep." Peasant mothers until very recently shielded their babies from a foreigner's unlucky glance and especially the black magic of his camera. All

---

* One devout Scotch opium-captain noted in his journal on December 2, 1832: "Employed delivering briskly. No time to read my Bible."

in all, the white peril in nineteenth-century China was a good deal more sinister than the yellow peril of the 1900's in America.

Moreover, since the white barbarians came by ship, the traditional Chinese defensive strategy was completely reversed. The sea now took the place of the steppe. China's frontier was no longer on the Great Wall or at the Jade Gate in Kansu, but at Canton and Shanghai. Age-old conceptions had to be reversed accordingly.

4. THE TREATY SYSTEM

The legal structure established by the unequal treaties in the period 1842–1860 resulted directly from the two wars fought by the British against the Ch'ing government. The first war in 1840–1842, which has been called, particularly in China, the Opium War, resulted directly from the doughty Commissioner Lin Tse-hsu's vain effort to suppress the drug trade at Canton. But the British expeditionary force was sent to Canton and thence up the coast to secure privileges of general commercial and diplomatic intercourse on a Western basis of equality, and not especially to aid the expansion of the opium trade. The latter was expanding rapidly of its own accord, and was only one point of friction in the general antagonism between the Chinese and British schemes of international relations.

The principles embodied in the Treaty of Nanking in 1842 were not fully accepted on the Chinese side and the treaty privileges seemed inadequately extensive from the British side. Consequently the treaty system was not really established until the British and French had fought a second war and secured treaties at Tientsin in 1858. Even then the new order was not acknowledged by the reluctant dynasty until an Anglo-French expedition had occupied Peking itself in 1860. The transition from tribute relations to treaty relations occupied a generation of friction at Canton before 1840, and twenty years of trade, negotiation, and coercion thereafter.

Although the new treaties were signed as between equal sovereign powers, they were actually quite unequal in that China was placed against her will in a helpless position, wide open to the inroads of Western commerce and its attendant culture. By the twentieth century, after three generations of energetic Western consuls had developed its fine points, the treaty structure was a finely articulated

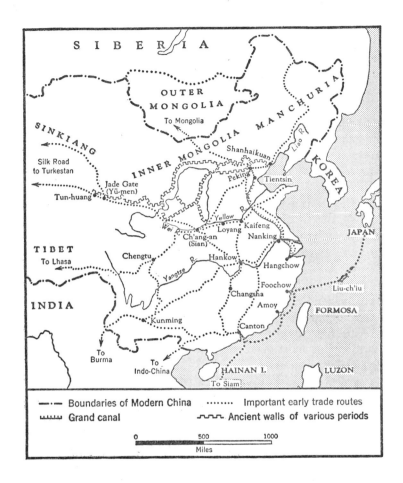

▬·— Boundaries of Modern China	········ Important early trade routes
⊔⊔⊔⊔ Grand canal	⌐⌐⌐⌐ Ancient walls of various periods

0   500   1000
Miles

and comprehensive mechanism. It was based first of all on treaty ports, at first five in number, and eventually more than eighty. (See map, page 179.)

The major treaty ports had a striking physical and institutional resemblance to one another. Each had a crowded, noisy bund and godowns (warehouses) swarming with coolies, who substituted for machinery, under the supervision of Chinese compradors (business managers), who managed affairs beneath the overlordship of the foreign taipan (firm managers), tea-tasters, and other personnel.

Each treaty port centered in a foreign section newly built on the edge of a teeming Chinese city and dominated by the tall white flagstaff of Her Majesty's Consulate. Its institutions included the club, the race course, and the church. It was ruled by a proper British consul and his colleagues of other nations and protected by squat gunboats moored off the bund. At Canton, Amoy, Swatow, and Foochow this foreign community got further protection by being established on an island adjacent to the shipping. At Ningpo, Shanghai, and other places the foreign area was separated from the Chinese city by a river, canal, creek, or other waterway.

Extraterritoriality. This legal system, under which foreigners and their activities in China remained amenable to foreign and not Chinese law, was not a foreign nor a modern invention. In a manner rather like that of the Turks at Constantinople, the Chinese government in medieval times had expected foreign communities in the seaports to govern themselves under their own headmen and by their own laws. This had been true of the early Arab traders in China. The British and Americans at Canton before the Opium War demanded extraterritoriality because they had suffered from Chinese attempts to apply Chinese criminal law to Westerners, without regard for Western rules of evidence or the Western abhorrence of torture. But most of all the foreign traders needed the help of their own law of contract.

As applied in the treaty ports, extraterritoriality became a powerful tool for the opening of China because it made foreign merchants and missionaries, their goods and property, and to some extent their Chinese employees, converts, and hangers-on all immune to Chinese authority. France in particular undertook the protection of Roman Catholic missions and communicants. All this was, to say the least, an impairment of Chinese sovereignty and a great handicap to China's self-defense against Western exploitation. The Japanese, who were saddled with the same system also, after 1858, made tremendous efforts to get out from under it and did so by the end of the century.

A further essential of the treaties was the treaty tariff which by its low rates prevented the Chinese from protecting their native industries. Since, for various reasons, the administration of the low treaty tariff was not effective in Chinese hands, a foreign staff was taken into the Chinese custom house. Under Sir Robert Hart as

Inspector General, the Westerners who served as commissioners of Chinese Maritime Customs became leading figures in every port, guardians both of the foreign trade and of the modest Chinese revenue of about 5 per cent derived from it.

Under the new dispensation of the treaties Western civilization brought to China a rich fare of good and evil. The opium trade which supplied 10 or 15 per cent of the revenue of British India went hand in hand with the Protestant missionary movement which was nourished by the shillings and dimes of devout congregations in the Christian West. Beginning about 1830 British and American Protestant missionaries found that modern medicine carried more weight in China than the scriptures. Missionary hospitals were soon attempting to repair the ravages of disease, including the effects of opium. In Chinese eyes this was no more anomalous than the general gap between Christian precept and imperialist practice.

By the most-favored-nation clause (the neatest diplomatic device of the century) all foreign powers shared what any one of them could squeeze out of China. The treaty system kept on growing as the fortunes of the Manchu dynasty deteriorated. The dynasty became increasingly dependent upon British administrative and diplomatic support. During the century of the treaties the Chinese people were consequently subjected to a most far-reaching, cumulative, and violent process of change. The opium trade that had begun as a joint Sino-foreign traffic was taken into the country. After the 1880's China's native opium production began to supplant the Indian product, importation of which ceased in 1913. From the treaty ports along the coast and up the Yangtze, Western ways as well as goods spread into the interior, aided in the remote centers by zealous evangelists like those of the China Inland Mission. Christianity opened the way for the acceptance of Western values which upset the old order entirely.

5. THE DEMOGRAPHIC MYSTERY

China's metamorphosis in the nineteenth and twentieth centuries has been intensified by the unhappy conjunction of two processes — Westernization and dynastic change. At the same time that the culture of the treaty ports was undermining the Confucian order, an accumulation of domestic problems was weakening the dynasty.

From the beginning of the nineteenth century the Manchus, already 150 years upon the throne, began to experience all the difficulties which had undone preceding dynasties. Prosperity seems to have brought overpopulation. The extraordinary and tremendous population increase since 1700 has contributed mightily to China's present problems.

The Record. Records of previous dynasties portray a peculiar stability of population from the Han period at the time of Christ down to the end of the Ming dynasty in 1644. The imperial registration of 2 A.D. recorded a population of 59.9 million. Population was then concentrated mainly in the Yellow River area with relatively little habitation south of the Yangtze. In the next millennium and a half these figures were hardly exceeded. At the end of the T'ang dynasty, around 900 A.D., the figure is about 53 million. Under the Southern Sung around 1200 A.D., when the north was under barbarian control, the figure is given as 45 million. In the Ming period, from 1368 to 1644, with China united and at peace, the figures vary between 50 and 60 million. The first records of the Manchu dynasty in 1651 record 10 million families or households, each of which was estimated by the Chinese authorities at 6 persons.

In the absence of definitive studies of these records it may be assumed as quite evident that the official population estimates of early dynasties erred on the short side of the facts. This was because tax payments were due from an administrative area partly according to the estimated population total. This created an incentive for short reporting both by the people themselves and by the Chinese authorities responsible for tax payments to the capital. On this assumption one may guess that the Chinese population in Sung times was already 100 million and by 1600 was at least 100 million and probably closer to 200 million. However, the Manchu records for 1659 report 19 million households. By 1734 this total had gradually increased to 26 million households.

At the beginning of the eighteenth century administrative changes were made in the method of estimating population totals. Among other things the Emperor declared in 1712 that the land tax and poll tax would thereafter never be increased (later tax increases therefore had to be made under other headings). This may have removed the normal incentive for short reporting. At any rate, beginning about 1741 population reports estimated the total of persons rather than of households. Possibly another incentive now came into play, to report constantly higher totals in order to indicate the prosperity of regions entrusted to the reporting official, and to please the monarch by demonstrating the beneficent effect of his reign.

Be that as it may, the figures from 1741 to the outbreak of the great rebellion in 1851 rise steadily and spectacularly, beginning with 143 million in the former year and ending with 432 million in the latter. Among these spectacular evidences there are some discordant notes. The totals for some years register a quite impossible jump over that of the preceding year — for example, 221 million in 1774 and 264 million in 1775, or 304 million in 1804 and 332 million in 1805.

Modern demographers probing into China's population growth do not lack for estimated totals for the empire and the provinces — the records abound in figures, but what do they signify? The difficulty is that there has never been a genuine census of the Western type, recording precise data as of a given date on age and sex distribution, marital status, migration, and all the other minutiae necessary for scientific analysis. The Chinese figures, on the contrary, have resulted from an administrative procedure of registration-and-estimation, conducted for government purposes to find out the number of persons capable of cultivating land, laboring on public works, bearing arms, or paying taxes. Many things have impeded accuracy. Popular cooperation was not to be expected. Whole categories of persons used to be omitted. Uniform schedules, accurate maps, trained enumerators, all have been lacking. The result is to cast a pall of extreme unreality over the whole body of estimates, which must be regarded as a product of bureaucratic ritual. The officials of Honan province, for example, during much of the nineteenth century reported an increase of 1000 persons every other year.

If, for the sake of argument, we accept the totals of 143 million for 1741, 313 million for 1793, and 413 million for 1849, we are confronted with a situation in which the Chinese population doubled in the fifty years between 1740 and 1790 and increased by one-third in the next fifty years from 1790 to 1840. If, with greater caution, we throw out the statistics and assume a total of 200 million in the early eighteenth century and only 350 million by 1850, we still face a startling fact: something like a doubling of the vast Chinese population in the century *before* Western contact and industrialization really got started.

Attempted Explanations. The Jesuit fathers, who were the leading students of China in their day, explained this increase by pointing to the common Chinese desire for sons as an expression of filial piety toward the ancestors. There is no necessary relationship, however, between such ideas and the reproductive rate of a population. The early age of marriage in China, facilitated by arranged marriages, would seem to have been a continuing factor. In short, to explain this sudden increase of the eighteenth century we cannot point to factors constant in Chinese society but must find conditions or a combination of factors which were newly effective during this period.

Among these the most obvious is the almost complete internal peace maintained under Manchu rule during the eighteenth century. With this general condition we know that there was associated an increase in foreign trade through Canton and possibly some improvement of transportation facilities within the empire. But in the absence of detailed monographic studies of other factors, there is one element in the situation which appears at present to have been of critical importance, namely, the food supply.

In eighteenth-century China it seems plain that the Malthusian principle applied and the population was ready to increase in proportion as it could find subsistence. Increased food production would both prevent the setbacks of famine years and strengthen resistance against disease, with the specific result of lowering infant mortality so that a greater proportion of infant females would survive to bear children.

The importance of a new crop to China's agrarian economy had already been demonstrated by the introduction of kaoliang. This tall-growing sorghum, not unlike corn in appearance, reached North China via Central Asia during the Mongol dynasty. It was relatively drought resistant and flourished on marginal soil of little value for wheat or millet. In one form or another it could be used to make porridge or wine, or for thatch, matting, fencing, and housebuilding, or as fuel, or as fodder. Grown in combination with other crops, such as soybeans, it is estimated that kaoliang now provides one-fifth of the food energy in many parts of North China.

Maize or corn was introduced from the American continent in the sixteenth century, and proved its value on the dry soil and marginal hill land of North China. Like kaoliang it had many uses for food, fuel, and fodder, and today provides something like one-seventh of the food energy available in North China.

More important was the sweet potato which came into South China from the Americas via the Spanish and the Philippines. The sweet potato had the special merit of growing on sandy soil and providing more food energy per unit of land than other crops. It has become the poor man's food in much of the South China rice area. The vines are used for fodder, the roots for fuel, and the surplus sweet potatoes can be dried and exported to breweries.

The essential point about these new crops was that they could be added to the crops already used, absorb otherwise unused labor power, intensify the use of the land, and so become integral parts of China's farm economy. Other crops introduced from America, such as tobacco and peanuts (as a source of peanut oil) proved useful to supplement this economy.

As further evidence of an increase in food production we find imperial edicts of the eighteenth century exhorting the farming population to use the land more intensively. Greater efficiency was also being achieved in rice production by the continued spread of early-ripening varieties of rice.

Whatever the explanation, we are faced with the amazing fact that the Chinese population seems to have doubled, and possibly increased four times, in the two centuries between 1650 and 1850, before contact with the modern world really began. Since the process of industrialization in nearly every other region of the earth has involved a rapid growth of population, this pre-industrial growth in China has set the stage in our own day for the greatest population problem of all time.

The Chinese Communists are saddled with this problem today. Their registration effort of 1953–54, still not a genuine "census" in our terms, gave a grand and appalling total of 586 million in mainland China. At their estimated rate of two per cent net increase a year, by no means an impossible rate, the Chinese people could total a billion by 1980. Small wonder that, despite its Marxist contempt for Malthusianism, Peking is promoting birth control!

8

The Revolutionary Process:
Rebellion and Restoration

THE BREAKDOWN of the old way of life in China and the building of new ways is the least known story of modern times, and one of the most dramatic. It has been marked during the last century by a series of phases. Each phase has seen the collapse of certain old forms and the emergence of new ones. The major periods of change, considered as a single revolutionary process, may be grouped to form two main stages — a period of anti-dynastic rebellion along traditional lines which was suppressed in a traditional fashion, and a period of reform and Westernization which merged into revolution. Indeed, rebellion, reform, and revolution have been intermixed, and the division of the revolutionary process into stages is merely an analytical device, to indicate how the elements of Chinese society have been remade and reorganized during the last century. Behind them all may be seen two types of change at work, one cyclical and one permanent.

By cyclical change I mean simple pendulum-like fluctuations, for example, from unity to disunity and back to unity again. This kind of change has occurred often in Chinese history with the rise and fall of dynasties, many of which ended with great rebellions provoked by the corruption of the bureaucracy, the rise of provincial warlords fighting civil wars, and the eventual reunification of the country under another strong founder of a dynasty. This process may be seen in the decline and fall of the Manchu dynasty, the warlord period which followed (1916–1928), and the rise of Chiang Kai-shek and Mao Tse-tung in succession.

By permanent (or secular) change we mean the reshaping of Chinese life through seemingly irreversible trends like the emanci-

pation of women, inauguration of government by parties instead of
dynasties, the increasing use of machines, and the spread of new
ideas. Obviously, these secular changes are much the more far-
reaching and fundamental. Yet they are obstructed at every turn
by the persistence of old cyclical patterns, like the re-emergence of
Confucianism as an ideological support for a new central government.

Here let us recall briefly (from Chapter 3 above) that when the
modern revolution began a century ago, the old China was still a
society containing two main strata, the literate upper class and the
illiterate mass of the peasantry. The gentry families included most
of the local degree-holders. Some of their sons became scholars,
some of them in turn became officials. Government was conducted
by the bureaucracy selected mainly from the literate upper class,
who were knit together by the Confusian ideology which they
imbibed from the classics. Thus an authoritarian monarchic government had for centuries held sway over a universal empire which
embraced the world of Chinese culture. But it rested upon intensive
cultivation of the soil by an earth-bound peasantry who did not
participate in the higher life of government and the arts. The politics, economy, and ideas of old China were still dominated respectively by bureaucratic authoritarianism, the landlord, and the Confucian ethic.

The first phase of the revolutionary process consisted of rebellion
in the traditional pattern against both landlordism and the alien
Manchu dynasty. Its fanatical religious leadership, however, was
anti-Confucian in ideology and failed to enlist the support of the
Confucian literati, who supported a restoration of the traditional
administration.

The Reform Movement at the end of the century was led by
the literati, who sought to retain Confucian values while strengthening the Chinese state by adopting Western methods. But these
scholar reformers sought change through the Emperor, from the
top down, and had no thought of mobilizing peasant support.

The Republican revolutionary movement was led by students of
the West and supported by the new merchant and military classes.
The transition from the Manchu Empire to the Chinese Republic
in 1912 marked both the end of a dynastic cycle in the traditional
pattern and a permanent change away from monarchy. But West-

ern ideas of parliamentary government did not take firm root and the peasantry still did not participate in politics — China relapsed into warlordism.

In the ensuing decade the student class, imbued with a new patriotism, became leaders of a true nationalist movement in politics and espoused social and cultural reform under the slogan of "Science and Democracy." The modern scholar class for almost the first time began to try to give political leadership to the illiterate populace.

This abbreviated preview of the summary which follows is offered here to indicate one thing — that political change in Modern China has been part of fundamental social developments in class structure as well as in the economy and system of values. These changes have been accelerating.

1. THE WHITE LOTUS AS A PROTOTYPE

Military power in agrarian China rested on the control of the countryside, its man power and its food supply. These were the sinews of warfare, which might be mobilized to unseat the reigning dynasty. Domestic rebellions therefore saw a struggle between competing groups, as to which side could control and use the men and crops in the villages. The dynasties relied first upon their professional striking forces, like the Manchu bannermen, and ultimately upon local gentry initiative in supporting the established order. The rebels usually found their initial organization in a secret society or religious cult.

This age-old pattern emerged once again, before the expansion of Western contact, in the savage rising of the White Lotus Society, 1796–1804. This secret society went back to the Mongol period. As a religious cult, it appealed to the superstitious faith of poverty-stricken peasants by its multiple promises that the Buddha would descend into the world, that the Ming dynasty would be restored, and that disaster, disease, and personal suffering could be obviated in this life and happiness secured in the next. In the late eighteenth century it had spread through the mountainous border region where the provinces of Hupeh, Szechwan, and Shensi join, in the region above the Yangtze gorges and on the upper waters of the Han River. This mountainous area, rather inhospitable to agriculture, had been opened to cultivation and settlement under official Ch'ing auspices only in modern times. Migration of poor settlers into these mountains, although encouraged officially, had not been accompanied by an equal development of imperial administration over them. The communities of settlers lived on the very margin of subsistence and tended to be a law unto themselves. The fanatical leaders of the White Lotus cult soon added to their popular appeal an anti-Manchu racial doctrine.

The outbreak of the rebellion in 1796 appears to have been as a movement of protest against the exactions of minor tax collectors. Though the imperial garrisons were able to come in and get each uprising under control in turn, new outbreaks continued to erupt and became too numerous to control. The populace had already organized self-defense corps against the aborigines to the south and had collected arms and food. The insurgents could move into easily defensible mountain redoubts and had time to establish their positions before the imperial forces could arrive. The systematic corruption permitted by the senile Emperor Ch'ien-lung handicapped the imperial military effort. While the rebels had little strategic plan and remained merely roving bands, the imperial forces lacked supplies, morale, and incentive as well as vigorous leadership. Both sides ravaged the populace instead of fighting.[*]

The White Lotus Rebellion was suppressed only after the Chia-ch'ing Emperor assumed real power in 1799 and supported vigorous Manchu commanders who restored discipline to their forces. By pursuing the rebels tenaciously, on the one hand, and getting control of the man power and food supply of the area, on the other, the Manchu generals eventually achieved an old-style suppression of the rising. Their methods indicate certain persistent problems in the military control of a densely populated countryside.

First of all, they mobilized the villagers to build several hundred walled enclosures in which the local peasantry could be concentrated. These walled villages were then protected by newly organized local militia who could by this time more easily be enrolled because the devastation of the countryside had seriously hindered

* A contemporary satire on this subject may be put into pidgin English as follows: "Bandits arrive, troops no trace. Troops come, bandits disappeared. How sad, the troops and the bandits! When will they ever get to meet each other?"

their farming and sustenance. Thus the populace were brought under imperial control. Meanwhile militia were trained to join in the campaign of extermination against the rebels, although it was found that these troops when properly trained became professional soldiers, warlike and dangerous, and subsequently an effort was made to recover their arms from them. At the same time a policy of conciliation was pursued toward the men the rebels had impressed into their bands, so as to secure their surrender; and other measures were taken to prevent refugees from continuing to join the rebels. By this combination of force and administrative arrangements, the imperial commanders gradually starved the rebels of their new recruits and supplies. The policy of "strengthening the walls and clearing the countryside" eventually sapped the strength of the rebellion and it died out. It had cost the imperial regime the equivalent of five year's revenue (200 million ounces of silver).

This pattern is reminiscent of many earlier uprisings and is even relevant to North China during the Japanese invasion of the 1930's and the Communist expansion of the 1940's. But the White Lotus, though an omen of dynastic decline, lacked one ingredient of power: the ideological and administrative leadership of scholars. In this respect it was a mere curtain raiser for the greatest struggle of the ninteenth-century world, a civil war in China which in numbers dwarfed our own Civil War.

The Chinese revolution of today really goes back to the Taiping Rebellion of 1851–1864, a full lifetime before Marxism entered China. The Taiping rebels were mainly peasants. They never heard of the Communist Manifesto. Yet modern China's revolution is unintelligible without reference to the Taiping effort to destroy Confucianism, and why it failed.

2. THE TAIPING HEAVENLY KINGDOM

This great upheaval arose from a background of population pressure, which had increased the insecurity of life and the vulnerability of the populace to drought, flood, famine, and disease. These in turn presented the creaking machinery of government with problems which it could not meet — flood control, famine relief, increased need for taxes, increased difficulty in getting them. Then, as now, official self-seeking produced inefficiency. Governmental incompetence bred loss of confidence on the part of the people.

The Emperor's inability to expel the British barbarians in 1842 or to check the connivance of Chinese merchants and pirates with the foreigner in the import of Indian opium, shook the imperial prestige. In 1846–1848 flood and famine were widespread among China's expanded population. It is not surprising that a great uprising finally began in 1851.

We can also understand why it should have begun in the southernmost provinces, which had been last conquered by the Manchus. The Canton region and its hinterland had been longest connected with the growing foreign trade, not only of the Western merchants at Canton but of Chinese traders with Southeast Asia. In this area, moreover, the Manchu power was at its weakest. Aside from the garrison of Manchu bannermen at Canton, the two provinces were loosely held by about 90,000 government troops which were by law supposed to be scattered widely in some 142 different camps as a sort of constabulary. In fact, they existed partly on paper only. Thus the Manchu power was weakest in the very region which had been most fully subjected to the upsetting effect of foreign trade.

The traditional pattern called for rebel leadership by a secret religious society. The natural candidates for this leadership were the established societies like the White Lotus in North China or the Triad in South China. The fact that the Taiping Rebellion did not join with these established agencies of revolt is one of the accidents of history and springs directly from the personality of the Taiping leader, Hung Hsiu-ch'üan.

How this disappointed scholar had visions and became a rebel Emperor of half China is a saga worthy of a great biographer. Hung was born in 1813. Three times he tried and failed in the provincial examinations at Canton. At the time of his third failure he suffered an illness and delirium. He believed that he saw a venerable sage who commanded him to save humanity. After this vision he returned from Canton to be a country schoolmaster, bringing with him a Christian missionary tract in Chinese entitled "Good Words Exhorting the Age." Curiously enough, Hung appears to have read this tract and its biblical quotations for the first time only six years later, in 1843. The correspondence between its teaching and his earlier vision gave him the conviction that God had called him. He baptized himself and soon afterward organized his followers into the God Worshippers' Society.

A subsequent visit to a Protestant missionary at Canton, the Reverend Issachar J. Roberts, in whose house he spent two months, added to his store of religious tenets and confirmed him in his sense of mission. With his followers he performed the rite of baptism, broke the idols in the local temples, and prayed to God. Forced by public opinion to leave his schoolmastering, Hung took his followers into the hills. For them he wrote hymns and religious tracts and preached his new religion. He soon had between one and two thousand baptized followers and began to give his religious teaching an anti-Manchu tinge. In the winter of 1850 a peasant disturbance was suppressed in Kwangsi and people escaping this suppression joined Hung's band. Already his lieutenants had created a military organization for protection against bandits. By this concatenation of seemingly chance elements, Hung's movement grew in strength. In 1851 the leaders gave it a dynastic title, *T'ai-p'ing t'ien-kuo,* "The Heavenly Kingdom of Great Peace," and thus raised the standard of open rebellion. Undoubtedly one essential ingredient in this development was Hung's faith in his divine mission.

Once launched, the rebellion rapidly expanded and its leaders conducted their forces on a great northern expedition into the Yangtze valley, comparable to the later northern expedition of the Nationalist forces under Chiang Kai-shek in 1926. The troops of the established dynasty held out in the Hunan capital, Changsha, but otherwise were routed or beat strategic retreats. Their "victories," which every imperial commander was bound by custom to report to the throne, occurred closer and closer to Peking. In the beginning of 1853 the Taipings captured and burned Hankow and started down the Yangtze by boat, half a million strong. In March 1853 they captured Nanking. An expedition continued northward and reached the Yellow River in June. By a trick of fate, however, the Yellow River in that year was in the process of shifting to its new course to the sea north of the Shantung promontory, instead of south of it. (See map, page 179.) The rebel forces were obliged to detour to the west through Shansi. In October they neared Peking and got within thirty miles of Tientsin. But this was the high tide of the rebellion. Turned back at this point, almost within sight of their goal, the Taipings failed to capture the symbol of dynastic authority, Peking, and gradually retreated to their base in the lower Yangtze. The next decade saw a continuing stalemate between the imperial and the rebel forces, finally broken by the suicide of Hung Hsiu-ch'üan as Nanking was assaulted and captured in 1864.

In this story of failure it is plain that the rebellion suffered primarily from inadequate leadership. As has been pointed out by Chinese students of all camps, the movement lacked guidance in terms of a political doctrine and political organization. Its ideological inadequacy can be seen by a brief glance at the use it made of Protestant Christianity.

Taiping Christianity. The Taiping use of the Christian Bible, as they received it in the form of Protestant missionary tracts and translations in Chinese, had at first inspired the American and British missionaries in the treaty ports with the fond hope that Christianity was about to sweep China and the "servants of God" take possession of the empire. The Reverend Issachar J. Roberts visited Hung at Nanking. Others made English translations of the Taiping Ten Commandments and other religious writings. Closer contact, however, was disillusioning. The missionaries found little in common with the Taipings and were not welcomed by them. They were forced to conclude that Hung's teaching was "all very unlike what might be expected to come from our Heavenly Father, and very different from anything ever uttered by Jesus."

Hung's selection of Christian doctrines, what he did and did not take from the Bible, makes a fascinating study.

As E. P. Boardman has shown, Hung adopted the ancient Hebrew concept of God as the creator. There was only one God. Ceremonial sacrifices should be made to Him. Individuals should pray to Him. There should be no worship of images. In ancient times, said Hung, the Chinese had followed God but since the foundation of the empire in 221 B.C. they had been deluded by the devil.

Also in Old Testament fashion, both the Taiping God and his son, the Elder Brother Jesus, communicated directly with two of Hung's principal lieutenants. In time of crisis the Taiping God might intervene on their behalf.

From the Old Testament the Taipings also took the story of the creation and the stories of the flood and of the flight from Egypt. The Ten Commandments were incorporated into the

Taiping social system and used with vigor. The rebels also used the conception of the Fatherhood of God, but they did not follow the New Testament very far in developing the story of Jesus and His teaching.

In general, in spite of the use of Christian and particularly Old Testament ideas and ceremonies such as baptism and the keeping of the Sabbath, they failed to take over many of the fundamentals of Christianity. Rewards and punishments they borrowed from the New Testament, together with descriptions of heaven and hell. But they omitted distinctive Christian teachings concerning the spiritual power of love and forgiveness, and of humility and concern for one's neighbor. It is plain that Hung took from the Bible the elements which were most useful to him in building his own theocracy. But it cannot be said that he really adopted the Christian religion, either for himself or for his followers. Instead, he set himself up as a new fount of pseudo-Christian revelation.

In spite of his attempts to fit his biblical ideas into the context of Chinese history and institutions, Hung did not succeed in making a mixture which would appeal to the scholar class. His failure to win the adherence of any body of Confucian literati was a primary element in his political failure as a whole. Moreover, the Taiping failure to join forces with the anti-Manchu secret societies, particularly the Triads, seems to have come partly from the antithesis between the Christian rites and doctrines used by Taiping fanatics and the Triad ceremonies derived from Chinese folk religion. The Triad ritual, for example, used esoteric characters not to be found in a Chinese dictionary, Triad members worshiped the Dipper, recited thirty-six incantations, stabbed their fingers to achieve a blood brotherhood, and performed ceremonies to represent the forces of heaven, earth, and man.

Since the Triad Society was widely organized in South China in five main lodges, of which the head was in Fukien and others in Kwangtung and Kwangsi, with a great number of followers among the lower military and civil officials, their aid to the Taiping cause could have been substantial. The Triads also had many members among the petty merchants and seafaring people connected with the foreign trade at the southern ports. In 1853 rebels connected with the Triads actually seized the walled city of Shanghai, next door to the young Foreign Settlement, and held it for seventeen months. Yet in this time the Taiping movement at Nanking failed to join forces with them. They also failed to court the friendship of the foreign trading powers at Shanghai.

Taiping Communism. The gropings of the Taiping leaders in the direction of a social and economic reorganization of Chinese life were visible in their use of ancient utopian ideas from pre-Confucian classics like the *Rites of Chou,* schemes to which earlier Chinese reformers had also appealed and which represented a native ingredient in their cosmology quite as important as Christianity. These ancient texts called for a sort of primitive communism in which each twenty-five households among the peasantry were to form one communal unit, each with its treasury and church and two superintendents. In these communities the fields were to be tilled in common, as on a communist collective farm today. Food, clothing, and money were to be used in common. The surplus from the harvest was to revert to the communal treasury. While this system seems to have been actually attempted only in Taiping military organization, it expressed their egalitarian interest.

In the same vein they advocated, although they could not make it effective, the redistribution of land so as to have it used according to need. Farm land was to be divided into nine classes and distributed among the people, with preference to men above sixteen and under fifty. At the same time the farming population was to be redistributed. In this way it was proposed to distribute land and people so that all would be equally well off. This was essentially a policy of equalization of land use, reminiscent of traditional reform efforts. It may be compared with the doctrine later put forth by the Chinese Communists, in the agrarian reform which preceded collectivization.

In other social teachings the Taipings advocated equality between the sexes. They inveighed against slavery, concubinage, foot binding, arranged marriage, cruel punishments, and the use of opium. These doctrines reflected popular desires which have found fuller expression in later decades.

Their military policy suffered from a lack of controlling leadership. The chief leaders usually acted on their own and became prey to feuds and jealousy. After 1854 they too often remained on the defensive and time after time squandered strategic opportunities. All the original leaders were eventually murdered or expelled, except Hung, whose fanaticism verged upon insanity.

The final collapse of this great rebellion, with all its latent potentialities, was an inevitable result of its early failures. Securing the support neither of scholar-gentry nor of anti-Manchu secret societies, it could not achieve a dynastic revolution of the traditional type. On the other hand its Christianity was too thin and its social and economic doctrines inadequate to take the place of Confucianism.

The Nien Rebels. During the period of Taiping control of the lower Yangtze region there arose on their north between the Huai and the Yellow Rivers another movement, of rebel bands called "Nien." Based on fortified earth-walled villages on the southern edge of the North China plain, these bands followed the White Lotus tradition, organized cavalry forces in their own banner system for raiding abroad, and controlled their territorial base by taking over the local militia corps. Though lacking dynastic pretensions, the Nien movement from 1853 to 1868 supplanted the imperial government in a sizable region and harrassed it with raids to plunder food supplies from neighboring provinces.

Imperial efforts to root the Nien out of their fortified nests repeatedly failed. Walls were leveled only to rise again. At last the scholar-generals who had defeated the Taipings developed a more-than-military strategy: to deprive the Nien of their popular support in the villages by promising security to the populace, death to the leaders, and pardon to the followers, many of whom shifted to the imperial forces. By taking over and reorganizing one village after another they cut the rebel cavalry off from their supplies of food and man power and eventually, with blockade lines and counter-cavalry, destroyed them on the plain.

In the aftermath of these revolts which convulsed Central and North China there were also sanguinary risings of Chinese Moslems in the Southwest and Northwest during the 1860's and 1870's — bitter struggles which are only now beginning to be studied. All in all, the movement for change in Modern China began by following traditional patterns of peasant-based rebellion and produced little but disorder and disaster, bequeathing to later revolutionists an egregious example of intellectual failure in popular leadership.

3. THE RESTORATION OF CONFUCIAN GOVERN-MENT

The constructive alternative to rebellion was to combine some degree of Western-style modernization with an old style revival of imperial administration. In 1860 the Ch'ing dynasty seemed on the point of collapse, beset by a recrudescence of Taiping military vigor in the lower Yangtze region and by the Anglo-French invasion and capture of Peking. Yet just at this point there emerged new Manchu leaders under the regency of the young Empress Dowager (Tz'u-hsi). By accepting the Western treaty system and supporting the conservative Chinese scholar-generals in the provinces, they achieved the suppression of the Taipings by 1864 and gave their dynasty a new lease on life. A small Sino-foreign mercenary army, led by an American and then a British commander (F. T. Ward of Salem, and the famous C. G. "Chinese" Gordon) helped defeat the rebels around Shanghai; but the victory was essentially a Chinese one.

As a result the 1860's saw a genuine conservative effort at a "Restoration," similar to those which had occurred after the founding of the Eastern or Later Han dynasty or after the great mid-T'ang rebellion of the 8th century. During the 1860's the components of the traditional Confucian state were energized to function again: a group of high-principled civil officials, chosen by examination in the classics and loyal to the reigning dynasty, sternly suppressed rebellion and ministered benevolently to the agrarian economy and the popular welfare. Order was restored in the central provinces, armies were reduced, taxes remitted, land reopened to cultivation, schools founded, and men of talent recruited for the civil service. While reviving the traditional order in this fashion, the Restoration leaders also began to Westernize. They set up arsenals to supply modern arms, built steamships, translated Western textbooks in technology and international law and created a proto-foreign office in the form of a special committee (the Tsungli Yamen) under the Grand Council. In these efforts they were aided by the cooperative policy of the Western powers, whose imperialist rivalries did not become intense until the 1870's. Yet in the end this renewed vitality within the Ch'ing administration showed both the strength and also the inertia of the traditional Chinese polity—it could not really be modernized but could function effectively only on its own terms, which were now out of date. As analyzed by Mary Wright, this successful revival within a context of inevitable failure makes an absorbing story.

The personal embodiment of the Restoration was the scholar-general Tseng Kuo-fan (1811–1872), who has been revered or condemned ever since as the great protagonist of Chinese conservatism. Tseng was loyal to the Manchu dynasty because it was an integral part of the Chinese social order. He was not racially nationalistic in the modern fashion but was patriotically culturalistic in the old tradition of the Middle Kingdom. Although trained as a classical scholar and civil official at Peking, during the 1850's he became a general in the provinces, organizing the famous Hunan Army which suppressed the Taipings along the central Yangtze by a strategy of gradual envelopment and mobilization of provincial resources. This first regional army of modern times was officered largely by local gentry-literati who followed Tseng Kuo-fan's example in leading peasant troops by the force of their personal moral character, their paternalistic sense of duty, and their faith in the Confucian principles of social order. Both in civil war and in later reconstruction, Tseng and his colleagues stressed the preëminence of "human abilities" or talent and character, which were partly inborn but partly could be cultivated by individual devotion to principle. They therefore stressed the revival of the examination system as a means of choosing talent and, for this purpose, the founding of academies and reprinting of classic texts.

Yet in spite of the influx of Western trade and the evident commercial power of the foreigners, the Restoration leaders clung conservatively to the economic principle of the preëminence of agriculture as the basis of state revenue and popular livelihood. They had no conception of economic growth or development in the modern sense but were austerely anti-acquisitive and disparaged commerce, including foreign trade, as non-productive. Rather, they tried to set before the peasantry and bureaucracy the classical ideals of frugality and incorruptibility, so that the product of the land could more readily suffice to maintain the people and the government. To assist agriculture, they reduced land taxes in the

lower Yangtze region, but did not try to lower rents or prevent
landlordism. They tried to revive the necessary public works for
water control, but could not control the Yellow River any better than their predecessors.

The Restoration lost vitality after the 1860's for many reasons.
Its leaders were conscientiously reviving the past instead of facing
China's new future creatively. They could not adequately inspire
the lower levels of their bureaucracy nor handle the specialized
technical and intellectual problems of modernization. The very
strength of their conservative and restorative effort inhibited China's
response to the West.

9

The Revolutionary Process:
Reform and Revolution

1. THE SELF-STRENGTHENING MOVEMENT

THE CONFUCIAN way of life was undermined first of all by the fire power of foreign cannon. During the first Anglo-Chinese war in 1840–1842 the British had used on the coast of China a shallow-bottomed paddle-wheel iron steamer called the *Nemesis*. It carried swivel cannon fore and aft and was capable of moving into the wind and against the tide in a manner disastrous to China's fortunes. Chinese officials like Commissioner Lin Tse-hsu, who were given the job of pacifying the new barbarians from the West, could not but be impressed with this mechanism. At Canton in 1840 Lin led the way in study of the West, securing translations of Western periodicals, patronizing an American missionary hospital, and experimenting in the construction of cannon and gunboats. Under the British impact Chinese officials in the coastal provinces made extensive preparations for coast defense, at least on paper, and several others followed Lin's example in studying Western geography and arms.

In contrast to the Japanese, however, these Chinese officials of the 1840's were unable to initiate changes to meet the foreign menace once the British had been pacified. During the two decades following the first war with Britain no fundamental progress was made in learning Western technology for military purposes, much less in accepting Western ideas generally. Lin himself, although plainly convinced of the need of Western arms by his experience at Canton, later hid his views because they were unpopular, and thus failed to warn his countrymen of dangers they refused to acknowledge.

Meanwhile, however, the great rebellion created profound changes in the Chinese government, primarily by shifting the center of gravity from the capital to the province both in financial and in military affairs. With Peking cut off from its richest provinces, it was left for local Chinese gentry leaders to raise the funds and the armies with which to suppress the rebels. The result was that trade taxes began to compete with the land tax as the government's staff of life, while personally-led regional armies began to supplant the effete imperial forces.

The chief new trade tax instituted at this time was *likin* (literally, a tax of "one-thousandth"). Beginning in 1853 in the lower Yangtze, provincial officials set up *likin* stations on the main routes of domestic commerce. They soon proliferated in all the provinces as a source of local revenue, beyond Peking's control and available for the support of regional armies. Meanwhile the new foreign-staffed Imperial Maritime Customs began to give the central government an increased revenue from foreign trade, which could be used partly to support the new office under the Grand Council for handling foreign affairs, the Tsungli Yamen.

Both in the provinces and at Peking the new trade revenues financed new efforts to deal with the Western invaders. Manchu and Chinese officials worked as one to strengthen the Chinese position by imitating Western mechanisms. This movement for "self-strengthening," as it was called, was posited on the attractive though fallacious doctrine of "Chinese learning as the fundamental structure, Western learning for practical use" — as though Western arms, steamships, science and technology could somehow be utilized to preserve Confucian values, instead of destroying them. In restrospect we can see that the latter was inevitable — gunboats and cotton looms bring their own philosophy with them. But the generation of 1860–1900 clung to the frustrating shibboleth that China could leap half-way into modernization. Under the slogan of "self-strengthening" they therefore began the adoption of Western arms and machines, only to find themselves sucked into an inexorable process in which one Western borrowing led to another, from machinery to technology, from science to all learning, from acceptance of new ideas to change of institutions, eventually from constitutional reform to republican revolution. The fallacy of half-way modernization, in tools but not in values, was in fact apparent to many conservative scholars, who therefore chose the alternative of opposing all things Western. With policy discussions dominated by these die-hards (who opposed Westernization as fervently as we oppose totalitarianism, but with much less chance of success) and the half-way modernizers (who usually had the responsibility for taking action), there was little chance for a third course of drastic revolutionary change.

The leaders in "self-strengthening" were those who had crushed the Taipings, scholar-officials like Tseng Kuo-fan and his younger coadjutor, Li Hung-chang. These men set up arsenals to make Western ships and guns. They supported the translation of Western books on science and spread the idea that Western methods must be learned and used for defense. As early as 1864, Li explained to Peking that the foreigners' domination of China was based on the superiority of their weapons, that it was hopeless to try to drive them out, and that Chinese society therefore faced the greatest crisis since its unification under the First Emperor in 221 B.C. Li concluded that in order to strengthen herself China must learn to use Western machinery, which implied the training of Chinese personnel. This simple line of reasoning had been immediately self-evident to the fighting men of Japan after Perry's arrival in 1853. But the movement for modernization in China was obstructed at every turn by the narrow ignorance and prejudice of the Confucian literati. This lack of responsiveness in China, during the decades when Japan was being rapidly modernized, provides one of the great contrasts of history and when more fully understood may offer one of its great lessons.

The difficulties of China's modernization were repeatedly illustrated. In the field of Western education, for example, the Jesuit missionaries of the seventeenth century had translated several dozen Western works on science, and the Protestant missionaries of the nineteenth century had continued to make translations of Western literature. Translators at Tseng Kuo-fan's arsenal at Shanghai during the 1870's produced Chinese versions of almost one hundred Western works on science. Yet this activity had to be conducted on the personal initiative of officials concerned with foreign affairs, not under guidance from the throne.

At the capital an interpreters' college had been set up in 1862 as a government institution to prepare young men for diplomatic negotiation. With an American missionary as head and nine foreign professors under him, this new college soon had over one hundred Manchu and Chinese students of foreign languages. Yet this innovation had to be defended vigorously against the attack of antiforeign literati who objected to the teaching of Western subjects. In 1865 we find the chief official in charge of foreign affairs defending these studies by the erroneous excuse that "Western sciences borrowed their roots from ancient Chinese mathematics. Westerners still regard their mathematics as coming from the Orient . . . China invented the method, Westerners adopted it."

The jealousy of a scholar class whose fortunes were tied to Chinese learning was most vigorously illustrated in the case of the first Chinese returned student. This man, Yung Wing, had been taken to the United States by missionaries in 1847 and graduated from Yale in 1854. When he returned to China after eight years abroad, he still had to wait almost a decade more before he was used by Tseng Kuo-fan as an agent to buy machinery and as an interpreter and translator. Yung Wing's proposal to send Chinese students abroad was not finally acted upon until fifteen years after his return. In 1872 he headed an educational mission which brought some 120 long-gowned Chinese students to Hartford, Connecticut. Old-style Chinese teachers came with them to prepare these prospective modernizers of China for the examinations in the classics, a preparation still essential to their becoming officials. Yung Wing was also given as colleague an obscurantist scholar whose mission was to see to it that Western contact did not undermine the students' Confucian morals. In 1881 the whole project was abandoned.

Similar attitudes handicapped the early industrialization effort. Conservatives feared that mines, railroads, and telegraph lines would upset the harmony between man and nature (*feng-shui*) and create all sorts of problems — by disturbing the imperial ancestors, by assembling unruly crowds of miners, by throwing boatmen and carters out of work, by absorbing government revenues, by creating a dependence on foreign machines and technicians. Even when modernizers like Li Hung-chang could overcome such fears they still faced enormous practical difficulties such as the lack of entrepreneurial skill and capital. Major projects had to be sponsored by high officials, usually under the formula of "official supervision and merchant operation." This meant in practice that enterprises were hamstrung by bureaucratism. Merchant managers remained under the thumb of their official patrons. Both groups milked the new companies of their current profits instead of reinvesting them. An ongoing process of self-sustaining industrial growth through reinvestment was never achieved.

Thus China's late-nineteenth-century industrialization proved generally abortive in spite of the early promise of many officially-sponsored projects. For example, the China Merchants' Steam Navigation Company founded in 1872 was subsidized to carry the tribute rice from the Yangtze delta to feed the capital. Almost every year since 1415 long flotillas of grain junks had moved these shipments up the Grand Canal. Now they could go quickly by sea from Shanghai to Tientsin. To provide coal for the steamer fleet the Kaiping coal mines were opened north of Tientsin in 1878. To transport this coal, China's first permanent railway was inaugurated in 1881. Yet by the end of the century these mutually-supporting enterprises had made comparatively little progress. The China Merchants' Company, plundered by its patrons, managers, and employees, lost ground to British steamship lines. The Kaiping mines, heavily in debt to foreigners, were taken over by Herbert Hoover and others in 1900. Railroad building was neglected by China and promoted by the imperialist powers in their spheres of influence after 1895.

How far China's slowness in modernization was due to foreign privilege and exploitation under the unequal treaties is a question awaiting impartial study. As Western imperialism in the Far East intensified in the late nineteenth century, Japan succeeded in throwing it off while China succumbed further and further. Certainly one main cause was the nature of Chinese society, including the fact of a big country with a comparatively weak central government.

2. CHRISTIANITY, IMPERIALISM AND THE REFORMERS OF 1898

During the four decades from 1860 to 1900 China was opened increasingly to foreign commercial exploitation and missionary endeavor. Foreign trade flourished, yet it never quite realized the persistent Western hope that if every "Chinaman" would only add an inch to his shirt-tail, the mills of Lancashire might be kept humming indefinitely. Likewise the Western evangelist found China remarkably self-sufficient and spiritual converts rather few.

The opening of the country in the 1860's facilitated the great effort to Christianize China. Building on old foundations, the Roman Catholic establishment totaled by 1894 some 750 European missionaries, 400 native priests, and over half a million communicants. By 1894 the newer Protestant mission effort suported over 1300 missionaries, mainly British and American, and maintained some 500 stations — each with a church, residences, street chapels, and usually a small school and possibly a hospital or dispensary — in about 350 different cities and towns. Yet they had made less than 60,000 Chinese Christian converts! Plainly, China was not destined to become a Christian nation. But the influence of mission schools and hospitals, of missionary ideals and activities in seeking out the common man, translating Western literature, initiating women's education, assisting in ancient tasks of charity and famine relief and in new tasks of modernization, was very considerable. No doubt future historians will conclude that this influence was highly disruptive to Chinese society, even though it was eminently helpful to the Chinese people.

The Peking fashion today is to belittle these good works of missionaries, who were the Communists' predecessors and rivals in the remaking of China, as "cultural imperialism." The argument that they were carried on by self-righteous foreigners under the protection of extraterritorial privileges backed by gunboats is undeniable. So is the fact that there were some 400 anti-Christian riots, sometimes with loss of life, up to the the Boxer massacres of 1900. Yet the fact remains that the missionary movement, whatever its spiritual-doctrinal result in this period, was a profound stimulus to China's modernization. The riots against it seem to have been generally inspired less by the superstitious fears of the populace in the first instance than by the jealousy of the Chinese gentry, whose privileged status in society was directly threatened — socially, ideologically, and in the end politically — by the new class of privileged cultural invaders from abroad.

As long as the dynasty and its traditional institutions survived, the penalty for China's complacent self-sufficiency and inertia became apparent mainly on the frontiers where the lesser states, traditionally tributary to China, were detached by imperialist powers. Japan took over the Liu-ch'iu Islands, Russia moved for a time into the Ili region in Central Asia, France seized Annam and created French Indo-China, the British took Burma, and Korea was opened to foreign intercourse. As these ominous developments continued to whittle away the Middle Kingdom's once-proud hegemony in Eastern Asia, the pressure for drastic action gradually accumulated, but institutional reform became fashionable only when disaster was imminent. Not until Japan had unexpectedly defeated the Chinese empire in 1895 and the European powers had extorted leaseholds and concessions in the three years following were genuine institutional changes attempted. Even then, the objective was still not fundamental change but merely intensified "self-strengthening" by the use of foreign methods. The reformers still took the position that the fundamental values in Chinese society should remain unchangeable but that the laws and institutions were changeable and must be made to take account of the West.

Thus the reformers of 1898 were merely reformers and not revolutionizers. They still wanted only "change within tradition." With great courage and even greater optimism they hoped that the bearers of the Chinese tradition could renovate it to suit modern needs.

Most famous of these men was the fiery Cantonese, K'ang Yu-wei, a scholar of high standing who startled the literati with his study, *Confucius as a Reformer*. This iconoclastic interpretation pictured Confucius as standing for the rights of the people as a check upon the authority of the ruler. Its publication roused some scholars to demand that K'ang be executed because, while his face was Confucian, his heart was plainly that of a barbarian.

K'ang Yu-wei's chief argument was that China must reform or perish, and that moderate reform still could not save her. He was intensely loyal to the dynasty and knew relatively little of the West, his knowledge of it being derived entirely from translations. In reforming, he believed China should learn particularly from Japan, whose experience was closer in time and space than that of Western countries. This led K'ang to advocate constitutionalism. He organized a rudimentary political party, the Society for the Study of Self-strengthening, to spread this point of view. His collaborator at this time was another Cantonese literary genius, Liang Ch'i-ch'ao, who edited a "self-strengthening" newspaper.

This group gained adherents after the disastrous defeat of China by the Japanese in 1895 and attracted the attention of the Emperor, for whose information K'ang prepared memorials and wrote two books. So convincing was his presentation that the young Emperor for a brief period of one hundred days in the summer of 1898 with his assistance issued a cataclysmic series of reform edicts.

These famous documents in the name of the Emperor ordered the remaking of the examination system, the administration, and many of the governmental institutions. The edicts aimed to inaugurate all the new services of a modern government and at the same time to wipe out the sinecures and corruption of the old. There were edicts dealing with medicine, agriculture, education, the penal code, the police, postal service, mining, commerce, the army, the navy, inventions, and study abroad. Seldom has the untrammeled power of an Emperor been more vividly exemplified, at least on paper.

The Hundred Days of 1898 produced consternation among the officials high and low. It mattered little that the constitution envisaged by the reformers would hardly limit the ruler's power, even though it espoused the rule of law — the fact was that too many officials felt themselves too closely endangered by these sudden changes. The Manchu Empress Dowager, Tz'u-hsi, who had been in retirement for the past decade, was able with military support to effect a *coup d'état,* depose the unfortunate Emperor, declare herself regent, and rescind all his edicts. Six of the reformers were executed. K'ang and Liang fled to Japan.

No incident could have dramatized more effectively the hopelessness of modernizing China through gradual reform from above. The defeat of 1895 and the fiasco of 1898 together gave the first great impetus toward revolutionary change. From then on, efforts at political revolution ran parallel to those for constitutional reform.

3. SUN YAT-SEN AND THE REPUBLIC

Sun Yat-sen (1866–1925) had the particular combination of abilities to talk and to act, to inspire and to organize, which made him the Father of the Republic. More than any other man he responded to the need of the times for devoted leadership. Equally important, he survived long enough to become a symbol.

The most remarkable thing about his early life was the degree to which, as a product of the peasant class, he achieved a Western scientific education and yet combined it with concern for the welfare of China's people. He was born near Macao in the region from which so many Cantonese emigrants have gone overseas. His father was a farmer who rose to the status of a village elder. Sun stated later with typical inaccuracy and sincerity, "I am a coolie and the son of a coolie. I was born with the poor and I am still poor. My sympathies have always been with the struggling mass."

Sun went to the village school and got his first contact with the West only in 1879 when at the age of fourteen he went from Macao to Honolulu on a British steamer as an emigrant to join his elder brother there. In Honolulu his brother placed him in a Church of England boarding school for Hawaiian boys. He studied English, mathematics, and English history and even sang in the choir, during a period of three years. This was a fundamental experience. When he graduated from this school in 1882 he was given the second prize in English grammar and had already conceived the desire to become a Christian. His return to his native village at the age of seventeen made him a radical.

Partly because he attacked the images in the local temple, he was sent away from his village and became a student at Queen's College at Hong Kong. Here he became a baptized Christian in the Congregational Church, in 1884, the same year that he dutifully married in the traditional manner a girl of his native village whom he had never seen and who remained there as a proper daughter-in-law.

The crushing French defeat of China in the undeclared war of 1885 roused Sun Yat-sen's interest in reform and national salvation. He appears already to have made some contact with the Triad Society. After another visit to his brother in Hawaii, Sun decided to study medicine. For five years from 1887 to 1892 he was a student of a young British missionary doctor, (Sir) James Cantlie, at Hong Kong. He studied chemistry, botany, physics, physiology, surgery, and clinical medicine, learned to play cricket with Cantlie, and assisted him in many missionary projects. After his graduation he began to practice as a surgeon at Macao and seemed well launched upon a professional career. The Portuguese who ran Macao, however, in order to preserve their medical monopoly forbade him to practice without a diploma from Portugal. In 1893 Sun abandoned his new profession and traveled to North China. There he vainly memorialized the authorities, urging programs for increased food and mineral production and a wider distribution of material goods and of education among the populance.

In 1894 Sun finally embarked upon his revolutionary career. He had already organized a secret society of his own, the Hsing Chung Hui (lit., "Revive China Society"). Its purpose was to save China by improving the livelihood of the people through education and the press and the use of modern methods in agriculture and industry. The members were sworn to secrecy by oaths written in blood, and Sun began to organize branches of fifteen or more adherents in other centers. Thus by the time that the Japanese defeat shook the Chinese state from its lethargy and precipitated the efforts at reform as well as the heightened imperialism of the powers, Sun had already become a leader in the cause of revolution. At this early date he appears to have met and got help from a Shanghai merchant, Charles Jones Soong, who had lived in the United States as a child, become a baptized Methodist, and studied theology three years at Vanderbilt University before returning to China. (His daughters married Sun Yat-sen, Chiang Kai-shek and H. H. Kung, respectively. Their brother was T. V. Soong.)

Sun Yat-sen's first revolutionary effort was made in 1895. Using Hong Kong as a base of operations, his group attempted to seize the Canton provincial government offices. The plot was discovered. Several of Sun's colleagues were executed. He himself escaped with a price on his head. It was then that he went into disguise, cutting his queue and adopting foreign dress. With a mustache he thenceforth passed easily as a Japanese. When in Japan he used the name Nakayama (meaning literally "central mountain"), pronounced in Chinese "Chung-shan," a name later applied to numerous institutions, streets, and even a style of clothing in Modern China. As Marius Jansen's fascinating study makes clear, Sun during the next decade got repeated and substantial help from Japanese patrioteer expansionists, including the Black Dragon Society and politicians of the Liberal Party. This included funds, arms, advice, and protection. Sun met Inukai, Okuma, and other Japanese leaders.

In 1896 Sun underwent in London an experience which confirmed him in his revolutionary mission. He was recognized at the Chinese Legation and locked up there incommunicado for twelve days. The Legation prepared to ship Sun back to China, where he would certainly have been executed. During the first days of his captivity Sun says that he prayed without ceasing and then achieved a greater peace of spirit. A few days later he got word to Sir James Cantlie, who lived nearby. Cantlie at once saw Scotland Yard, the press, the courts, and the Foreign Office. Through official British intervention, Sun was saved. He found himself at the age of thirty world-famous as the leader of the anti-Manchu revolutionary movement.

During the next two years he studied in London and on the Continent and evidently in this period acquired his background of political and social theory. From 1900 to 1905 he was constantly on the move in the Far East, organizing revolutionary activity, sometimes in the disguise of a coolie or a peddler, at other times as a Japanese carrying a forged Hawaiian birth certificate. He moved between Shanghai, Hanoi, Malaya, Honolulu, and Japan. In China he developed his connections with the Triad Society and worked particularly among the officers of the newly modernized imperial army. Sun declared that three groups could be enlisted to help the revolution — idealists, Chinese with racial bias against the Manchus, and all those whose livelihood had been destroyed by official corruption and extortion. By 1911, ten revolutionary outbreaks had been engineered, all in vain.

Sun Yat-sen's first statement of the Three Principles of the People (San Min Chu I) which still form the dogma of the Kuomintang (National People's Party) was made in 1905. Roughly translated, they are Nationalism, Democracy, and the People's Livelihood. In that year Sun also amalgamated his own revolutionary society with others to form the T'ung Meng Hui (lit. "Together Sworn Society"). Sun already had over forty branches of his earlier society in China. In the new organization he became president. Four hundred members attended the first meeting in Japan and took an oath to overthrow the Manchus and establish a republic. Sun also added to his credo some rather vague ideas of non-Marxist socialism, particularly Henry George's proposal to expropriate future increases in land values, effecting an "equalization of land rights."

This new and more powerful organization continued its secret activity using traditional techniques. Members were known by number only and communicated verbally rather than in writing. They made themselves known to one another by such devices as lifting a teacup with a thumb and two fingers, placing an umbrella on the window sill, or pausing on the threshold of a room and advancing with the left foot first. Using Japan as their base, they began publication in 1905 of a monthly newspaper, *The People (Min Pao)*, smuggling two thousand copies regularly into China to feed the discontent of the student class.

The dramatic story of Sun Yat-sen's political work should not eclipse other long-term developments which led to revolution. In the decade preceding the birth of the Chinese Republic in 1911, intensive reformist activity prepared the ground for it.

Liang Ch'i-ch'ao. After the fiasco of 1898, K'ang Yu-wei had remained a monarchist. He was left behind in the development of the reform movement while Liang Ch'i-ch'ao through his writing and editing in Japan became one of the founders of the modern Chinese liberal tradition. Liang was a classical scholar, a graduate of the provincial examinations, and a powerful writer. As Joseph Levenson's study makes clear, he was essentially a reformer of ideas rather than a political revolutionist. His limited knowledge of the West and his preëminent literary abilities made him fundamentally a man to reinterpret the Confucian tradition rather than destroy it.

After travel in the West he began in 1902 in Yokohama to publish the *New Citizen (Hsin Min Ts'ung Pao)*, a journal devoted to the theme of the "renovation of the people" *(hsin min)*. In the first few issues were articles by himself on Hobbes, Spinoza, Montesquieu, Bentham, Rousseau, and the history of Western political thought. He extolled Anglo-Saxon individualism and pointed out that personal freedom is possible only under the disciplined acceptance of law and order, tempered by common sense. The new Chinese citizen, said Liang, should learn to be public-spirited, to have a spirit of enterprise, to assert his rights and forget the Emperor's benevolence; he should achieve and maintain his independence of social custom, take an interest in his community, and demand self-government. This was a direct attack upon the ancient dogma of the five relationships.

Liang's reinterpretation of the Confucian ethic may be illustrated by his use of loyalty and filial piety. Since the state had now become the community in which the fortunes of the people were involved, it, he said, instead of the monarch, should now become the focus of loyalty. Confucian loyalty should be metamorphosed into modern patriotism through the redirection of human feeling, not by coercion.

Thinking along these evolutionary lines, Liang argued that republican constitutionalism was still impossible; the educational standard of the Chinese people was still too low to permit their participation in representative government. Moreover a revolution would bring great dangers of dictatorship and invite foreign aggression and the partition of China. He therefore advocated a benevolent monarchism under which education for the new citizenship and the establishment of provincial and national assemblies would permit gradual progress. The political party which Liang organized at Yokohama in 1907 advocated the setting up of a national assembly with a cabinet government responsible to it, new law codes and an independent judiciary, local self-government, a division of powers between local and central government, and the achievement of diplomatic equality through the abolition of the unequal treaties. This enlightened and gradual, though utopian, program represented the most humane and sophisticated political thought of the period and had wide influence.

The Boxer Rebellion and Late-Ch'ing Reforms. The activity of revolutionists and reformers abroad was paralleled in the 1900's by the belated reform efforts of the dynasty at home. In this effort to save itself by changing its spots, the Manchu government was given a compelling impulse by the Boxer uprising of 1900, which had the makings of a traditional peasant rebellion but lacked the social objectives of the Taiping movement. It was led by fanatical members of a secret society, who eventually got support from xenophobic officials and gentry. The latter violently resented both the obvious aggressions of imperialism and the less spectacular rise of the new class of Christian converts and protégés under the wing of foreign missions and the protection of extraterritoriality. Manchu princes finally supported this bitter and superstitious effort to expel the foreigner by relying on the magic "invulnerability" of Boxer braves.

In the end armed provocation by foreign troops was partly responsible for the outbreak of violence against foreigners. In this sudden frenzy the Boxers killed some 242 missionaries and other foreign civilians in North China and Manchuria. For two months in the hot summer of 1900 they besieged the foreign community in the Peking legations, yet the attack was never pushed home because leading Manchus realized its suicidal futility. Chinese officials in the southern provinces quickly asserted that this was a domestic rebellion, not the anti-foreign war which Peking had declared it to be. By this fiction the dynasty was preserved for another decade, though further humbled by the Boxer Protocol and indemnity of 1901. But the powers egregiously failed to demand or support genuine reform. Once again they used their influence to prop up a profitable though decadent *status quo*.

The Empress Dowager, on her return early in 1902 from her flight on a "tour of inspection" to the western provinces, took full responsibility for the Boxer trouble and announced a reform program. During the next decade the Manchus attempted, too late, to carry out many of the reforms which had been proposed during the famous Hundred Days of 1898. But history left them behind. The net effect of their reluctant reform efforts was to prepare the ground for the revolution.

The apparent inevitability of this process, in which the incompetent leadership of the Manchu dynasty seemed capable only of leading it to disaster, is well illustrated in its program for educational reform, which succeeded just enough to undermine the established order.

In 1905 the ancient examination system was abolished, marking the end of an era. New schools and new studies were planned hopefully to take its place, though the funds and the teachers were alike inadequate. Students were sent abroad, principally to Japan, both by Peking and by the provincial governments. An elementary school system was inaugurated, modeled on that of Japan. Colleges were opened in many centers. By 1911 there were said to be 57,000 schools with 1,600,000 students (out of perhaps 65,000,000 young people of school age). In higher education the Imperial University at Peking was formally established, incorporating the interpreters' college founded in the 1860's. As of 1911 there were abroad in the United States some 800 Chinese students and in Europe about 400. Meanwhile, however, Japan had been the chief training ground for Modern China. During the decade of the 1900's and particularly after Japan's great victory over Russia in 1905, every year saw 10,000 or even 15,000 Chinese students securing a modern education in Japan. Much of the top leadership of China today has come from this group. But from the point of view of the Chinese government the net effect of this decade of educational beginnings was to create in China a student class with radical ideas.

The students' dangerous thoughts came partly from their having a little learning, an awareness of China's backwardness, without any very fundamental understanding of the relation between a society and its institutions. Many of them on their return to China were appointed to official position in the traditional manner. Others became teachers in the new colleges on which Chinese local authorities prided themselves. Some were poor and others were idealists and many joined the revolutionary movement secretly.

In yielding to the pressure for reform the court accepted the idea of constitutionalism, as had the ruling oligarchy in Japan. The constitutional commission sent abroad after 1905 quickly copied the Japanese constitution. A reorganization of the government's ministries in 1906 established a cabinet system. Reorganization of provincial government in 1907 was followed in 1908 by the proclamation of a set of principles looking toward full constitutional government at the end of a nine-year period of preparation. It was proposed to establish assemblies in the provincial and central governments, which, however, should be purely consultative. When they met in 1909 they became natural centers of agitation for change.

Many of the Manchu reform efforts got no further than the paper stage. This was particularly true of the navy and the Western-type legal system, both so foreign to Chinese ways. Efforts at tariff revision as provided in the Boxer protocol were impeded by the difficulty of securing agreement among the powers. Currency reform was attempted but made little progress. Of all these efforts perhaps the most significant was the development of the New Army, the lead in which was taken by a vigorous Chinese official, Yuan Shih-k'ai. Following the precedent of Tseng Kuo-fan and Li Hung-chang, he became in effect the head of a personal army organization, the officer corps of which felt loyalty to him rather than to the state.

By using Japan as their base in the early 1900's, Sun and his co-revolutionaries were well situated to enlist both the idealists and the adventurers among the thousands of Chinese students who came to Japan. One of the most gifted of these new recruits was Wang Ching-wei, a Cantonese born in 1883 into the family of a scholar. Wang was a man of pronounced literary gifts. He passed the provincial examination in 1902 and was sent to Japan as a government scholar. In Tokyo he took a degree in political science and began to write for Sun's journal, proving himself a brilliant controversialist. During 1906–07 Wang Ching-wei contributed about one-quarter of the contents of this pro-republican organ, in a literary duel with Liang Ch'i-ch'ao. When Sun organized his new society (the T'ung Meng Hui) with three councils at the top, Wang became the head of the legislative council.

As this subversive movement gained strength, the Chinese government was able to strike against it. The revolutionary attempt of 1906 in Hunan province failed. Diplomatic representations from Peking moved the Japanese government to refuse further shelter to the revolutionists. Dissension arose within their ranks against Sun himself, who was denounced to the Japanese. When Sun set up headquarters in Hanoi, he was expelled by the French in turn. By 1909 the organization was in danger of disruption and demoralization. Further putsches had failed. To meet this crisis Sun Yat-sen in 1910 made another world tour while Wang Ching-wei determined to restore morale by a spectacular deed.

This was the origin of the famous attempted assassination of the Prince Regent in Peking in 1910. Wang placed a bomb under a bridge over which the Prince was expected to pass. The plot was discovered. But Wang when seized freely acknowledged his desire by this sensational act to rouse the Chinese populace in support of the revolution. By this courageous stand Wang Ching-wei (who at the end of his career went over to the Japanese in 1938) became a national hero and perhaps for this reason was only imprisoned and not executed.

The Revolution. A revolutionary attempt at Canton in April 1911 was put down with the execution of the famous seventy-two martyrs. This constituted Sun Yat-sen's tenth failure. The next plot was planned in Hankow in October 1911. The plot was accidentally discovered when a bomb exploded in the revolutionists' warehouse. This precipitated the uprising of October 10, since celebrated as the birthday of the Republic, the "double ten" (tenth day of the tenth month).

Sun Yat-sen meanwhile was traveling in the United States to

raise funds. He received a coded cable about the plot but had shipped his code book ahead and could not decode the message until two weeks later. He read in a newspaper that the Chinese revolution had been begun by Sun Yat-sen, who was to be the first President of the Chinese Republic.

The outbreak on October 10, following widespread unrest, especially in Szechwan, had been the signal for similar risings in other provinces. Within a few days revolutionary groups in the leading centers of South and Central China had declared their provinces independent of the Manchu dynasty at Peking. Once started, this anti-Manchu movement swept the country with comparatively little bloodshed. The ease with which the revolutionists finally succeeded in overthrowing the dynasty was, however, deceptive, for the groups and classes who joined in the movement soon proved to have little in common but their opposition to the Manchus.

Sun Yat-sen had derived his main support from the new merchant class among the overseas Chinese and from parts of the new student and officer classes within the country. His movement had been joined with another movement, inside China, which sought provincial autonomy in economic development. On this issue the leading landlord gentry and commercial interests in the provinces had united in opposition to the belated efforts of the Manchu central government when it tried to reform China from the top down. This whole issue of provincial autonomy against monarchic centralization of power had been raised in the new provincial assemblies and also in the provisional national assembly at Peking. It had been brought to a head by the dispute over railroad development, particularly the financing of railroads through Hankow and into Szechwan. On this railroad issue the provincial leaders had ranged themselves in public statements against the element of foreign control implicit in Peking's railway loan agreements. In actual fact they had been jealous of the prospect that central government officials would chiefly profit from these new developments.

The revolution of 1911 thus represented a good deal more than the revolutionary leadership supplied by Sun Yat-sen and his colleagues. By the same token, Sun, though the nominal leader of the revolution, had relatively little power to control the forces behind it. He was inaugurated as provisional President of the new Republic on January 1, 1912, at Nanking. But several considerations combined to make him decide to step aside within a few weeks in favor of Yuan Shih-k'ai, as a strong administrator better fitted to succeed to the position of the Manchu Emperor. For one thing, Yuan was the leader of the New Army in North China, where he had been called to run the Peking government when the Manchu regent resigned in December 1911. With this beginning Yuan was able to improve his position as the only man prospectively capable of maintaining order in the country. He negotiated with Sun but used delaying tactics.

Meanwhile time favored Yuan, for it became increasingly apparent to all that a China which continued divided would invite foreign aggression. The foreign trading powers, led by Great Britain, encouraged peace within China because they feared the possibility of intervention by her territorial neighbors, Japan or Russia. The revolutionists themselves were aware of this danger and tried to secure from Yuan assurances which would safeguard the Republic.

Agreement was soon reached in the negotiations between Yuan at Peking and Sun at Nanking. On February 12, 1912, the Manchu Emperor formally abdicated to Yuan Shih-k'ai as provisional President of the Republic of China. In this new post Yuan was to work with a parliament, and a cabinet responsible to it, under the terms of a new constitution.

Failure of Parliamentary Democracy. In this way the Chinese Republic was inaugurated to succeed the Manchu dynasty without any settlement of the fundamental institutional problems which confronted it. The provisional President was a military leader who represented the old style in Chinese politics, a strong man who was capable of taking personal responsibility for his regime and who soon became enamored of the idea of assuming an imperial title. Harnessed with him were new-style institutions of a parliament and a cabinet which were supposed to represent the people after the fashion of Western democracies. But these new institutions had as yet too little foundation in Chinese political practice.

The idea of political parties, for example, was contrary to the tradition by which the Emperor had ruled through his bureaucracy with a monopoly of political organization while opposition groups had had to become secret societies in order to survive. Not only were party programs a new alternative to personal leadership as a principle of group organization; the very idea of a cabinet responsible to parliament was a further anomaly, since the cabinet ministers were at the same time confronted with the Confucian tradition of the ministers' fundamental loyalty to the head of the state. The old-style landlord interest in the provinces was not accustomed to participation in the settlement of national problems, and the new commercial interests of the treaty ports were still not strong enough to dominate their society. The genuinely modern-minded revolutionists who were led by Sun Yat-sen formed but a slight leaven in the Chinese mass.

Yuan as the chief executive steadily strengthened his position. He got his own men into the cabinet, disregarded the spirit of the constitution, attacked and proscribed Sun Yat-sen's new political party, the Kuomintang (successor to the T'ung Meng Hui), and finally dissolved the parliament entirely. Led on by his entourage, he eventually attempted in 1915 to establish himself as Emperor, was thwarted by the opposition of the revolutionists, abandoned the project, and died in June 1916. After his death China broke up into rival warlord areas and for more than a decade, from 1916 to 1928, suffered disunity even though the government at Peking continued to receive international recognition.

For the student of Modern China it is most instructive to analyze the reasons why the 1911 revolution failed to build a new Chinese state on Western lines. As already noted, the elements that combined at the time of the uprising had no common objective beyond the overthrow of the Manchus. Anti-imperialism as a unifying sentiment was not yet widesperad and was not used as a motive force. This fact doubtless bespeaks a more fundamental factor, the retarded development of national consciousness. The revolutionists, moreover, in their secret plots had not been able and indeed had seldom attempted to mobilize mass 'support either in the cities or in the countryside. The conservative gentry class who cooperated against Peking were at heart the opposite of revolutionary. They readily acknowledged the superior armed force which Yuan was able to put into the field. In addition all patriotic Chinese at this time feared active foreign intervention. As an alternative to Japanese troops at Peking they were inclined to acquiesce in the stabilizing efforts of other foreign powers led by the British, who backed Yuan Shih-k'ai. The reorganization loan of £25,000,000 in 1913 (from which the United States abstained) represented the powers' inveterate support of stability, which Yuan then embodied.

Against this combination of foreign finance and domestic arms, Sun Yat-sen could do little. The ideas of political organization through a constitutional parliament and cabinet, which the Chinese Republic had borrowed from the West, could not be linked up with the Chinese political tradition. They did not even become a useful vehicle for Dr. Sun's revolutionary philosophy of the Three Principles of the People. It seems plain that in this period the effort to transplant Western institutions played China false.

10

The Rise of the Kuomintang

THE KUOMINTANG ("National People's Party") and the Chinese Communist Party (Kungchantang) have experienced a curious parallelism in their life histories. Each party soon after its formation came close to power and then met disaster. Each spent a long period in the wilderness before reaching the top at last.

After Sun Yat-sen's resignation as first President of the Republic in 1912, the Kuomintang as an open political party had been formed from the revolutionary T'ung Meng Hui and other groups by Sung Chiao-jen, a young political leader of such brilliant promise that Yuan Shih-k'ai promptly had him assassinated in 1913. The Kuomintang spent the next decade largely in eclipse. After the founding of the Chinese Communist Party in 1921 and its early effort to seize control of the Nationalist Revolution, the split of 1927 drove it out of the cities into the mountains of South China. Its final triumph came twenty-two years later.

This superficial similarity in their careers is not the only common characteristic of these rival parties. Robert North's study of their leadership indicates that in both parties the original elite were men from upper class, not peasant, backgrounds who had had some higher education. They were typically "alienated intellectuals," whose modern education pulled them out of the traditional society, restless misfits who found careers as full-time professional politicians and military or party organizers. Naturally they were young. Many got their start as specialists in violence, suited to a revolutionary era.

The early Kuomintang and Communist leaders differed less in social than in geographical origin. Dr. Sun's followers were city men, often from merchant families and hence from the big coastal treaty ports, particularly Canton. More of the Communists were from rural areas, particularly the central Yangtze basin. As time went on, the Communists recruited leaders of true peasant origin, the Kuomintang did not. Another difference beteen them was chronological. The founding fathers of the Kuomintang grew up in that ancient time before World War I. The Communists belonged to the wartime and post-war generations of an entirely different age, responsive to new pressures and new ideas. It is not surprising that the older generation of republican revolutionists were destined to do a part-way job, leaving the potentialties of change in Modern China to be exploited more thoroughly by a younger group.

Since the Kuomintang and the Communists both rose to power as exponents of modern mass nationalism, the competition between them must be traced from its first widespread articulation at the end of World War I.

1. THE MAY FOURTH MOVEMENT

This is the name given in China to the intellectual movement which crystallized in the Peking student demonstration of May 4, 1919. By extension the term has come to represent the whole development of thought and activity among the Chinese scholar class in the years immediately before and after that date. In its historical setting this intellectual movement was a necessary preparation for the successful Nationalist revolution of the years 1925 to 1928. To be properly understood, the May Fourth Movement must therefore be examined against the background of warlordism, industrialization, and rising patriotism which characterized the first decade of the Chinese Republic.

This decade from 1911 to 1921 was influenced by three circumstances. First, the central power of the dynasty was gone and nothing equally vigorous could be maintained in its place. There was therefore a lessening of efforts at reform or at repression from the top, and widespread opportunity for local change and innovation. Secondly, the foreign powers became absorbed in World War I. Industry in China had a breathing space in which to develop in relative freedom from the pressure of foreign commercial competition. Thirdly, the World War gave Japan an opportunity for political aggression. After ousting the Germans from Shantung in

1914, the Japanese presented to China in 1915 the notorious Twenty-one Demands. This brazen diplomacy backed by the threat of force consolidated the Japanese position in Shantung and Manchuria but failed to achieve a Japanese protectorate over China. In the process it roused Chinese nationalist sentiment to a new height.

China's new nationalism, of course, was rooted deep in her ancient pride of culture, which amounted to a sort of "culturalism," so profound as to be assumed without the need of explicit statement. The Middle Kingdom had been the known universe. A great source of patriotism was therefore at hand to draw upon, once modern Chinese individuals came into contact with patriotic nations which not only destroyed China's superiority but actually menaced her existence.

Warlordism. Warlordism was an old-style political phenomenon. It was based on the fact that coolie armies are easy to conscript and that Chinese provinces in many cases have natural geographic boundaries and can easily be made into military satrapies relatively independent of outside authority. Shansi province with its mountain escarpment on the east, the Yellow River on the west and south, and the Great Wall in Mongolia on the north is a prime exemplar of a unit based on geographic boundaries. It is not surprising that it remained almost continuously from 1911 to 1949 under the domination of a single warlord, the so-called "model governor," Yen Hsi-shan. Other warlord areas were centered about key economic regions such as the Canton delta, the Chengtu plain in Szechwan, or the lower Yangtze valley around Shanghai and Nanking.

Using these geographic bases it was the purpose of each warlord to enlarge his army and economic resources, conquer his rivals, and so succeed to the Mandate of Heaven in the traditional manner. The military leaders who aspired to follow this customary pattern represented in their origins the social fluidity of an interregnum between dynasties. Of the ten or a dozen leading warlords of this period, one began life as a peddler, another as a fiddler, two rose from the rank of private, one had been a bandit and another a coolie. Of them all perhaps the most famous was the "Christian General," Feng Yü-hsiang. He had been converted to Methodism by Dr. John R. Mott and set his men an example of puritan living and strict discipline. A man of unusual height and bodily physique, Feng prided himself on his peasant origin and led his troops by the quality of his personal example. It may be untrue that he baptized them with a fire hose. But this and many other bits of folklore concerning him testify to an unusual vigor of personality. It was symptomatic of the general struggle for power that Feng should be found switching allies and fighting first on one side and then on another among the shifting warlord factions. In 1925-26 he accepted Russian aid. In 1927 he joined Chiang Kai-shek but in 1929 was arrayed against him. In the end he became Marshal Feng, an honored and powerless captive of the Kuomintang, obliged to spend his time during World War II in scholarly calligraphy.

During the height of the warlord period Sun Yat-sen tried repeatedly to achieve his revolutionary objectives through warlord channels. He had soon become disillusioned as to the efficacy of the Western parliamentary system. In 1914 he had withdrawn from the vain and futile competition of the cliques and parties in Chinese politics and had organized again a secret revolutionary party, loyal to himself personally, through which to complete the unfinished task of revolution. In 1917, accompanied by the main body of the Chinese navy, he went to Canton and sought to cooperate with the local warlords. Thwarted at first, he nevertheless continued his efforts to unify China through military means. In the summer of 1920 Sun was cooperating with the Kwangtung governor to fight the Kwangsi governor. In early 1922 he launched his first, but abortive, northern campaign to invade Hunan on the same route as that followed by the Taiping rebels seventy years before.

In these old-style efforts to compete with the warlords by cooperating with some against others, Sun opposed the idea of federalism which was then current. This conception has sometimes been raised in Modern China, by analogy to the experience of the United States. In 1922 there was a widespread "federated provinces self-government movement." Intellectuals at this time argued that democracy in China must develop on the level of the provincial assemblies, after which a national government could be built on federal lines. Warlords supported the idea of a federal constitution as a basis for their own local autonomy. It is a striking fact, however, that the logic and apparent expediency of this federalist movement were unavailing. One may surmise that China did not follow the foreign example of the thirteen American colonies for two main reasons. First, the great weight of tradition, that there is "one sun in Heaven, and one ruler on earth," has dominated political thinking and ambitions. Second, the dangers of foreign intervention in China mobilized all the forces of nationalism in support of national unity, to be attained under a strong central government.

The New Labor Class. The nationalism of this period derived its impetus partly from the spread of industry in the great Chinese cities. World War I gave Chinese industrial production an opportunity to expand. Building on earlier beginnings, China developed her own industries in cotton textiles, flour milling, and the production of matches, cigarettes, cement, canned food, and similar mass commodities. Heavy industry and highly technical processes were still retarded. But the use of cheap hand labor to tend cotton spindles or sort tobacco developed steadily. Newly important towns like Tsinan, Hsüchow, and Chengchow grew up at railroad junction points. Shanghai, Tientsin, and Hankow became genuine industrial centers with a large factory labor class.

The growth of industrial cities, large and small, in turn began to provide alternative opportunites of employment for the peasant masses of the countryside. The new cities and the railroads leading to them opened a way of escape from the strait jacket of peasant life. The son of a farmer, for example, no longer had to depend so completely upon his family situation and particularly upon his filial rectitude toward his father as the only road toward a good life. Similarly, peasant women, accustomed to male domination, were offered an alternative to depend upon, in the form of factory wages. The old Chinese family system began to crack.

The vital significance of this process will be apparent if we recall how the family had been not only a social but also an economic institution, each peasant household functioning ideally as a self-sufficient unit. The members of the family, tilling their soil and managing their home in common, had sought to maintain security by relying on the outside world as little as possible. Custom as well as circumstance had long enforced the family bond and the personal relationships of status, in which each individual found himself placed by fate. The new life of the industrial cities, however, was based on utterly different principles of organization, on function rather than status. There the wage-earning individual could be the economic unit of subsistence, not the family. Moreover, individuals were hired and fired by impersonal criteria of the labor market without reference to personal or family connections. No one should idealize the life of unskilled laborers in an industrial city. The point is that with all its evils this new life provided an alternative to the old. More than that, it created a new class of people to whom the old loyalties and customs no longer applied, a nascent proletarian class ready to give their allegiance to mass movements such as nationalism and Communism.

The New Merchant Class. The growth of the cities had its most immediate effect upon China's merchant class, for whom the treaty ports of the nineteenth century had opened a new era of opportunity. The term "comprador" (of Portuguese derivation) had become well established in the pidgin English of the China coast to designate the "general manager" who represented a foreign merchant in all his operations in China. Following the example of the celebrated hong merchants who had monopolized the Chinese side of foreign trade at Canton until 1842, the compradors of foreign firms in the treaty ports soon became merchants in their own right. This new merchant class grew up under the wing of the foreigner. It was trained in his ways, and frequently protected by the operation of his laws under the system of extraterritoriality. In its later phase this merchant class had begun to exchange the sheltering wing of the foreigner for that of the modern Chinese official.

The disparity of values attached to both goods and currency in the trade between China and the outside world gave ample opportunity to the Chinese middleman's genius for speculation and manipulation. Chinese merchant capital was amassed in the treaty ports. Absorbing Western ideas, these merchants began to share the concern for national independence and unity which have typified the modern bourgeoisie in other countries.

One evidence of this growing patriotism among the Chinese merchant class was the increasing use of boycotts against foreign goods. In Chinese life the boycott had been a widely used form of passive resistance, or non-violent coercion, by which organized groups such as merchant guilds could exert their influence upon officialdom. In the twentieth century they began to be used as expressions of anti-foreignism. In 1905 a boycott sponsored by the merchant guilds of Canton had protested against the American exclusion of Chinese labor. In 1908 another Cantonese boycott expressed patriotic resentment against Japan over a diplomatic incident. The Twenty-one Demands in 1915 provoked a nation-wide movement to boycott Japanese goods and to encourage the purchase of Chinese goods and the growth of Chinese industries. For a few months this movement had a visible effect on Japanese trade.

The New Scholar Class. All these elements were in the background in 1919. The May Fourth Movement of that year gave them intellectual direction and leadership. The scholar class now for a brief time assumed the active leadership of the Chinese revolution. This reflected the fact that China's problems lay so deep that the analysis and understanding of them were more than ever prerequisite to effective action. The failure of the constitutional reform movement of 1898 and of the parliamentary movement after 1911 had demonstrated that no mere imitation of the West would suffice to remake China. Yet the national humiliations of the Japanese victory of 1895, the Boxer Protocol of 1901, and the Japanese demands of 1915 had strengthened the realization that Chinese society must be somehow revived and reorganized by the most fundamental changes.

One point of attack upon this problem of change was the classical written language. In the twentieth century a script and even a vocabulary which had been largely created about the time of Christ were still being used. In the minds of Western educated Chinese it inevitably became a question whether this language, like Latin in the West, had not become outmoded and insufficient for modern needs. Like all languages, Chinese has been the creation as well as the creator of those who studied it. Like Japanese, it had begun to absorb modern technical terms. The fundamental question was not the technical one, whether the classical language could be used for modern purposes of scholarship, but the social one, whether its use could be spread among the great mass of the Chinese people as a written medium.

Since the Chinese written language has been one of the tools by which the upper class has enjoyed the fruits of Chinese culture and maintained its social dominance, language reform and the mass literacy which it might make possible have been a fundamental problem in China's revolution.

The first stage in the linguistic revolution was to use the everyday vernacular speech in written form — the step taken in Europe at the time of the Renaissance, when the national vernaculars supplanted Latin. In China leadership was taken by the noted scholar and writer who later became known to Americans as China's wartime ambassador, Dr. Hu Shih. While a student at Cornell and Columbia during World War I he had advocated the use of the *pai-hua,* or Chinese spoken language, as a written medium for scholarship and all purposes of communication. Many others joined in this revolutionary movement, which denied the superior value of the literary style and made the Confucian classics into works of reference for the scholar rather than textbooks to be memorized by every student. The use of *pai-hua* spread rapidly, carrying with it the acknowledgment that the tryanny of the classics had been broken.

Hu Shih, a student of John Dewey and of pragmatism, also became a leader in the advocacy of scientific methods of thought and criticism. The value of science in technical studies had long been incontrovertible. Its application, as a way of thought, to Chinese literary criticism and historical scholarship now marked a further step in the revolutionary process. The new scholarship vigorously attacked the myths and legends of early Chinese history and reassessed the authenticity of the classics.

With science came democracy as the other watchword of the new learning. Leadership in the propagation of the new doctrine of Science and Democracy was taken by the son of a rich family, Ch'en Tu-hsiu. He had absorbed in France the tradition of the French Revolution and returned to found a magazine in Shanghai in 1915 called *The New Youth (Hsin Ch'ing Nien,* or *La Jeunesse).* In this and a score of similar journals which soon sprang up in the cities, the scholars of this revolutionary generation debated and discussed the application of Western ideas to China's ancient culture. Hu Shih stood forth for a critical attitude toward all things and the necessity of a healthy individualism. Ch'en Tu-hsiu, in the name of human rights and social equality, attacked Confucianism. Like Liang Ch'i-ch'ao, these scholars pointed the way toward an ethical revolution at the very roots of China's ancient society.

Beginning in 1917 this intellectual ferment became centered in the National University of Peking (commonly abbreviated in China as Peita), where the chancellor, Ts'ai Yuan-p'ei, a courageous advocate of freedom of thought and expression, invited Ch'en Tu-hsiu to serve as dean of literature and Hu Shih to lecture as a professor. (Mao Tse-tung about this time became an assistant in the Peita library.) With this leadership it is not surprising that the May Fourth Movement originated in the Peking National University.

The Student Movement. The incident of May 4, 1919, was provoked by the decision of the peacemakers at Versailles to leave in Japanese hands the former German concessions in Shantung. After learning of this decision, some five thousand students from Peita and other Peking institutions held a mass demonstration at one of the palace gates. They burned the house of a pro-Japanese cabinet minister and seized and beat the Chinese minister to Japan. Police attacked the students. They thereupon called a student strike, sent telegrams to students elsewhere, and organized patriotic teams to distribute leaflets and make speeches among the populace. Similar demonstrations were staged in Tientsin, Shanghai, Nanking, Hankow, Foochow, Canton, and elsewhere. A few students were killed and others were wounded. The prisons were soon full of demonstrators.

The spirit of protest spread among the merchants, who joined the movement by closing their shops in a merchants' strike which spread through the major centers in June of 1919. This developed into a boycott of Japanese goods attended by clashes with Japanese residents. For more than a year student patriots continued the agitation for the destruction of Japan's market in China, with an appreciable effect upon it. Meanwhile strikes were staged among the recently organized labor unions, which joined in the broadest demonstration of national feeling which China had ever seen.

The startling thing about this movement is the fact that while the traditional ruling class of officials and gentry had little to do with it, as might be expected, its leadership was also neither among the new militarists nor among the new politicians. It was led by intellectuals who were quickly supported by organizations of retail merchants, industrial and craft workers, and similar groups. The movement was particularly significant in that it brought both the new cultural ideas of science and democracy and the new patriotism into a common focus in an anti-imperialist program. More than ever before in modern history the student class assumed responsibility for China's fate and made an effort through their student organizations to reach the common people in the villages. It is not too much to say that this was the beginning of the modern effort to bring the Chinese scholar into touch with the peasant in a common cause.

2. THE NATIONALIST REVOLUTION

In a general way it can be said that the Nationalist revolution of the 1920's combined the traditional trend toward reunification of the country under a strong leader (in this case Chiang Kai-shek) with a new trend toward modernization of the government through the use of Western administrative methods, the inculcation of a new loyalty to the nation, and the monopoly of power by a party dictatorship (rather than a new dynasty). The dominant sentiment behind the revolution was a nationalism which sought both unity within China and independence from foreign domination. Its class basis was still, however, the literate upper stratum. Essentially, the Nanking Government in the decade after 1927 led the way in the modernization of China's upper class institutions. But it was unable overnight to revolutionize the life of the common peasant.

This part-way nature of the Nationalist cause, its limited aims in the reorganizing of Chinese society, emerged quite clearly in the 1920's. The occasion was provided by Sun Yat-sen's decision in 1922 to learn from, and Chiang Kai-shek's decision in 1927 to break with, Soviet Russia.

The Kuomintang-Communist Alliance. It was no doubt inevitable that the Chinese Nationalist revolution in its effort to shake off the unequal treaties and other bonds of imperialism should be deeply influenced by the doctrines of Marxism-Leninism and the example of Russia. Communist theory put anti-imperialism on a more than national basis and made it a part of the world-wide trend of history. According to this doctrine China could develop as a nation only by breaking the influence of foreign capitalism. Since political thinking in China had always been based on universal principles, and the Chinese empire had traditionally embraced the civilized world, Chinese revolutionists readily sought to base their cause on doctrines of universal validity. Ch'en Tu-hsiu became one of the founders of the Chinese Communist Party which was organized in the summer of 1921 in Shanghai. Sun

Yat-sen, while not subscribing to Communism, in the last years before his death (in March 1925) fully recognized the usefulness of Communist methods and accepted Communist collaboration in his Nationalist cause.

The Comintern (Communist International) or Third International was a successor to the First and Second Internationals which had been organized in 1864 and 1889, respectively, to bring together the various elements of the socialist movement in Europe. In 1914 the Second International succumbed to militant nationalism. After the war the Russian Bolsheviks had organized the Third International out of scattered groups in various countries. Their first Comintern congress in 1919 was followed by six other international congresses before the outbreak of World War II. In general it was the function of the Comintern to represent the Russian Communist movement in its world-wide aspect. This was particularly true in the first years after World War I when the Bolsheviks were encouraging active revolution in many countries in Europe. After 1921, when Lenin turned the Soviet Union to his new economic policy, the Comintern competed with the revived socialist parties of Europe but was less actively revolutionary, except in China.

Lenin held that Western capitalism was using the backward countries of Asia as a source of profit to bolster the capitalist system. Without imperialist exploitation of Asia, which allowed continued high wages for the workers of the West, capitalism would more rapidly collapse. Nationalist revolutions in Asia, which would deprive the imperialist powers of their profitable markets and sources of raw materials, would therefore constitute a "flank attack" on Western capitalism at its weakest point — that is, in Asian economies where imperialist domination exploited the working class most ruthlessly. From the very beginning the Bolsheviki had therefore called upon the colonial peoples to rise against their Western masters. From this time on, Lenin's explanation of imperialism was to gain increasing acceptance among Asian intellectuals.

In China the Soviet government had capitalized upon its own impotence by grandly renouncing the privileges of the Tsar's unequal treaties. But it subsequently proved a hard bargainer over Tsarist rights in Manchuria and it continued to deal with the Peking government and warlords in North China, while the Comintern worked for revolution. Soviet propaganda concentrated upon British imperialism as its chief target. The Comintern picked China as the chief area of foreign struggle in the years from 1922 to 1927.

On his part Sun Yat-sen by 1922 had reached a low point in his fortunes after almost thirty years of agitation. He had seen the Manchu dynasty collapse and had been proclaimed President of the Chinese Republic only to see his country disintegrate into war-lordism and become more than ever the prey of foreign powers. His effort to unify China through warlord means had led him into dealings with opportunist military leaders at Canton. In June 1922 a Cantonese militarist whom he had attempted to outmaneuver had turned the tables upon him. Sun was forced to flee, and reached Shanghai in August. It was just at this moment, when Sun had demonstrated his preëminence as China's Nationalist leader but his incompetence to complete the revolution, that he joined forces with the Comintern. In September 1922 he began the reorganization of the Kuomintang on Soviet lines.

This was purely a marriage of convenience. The entente announced in a joint statement by Dr. Sun and Adolph Joffe in January 1923 was a strictly limited arrangement. It stated that Sun did not favor Communism for China since conditions were not appropriate to it, that Joffe agreed that China needed unity and independence, and that Russia was ready to aid the Chinese Nationalist revolution. As Sun Yat-sen wrote to Chiang Kai-shek at the time, he had to seek help where he could get it. The Western powers offered no aid. But although Sun now sought and accepted Soviet Russian aid, Communism in his mind did not supplant his own *Three Principles of the People* as the program for the Chinese revolution — even though he found it useful to incorporate in his ideas the Communist emphasis on a mass movement fired by anti-imperialism.

On the basis of this uneasy alliance, Soviet help was soon forthcoming. Chiang Kai-shek spent three months in Russia in late 1923 and returned to become the head of the new Whampoa Military Academy at Canton in 1924. Meanwhile Michael Borodin, an able organizer who had lived in the United States, was sent from the Comintern to be political adviser and became the Kuomintang's expert on how to make a revolution. He helped to set up a political institute for the training of propagandists and to teach Kuomintang politicians how to secure mass support. On the Soviet model the Kuomintang now developed local cells (*tang-pu*) which in turn elected representatives to a Party Congress. The first national congress was convened in January 1924, and elected a Soviet-modeled Central Executive Committee as the chief authority in the Party. Borodin wrote its new constitution.

In addition to aiding the Nationalist revolution, the ulterior objective of the Comintern was to develop the Chinese Communist Party and get it into a strategic position within the Kuomintang, so as eventually to seize control of it. Members of the Chinese Communist Party were, by eventual agreement with the Kuomintang, admitted to membership in it as individuals, at the same time that the Chinese Communist Party continued its separate existence. This admission of Communists seemed feasible to Sun Yat-sen because they were so few in number and because the two parties were united on the basis of anti-imperialism and the Kuomintang aimed to lead a broad national multi-class movement avoiding class war. Sun also felt that there was little real difference between the People's Livelihood and Communism, that the Chinese Communists were only a group of "youngsters" who hoped to monopolize Russian aid, that Russia would disavow them if necessary to cooperate with the Kuomintang.

On their side the Chinese Communists were seeking definite class support among urban workers, poor peasants, and students. But they recognized that this class basis was still weak and backward. They therefore sought to go along with and utilize the Nationalist movement without antagonizing the major non-Communist elements within it. It should not be forgotten that the Communist Party in China at this time was still in its infancy. It numbered hardly more than 300 members in 1922, only 1500 or so by 1925, whereas the Kuomintang in 1922 already had 150,000 members. As in other countries the Chinese Communists of this period were significant for their ideas and methods of organization rather than their numbers.

Thus from the beginning the Kuomintang-Communist entente was a precarious thing, held together by the usefulness of each group to the other, by their common enemy, imperialism, and also while he lived, by Sun Yat-sen's predominance over the more anti-Communist elements of his party.

The Nationalist Accession to Power. After Dr. Sun's untimely death at Peking in March 1925, the third and final military effort of his followers achieved, in 1926–27, the successful northern campaign from Canton to the Yangtze valley. The newly trained propagandists of the Nationalist revolution preceded the armies of Chiang Kai-shek, who was aided by Russian arms and advisers. This military effort was the climax to the great wave of nationwide anti-imperialist sentiment which had been roused by student demonstrations and police gunfire in incidents at Shanghai and Canton (May 30 and June 23, 1925, respectively). These provocative and dramatic proofs that the unequal treaties and the foreigners' privileges still persisted, had been followed by a prolonged boycott and strike against the British at Hong Kong.

Thus Chinese nationalism in the years from 1925 to 1927 had reached a new height of expression and was focused against Britain as the chief imperialist power. To defend their position the British on the one hand restored to China their concessions at Hankow and Kiukiang on the Yangtze and on the other hand, with the support of the powers, built up an international force of 40,000 troops to protect Shanghai. In fear of anti-foreignism, most of the missionaries evacuated the interior. In March 1927, when the revolutionary troops reached Nanking, foreign residents were attacked, six of them killed, and the others evacuated under the protecting shellfire of foreign gunboats in the river.

It was at this point in the spring of 1927 that the latent split between the right and left wings of the revolution finally became complete. For two years the right and left within the movement had generally cooperated, although as early as March 1926 Chiang Kai-shek had arrested leftist elements at Canton to forestall a plot to kidnap him. His three-months view of Russia in 1923 had left him aware of Soviet methods and suspicious of Communist aims. The success of the northern expedition finally took the lid off the situation.

In brief, the left wing of the Kuomintang together with the Communists by March 1927 dominated the revolutionary government which had been moved from Canton to Hankow. Here were collected, among other leaders, Madame Sun Yat-sen and Wang Ching-wei, the widow and the chief disciple of the founder, and Borodin, the chief adviser on revolutions. Hankow had been proclaimed the new national capital. This suited the strategy of the Communist proletarian revolution because it was a large industrial center. Two members of the Chinese Communist Party had actually been made cabinet ministers. But this Hankow government was weak in military strength.

Chiang Kai-shek with the support of the more conservative leaders of the Kuomintang had aimed at the rich strategic center of the lower Yangtze. Once the Shanghai-Nanking region was in his grasp, Chiang was able by military force to forestall the Communists, take over the leadership of the revolution and consolidate his position. He crushed the vigorous Communist-led labor movement in Shanghai and set up his capital at Nanking in April 1927. Shortly afterward a local general seized power at Hankow and broke up the left-wing government. Some of its leaders fled, like Borodin, to Moscow. The new Nanking Government expelled the Chinese Communists from its ranks and instituted a nationwide effort to suppress the Communist revolution. In this effort it was, for the time being, largely successful. Small contingents of Communist-led troops revolted, and in December 1927 the Communists attempted a *coup d'état* at Canton. But after this failure to seize power, they withdrew to the rural mountain area of Kiangsi province in Central China.

This ignominious failure of the Comintern's laboratory experiment in revolution in China had been part of a power struggle in Moscow. Trotsky and his followers had criticized the Comintern effort to work through the Kuomintang. They foresaw Chiang Kai-shek's "betrayal" and urged an independent program to develop workers' and peasants' soviets in China under purely Communist leadership. Stalin and his supporters, however, had argued that an independent Communist movement in so backward a country would invite suppression all the sooner. They had looked forward to the time at a later stage of the revolution when, in Stalin's phrase, the Communists could drop their Kuomintang allies as so many "squeezed-out lemons." Whatever the merits of these competing strategies, it is plain that the right-wing Kuomintang squeezed first.

Much of the Comintern's ineptitude undoubtedly came from its remoteness from the scene of action. Lacking instantaneous radio communication, Stalin and his colleagues could hardly succeed in

masterminding by the aid of Marxist dialectics the confused and unprecedented stirrings of revolution in a place like Shanghai. The
Comintern plot in China was also frustrated by the Comintern's
own prior act in giving the Kuomintang a centralized Soviet-style
party apparatus, which was much harder to infiltrate and sub-
vert than an open Western-style parliamentary party. In the end
the Comintern made Ch'en Tu-hsiu, who had been a founder and
leader of the Chinese Communist Party, the scapegoat. He was expelled in 1929.

Chiang Kai-shek's break with the Communists represented an
effort to consolidate the gains of the national revolution at a certain level in the revolutionary process, stopping short of the remaking of peasant life in the villages. This consolidation in the
Nanking Government, combined with his military campaigns to
check revolt, enabled Chiang and the Kuomintang leaders to
achieve a degree of national unity, secure the recognition of the
powers, and begin the process of administrative development which
would be a necessary prerequisite to the abolition of the unequal
treaties. In the spring of 1928 Chiang led a further northern expedition from the Yangtze to Peking, which was occupied in June and
renamed Peiping ("Northern Peace"). In November the young
warlord of Manchuria completed the nominal unification of all
China by recognizing the jurisdiction of the Nanking Government.
Meantime the foreign powers one by one made treaties with it and
so gave the Nationalist revolution international recognition.

In the historical perspective of thirty years afterward, these
achievements can be viewed as a necessary phase in a long process
which had not yet been finished — the gradual mobilization of the
Chinese people in their national political life. The fact that the
Nationalist revolution went only part way in realizing this poten-
tiality of popular mobilization gave the Communists their later
opportunity. But the Communists did it quite differently than the
Nationalists might have done it.

3. THE NANKING GOVERNMENT

The Nationalist Government of China at Nanking in the decade
from 1927 to 1937 was the most modern that China had known. It
was controlled by the Kuomintang on the basis of party dictator-

ship. Financially its strength lay in the new Chinese mercantile and financial circles which centered in the International Settlement at Shanghai. Militarily it sought the creation with the help of German advisers of a modern type of army imbued with loyalty to nation and party leader rather than to a warlord. Many fine new buildings, including Sun Yat-sen's white marble mausoleum, were constructed at Nanking to make it, in the traditional manner, a fitting symbol of the government's power as well as a focus of the modern national spirit. Sun's writings were made a sacred canon. A cult of Sun Yat-sen replaced the state cult of Confucius, long since in desuetude. In this new era, which the new Nanking symbolized, ancient and modern institutions and ideas were juxtaposed and sometimes fused. The result gave China a decade of relative progress before the forces of imperialism and revolution again engulfed her.

In Chiang Kai-shek the new government had a leader who seemed to meet the demands both of ancient tradition and of modern politics. Born in 1887 in a gentry family near Ningpo, Chiang had entered China's first military academy at Paoting near Peking in 1906. After a year there he went to Japan and spent four years in the imperial military college at Tokyo, where he learned Japanese. By 1910 he had become a convert of Sun Yat-sen and he participated in the military efforts of 1911 and 1913. During the first World War he appears to have led an obscure existence as a small broker in business in Shanghai before he again became active as a military man in Sun Yat-sen's behalf. His career really began when Sun sent him to Moscow in 1923.

After his rise to power he provided the Nationalist movement, through his political astuteness and ruthless determination, with a military leader who could deal with and outdo the warlords. In this respect he typified the traditional strong man who founds a dynasty by the sword. At the same time, however, Chiang Kai-shek was a party member, austerely and fervently devoted to the cause of Chinese Nationalism, which he came to regard as indistinguishable from his own career.

Party Government. The objectives and principles of the Kuomintang had been inherited from Sun Yat-sen. Thus the Nanking Government set up his five-power division of the government among executive, legislative, judicial, civil service, and censorial

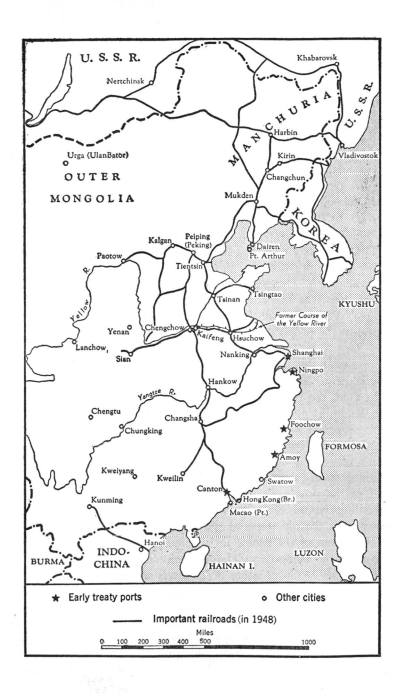

U. S. S. R.

Nertchinsk

Khabarovsk

MANCHURIA

U. S. S. R.

Harbin

Kirin

Urga (UlanBator)

OUTER

MONGOLIA

Changchun

Vladivostok

Mukden

KOREA

Kalgan

Peiping
(Peking)

Paotow

Tientsin

Dalren
Pt. Arthur

Tsinan

Tsingtao

KYUSHU

Yellow R.

Yenan

Chengchow

Kaifeng

Former Course of
the Yellow River

Lanchow

Sian

Hsuchow

Nanking

Shanghai

Ningpo

Hankow

Yangtze R.

Chengtu

Changsha

Chungking

Foochow

FORMOSA

Kweiyang

Kweilin

Amoy

Swatow

Canton

Kunming

Hong Kong (Br.)

Macao (Pt.)

Hanoi

LUZON

BURMA

INDO-
CHINA

HAINAN I.

★ Early treaty ports   o Other cities

——— Important railroads (in 1948)

Miles

0   100   200   300   400   500   1000

agencies (*yuan*). Of these, the Executive Yuan with its dozen ministries of Foreign Affairs, Economics, Communications, War, and the like at once became dominant and overshadowed all the others. The last two Yuan, known as the Examination Yuan and the Control Yuan respectively, were derived by Sun from the imperial traditions of the examinations and the censorate. In practice this latter tradition was carried further by the extensive growth of the secret police, both of the government and of the party.

Sun's theory of the three stages of the revolution (military unification, political tutelage, and constitutional democracy) was carried out by the proclamation in 1928 of the beginning of the period of political tutelage under the Kuomintang party dictatorship.

The first Party Congress had met in January 1924 and adopted a Soviet-style organization. From that time onward, in the interim between Party Congresses, the Kuomintang Central Executive Committee was the chief repository of political authority. The People's Political Council set up in 1938 as an advisory body to represent the people's voice had its membership partly arranged by this Party C.E.C. Meantime the high officials of the government were chosen by the C.E.C. and usually from it. Constitutional government was postponed.

In short, the Nationalist Government at Nanking was set up by the Kuomintang and was legally responsible to it, not to the Chinese people directly. The four political rights of the people — election, initiative, referendum, and recall — which had caught Sun's fancy and become enshrined in his teaching, were to be retained during the period of political tutelage by the Party on behalf of the people. During this period the Party, having in the preceding period of military government taken political power away from the old imperial system and the warlords, was to act as the parent of the people in instructing and preparing them for constitutional democracy. The Kuomintang's complete control of the Nationalist Government at all levels was later typified by the growth of Party ministries, such as the Ministries of Information, Social Affairs, Overseas Affairs, or Party Organization, which functioned as part of the central administration and yet were in form under the Kuomintang, not the Government. Party and Government thus became indistinguishable.

The Party Leader. After sharing power in the early 1930's with Wang Ching-wei and other party stalwarts, Chiang Kai-shek eventually emerged as the one indispensable man. Japan's aggressions in Manchuria in 1931, at Shanghai in 1932, and her infiltration of North China thereafter, all combined with Nanking's domestic problem of suppressing warlord and Communist armies to make a military leader essential. Chiang has been aptly characterized as a "military politician," supremely capable of holding power in a country where armies and generals, not electorates, provide the final sanction. Unhappily, his record and his writings betray no grasp of China's modern economic life and problems. The farmer's increasing dependence on a precarious market, his need for capital, literacy, and technology, the intellectual's vision of socialist industrialization to build a modern nation — these considerations did not enter into Chiang Kai-shek's daily thoughts, though they became more and more important among the Chinese people.

In the end the Generalissimo's power rested on a tripod of Army, Party, and Government. Surviving graduates of the first classes at the Whampoa Military Academy formed a "Whampoa clique" of generals personally loyal to him, which dominated China's new armies. In 1939 he became permanent Party Leader. Any office he held was the point of governmental decision-making. All this reflected not merely Chiang's ability but even more the demand of the Chinese political scene for personal rule by a modernized Son of Heaven. His institutional role, as the one man at the top to lead the nation, was as significant as his personality.

Rights Recovery. Nationalism received its first expression after the unification of 1928 in the "rights recovery" movement. This was an effort to wipe out the unequal treaties bit by bit. The Washington Conference in 1922 had provided for modifications in extraterritoriality and the customs tariff. By 1930 the Nanking Government had secured treaties which placed many minor foreign nationalities under Chinese legal jurisdiction. New civil and criminal codes had been issued. The old Sino-Foreign Mixed Court at Shanghai had been abolished, although the major powers, Britain, the United States, France, and Japan, had not yet given up extraterritoriality. This promising beginning came to a halt when the Japanese aggression of 1931–32 gave both the Chinese and the other foreign powers a common interest in the preservation of the latter's legal position.

Similarly the new Nationalist Government sought to realize the promise of the Washington Conference regarding tariff reform. Under the unequal treaties China had been prevented from protecting her native industries or taxing foreign trade for revenue beyond nominal rates of about 5 per cent. Most of the available customs revenue had become earmarked to pay foreign loans and indemnities. After 1911 the customs duties had been collected, in effect, for an international commission of bankers. The Nanking Government at once moved to recover tariff autonomy and by 1930 had done so. Boxer indemnity payments by that time also had been largely remitted by the powers, on the understanding in the cases of Britain and the United States that the sums due would continue to be made available by China mainly for educational purposes.

The foreign concessions which had been the embodiment of the unequal treaties began to return to Chinese sovereignty. By the outbreak of the war with Japan in 1937 the maximum of thirty-three concession areas leased to foreign powers had been reduced to thirteen, in addition to the continuing International Settlements at Shanghai and Amoy. The rights of the foreign powers to station troops and warships in China and navigate her inland waters still persisted. But this was mainly because they had become measures of international opposition to Japanese encroachment. In general the Nanking Government had begun to satisfy the demands of Chinese nationalism for the assertion of Chinese sovereignty and international equality. By 1937 the chief impairment of China's national unity and independence came not from the unequal treaties (which were finally abolished in 1943) but from Japan.

National defense was thus the over-riding concern of the day, but behind it lay a larger issue — how far China's resistance and salvation were to be achieved by a revolutionary mobilization of the populace, by a realization of some form of democracy and people's livelihood in addition to nationalism.

11

Authoritarianism and Liberalism under the Kuomintang

1. THE SPREAD OF CENTRAL POWER

IN RECONSTRUCTING China domestically the Kuomintang was to follow Dr. Sun's Three Principles of the People. Unfortunately these principles had been left by Sun to his followers chiefly in the form of a series of lectures delivered at Canton in 1924 and copied down by his hearers. The resulting volume, the *San Min Chu I*, suffers from this oral origin. Its use as the Kuomintang bible perpetuated many naïve views — for example, that "Japan is an excellent model . . . China's ancient virtues are superior to foreign virtues . . . Europe looks to China for the fundamentals of political philosophy . . . The yellow races of Asia may, before long, be wiped out."

Nevertheless the *Three Principles* was a textbook which vigorously proclaimed the spirit of nationalism and the task of national reconstruction. As an expression of Sun's personality it indicated the breadth of his intellectual interests, also something of his impracticality regarding China's fundamental problems of democratic institutions and the people's livelihood.

National Unity Versus Democracy. Sun Yat-sen and his followers labored first under the shadow of the Manchu autocracy and therefore began their thinking with the idea of republican institutions as opposed to monarchy. But after the Manchus had departed in 1912, the revolutionists found themselves laboring under the burden of imperialism. Consequently nationalism came to dominate their thinking. In the domestic scene their immediate political problem was warlordism, which prevented their accession to power. This led them to put a great premium upon national unity. From either the foreign or the domestic angle, nationalism, unity, a strong central government became immediate goals, without much reference to democracy.

In the Nationalist Revolution of the 1920's Dr. Sun and his successors learned that the road to national unity and central power lay through popular movements and mass mobilization, which utilized doctrines of democracy and the people's livelihood. They learned this partly from the Russians. But once it had come to power, the main body of the Kuomintang found that national unity and central power, under the heading of nationalism, took precedence over the other two principles of the revolution (democracy and the people's livelihood). The Russian example, in fact, confirmed Sun's idea of party dictatorship whereby democracy was to be postponed until nationalism had been firmly achieved. The Kuomintang as a party dictatorship therefore found its main sanction in the principle of nationalism.

In the twenty years after they came to power, the Kuomintang leaders became conservatives increasingly concerned with the preservation of power. This is one of the oldest political phenomena in history. Beginning as revolutionists seeking to construct a new order, they became oligarchs in defense of it, or rather of their power, displaying all the virtues of fixity of purpose and ruthlessness characteristic of self-made men. Unlike successors to the presidency or premiership of established Western states, they did not originally gain power by moving through established channels in an accepted pattern, but had to improvise both in methods and in ideas. They therefore found it easy to adapt their ideas to their needs. Perhaps this explains the Kuomintang's progression from revolution to reaction.

In this drift to the right, bureaucratic power developed faster than democratic processes. Sun's revolutionary organization, before the Kuomintang, had begun as a secret society; it had a leader, executive committee, and membership, but no tradition of an elective process or political campaigning. The T'ung Meng Hui operated from the top down before 1911; there was little chance for the Kuomintang to reverse the system thereafter.

Sun Yat-sen's failure to make progress in the futile parliaments of the early Republic gave him bitter memories. By 1924 he could think of no democratic institutions more powerful or effective than the four "people's rights" of election, initiative, referendum, and

recall. Of these the last three were technical devices which had
been publicized by American progressives but never very thoroughly institutionalized even in the United States.

Sun's argument presents a curious bifurcation concerning these
people's rights. In his lecture on democracy in the *Three Principles
of the People* he advocates a separation of sovereignty (*ch'üan*) and
ability (*neng*), and a corresponding separation of the political
sovereignty of the people and the administrative power of the
government.

The political power will be given into the hands of the people, who
will have a full degree of sovereignty and will be able to control directly
the affairs of state; this political power is popular sovereignty. The other
power is government, and we will put that entirely in the government
organs, which will be powerful and will manage all the nation's business; this political power is the power of government. If the people have
a full measure of political sovereignty and the methods for exercising
popular control over the government are well worked out, we need not
fear that the government will become too powerful and uncontrollable.

With this naïve premise Dr. Sun proceeded on the theory that
he could "make the government the machinery, and the people
the engineer." He acknowledged that the Chinese people did not
as yet understand democratic processes and must be trained to do
so. But under the sway of his analogy to the machine and the engineer, he concentrated upon the creation of new machinery. Having
been struck by the imperfections of the Anglo-Saxon parliamentary
process which pre-revolutionary China had once so admired, he
abjured the idea of representative government and took refuge in
a utopian conception of direct democracy.

Before there was any complete democracy people elected their officials
and representatives and then could not hold them responsible. This was
only indirect democracy or a representative system of government. The
people could not control the government directly but only through their
representatives. For direct control of the government it is necessary that
the people practice these four forms of popular sovereignty . . . This
means that our four hundred millions shall be king . . .

Few causes have been more completely betrayed by an excess of
idealism. The people's rights remained on the statutes, but were
never realized.

Central Control Versus Local Self-Government. Local government under the Kuomintang, as under the empire, spread downward from the *hsien* (county or district). Under the Manchus there were about 1400, under Nanking about 2000, of these units. The tradition which Nanking inherited is worth examining.

Under the empire each *hsien* was staffed with the lowest rank of imperial official who with his supernumerary assistants and underlings formed the point of contact with the customary institutions, the gentry, elders and headmen, of the villages and market towns. The working relationship between district magistrate, gentry, and village headmen bridged the gap between the imperial bureaucracy and the masses. The headman on his side was but one among many spokesmen for local interests. These included the leading gentry families, best represented by degree-holding scholars or retired officials, and the representatives of merchant or craft guilds and of secret societies. The center of gravity in Chinese government lay at this district-village level, where the interests of the imperial superstructure were harmonized with those of the local substructure.

On the side of the imperial bureaucracy, after the maintenance of order and necessary public works and ritual observances, the chief task was to collect the revenue: land tax, grain levies, salt revenue, customs duties, and miscellaneous taxes on goods in transit. Only a fraction of this revenue which the officials secured from the villages ever reached Peking. Collections were pooled in each provincial treasury, a regular quota went to the capital annually, and transfers were made to other provinces as Peking might require. But Peking received no more than a proportion, say perhaps a quarter, of the reported tax collection; and the collection reported was no more than a part, say possibly one-quarter, of the revenue actually received. In short, the officials lived on their take. Under a weak regime they waxed fat while the central government went bankrupt.

Underneath this predatory bureaucracy, however, it has long been held that the Chinese village enjoyed a degree of self-government amounting to local democracy. Critics irked by the mandarins usually had a good word for the common people and extolled the "democratic" process by which village public opinion influenced the village elders and headmen. In fact, however, this local self-government must be considered another of the old China's official myths — though such a good one that the common people themselves may sometimes have believed it. From any modern point of view as to who gets what and how, the customary democracy of the Chinese village was highly superficial. It operated at the social rather than the economic level and avoided politics entirely. The local gentry and village elders settled neighborhood disputes more easily than they modified the tax rates. They took care of local problems of the market place — drainage, temple repairs, schooling, public nuisances — and kept them out of the sticky hands of the officials. If this is to be called "democracy," it must be admitted that it was truncated and in a strait jacket, with no outlet at the top. It constitued at most a negative defense against extremes of tyranny, not a participation in the real government.

The local gentry had a common interest with the bureaucracy in maintaining local order, property rights, and prosperity. To protect their class interest as owners of wealth they had several means of defense — first, their participation in the official class itself, then, less directly, the type of public opinion they could mobilize in the memorials or protests of scholars, the weight of community feeling when organized in stoppages of work or trade, and finally an even more effective agency, the secret society, a political institution which existed in secrecy because it defied the bureaucracy's monopoly of political organization.

Fundamentally, an organization like the Elder Brother Society (Ko Lao Hui) was a mutual association for the safeguarding of the members' property and security both against the disorder of the rabble and the exactions of officials. Like the White Lotus Society of an earlier day, it was highly organized in a network of branches, each with its director, secretariat, and treasury. The members of various ranks swore to be blood brothers under grievous penalties, participated in formal rites, and learned esoteric symbols and a secret language. But secret societies existed for practical, not esoteric purposes. Some, like the Triad Society along the southeast coast, served the merchants. Others, like the Red Spears (Hung Ch'iang Hui) of Shantung, served the landed gentry.

With an agency like the Elder Brother Society as their tool, the families of wealth and standing in a rich inland enclave like the Chengtu plain could dominate the villages. For a secret society had its executive arm in the person of professional thugs, as well as its income from the protection of illicit activities — gambling houses, brothels, opium dens, or illegal markets where government taxes were evaded. The combination of this darker side with the protection of respectable rank and file members in their daily pursuits, and with clandestine leadership by some of the wealthiest landlords and officials, was all very reminiscent of the bossism and rackets of a Western city.

Modern Centralism. When the Kuomintang inherited the mantle of central government, it was unlike its imperial predecessor in that it possessed modern facilities for bringing its control down to the village level. The telephone and telegraph, motor roads and bus routes, linking local areas with the capital, gave Nanking and later Chungking the means of conveying their orders at once to the smallest hamlet, just as the growth of the modern money economy made them interested in revenue collected directly in all parts of the country. The new Nationalist Government became a center for the spread of reform to the villages through agricultural extension, crop improvement, and other programs. Simultaneously it tried to choke off peasant-based rebellion by an intensified police control. But once it ceased to foment violent social change, it was foredoomed to govern from the top down. Trained modern personnel were lacking to build local self-government up to the provincial level; moreover such an effort might open the door to popular agitation and dissident movements; so Nanking sought to build its central administration down through the provinces to the village level.

This acknowledged the upsetting of the traditional balance in Chinese politics between local and central government. Where minor administrative problems had been kept below the imperial administration, which to that extent permitted a kind of local self-government under gentry influence, now the gentry class had largely ceased to function. In the narrow sense of degree-holders, it became vestigial after the abolition of the classical examination system in 1905. Its many activities in the local community gradually ceased to be performed as before. The subject has been little studied, for all its importance. But it appears plain that the modern scholar class of middle-school and college graduates gravitated to the urban centers and failed to take the place which educated men, the degree-holders of gentry status, had traditionally held in the rural communities. With the disappearance of the gentry, local government had deteriorated and fallen more and more into the hands of petty militarists or unqualified political appointees.

In place of the gentry of imperial times, the new administrators from Nanking tried to spread their reforms, and the secret police organized their anti-Communist net, radiating from the capital. The energy of both carried them further into the local scene than had been the custom under the empire. Where the Emperor had appointed the *hsien* magistrate but left him under the provincial authorities, the Central Government now developed direct contact with him. *Hsien* magistrates were a chief element among the trainees brought to the capital for indoctrination in Chiang Kai-shek's Central Training Corps. Meanwhile the Central Government established local administrative organs in charge of military, customs, transportation, or other matters, independent of the regular structure of *hsien* government. The Kuomintang set up its local cells (*tang-pu*) under central Party control, parallel to the official system. Below the *hsien* were subdistricts including groups of villages and towns, and still smaller divisions below them, leading down to the groups of households which formed the *pao* and *chia*.

The idea of this *pao-chia* system went back to the Legalists in ancient China, where families were grouped in units for mutual guarantee, each unit responsible for the acts of all the others — a surveillance system par excellence, which set neighbor to spy upon neighbor and kith upon kin. Ideally, one hundred families formed a *chia* and ten *chia* formed a *pao*. The Kuomintang theory was that through this hierarchy of subunits the government could train the people during the period of political tutelage to prepare them for local autonomy. In 1939 the Nationalist Government issued a new statute to reorganize the *hsien* and areas below it, in an attempt to check the increasing tendency toward bureaucratic government from the top downward. Beginning with the family household it was provided that families should be grouped more flexibly, on community lines, to form *chia* and *pao*. A number of *pao* should then form villages or towns, which would in turn be under the *hsien* government. The villages and towns were now to become incorporated legal persons able to operate their own local administrations. Each *pao* should form an assembly and elect two representatives, who would in turn function in a village or town assembly. The latter would assist the head of the village or town government, who would himself be elected.

The result of this effort to inculcate some kind of democracy or at least popular participation through reform of administration was disappointing. Wartime circumstances were highly unpropitious. More fundamental was the fact that this political reform was confined to the political sphere, unattended by change in the local social and economic structure in which it was expected to operate. On paper the law of 1939 was put into effect in nearly all the districts in Free China. Yet in the same period the military and police authorities dominated the scene. There is little record of the election process taking hold as a factor for active change. One essential distinction between the Kuomintang and Communist party dictatorships lay in this — that the Kuomintang maintained itself by supporting the landlord regime in local government, while the Communists expanded by opposing it.

2. ECHOES OF CONFUCIANISM

The growth of political controls through local gendarmerie, secret police, press censorship, subsidizing of education, the *pao-chia* and other devices, all supervised by the local Party office, was accompanied in Kuomintang China by a revival of traditional Confucianism. This doctrinal metamorphosis began by stressing the principle of nationalism and from it going back to the national heritage to find political doctrines which would support central power. Even as commandant at Whampoa in 1924 Chiang Kai-shek had taken the victor over the Taipings, Tseng Kuo-fan, as his model. As Mary Wright has shown in her study of the post-Taiping Restoration, the example of revived Confucian government in the 1860's had a fatal fascination for the Kuomintang leaders of the 1930's, even though the Restoration had failed to preserve that traditional Confucian order which by its nature could never have been modernized. The fact was that Nanking's new leaders had not been able to modernize their own thinking. Culture-bound, they sought intellectual sanction for a new stability in the classical doctrine — rule by leaders of impeccable moral virtue, obedience by a people disciplined in personal loyalty and filial piety.

By 1934 the state cult of Confucius was nominally revived. In the same year Chiang launched his New Life Movement to instill in his people a new social consciousness and martial spirit through a revival of the ancient virtues of moral conduct. These were *li,* variously defined as propriety, the principles of social usage, "proper behavior according to status," a regulated attitude; *i* (or *yi*), right conduct, justice; *lien,* integrity; and *ch'ih,* conscience, the sense of shame. Since these classical concepts were now vague at best, 96 specific rules were issued to apply them to the categories of food, clothing, shelter, and action: for example, do not eat noisily, correct your posture, stop smoking, keep your gown buttoned, do not spit, kill rats and flies, be prompt, use native products. Through a nation-wide network of some 1300 local associations, the movement sought paternalistically to lead each individual to practice orderliness and cleanliness. Many other activities proliferated under it in 1934–1937. Some of them were easy to ridicule but they represented nevertheless a direct attack on China's problem of social regeneration — in just the way that the commandant of a military academy might be expected to attempt it.

Chiang Kai-shek's thought was a syncretism derived from many sources — Tseng Kuo-fan's view of moral purpose as the arbiter of human affairs, Lenin's interpretation of imperialism, the Methodist piety of a practicing Christian, influences from Japan, Russia, America, and the Axis powers, all within the framework of a conservative nationalism. Much of this appears in the book that he published in Chinese, not for foreign consumption, in 1943.

China's Destiny. This volume celebrated the abolition of the American and British unequal treaties in 1943 and became required reading for Free China's youth in the compulsory study of "Party principles." It began by interpreting China's modern history and contact with the West. The substance was that China's national humiliation and other modern ills have been caused almost entirely by the unequal treaties. Chiang gave an impressive list of the evils in the treaties — extraterritoriality, the 5 per cent tariff, inland navigation, concessions and foreign garrisons, indemnities and spheres of influence. Foreign imperialists caused China's civil wars, instead of merely aiding them. Foreign courts in the concessions were even worse than unreformed Chinese courts. The treaties and treaty ports caused the spread of famine, stock market panics, the breakup of the family, selfishness, the use of narcotics, profit-seeking materialism, Chinese self-abasement, and the slavish copying of Western ways. In effect Chiang attributed to the treaties and foreign concessions all the manifold social, psychological, and economic maladjustments which have come upon China in modern times.

China's Destiny also sought by exhortation to revive the ancient Confucian virtues of benevolence, sincerity, loyalty, filial duty, proper human behavior, the sense of justice, personal integrity, and the sense of shame and self-respect. While publishing this work to urge national revival by moral regeneration and the patriotic subordination of the individual to the state, Chiang also produced in 1943 a work restricted to official circles entitled Chinese Economic Theory. In it he derived from the ancient philosophers a sanction for the state control of economic life. Against Western free enterprise this work called for an anti-Marxist Confucian totalitarianism. Chinese Economic Theory in its restricted circulation provided the inner rationale of the ten-year industrial program which was laid before the millions in China's Destiny. It sought to direct China's industrialization toward building a defense state, rather than toward mass welfare.

This plan for industrialization had the utopian statistical character of Sun Yat-sen's earlier blueprint, The International Development of China. It gave totals of machinery, minerals and other things to be produced and of technical personnel to be trained in various specialties in order to adapt China's economy to national defense. Agricultural development, which would benefit over three-quarters of the people, was noticeably an afterthought added in the revised edition. Chiang called for the training of some 206,000 higher graduates in various kinds of engineering and technology, plus 232,500 in medicine, 25,000 in architecture, and 55,000 in agriculture. To these totals he added only 31,000 in "arts, law, commerce, economics, and other courses." In effect, this training program would try to give China the new technology of a modern state. But it would slight the study of China's social transformation, in terms of which the use of all new technology would have to be directed. Specifically, Chiang asserted that Western economic theory is unsuited to China and tried to reconstruct

China's traditional economics by quoting the sages. This opened the door to several non-Western conceptions — for example, that land and labor are factors of production in China, but not capital, and that economics should not study how to fill the individual's personal wants, but how to make the nation strong.

Most important, the people's livelihood of Sun Yat-sen was now bracketed with national defense as the dual objective of state control of economic life. They constituted a single problem. The solution proposed for it was to conscript China's farmers onto collective farms where they would also be soldiers. If the masses were farmer-soldiers, China would be strong. This was reminiscent of the Legalist philosophy used by China's first unifier in 221 B.C. It was of a piece with the idea that Sun's conception of "local self-government" could best be realized by reviving the *pao-chia* system of collective local responsibility. In general, Chiang castigated the liberal tradition in economics as advocating government noninterference in the people's economic life. In China he believed the government should not only plan the people's livelihood but also control and restrict their wants, thus combining "benevolence" with "justice." These blueprints called for a power-state in Confucian dress.

The New Neo-Confucianism. The revival of Confucianism was most actively promoted by Ch'en Li-fu, whose uncle had been Chiang Kai-shek's patron and who became Chiang's most loyal political organizer. Ch'en Li-fu had studied Western science briefly at the Pittsburgh School of Mines. For twenty years he specialized in party personnel management, together with his elder brother, Ch'en Kuo-fu, the patriarch of the Central Political Institute for the training of civil servants. The Ch'en brothers led the "CC" clique which dominated the right wing of the Kuomintang. At various times they headed the central secretariat and the Party Ministry of Organization, paying special attention to the development of personnel, financial controls, and the secret Party police.

In general Ch'en Li-fu called for the fusion of Western technology and Confucian social values. This echoed the nineteenth-century slogan, "Chinese studies as the fundamental structure, Western studies for practical use." Ch'en argued that ancient Chinese culture is the cure for modern China's ills. "The spirit of Confucianism is the means of adjusting our culture to the modern age." He urged that the dicta of famous Confucian scholars be systematically arranged and explained to the people. "Confucianism belongs to no specific class." It is actually in keeping with Sun's Three Principles.

In active politics Ch'en Li-fu concentrated on the struggle against Communism. To compete with it on the plane of ideology he propounded a theory of "vitalism," set forth in a work of cosmology first presented as lectures at the Central Political Institute in 1933.

In accordance with the principle of synthesizing ancient Chinese values with conceptions of modern science, this book runs the gamut of knowledge. It begins with the dubious point that "Einstein's discovery of the fourth dimension" was anticipated by the ancient Chinese idea of the universe of space and time (*yü-chou*). It then carries the reader through an eclectic analysis of the atom and hydrogen nucleus, the life principle, the animal, vegetable, and mineral kingdoms, the true, the good, and the beautiful, the six ages of man, and the six stages of political development — a peculiar list which runs as follows: leadership, feudalism, monarchy, democracy (*min chu,* which is evidently improved upon by) party dictatorship, and finally "government of all the people." Ch'en believes in organic evolution and after analyzing the principles of psychology and sociology, he finds the creative life subsumed under the Confucian virtue of sincerity (*ch'eng*). This whole disquisition of 162 pages was illustrated by numerous charts and formulae and the Chinese text included from time to time English phrases such as "starting torque," "state of equilibrium," or "the golden mean."

These ideas of Chiang and his henchman made no contribution to Chinese thought but had importance because they were held by the wielders of Kuomintang power. Modern-minded Chinese scholars could not find in their confused atavism any solution to the fundamental problems of China's adaptation to modern life. The right-wing authoritarianism of Chiang and Ch'en, though widely spread through school and Party, lacked the intellectual vigor to gain the allegiance of thinking Chinese.

The New Militarism. Modern Chinese militarism, manifest in the growth of larger and larger armies, was a new political factor supporting authoritarianism. At first the modern armies, organized on personal lines of loyalty to leading officials or warlords, were largely mercenary and fought with a minimum of ideology. This contributed to the instability of warlord politics, since armies and their commanders could be so easily bought or neutralized. But the new officer corps trained under German advisers at the Central Military Academy at Nanking achieved a new mixture of patriotic sentiment and personal loyalty to the Generalissimo.

Modern militarism came to power on the crest of the new technology which has accompanied modernization. The "foreign gun corps" and steam gunboats of the 1860's, first product of the scholar-officials' efforts at Westernizing, were followed by the abortive navy building of the 1880's and 1890's, under British guidance, and the New Army of the 1900's. This produced a trained military class which was useful to the revolutionists in 1911.

In the end these factors of ideology and technology coincided in a technically trained and patriotically inspired new officer class with a new social status: for it could not be denied that military cadets were students, who after their graduation possessed a certain type of learning and deserved respect accordingly. Patriotic youth acknowledged the sanction which patriotism gave for a military career. In the 1940's the Chinese air cadets often came from the best families and universities, received a highly technical education, and after training in the United States had the status of returned students as well as soldiers. These young pilots of the nascent Chinese air force were idolized by Chinese youth and were an entirely new social phenomenon. The inertia of tradition, however, was evident in the gulf which separated them from their mechanics.

Needless to say, the fifteen long years of Japan's aggression, from 1931 to 1945, provided the need and the excuse for the growth of Chinese militarism. Finally, in addition to the sanctions of patriotism, technical learning, and defense, the power of the new military class rested on the brute size of the military establishment. The millions of troops (Chungking claimed to have 5,000,000 mobilized at one time), with their half million officers, required thousands of military bureaucrats and all the institutions of bureaucracy. Militarism became an enormous vested interest. The gigantic Military Affairs Commission (later revamped as the Defense Ministry) with its congeries of subministries formed part of the real governing trinity — army, Party, and civil administration. Being essentially an authoritarian institution, the army inhibited political democracy, even though, as in Japan, it provided a channel for upward social mobility. The military, gendarmerie, and police forces became an inexhaustible reservoir from which authoritarian-minded politicians like the Ch'en brothers could find their reinforcements.

3. LIBERALISM AND EDUCATION

The scholars of Peking (Peiping) represented a quite different tradition from the party dictatorship and militarism developing at Nanking. While not stemming from Western liberalism, which depends upon the supremacy of law to safeguard the individual in his rights of property and personal freedom, the Chinese tradition of humanism still offered certain rudiments upon which returned students from the West could try to build. The first was the ideal of the cultivated man (the "superior man" or *chün-tzu*), who through the centuries had trained himself to act correctly as a Confucian gentleman and scholar. His ideals of self-respect and propriety were communicated to each individual farmer and coolie and became evident in national traits of politeness, concern for face, and the Chinese sense of responsibility. More importantly, the Confucian moral code stressed personal integrity in the pursuit of virtuous conduct, which meant that the civilized individual was not infrequently called upon to sacrifice himself for a convention or principle. The famous stories of filial piety in which sons sacrificed themselves for their parents — Tung Yung of the Han dynasty who sold himself to bury his father properly, Chu Shou-ch'ang of the Sung who resigned official position so that he could search for his mother — like other classic examples of loyalty, attest the self-sacrifice demanded by the old moral code. With this self-discipline was associated the reverence for education, which gave the learned man a responsibility not only to know the truth transmitted through Chinese literature, but also to speak out on public matters. The modern scholar has continued to feel it a duty to advise the government.

In this framework the predecessor of the modern liberal was the Chinese scholar who courageously stood forth and denounced the evils of bureaucracy or tyranny. The censorate had been in fact an institution created to give learned men who were loyal officials the duty and opportunity of attacking political evils. More than one censor lost his life for it. Though in a different context, these brave scholars in Chinese history had corresponded to tribunes of the people and martyrs for personal faith in the West. Leaders of the modern student movement therefore had a native historical precedent to follow, even though it has been little studied and less publicized. Likewise the Chinese journalist who denounces corruption or despotism harks back to a very ancient past.

The modern liberal tradition in China stemmed directly from Peita (Peking National University) in the time of the May Fourth Movement. In the decade from 1917 to 1927 the spirit of criticism in scholarship and in politics flourished there with relative freedom from official control. Freedom of expression, with all that it implies for social change, became particularly associated with the new learning. Over the years the surge and conflict of new ideas found expression in vigorous journals of opinion. *The New Youth, The New Tide, The Modern Critic, The Independent Critic,* and others like them were each in their day forums of discussion. In the absence of lecture platforms, radio, or political rallies and campaigns, these journals gave men of scholarship and talent their opportunity to be heard. Professors entered government service by this route.

Western missionary education in China also nurtured the new liberalism. It had begun with the early work of pioneers on the China coast. Supported by Protestant constituencies mainly in the United States, Britain, and Canada, Christian education produced a great variety of schools in different parts of China which by degrees merged and developed into the Christian colleges. Before postwar reorganizations, these included the following Protestant universities: Cheeloo at Tsinan in Shantung, Yenching outside Peiping, St. Johns at Shanghai, Lingnan near Canton, a trio of institutions at Hangchow, Soochow, and Shanghai, West China Union University at Chengtu in Szechwan, Nanking University and Ginling College for Women at Nanking, two institutions at Foochow, and a group of colleges forming Central China University at Hankow. These institutions represented the cooperation of twenty-one Protestant societies and a dozen American universities.

In 1936–37 their faculties totaled 652 persons including 466 Chinese, their student bodies 6424. Chinese sources including tuition fees provided more than half their total income. Missionaries of the Catholic Church had more converts but fewer institutions of higher education than the Protestants, their leading universities being Fu-jen at Peiping and Aurora at Shanghai. All in all, this Western missionary education was on a small scale but of wide influence in setting an example and training leaders.

Against this background one can understand why the old traditions and the Western example produced liberal individuals in Modern China, but no liberal movement. Liberalism could not become institutionalized.

As one factor, the concept of freedom under law was not adequately developed. There was no real acknowledgment by those in power of the civil liberties and basic freedoms of speech and person, habeas corpus and jury trial, in short the supremacy of law — to which Westerners are all too unconsciously accustomed. Inclusion of such guaranties in constitutions and law codes was but a first step on a long hard road. The liberally-inclined individual did not enjoy the legal security of liberals in the West.

Closely related to this weakness was the lack of a strong middle class of the Western type. Private property, like the individual himself, had little legal protection against an inveterately corrupt officialdom. Liberals in China generally lacked the security of private economic means which has sustained the Western liberal movement.

Lacking the defenses of law and property, the Chinese liberal found an uncertain security in the superior social status accorded the scholar. The fate of liberalism in China was therefore closely bound up with the fate of education.

Progress in Education. The modernization of higher learning made great progress during the decade of uneasy peace from 1927 to 1937. The leading universities like Peita and Tsing Hua at Peiping were able to dispense with foreign staff members and to set standards of scholarship in many fields superior to those of the Christian colleges. The fine new buildings in modernized Chinese architecture, the broad campuses and thousands of students in these new government universities dwarfed the missionary institutions. Their staffs belonged to a generation trained abroad.

(Even after six years of war, the faculty of the Southwest Associated University created at Kunming by the cooperation of Peita, Tsing Hua, and Nankai Universities had more than 170 professors, out of 200 in all, who had received advanced training abroad. Of this 170, more than 100 had taken doctoral degrees in the United States.)

The new Chinese scholarship was led by new agencies. The Geological Survey of China surveyed the natural resources and mapped the terrain of the country. Eventually, it and the other new institutions such as those for research in Chinese architecture, the social sciences, or in various aspects of the physical sciences, became parts of China's modern national research academy, the Academia Sinica. Its dozen institutes, maintained on all too meager government funds, became leading centers of pure research in all the departments of learning.

In this period archaeological excavations uncovered the story of Peking man at Chou-k'ou-tien and found China's most ancient capital at Anyang. The palace of the Manchus was made into a national museum. Publications were made from their archives. With American help the new National Library of Peiping and the Peking Union Medical College set new standards of scientific technique and social service and stimulated, respectively, the development of other national libraries and of a national health administration. By the end of the decade the new scholarship was producing new critical editions and indices to classical sources, and critical monographs with specific footnote references — both indices and footnotes being modern additions to a scholarly tradition formerly based on verbatim memory of the classics.

The Chinese scholars who worked and taught in the government-supported universities and research institutes had their counterparts in the Western-trained administrative staffs gathered at Nanking who undertook the reform of the administrative process of the government. They were able to build on the older parts of China's modern administration, like the Maritime Customs Service, the Post Office, and the Salt Revenue Administration, which had been inaugurated under foreign guidance. Recruiting of foreign personnel was stopped at the same time that training programs were developed for Chinese personnel. Academic specialists were drawn into government service.

Behind these developments in the 1930's, however, there was already evident the effort of Kuomintang bureaucrats to bring education under their control. The new liberalism, centered in Peiping, came under increasing pressure from the new bureaucracy at Nanking. Party agents were planted in the universities. Students who criticized the government were seized by police squads raiding their dormitories at dawn, and carted off to prison. Teachers and editors were intimidated. This was a foretaste of the 1940's.

Politics in Education. It was no accident that Japan began in 1937 by bombing Nankai University at Tientsin as a symbol of Chinese nationalism. But the Japanese bombings and the spectacular scorched-earth policy of the Chinese resistance to Japan were probably less disastrous to the country than the undermining of liberal institutions and ideas which the war facilitated. The fine beginnings of the preceding decade came under wartime pressures which all but destroyed them. The independence of teachers and students succumbed to twin evils of inflation and domination by political authorities.

When war came in 1937, most of the universities were in the coastal area. They were either destroyed by the Japanese or abandoned by patriotic faculties and student bodies, who moved inland with the government. Some institutions in Nanking and Hankow were able to take much of their equipment directly up the Yangtze by boat. Similarly the Academia Sinica was able to transport its unrivaled Sinological library via Indo-China to a village on the Yangtze in Szechwan. But the universities in Peiping suffered badly. Peita and Tsing Hua, for example, moved in 1937 to a campus at Changsha in Hunan which was soon bombed by the Japanese, necessitating a further removal by truck and on foot overland through the mountains to Kunming in the Southwest. There the French railway from Indo-China formed the only real link with the outer world during the first years of war, like the Burma Road at a later date.

In these circumstances of flight and reëstablishment, each institution was obliged to lean more heavily upon the Central Government. Ch'en Li-fu had become Minister of Education in 1938. During the next seven years of wartime austerity he came increasingly under liberal attack because of his evident use of the educational system for partisan political ends.

Ch'en's policy was to expand the system as well as to control it. In 1936, for example, there had been 108 institutions of higher education with 41,000 students. In 1937 the war and evacuation had reduce the total to 91. One might have expected the number to drop still further as universities in exile joined to pool their meager and inadequate resources. But the Ministry of Education attempted a rapid expansion. By 1940 through the founding of new institutions and the reorganizing of old ones in Free China, it pointed with pride to a new total of 113 universities, colleges, and technical institutes under its aegis. By 1941–42 there were 132 institutions with 57,000 students. By 1945 there were 145.

But after five years of war the purchasing power of the Chinese dollar was hardly more than 1 per cent of what it had been in 1937. Budgets of the old established universities not under Kuomintang control had shrunk out of sight. Government rice stipends by no means made up the difference. The educational system had no sooner expanded than it was left penniless.

Students and faculties survived mainly because the government rice allowances gave them something to eat, roughly on the standard of concentration camps. They had to sell or pawn books, clothes, or furniture in order to keep alive. Ch'en Li-fu claimed that the Ministry's minute prescription of standard courses, in the new institutions he founded or took over and in the old ones now dependent on his budgets, was a great improvement — "the standard of instruction was equalized." It would be more accurate to say that the expansion of instruction, when the stuff of education in training and equipment was lacking, was an educational inflation. From the political point of view, however, it brought a greater number of impoverished intellectuals under Party influence.

The real meaning of the Ministry's fine record on paper was seen by all observers who came in contact with the Chinese universities during their wartime exile. Textbooks were largely lacking. So were all but the bare essentials of housing. Laboratory work was almost impossible. The small libraries of precious books that remained were often locked up for safekeeping. Instruction was in large part oral, sometimes with improvised mimeographed materials put together by devoted teachers from memory or from the few books available. Malnutrition became rife among the students. Children of faculty members died of tuberculosis. The bottom dropped out of Chinese liberal education and standards declined even faster than enrollment increased.

Chinese faculties preserved themselves by their pride, patience, and fortitude. Three faculties joined forces in the Southwest Associated University in Kunming, five mission institutions used the campus of West China University in Chengtu. Others, like the National Central University in Chungking, which had a complement of modern trained scholars and established standards, were also able by the personal quality of their instructing staffs to maintain a semblance of college teaching. But only in a few places like Kunming was it possible for a handful of courageous scholars to preserve the modern liberal tradition of speaking out on political issues.

It had been apparent from the beginning that the Kuomintang considered education to be a tool of the state. The political thinking of the students of Free China was intimidated increasingly through the mechanism of the Kuomintang Youth Corps founded in 1938. Its branches were established within every student body with official support. As the Chungking government felt itself more and more on the defensive against the Communists, these branches made it their business to exalt the official ideology and control thought.

Mass education was meanwhile discountenanced. As a single example, take the experience of Dr. T'ao Hsing-chih (Heng-chi Tao), one of the great figures of modern Chinese education. After studying at the University of Illinois and with John Dewey at Columbia, T'ao had gone into rural education in China and helped develop the system whereby school children became teachers to other illiterates. This "little teacher" movement spread rapidly. As Dr. T'ao put it, "the school became a powerhouse and every child a wire reaching out from it to electrify the minds of the people." A student who had taught another person to read was entitled to wear a star, and when that person had taught someone else, two stars. This literacy movement turned into a chain reaction, particularly during the united front of 1937–38 when the government was at Hankow. Evidently it seemed like political dynamite. Ch'en Li-fu called T'ao in and offered him the presidency of an agricultural college, suggesting that he should change his line of work. The little teacher movement was suppressed. T'ao opened a school for orphan children. At the time of his death in 1946 he was being threatened by the secret police for objecting to civil war. His genius as an educator inspired a whole generation, quite independently of the Communists, who now exploit his name.

After the war when the Nationalist Government moved back to the coastal cities, its problem of thought control was sharply intensified. The first jubilation over victory gave way to disillusionment, for liberation from Japan brought only further inflation and civil war. Middle schools and universities became centers of "dangerous thought," anti-corruption and anti-civil war. Arrests and disappearances of students and professors became frequent. Chinese education was turned into a battleground where indoctrination, secret police surveillance, starvation, terror, and the stirrings of revolution all but wiped out the nascent liberal tradition.

Liberals in Politics. The Kuomintang, although operating a party dictatorship, permitted the existence of several small political groups. A number of "minor parties" grew up, each consisting of a small nucleus of persons with a few thousand followers. These groups were consequently quite different in kind from the Kuomintang and the Communist Party. In 1941 several of them formed a Federation of Democratic Parties to oppose one-party government, party armies, secret police, and corruption. Later organized as the Democratic League, they stood primarily for a joint program: "democratization of the government, nationalization of the army." In the negotiations of 1945 and 1946 the Democratic League was recognized as a third element standing between the Kuomintang and the Communists, potentially in a position to hold a balance if a coalition government were formed. Even before the breakdown of negotiations, however, the right-wing Kuomintang began to intensify its coercion of intellectuals, particularly those of the Democratic League. One of its leaders was a scholar of Chinese literature, Professor Wen I-to, a graduate of the University of Chicago, who had led the Peiping students in their march overland from Changsha to Kunming. His open assassination in July 1946 was only the most prominent of many beatings, abductions, and assassinations aimed at the intimidation of Chinese liberals.

By pressure and cajolery, two of the minor parties were brought into the National Assembly organized by the Kuomintang in November 1946. The great part of the liberals in politics, however, remained aloof from these window-dressing efforts at multi-party government. The new constitution then adopted was a generally liberal document but it expressed worthy ideals, not political realities. In no part of China could an election process by secret ballot become established.

Given the record of corruption and terrorism which overtook the Kuomintang government in proportion as its problems multiplied and its leadership moved to the right, it is not surprising that the Chinese intelligentsia in their political thinking became steadily more estranged from it. The Chinese Communist Party was able more and more easily to recruit personnel from the student class, at the same time gaining the widespread tacit sympathy of intellectuals in education, the professions, and the lower levels of the bureaucracy. The Communist appeal to the intelligentsia was typically expressed in terms of the civil liberties and social justice so openly flouted by the Kuomintang police and bureaucrats. The resulting "desertion of the intellectuals" became a plainly marked phenomenon of the 1940's. In a country where the literati still stand so close to the government, this classic harbinger of revolution was more than usually significant.

The attraction of the Chinese Communist movement for the liberal-minded idealist in China cannot be understood in purely American terms. The liberal intellectual generally abhorred the police state and was patriotically opposed to Russian domination. The Kuomintang regime, however, was very different from the United States Government, and the Chinese Communist Party very different from the American Communist Party. Chinese liberals by their own liberal principles were often pushed into the opposition, where the Chinese Communists eagerly tried to recruit them into their totalitarian cause.

Moreover, the Communist regime, operating entirely in the countryside, had become a functioning government with a record on which it could be judged. Given the hard conditions of Chinese life and the record of the Kuomintang as a point of comparison, the Communist record in its moderate Yenan phase was one of considerable achievement and attracted a great number of the student youth of the country. In this situation a Chinese liberal who as an individual subscribed to much the same ideals of freedom as his American counterpart, might be more nearly on the fence than the average American would think possible.

12

The Nationalist Government
and the Economy

ONE KEY to the decline and fall of the Nationalist Government was in the economic problems it faced and how it dealt with them. Three decades later, when economic development has become a major field of scholarly study and government activity, we can easily forget how recent is our new knowledge. In the early 1930's the New Deal was still to come in the United States. No foreign aid bills gave millions of American dollars annually to small countries of Asia. Modern economic science had hardly been applied to underdeveloped areas, which were then simply called "backward." Nanking's economic policies must be judged in this historical context.

Ideally, Nanking should have attacked the key problem of agricultural production, which gave the Chinese people their living, by inaugurating programs to improve farm technology. Simultaneously it should have funneled more of the national income into industrial development and expansion of "social overhead" facilities, such as transport and communications. Capital and trained skills were the first requirement, with transportation a close second — as one may find spelled out in any textbook today. Lacking a clearly articulated plan and efficient administration, however, the new Nationalist regime achieved a mixed record. A look at this record today may give us some perspective on the present appeal of the Communists' program for industrialization, and on the real failure of their predecessors.

Nanking early sought technical aid from the League of Nations for public health work, and from this contact was stimulated to set up in 1933 the National Economic Council as an advisory body to coordinate efforts at development. Many fine blueprints were offered in the 1930's and 1940's for China's economic regeneration. Land reclamation, reforestation, water conservancy, hydro-power, crop and animal breeding, better tools, improved land use, pest control, crop storage facilities, land redistribution, rent reduction, light and heavy industrialization, rural industry and cooperatives, cheaper farm credit, mass education, public health, transportation, law and order — all had their advocates and their obvious rationale. The first and foremost object of all such efforts was to increase the productivity of the farmer. This was the crux of China's modernization effort but the government was unable to get at it. To tackle a diffused and multifarious set of interrelated problems no comprehensive plan was ever devised, much less given effect. Looking back we can see that the Nanking decade was the time for Western aid to China's vigorous economic development. But America was absorbed in the Depression and New Deal. Kuomintang China in these years made halting and spotty progress along many lines, to no particular end.

1. BEGINNINGS OF ECONOMIC CHANGE

Poverty as a Social Institution. The brilliant social anthropologist, Fei Hsiao-t'ung, described the quagmire of old agricultural conditions and practices as a "closed economy" or "economy of scarcity." We might also call it an economy of struggle for physical survival. Fei pointed to the social attitudes and values that maintained the inertia of this long-established low-level man-power economy, perpetuated by the Chinese emphasis upon the virtue of contentment and limitation of wants. In the old Confucian saying, "Acknowledgment of limits leads to happiness." This age-old acceptance of the institutionalized penury of peasant life, for want of any alternative, was a means by which the individual could fit himself into his kinship group, sustain his lot in life, and actually achieve a high degree of "social integration" of himself in the community. Indeed the narrow horizon, low efficiency, poor diet, and chronic diseases of the Chinese peasant, which struck the eye of the modern investigator, were always an integral part of the old society which has been described above in Chapter 3, just as they were part of premodern society in Europe. One could expect the Chinese peasant, like his European predecessor, to join eventually in an effort to better himself. But one could not expect this process to create any less disorder, violence, and bloodshed than it did in Europe.

Not only did the old farm economy produce a relatively small surplus. The surplus, once produced, was poorly distributed — little or none of it could be invested in improvements. Here again an appreciation of Chinese social values, of the expectations and assumptions in a farmer's mind, is necessary to any understanding of how the product of the land was distributed. As already noted, landholding relationships in China were generally complex; tenantry, share cropping, and various forms and degrees of indebtedness were intermixed. The simple terms, rent and taxation, included a great variety of payments, exactions, and charges by which the farmer was separated from his surplus, if not his actual subsistence. Landlordism was generally small-scale and there were few large baronial estates. Probably the majority of peasants were independent landowners, not tenants at all. Yet they were handicapped by the minuscule size of their holdings and by their lack of capital and were consequently vulnerable in time of stringency vis-a-vis the small-scale landlord moneylender with his extra, though meager, resources. One careful American expert concluded that rents in China took from 45 to 60 per cent of the crop, not counting other payments. Indebtedness was endemic, but probably half or more of farm loans were for unproductive purposes, to buy food or repay debts, or to meet the compelling social obligation of ceremonial display and hospitality on vital occasions of marriage and death.

Only the firmest code of social conduct could have kept this old system operating and induced the peasant to make his rent, tax, or interest payments, or acquiesce in perpetual indebtedness and poverty. Plainly the sanctity of title to landed property, backed by the power of the landlord-official class, was one potent factor. But concern for social display and for filial piety, for an honest name and avoidance of conflict with the law, were other factors, to say nothing of ignorance born of illiteracy, and the ancient virtue of contentment. In other words, the distribution of the surplus on the land was an integral part of the old social process. It could hardly outlast the ideas and values of the old China.

Rural Reconstruction. In the early 1930's the lack of large-scale and effective Central Government aid for the villages was highlighted by a growing interest in the reconstruction of village economy. Several programs were set going in selected areas where the problems of peasant life were studied and methods developed for the promotion of literacy and improvement of living standards. In many of these efforts Christian missionaries had led the way. Best known to Westerners was the experiment financed partly by the Rockefeller Foundation at Ting-hsien in North China under the leadership of the dynamic Dr. Y. C. James Yen. Another model county was developed by the government near Nanking, and a pioneer effort of this type was also made by the scholar Liang Souming in Shantung. Fundamentally, these were all reform efforts which tried to give the peasantry some education for citizenship, some public health service, and scientific improvements as in crop and animal breeding — precursors of India's community development programs of today.

The movement for rural reconstruction discovered very soon that the problems of economic livelihood were deeply imbedded in social and political institutions. It became plain that a higher standard of living was a prerequisite for any democratic processes of a Western type. Improvements in living standards in turn depended upon social change. For example, the scientific reforms attempted at Ting-hsien needed financial support greater than the peasantry could provide, peasant organizations in support of local improvements required official permission, the improvement of crops raised questions of rent and land tenure, an increase of literacy was likely to make the populace more vocal in the pressing of grievances.

In short, any real change in one aspect of the old order on the land implied fundamental changes in the whole system. The problems of the Chinese countryside were so far-reaching and the pressure for change so great that reforms were always likely to set off a chain reaction toward revolt. This interdependence of democracy and the people's livelihood was probably what led the Nationalist movement to stop short in its democratization program, after the achievement of power, lest it should provoke a political and economic revolution among the Chinese masses.

Transportation. Lack of transport was one major obstacle to agrarian development. Once a Chinese farmer had his crop, he could usually offer it for sale only within the region he could reach by carrying it on a pole or wheelbarrow. Where the United States had one mile of highway for each square mile of area, China had perhaps seventy feet — transportation was by paths, not roads. Manpower transport was the norm. Animals were in the minority. One estimate was that three-fifths of all farm produce was sold locally or at nearby villages, while another investigator concluded that, even so, transportation accounted for the great part of marketing costs. Consequently every locality had to be largely self-sufficient. It seldom could specialize in production or count on outside help in time of shortage. The farmer had to sell to the merchant at hand and could not bargain in a wide market nor store his produce to await a higher price.

The major means of transport in Central and South China was the ancient system of waterways, which make the great Yangtze River still the life line of the country. The inland waterways of the delta regions around Shanghai and Canton, for example, fed the growth of those modern cities. The old China was not able to defend herself on these routes, and the opening of China began with the British and American invasion of the junk trade along the coasts and up the Yangtze. Foreign treaty rights of inland navigation gave British firms like Jardine Matheson and Company for a time almost a monopoly of modern water-borne commerce. Even as late as 1936 two-fifths of the steam tonnage in China's domestic coastal and river trade was still under the British flag. Chinese vessels carried less of this domestic trade than did those flying the Union Jack. Compared with the United States, transportation in China was still entering the age of the railroad and steamship. In the absence of private purchasing power, the automobile had not yet come into its own, even though Nanking sponsored an extensive program of road building for public bus lines.

Railways had been delayed as long as possible because officials of the Manchu period were fully aware of their strategic importance and wanted them, when built, to be under Chinese control. They became a key factor in China's modern history. The first railroad from Shanghai to Woosung was proposed in 1865, constructed by foreign merchants in 1876, purchased and destroyed by the Chinese

government in 1878. By 1894 China still had only 195 miles of railroad in the whole country. After the imperialist powers' scramble
for concessions in 1898, this mileage was increased to 2700 by 1903
and 5800 by 1911. Thus the decade before the Revolution was the
first great period of construction. It saw the completion of the network from Shanghai to Nanking and thence to Tientsin and Peking and the parallel line on the west from Hankow to Peking,
which provided two main north-south arteries, north of the
Yangtze. The first Chinese-built line had also been started along
the southern border of Inner Mongolia, west from Peking. A
beginning had been made on the Lunghai Railroad, the main east-
west line just south of the Yellow River. (See endpaper maps.)

After 1911 the combination of warlord rivalry, foreign absorption
in the World War, and the international bankers' consortium
arrangements (which tended to act as a brake on the investment
both of Japanese and other foreign capital), all contributed to the
retardation of railroad development. By 1926 the total mileage in
China including Manchuria was only 7683 and by 1935 it was still
under 10,000 miles. Railway construction in North China was far
ahead of South China, yet it was equally far behind the railroad
development in Manchuria. The railway accompanied the expansion of the frontier of Chinese settlement into Manchuria more
easily than it could be introduced into the crowded countryside and
rough terrain of South China. As a result, more than a third of all
China's railway construction was in Manchuria (3726 out of 9773
miles as of 1935), serving less than one-tenth of China's population.
(By 1945 Japan's heavy investment in a strategic and economic
rail network made the total mileage roughly equal to that in China
proper.)

The history of Chinese railroad construction suggests that it was
retarded by the relative adequacy of the water transport network as
well as by an unfavorable social environment in general and,
specifically, by lack of capital for investment. The provincial gentry
demanded control over railroad construction before the Revolution
of 1911. But although projects were put forward in fourteen provinces, they were unable to mobilize the requisite capital for actual
construction. After the Nationalist Government came to power its
program also suffered a stalemate because of the patriotic aversion
to foreign financial control and the foreign hesitation to invest

without more definite security. Under an energetic Minister of Railways, Chang Kia-ngau, a solution finally was developed by which foreign firms were asked to finance the foreign-built equipment for new roads while Chinese sources financed the local building costs. Foreign loans, which had been in default, were refinanced and a new period of growth was just beginning when Japan struck. The major achievement of the Nationalist Government in preparation for its struggle against Japan was to complete the Canton-Hankow Railway, connecting the Yangtze with Hong Kong, and build an east-west (Chekiang-Kiangsi) line from Shanghai south of the Yangtze westward to meet the Canton-Hankow line.

The Japanese invasion of China, like the subsequent effort of the Nationalist Government to quell the Communist rebellion, was dominated strategically by the problem of transport. In each case the higher striking power of modernized armies could be made effective only over a transportation network. So the Japanese campaign in China during its first year and a half was a railroad campaign. The Japanese first brought their troops in over the Peiping-Mukden line and advanced from Tientsin southward and from Peiping both south and west along the main trunk lines. They overran both Shantung and Shansi provinces. They moved from Shanghai up the railway to Nanking. Eventually they converged on the railroad junction of Hsuchow, where the line from Tientsin to the Yangtze is bisected by the Lunghai artery from east to west. It was near here in 1938 that the Chinese under General Li Tsung-jen, later vice-president, gained their victory at Tai-erh-chuang, though at the cost of heavy losses in rolling stock.

The wartime destruction of China's railways began with the scorched-earth policy of all-out national resistance, typified in Chinese destruction of the Yellow River bridge north of Chengchow and the new Chientang River bridge at Hangchow. Railway installations which were dismantled and shipped to the interior contributed to the industrialization of the Southwest but only at great cost in wastage during the process. During the war the Japanese built some useful branch additions to the railroad net in North China, where they intended to remain.

Thus the railway in crowded China has not played the role for which it gained fame in the wide open spaces of the American West. Unable to supplant the established water routes, it did not precipitate a commercialization of agriculture nor did it markedly stimulate industrialization, except in the most modern economic region, Manchuria.

Industry. As a power resource for industry, China's coal reserves were conservatively estimated during the Nationalist period at 240 billion tons, three-quarters bituminous and one-quarter anthracite, with coking coal available in several places. This made China's reserves perhaps the fourth largest in the world, comparable to those of Germany and surpassed only by Canada, the United States, and the USSR. Four-fifths of China's coal appeared to be in the northwestern provinces of Shensi and Shansi. But production had centered mainly in the region of North China and Manchuria, where the coal supplies were more accessible to the railroad network.

China's iron resources had been variously estimated, by pessimists and optimists. The Germans once believed Shantung to contain 100 million tons. This was later revised to 14 million tons. Postwar estimates placed China's resources at between 1.4 and 1.8 billion tons of iron ore, of which three-fifths were in Manchuria. This would make China's reserves comparable in quantity to those of the Lake Superior district in the United States or about half those of European Russia. But in quality China's ores seemed generally low-grade. Thus by Western standards China was not rich in iron but had enough for more than one generation of active industrialization. Meanwhile for the production of light metals she had the largest magnesite reserves in the world and extensive bauxite deposits. In the past she had supplied half or more of the world's tungsten and antimony. Oil and oil shale reserves appeared relatively small. (Results of Communist prospecting, though not known in detail, have not yet revolutionized this picture.)

The use of coal and iron by heavy industry in China had been impeded by problems of politics, management, and capitalization. An industrial base was inaugurated by Chang Chih-tung in Central China near Hankow in the 1890's. British interests developed the Kailan coal mines north of Tientsin in North China. But the chief development was left for the Japanese in the Mukden region of Manchuria. Because Manchuria through its resources and circumstances was China's potential center for heavy industrial development, it received special attention from the imperialist powers.

While Manchuria (called by Chinese "the Northeast") is unquestionably a part of China, inhabited over 95 per cent by Chinese people, it is very different indeed from the more settled regions south of the Great Wall. Except for the Chinese pale south of Mukden, Manchuria remained in large part a Manchu preserve down to the late nineteenth century. Beginning as an area of friction among Russia, Japan, and China, it became a Japanese puppet state and subsequently a meeting point of Russian and Chinese interests.

As a new country Manchuria profited by its low density of population. Its area of 500,000 square miles (including Jehol, the mountainous province north of Peking) is between one-quarter and one-third the size of China proper, yet the population as estimated in 1900 was only 17 million and today is possibly 50 million. In spite of its rapid growth through migration of Chinese farm laborers from North China, it still has less than one-tenth of China's total population.

When the Japanese grabbed Manchuria in 1931, it accounted for one-fifth of all China's trade. The raising of soy beans for export and Japanese development of coal and iron resources had made Dairen the second port to Shanghai. This was only a beginning. The Japanese rapidly developed a communications network, reformed the currency, and pushed industrialization for strategic purposes.

In the fourteen years of their occupation, they are estimated to have invested something like US $2 billion, a large amount considering Japan's resources. By 1945 Manchuria had some 60,000 miles of motor roads in addition to some 6000 miles of railway. Dairen had three-quarters of a million people, Changchun (Hsin-king) 850,000, and Mukden over 2 million. Coal production had reached 30 million tons a year. The steel works at Anshan near Mukden could produce 2 million tons of pig iron and 1.5 million tons of steel. On the basis of an efficient coal and iron combine, great factories had been built in Mukden where machinery, chemicals, automobiles, and even aircraft were produced. As an industrial base Manchuria under Japanese exploitation had outstripped all the rest of China put together.

Meanwhile in China proper, textiles and light industries had concentrated in Shanghai and a few other treaty ports like Tientsin and the Yangtze cities. Here again, foreign finance and entrepreneurship combined with cheap Chinese labor to produce a mixed Sino-foreign management of the modern economy. Foreign distribution of kerosene and tobacco from abroad was still a major industry. China's was still a commercial economy, with "semicolonial" features. The cotton mills, silk filatures, small shipyards, cement works, canneries, and cigarette factories of Kuomintang China did not add up to a heavy industrial base. Machines to make machines were still lacking. The nearest thing to the contemporary Soviet, German, and Japanese economic plans was a program for developing arsenals and military production under Nazi tutelage.

That these many beginnings of industrial growth were not refashioned into a centrally planned program of national development was no surprise to Americans, who did not then and do not now believe in the state control of the economy which such a development would have entailed. But the result for the Kuomintang, in the conditions in which the Chinese people found themselves, was to forfeit the Mandate of Heaven. The inadequacy of its performance was evidenced particularly in its fiscal and monetary policies.

2. *KUOMINTANG FISCAL POLICY*

The Banking System. China's old-style "native" banks were local institutions, usually partnerships, which existed for the purpose of handling money — lending, saving, transmitting, or exchanging it — but not for purposes of productive investment. Although organized in guilds, the native banks were decentralized and conducted a form of small private business, mainly in supporting small merchants with unsecured personal loans. Country-wide remittances had been handled by the famous Shansi banks and their many branches. But after 1911 these traditional institutions proved inadequate. The native banks generally had depended on methods of personal contact under the wing of official patronage instead of modern legal forms, and had profited by speculation rather than investment. Their financial resources were inadequate to serve a growing money economy.

The second element in the financial structure of Kuomintang China was the foreign banks which grew up in the treaty ports under the protection of extraterritoriality to finance foreign trade and handle foreign exchange. By 1936 there were some thirty-three foreign banks in China, many of which had issued their own bank notes. The most important of them historically was the Hongkong and Shanghai Banking Corporation, established in 1864 with a capital of Hongkong (HK) $2,500,000. By the 1930's its paid-up capital was HK $20,000,000 with a reserve of HK $100,000,000 and assets of HK $1000 million. Until 1927 the foreign banks had dominated the Chinese financial scene not only because they financed foreign trade and after 1911 held the official funds derived from the Chinese Maritime Customs and other sources to pay off foreign debts and indemnities, but also because they served as repositories of the private funds of politicians and militarists. Fundamentally, their position rested on their monopoly of foreign exchange and international transactions. At times they held as much as half the total silver stocks in Shanghai.

Government Banks. Under the Kuomintang program after 1927 the unification of the country went hand in hand with financial modernization, in which the modern government banks led the way. This long and arduous process of reform included the introduction of new credit instruments and new business habits. It was impeded by stubborn ubiquitous things like the old currency, the confusion of which was truly remarkable.

Under foreign prompting the Manchu government had finally opened in 1905 a Board of Revenue Bank to issue notes and conduct modern central banking operations. This early institution eventually in 1913 became the Bank of China. Its chief competitor was the official Bank of Communications set up in 1907. During the warlord period provincial banks were also established on modern lines, often issuing great quantities of rapidly depreciating bank notes. Modern private banks were also established. By 1926 the total of modern government, provincial, and private banks had grown to 102 institutions, most of them mercantile in character and dealing in short-term liabilities rather than long-term investments. As part of their chief business these modern banks had begun to finance the government both by issuing loans and by direct advances. From 1913 to 1926 the Peking Government had issued some twenty-seven loans. The Nanking Government after 1927 hastened to develop its financial agencies.

The Kuomintang had begun in Canton in 1924 by setting up the Central Bank of China to finance the Nationalist Revolution and conduct the fiscal unification of its resources. T. V. Soong was the first manager. It was reorganized in Shanghai in 1928 to act as a central bank of issue and a government treasury. In the same year the Bank of China was reorganized in order to make it dominant in the business of foreign exchange, in the same way that the Japanese had set up the Yokohama Specie Bank back in the 1880's to compete with foreign banks in this line. The Bank of China proceeded to handle about half of all the foreign business done by modern Chinese banks, although its functions were never entirely differentiated from those of the Central Bank of China. The Bank of Communications, also reorganized in 1928, was intended to foster the growth of transportation and industry but failed to develop as an industrial bank. The Farmers Bank of China was established in 1933 to facilitate agricultural credit, and set up its branches in the wake of the military campaigns against the Communists.

These four goverment banks acted as a central banking group. In spite of their intended differences they all issued bank notes and in various ways duplicated one another's activities. The functions performed by a single central government bank in most European countries were distributed among them. Their deposits, which totaled CN $553 million in 1928, grew to CN $2472 million in 1936 in a period when the flow of silver funds to the treaty ports led to a heavy concentration of capital in Shanghai and a consequent deflation in the rural economy. In 1935 the four government banks had two-fifths of the total capital and reserves of all the modern Chinese banks and more than half of the total deposits. Their note issue policy had remained conservative and their bank notes therefore exchanged at par with silver.

Thus in its first years the Nanking Government, led by T. V. Soong as Minister of Finance until 1933, had succeeded in creating a government banking mechanism which greatly aided its program of unification. The readjustment of internal loans and external debts, reforms of taxation, and the suppression of the *tael* (the old unit of account) in 1933 were all aspects of a program whereby the modern sector of the economy was brought increasingly under the financial domination of the central government. By 1937 there was a marked concentration of the national capital resources under government influence, which could pave the way for government control of credit.

The monetary reform of November 1935, with the support of Britain and the United States, was a final essential step in creating the modern banking structure. The American silver-buying program had already exacerbated the depression in China and was sucking out her currency in a most disastrous manner. This reform nationalized all the old silver currency in China, thus taking it out of circulation, and substituted a managed currency. The foreign banks, even with extraterritoriality, were put in a position of "necessary cooperation" with the Chinese Government. The latter was now able to unify and administer the financial reserves which it held against note issue. These reserves were gradually changed from silver into foreign exchange. The effort was to nationalize control of foreign exchange and build a national banking system independent of foreign powers. The notes of the four government banks were substituted for silver and other notes. In 1936–37 there was still no inflation.

This modernization of Chinese banking entailed the development of branch banking, interbank cooperation, long-term financing of industry, and the organization of bankers associations (beginning with the Shanghai Bankers Association in 1917).

But it must be admitted that this modernization was most rapid on the fringe of China where the money economy centered, in the treaty ports. For four-fifths of the people the greater problem was agricultural credit and how the government or the modern banks could take the place of the rural moneylender. Some city banks atempted to counter the preference for financing treaty port activities and tried to channel bank credit into rural areas through credit cooperatives. This had been aided by the China International Famine Relief Commission, which by 1927 had set up more than 500 cooperative credit associations in the province around Peking. In 1937 the government organized the Agricultural Credit Administration. Many expedients were tried. But the tendency was to use rural bank credit for seasonal short-term needs, in the same way as the loans of old-style usurers, not for long-term productive investment. Moreover, the official class who controlled bank credit flowing through government channels had many common ties at the local level with the landlord moneylenders.

Public Finance. The financial activities of the Nanking Government undoubtedly improved upon those of the corrupt Peking regimes of the warlord era but, as analyzed by economists like Douglas Paauw, they do not form a bright page of history. The half-way nature of the Nationalist Revolution was nowhere more evident than in these fiscal policies. The Central Government from the first renounced its claim to the land tax, the chief potential source of revenue, and left it for provincial administrations to exploit. Instead, Nanking financed its regime by taxing the trade and industry of the modern sector of the economy, thus living off that very sector that it should have tried by all means to develop.

About 50 per cent of the revenue came from the Maritime Customs (as compared with about one per cent in the United States). The second source was consolidated excise taxes on consumer staples like tobacco, kerosene and flour, and the government salt monopoly. This was regressive taxation, crippling the purchasing power of the masses at the lower income levels. The ancient tradition of bureaucratic revenue-grabbing still continued, for example, in the form of export duties which penalized native industry instead of subsidizing its development.

In this context, the fiscal reforms led by T. V. Soong remained superficial and indeed took on an ambiguous air. The *likin* tax on local trade was finally abolished along with the intricate *tael* system, and the currency was unified. But it proved impossible to install an effective budget system or keep military expenditures anywhere within bounds. Constant deficits were met by borrowing about 25 per cent of the sums expended from the four government banks, which in turn issued bonds on the domestic market. Debt payments to domestic bondholders soon exceeded those to foreigners, which had been extensive, and the service of these debts took a third of the government expenditures.

The net result was to tax the consumption goods of the poor in order to pay interest to the rich bondholders, many of whom were Nanking bureaucrats. Productive investment at home and capital loans from abroad were both discouraged by these anti-developmental policies. The best guess of economists now, in the absence of thorough statistical information, is that the Nanking decade saw continued stagnation in the agrarian economy, with no appreciable increase of production. This was accompanied, moreover, by a stultifying growth of "bureaucratic capitalism," that is, domination of industry and finance by officials and political cliques who feathered their private nests by manipulating government monopolies, finances, development schemes and agencies.

As a result of these aims and practices in the immemorial tradition of *sheng-kuan fa-ts'ai,* "become an official and get rich," the modernizers at Nanking failed to maintain a healthy and solvent fiscal regime, much less achieve a breakthrough into a genuine process of self-sustaining reinvestment and industrialization. Their unified government banking structure was used, not to provide cheap credit for purposes of economic development, but to pay high interest rates (20 to 40 per cent after allowance for discounts) to government bondholders, and to finance the very heavy military expenditures. Savings were thus channeled into current government use or private speculation. The nation's capital resources were not mobilized, even for military purposes. Industry was not protected nor investment encouraged. Dr. Paauw finds it "doubtful that the Kuomintang could have solved China's traditional problems of economic stagnation (even) with more political control and less Japanese aggression."

3. THE LOSS OF MORAL PRESTIGE

Wartime Decline. Given the limited economic base of the Nanking Government, the absorption of its meager revenues in military costs, and the unwisdom of its fiscal policies generally, it is a question whether both it and the Chinese economy as a whole were not worse off in 1937 than in 1928. By the end of World War II the disruption of the traditional economy, under way for a century, had been compounded by eight years of continental warfare. The Nationalist Government faced difficulties, including a run-away inflation, which it lacked the resources, the methods, the personnel, and the will to overcome.

The apparent wartime prosperity of some of China's farmers, during a decade which decimated the city salaried class, could not offset the over-all disaster and disinvestment which warfare brought upon the farm economy. The number of draft animals was seriously depleted over wide areas; the farms lost labor power, and the soil its necessary fertilizer. Man power had been similarly depleted by conscription. Loss of men and animals reduced transport resources and impeded marketing and trade. The farmer's usual handicraft industries were depressed. Instead of raising modern cash crops like cotton and tobacco, he had to go back to cereals and subsistence farming. His standard of living suffered accordingly.

In retrospect it seems plain that the government at Nanking, as the first fruit of the Chinese Nationalist movement, had been caught between two forces. The one was aggressive Japanese militarism which sought to shatter its new unity and check all that it might accomplish in the upbuilding of a powerful Chinese state. The other force was that of a mass discontent which sought to remake the life of the Chinese people on the land.

Unhappily the very factors which gave Nanking its strength as a focus of nationalism seem to have prevented it from taking the leadership of the nascent mass revolution. For the spirit of patriotism had arisen first among the merchants and students of the upper class who consituted the modern face of the traditional landlord gentry. Compradors, merchants, and bankers in the treaty ports used capital derived from the rents of the hinterland and the perquisites of old-style officials. Modern students who led the way in partiotism came necessarily from upper-class backgrounds, rather than from the peasantry. China could not be remade in a day, and Sun Yat-sen's followers, after the overthrow of the imperial system and the warlords, had their hands full in creating the political superstructure of a new nation, with the support of the more modern elements of the old ruling class. In the long course of the revolution, Nanking represented the partial modernization of China's central government more than a broadening of its base.

When the Nationalist Government after 1937 moved from the seacoast to the interior of Szechwan, there was a corresponding shift in the nature of its support. The Szechwan landlords and militarists took the place of the Shanghai bankers. Although the financial and mercantile class of the treaty ports had maintained close ties with landlordism, it had been in the forefront of modernization and of the Nationalist movement and had supported reform, though not revolution, in the countryside. The landed magnates of the interior, on the other hand, were conservatives of an earlier generation. They interpreted the wartime slogan of "Resistance and Reconstruction" to mean resistance to social change and consolidation of their position, while the Communists interpreted it to mean the acquisition of power through resistance, revolution, and mass mobilization. As a result when the Nationalist leaders settled down at Chungking in 1938 they had to face the question whether to follow the current trend of the united front and base their power upon mass mobilization, or to leave the old order intact upon the land.

In unoccupied China there had of course been no Japanese invasion and consequently no shatttering of the local structure of authority, nor any rousing of the common people to organize in self-defense under the sanction of patriotism. Since the Nationalist Government in its Szechwan base was forestalled from revolution, having no taste for it in any case, it had to rely heavily upon the established order. It opposed a mass mobilization which would arm the peasantry. This left the remnants of the landlord gentry families and local warlords to act in the ancient manner as the local ruling class.

The economy of Free China, compared to the new money economy of the Yangtze delta, represented a reversion to barter and self-sufficiency. As wartime inflation was fanned by the output of steadily depreciating banknotes, the government resorted to collection of the land tax in kind. Soon the bureaucracy and other salaried workers were dependent upon government rice stipends and inflated paper money. Meanwhile the peasant in Free China, though better off than city dwellers, found himself taxed and conscripted as much as ever and in no way emancipated by the war of resistance.

To those who saw the old China before the Kuomintang came to power and can recall the idealism, vigor, and efficiency of some of that Party's early administrators, the evils which grew up within it during the Japanese war are hard to believe. The Nationalist Government which in 1937 was forced into exile beyond the Yangtze gorges among the mountains and paddy fields of Szechwan, had become a rallying point for the best talent of Modern China, the first fruit of the new patriotism and technical training. Eight years later the leadership which returned down the river to Nanking and Shanghai in late 1945 was worn and demoralized. In its exile in the mists of Szechwan the top personnel of the government had changed very little. Cabinet reshuffling only brought the same faces to different windows. The heads of the Legislative, Judicial, Examination, and Control Yuans were the same in 1945 as in 1938. Chu Chia-hua had been secretary general of the Kuomintang, then minister of Kuomintang organization, and was now minister of education. Ch'en Li-fu had been minister of education and was now minister of Kuomintang organization. Chang Ch'un was vice-president of the Executive Yuan in 1939 and president (or premier) in 1947. Weng Wen-hao was minister of economic affairs in 1938 and still held that post in 1945. The deputy secretary general of the Kuomintang at the start of the war (Kan Nai-kuang) was vice minister of foreign affairs at its end, the assistant chief of the organization department (Ku Cheng-kang) was now minister of social affairs. Examples could be multiplied.

By retaining personal power, the Kuomintang leaders devitalized their organization. Politically they marked time while waiting for the war to end. The best men among them knew how to modernize China technologically. But they were unable to mobilize the back country in a continuing social revolution. The revolution consequently passed them by.

The Loss of Heaven's Mandate. Wartime politics in China had some overtones of the passing of the Mandate of Heaven, modern style. The Nationalist Government's currency depreciated in a vicious spiral in which production was depressed in favor of speculation and hoarding, while unproductive expenditure was increased to finance the war. But this monetary inflation went hand in hand with a no less tragic depreciation of the government's prestige.

It is still true in China that a regime is sanctioned by its moral worth. A morally unworthy regime must rely upon force, instead of poplar acquiescence in its rule. Like the old imperial administration, the Kuomintang government, in spite of the expanded number of its officials and the greater mobility and fire power of its armed forces, was still a rather small organization for so large a country. Its grip therefore depended partly on its prestige; and one constant aim of its Chinese Communist opponents was to undermine its moral repute, through radio and press as well as by more ancient methods of rumor and propaganda. In this the Communists had the greatest help from the bad record of the government itself. In meeting China's limitless problems it committed, through the person of its corrupt administrators, infinite mistakes. The postwar take-over process, when carpet-bagging generals and politicians returned to the coastal provinces and Formosa, was as shameful a record of official looting as modern history has displayed. The inflation made official salaries shrink out of sight. Graft took their place. But self-seeking and corruption seem to have been intensified by the officials' loss of confidence in the government's future. The result was a cynical *sauve-qui-peut*.

The government was thus obliged to shift from a reliance on its moral prestige to an increasing reliance on naked force. Wartime and postwar dangers seemed to give the balance of power at Chung-king to those persons or groups who were most interested in the preservation of the regime at all costs. Faced with disaster, the whole regime relied on its organizers, as Chiang relied on the Ch'en brothers. Unfortunately the organizers were those who, through loyalty or personal ambition, placed the fortunes of the regime above all other considerations, including those of principle. Men who believed in secret police, thought control, and suppression of opposition gained an ascendancy. This produced government action, like the punishment of critics, not justifiable in principle but based purely on force. The result was to antagonize formerly loyal elements. This weakened the regime. This increasing weakness being perceived, further reliance was placed upon force.

Only some such theory can explain the repeated acts by which the Kuomintang right wing lost the support of the intellectual and professional classes. Time after time government use of force against intellectuals served only to weaken its position among them. The public humiliaton and beating of demonstrating students, who were mostly non-Communist, turned them toward Communism. In this way, the advocates of force obliged the government to rely on nothing else. Party dictatorship, while not an absolute power, became absolutely corrupted.

This corruption of the holders of Kuomintang power consisted in their sacrificing the general welfare to their own interest as a political group. By a more democratic rural program the Kuomintang could have competed against Communism at any time since 1927. After enveloping and expelling the Communists from Kiangsi in 1935 they sought to make it a model province but were unable to create a dynamic peasant movement. After the united front in 1937 the Kuomintang soon came to a turning point. Mass mobilization in the war of resistance was arousing the country and through it the Communists were extending their influence. The Kuomintang faced the alternative of competing directly with the Communists by encouranging mass resistance through social revolution, or fighting on two fronts against foreign invasion and domestic revolt at the same time. About 1938 they chose the latter course. This obviously sprang from a deep bureaucratic distrust of mass movements and popular initiative, and an easily rationalized determination to retain power at any price. This attitude, however, conduced to the loss of that moral prestige which was still one of the necessary ingredients of power. More and more people became prepared to turn against the government.

13

The Rise of the Communist Party

ONE long-term factor in the Communist rise to power was Japan's continuous effort at military conquest, which roused the Chinese people for patriotic political action but weakened the Nationalist Government's capacity to lead them in other than military ways.

Japan's attack, from 1931 on, obliged the Kuomintang to continue militarizing in self-defense. Its resources went into its armies, its leadership into the hands of a Generalissimo, its policies became more conservative and militaristic — "unify before resisting" rather than "unify by resisting." During the long years of warfare Whampoa generals and CC-clique party organizers came to dominate its councils and control its actions as they might not otherwise have done.

Meanwhile Japan's war machine, conquering cities with torture and rapine, burning villages, squeezing the economy, bombing Free China, roused the student youth and the peasant populace for a movement of resistance and national survival which went far beyond the military sphere. Millions of persons were displaced, some 14 million men conscripted, families were broken up, vested interests destroyed, markets lost — the social order over wide areas was thoroughly disrupted. The student youth and the peasant populace were both subjected to violent social changes and so prepared for revolutionary programs of action.

The immediate underlying factor in the Communist rise to power was the Kuomintang's failure to lead the country in a program of creative action. Free China had the wherewithal in men and ideas. The rural reconstruction movement of James Yen, the little teacher movement of H. C. T'ao, the Industrial Cooperatives, the plants of the National Resources Commission, the trained workers of the Public Health Administration, the army medical corps (energized by a Peiping physiology professor, Dr. Robert Lim), all these and a hundred other groups and agencies existed in free China. They were the product of modernization through contact with the liberal West, and formed a reservoir of trained talent and public-spirited citizens, eager to participate in their country's inevitable modernization.

The Nationalist Government lacked the vitality to mobilize and lead them. Intent on holding power, it distrusted the enthusiasm of private agencies and individuals. It feared change in a rapidly changing world. Its failure in political leadership gave the Communists an opportunity which they otherwise might not have had.

The Attraction of Communism. This naturally cannot be understood in Western terms but only by an imaginative effort to understand it in its Chinese context — the authoritarian political tradition, the worsening circumstances of the 1930's and 1940's.

First of all, several aspects of China's past favored the Communist approach. Confucian tradition gave the modern student the sanction and indeed the moral imperative to take the lead in public affairs as a member of the scholar-elite and in terms of ideological principles. The authoritarian tradition by which the official class monopolized all overt political activity made it natural that an opposition movement must be secretly organized. Rebellion in the past had usually been energized by utopian and messianic doctrines (usually of Buddhist derivation but in the case of the Taipings both pseudo-Christian and pre-Confucian). Rebels had usually found in their sworn brotherhood a substitute for the support given each individual, in the absence of legal safeguards, by the old family system. Chinese folklore and literature had a romantic Robin Hood tradition of banditry in the cause of the downtrodden.

China's experience in modern times also reinforced traditional tendencies. As the economic plight of the farmer grew more apparent, if not in fact steadily worse, it was naturally assumed that government action should be taken to remedy it. The job was too big for individuals and must be the primary responsibility of those in power — all of which suggested some kind of state socialism. Sun Yat-sen had vaguely pointed in this direction. The Marxian socialist ideal in China, however, had been from the first a Communist Party monopoly. No social-democratic movement preceded it, to spread the socialist creed as in Europe on a gradualist, reformist basis. For those attacted to socialism there was nowhere to go but into a Leninist party. Leninism, finally, provided an explanation of the great fact in any Chinese patriot's political life — imperialism. When it proceeded to identify those ancient twin evils of landlords and warlords as "feudalism," the Marxist-Leninist scheme of history seemed to many sufficiently applicable to China to deserve their belief and faith. It claimed to be "scientific" and strictly "modern." It would allow China to expunge her modern humiliations by leaping over the capitalist phase of universal development to stand as she should in the forefront of the nations. For the faithful believer the Party would provide. A new China would result.

To offset these favorable factors there were several reasons why the Communist movement was checked and almost suppressed, before the Japanese war facilitated its resurgence. One reason was the success of the Kuomintang (hereafter KMT) at Nanking in mobilizing talent and support for its new government. Another was the KMT effort at suppression which killed thousands, if not tens of thousands, of leftist youth. But perhaps the most fundamental reason for retardation lay with the Chinese Communist Party (hereafter CCP) itself and the orthodox urban orientation given it by the master minds of the Comintern in Moscow. This can be seen if we trace the early vicissitudes of the party line — that ingenious device for maintaining inner unity while choosing allies and isolating enemies by "class analysis" according to alleged "laws of history."

1. THE COMINTERN'S DECADE OF FAILURE

After the Comintern agent Gregory Voitinsky in 1920 had prompted Ch'en Tu-hsiu to call together a mixed group of intellectual-revolutionaries to form a Communist party, it required some time to mould them into a genuinely Bolshevik organization. They early became active in the labor movement but, as C. M. Wilbur's recent study points out, their membership remained less than a thousand until the May Thirtieth Movement of 1925 roused a great surge of anti-imperialist feeling and gave them a tenfold increase of numbers. The immensely greater size of the Kuomintang intensified the Communists' persistent problem: how to seize political opportunities on a basis of theoretical principles, thereby avoiding a mere unprincipled opportunism. This necessity for rational flexibility, for reasoned opportunism, is what makes the party line so interesting a study.

For most Americans the Marxist-Leninist dialectic makes dry reading, about as palatable as packaged cereal without milk or cream. We must remember, however, that this rather tasteless fare has vital significance for the initiated — indeed, for all who have to deal with Communism. A change of line, redefinition of a term, may make or break human careers more decisively than the fluctuating statistics of a stock exchange in time of panic. Lives depend on the turn of the dialectic.

Early Twists in the Party Line. The Chinese Communists had begun by dividing Chinese society into the classes of workers (proletariat), peasants, petty bourgeoisie, national bourgeoisie (capitalists) and other, reactionary classes (militarists, "feudal" landlords, *et al.*). Their first manifesto of June 1922 (a year after their formal founding) called for a united front against the militarists in which the CCP would represent the workers (assuming with Marx that a party can really be an organ of only one class) and also poor peasants, while the "democratic party" (the KMT) would represent bourgeois elements. This concept was abruptly overruled when the Comintern shortly declared that the KMT was actually, and quite anomalously, a "bloc of four classes" (bourgeoisie, petty bourgeoisie, workers, and peasants) and that the CCP, instead of seeking a united front with it as a "bloc without" (*i.e.* from outside) should do so as a "bloc within," *i.e.* by having CCP members as individuals become KMT members while still remaining part of the CCP apparatus. The CCP Third Congress in June 1923, in confirming this ingenious idea, echoed the Comintern declaration that the KMT "should be the central force of the national revolution." When dual membership was accepted by the KMT in January 1924, the race began to see which party apparatus could make more use of the other. Communists gained key posts in the KMT organization.

Adhering to this approach (advocated by Stalin, criticized by

Trotsky), the Comintern in December 1926 ordered the CCP to join the left wing of the KMT in the Nationalist Government at Hankow, which it now defined to be a "bloc of three classes" (workers, peasants, and petty bourgeoisie). The aim was to effect a transition by which the national bourgeoisie would be excluded from the revolutionary movement. As a result the CCP continued to seek power as a "bloc within," even though its subordination to Hankow prevented its exploiting the peasant unrest of the time. The final fiasco of the Comintern's "bloc within" strategy was signalized first by the split between the left KMT at Hankow and the right KMT at Nanking (February–April 1927) and then by Hankow's explusion of the Communists (July 1927).

Under Comintern orders the CCP now reoriented itself (August 1927). It condemned Ch'en Tu-hsiu (who later was expelled) and "the Party's leading cadres" (who themselves participated in the condemnation) for "opportunism." "Their constant vacillation, their false, unrevolutionary theories . . . in complete contradiction to the resolutions and instructions of the Comintern . . . in reality betrayed the revolution." At the same time the CCP accepted Stalin's view that the revolution was entering a "higher" stage which must be marked by secret conspiracy and armed insurrections in city and countryside. Yet lip service was still paid to the necessity of achieving "hegemony within the KMT," a statement without meaning except as support of Stalin against Trotsky.

Following this new line the CCP staged the Autumn Harvest uprising in Hunan (led by Mao Tse-tung) and seized the South China port of Swatow for a week, in September 1927. In December it contrived a four-day uprising in Canton (the "Canton Commune"). These and similar efforts all failed.

The Sixth Congress of the CCP, meeting in Moscow with 16 or more members present in July–September 1928, again condemned Ch'en Tu-hsiu for his "opportunist" right deviation mentioned above, and now equally condemned his successor for the "putschist" left deviation which had resulted in unsuccessful uprisings. The new line stated that the revolution was now in a "trough between two waves" and the CCP must prepare for armed insurrections in view of the inevitable arrival of a new "revolutionary rising tide." This laid the basis for the disastrous "Li Li-san line" of 1929–30.

The Sixth Congress of 1928 had decreed that the agrarian revolu-

tion was the main "content" of the Chinese revolution as a whole,
but that the agrarian revolution could be achieved only under
"proletarian hegemony." This meant that the CCP must recapture the leadership of the urban proletariat. At the same time it
must prepare armed insurrection so as to be ready for the new
"rising tide" of revolution. The result was that under Li Li-san,
as secretary general appointed by Moscow, the CCP apparatus had
to organize city workers for political strikes and armed uprisings,
exploiting the labor union members for party ends rather than
representing their economic grievances. In the face of the KMT
white terror and its competing "yellow" labor union movement, Li
Li-san and his close ally in this period, Chou En-lai, got nowhere.
No tide rose, least of all in the cities. In 1926 two-thirds of the
party had been classed as proletarian and another fifth as intellectuals. In 1930 Chou En-lai reported that out of 120,000 party
members, only about 2,000 were industrial workers.

The climax of Li Li-san's insurrectionary effort came in July
1930 when Communist forces made front-page news by seizing
Changsha, the capital of Hunan, only to be expelled a few days
later. Li Li-san's downfall followed in the usual way. He was condemned for both "opportunism" and "putschism." He had struggled
"against the Comintern line, disobeyed Comintern discipline, and
adopted the arguments used by the leftist and rightist rebels against
the Comintern by saying that the Comintern did not understand
the Chinese situation," et cetera. Li Li-san recanted and went to
Moscow "for study" (to reappear in Manchuria in 1946). Chou
En-lai, after confessing his "cowardly rotten opportunism," remained on the Central Committee. The latter was now dominated
by a "returned-student" group of comrades newly trained in Moscow who still assumed that the urban proletariat must lead China's
revolution.

The failure of the first decade of Chinese Communism reflected
the difficulty of importing and adapting a foreign faith and its
institutions. Leninist party discipline included the fiction that
Moscow could not err and that the faithful executor of the Comintern line, if he failed, was himself at fault. The irrationality of this
latest importation from the West was not attractive to most
Chinese intellectuals, even though reminiscent of the Emperor's
holding a local mandarin responsible for acts of God within his

bailiwick. In Chinese politics the CCP leadership was something new, a band of professional revolutionists, disciplined and trained to concentrate in Leninist ideological terms upon the organization and seizure of power. The decisive feature of their party was that, unlike the Kuomintang which had borrowed a similar Leninist structure, it functioned as an ideological entity. The line set by the leadership on reasoned "dialectical" grounds, was capable of shifts and reversals, resilient in adversity and flexible when opportunity offered, always sacrificing individuals as expendable in the total cause.

Comintern directives, often concocted with one eye on Stalin's enemies in Moscow, had been disastrously doctrinaire. Yet as political platform documents they regularly included contradictory alternatives which could later be cited to prove wrong those who, like Li Li-san, had followed their main tenor. For example, the CCP Sixth Congress of 1928 in Moscow had foreseen "a war in the Pacific for the partition of China . . . the coastal provinces . . . will become the battleground." It declared that "the reformist devices of the bourgeoisie cannot solve the agrarian problem." It called for "alliance with the petty bourgeoisie and the rich peasants" (without, however, abandoning "the class struggle against the rich peasants"). It urged support of peasant guerrilla warfare, development of the Red Army, organization of peasant women and youth, the setting up of Soviet bases. In short, like a campaign platform, it covered all eventualities and so in later retrospect could be cited to prove Moscow's foresight, even though its main directive had led to defeat.

Thus by 1931 the first decade of Communism in China had created a Leninist party, in spite of the failure of Comintern policy. The second decade was to see an indigenous adaptation of Marxism-Leninism to Chinese potentialities. (One cannot help thinking back, in a general way, to the adaptation of Buddhism some 14 centuries before, to find points of comparison and of contrast.)

2. THE RISE OF MAO AND THE YENAN PERIOD

The Rise of Mao Tse-tung. The Comintern had reiterated that only the proletariat could lead the peasantry. It regarded peasants, in orthodox Marxist-Leninist fashion, as capable only of auxiliary action. But Mao Tse-tung's famous report on the peasant movement in Hunan foreshadowed what Benjamin Schwartz has called "the Maoist strategy." Written in February 1927, before the debacle of that year, this report asserted heretically that the "revolutionary vanguard" in China was not the proletariat but the "poor peasantry." When Mao's Autumn Harvest uprising of 1927 failed, he was temporarily dismissed from the CCP Politburo but he continued his work in the Hunan countryside. Convinced that mass revolution in China must be based on the peasantry, Mao learned from experience the necessity of combining mass organization with military power. Building up rural guerrilla forces, he began to create "soviets" (as Trotsky had advocated) even before the Comintern sanctioned it. With Chu Teh as military commander he took refuge in the winter of 1927–28 in the mountainous Chinkanshan region on the Hunan-Kiangsi border, collecting some 10,000 men, together with arms for perhaps 2,000.

Here developed a territorial base, to be fused with the other components — a Leninist party, support from the peasant masses, a Red Army — in the "Maoist strategy." The territorial base, Mao declared in 1928, must have a food supply and a strategic location, preferably on the rugged natural border between two provinces. Collecting here the traditional sinews of rebellion, man power and grain, Mao kept his movement ideologically orthodox in form if not in substance. The Chinese Soviet Republic was proclaimed at Juichin, Kiangsi, in November 1931 as a "democratic dictatorship of the proletariat and peasantry," using Lenin's formula of 1905 in utterly different circumstances. The non-existent "proletariat" were favored by excellent labor laws on paper and given greater representation than the peasantry in the system of soviets, the same as in Russia. The Red Army was specially privileged as a political class army. Land was violently redistributed, both in the time-honored fashion of peasant uprisings and also in terms of class warfare and for purposes of establishing political control. Collectivization, then the Russian fashion, was not pushed. In fact the Soviet Republic in Kiangsi was in no position to coerce all the soviets organized in and around its base area. Some rich peasants and landlords organized soviets so as to make peace with it. But Mao's rural strategy was like Lenin's: rely on the poor peasants and destroy the landlords, treating the middle peasants (until later) as allies and the rich peasants usually as class enemies.

Mao Tse-tung's ascendancy came slowly, some time after KMT

arrests and executions had forced the Central Committee to abandon Shanghai for Kiangsi in the autumn of 1932. Chiang Kai-shek's extermination campaigns, in late 1931, May-June and July-October 1932 and again in 1933 had been checked by guerrilla tactics which drew KMT columns into the mountains and concentrated superior force against isolated units. In 1934, however, a systematic, German-devised, KMT blockade with networks of blockhouses began to strangle the Soviet base. The Red Army's efforts at positional defense proved disastrous. After receiving permission from Moscow by radio, over 100,000 CCP personnel in October broke out of their Kiangsi redoubt, moving swiftly by night on the beginning of the Long March. Only now, when Chinese Communism was out of touch with Moscow and irrevocably committed to survive in the countryside or not at all, was the Moscow-trained element in the party leadership obliged to acknowledge Mao's dominance. Mao's rise was not decreed from the Kremlin.

Yenan and Wartime Expansion. After marching and fighting on a circuitous route of 6000 miles or more through half a dozen provinces of Southwest China, surviving perils and hardships now legendary, most of the CCP leaders and probably less than 20,000 troops reached northern Shensi province in the latter part of 1935, transferring their headquarters to Yenan at the end of 1936. Here in the arid, sun-baked Northwest, half-way from Nanking to the border of Soviet Outer Mongolia, a new chapter opened with the second united front, this time against Japan.

Since general Chinese resistance to Japan would serve a dual purpose, diverting Japan from attacking Russia and Nanking from attacking the CCP, it is not surprising that at the beginning of August 1935 both the CCP and the Comintern called for nation-wide resistance in a new united front. With some exceptions the CCP statements now offered to join with the arch-enemy, Chiang Kai-shek; but he remained deaf to this proposal until after his spectacular kidnapping at Sian in December 1936 by Manchurian troops who chafed to fight Japanese invaders, not Chinese rebels. Chou En-lai on Russian orders mediated to secure the release of Generalissimo Chiang, who now reached the zenith of his career as the indomitable symbol of national resistance.

Subsequent pourparlers and the unleashing of Japan's attack near Peiping on July 7, 1937, led to a second KMT-CCP marriage of convenience, an uneasy armed truce which began in an atmosphere of patriotic enthusiasm but soon deteriorated. The Communists now met Nanking's demands and promised to support Sun's *Three Principles,* to give up overthrowing the KMT by force and abandon the soviet campaign against landlordism, to democratize their local regime, and to put their troops under Nationalist command. These were of course temporary tactical expedients by which to expand CCP power in the wholly new context of a national war of resistance.

This relatively moderate program, during a period when violent change was being brought about by the Japanese invasion, recognized that China's war of resistance was in itself a revolution. The Communists had only to go along with it and give leadership in the mobilization of a people's army, the organization of local government, and the coordination of autonomous popular movements. By riding with the patriotic tide and on the crest of the popular wave, the Communist organization soon became the over-all government, the only coordinating mechanism, in the densely populated countryside of North China within and without the Japanese strong points and lines of communication.

This process of expansion was first of all military. The name of the Red Army was abolished in 1937 and it was put nominally under the orders of the Central Government, which named it the Eighth Route Army. By degrees its forces pushed into the mountain-ringed province of Shansi and thence out onto the North China plain. In the second year of the war the Communists organized the New Fourth Army from remnant forces left in the lower Yangtze region and extended their organization also into the sea-coast province of Shantung. The war bases which they organized centered in the less accessible border areas between provinces, beginning with the Shansi-Hopeh-Chahar Border Region set up in 1938, which eventually contained roughly 20 million people. By 1941 the last area of the Nien rebellion of 1853–1868 on the Shansi-Hopeh-Honan-Shantung borders was unified as another such Region with a population of perhaps 30 million. By war's end there were 19 bases, mostly called Liberated Areas, with a total population of 70 to 90 millions, protected by about 2 million militia and by Communist armies said to total 910,000 troops.

The Nationalist Government, never locally dominant in much of

North China, could not prevent this expansion. Its modernized forces, absorbed in stemming the main Japanese war effort in such areas as the Hunan rice-bowl, were trained for positional, not guerrilla, warfare. Chiang Kai-shek's troops were also handicapped by the Chinese military tradition which kept the army separate from the people.

Throughout Chinese history an armed populace had invariably endangered the established order, while the soldier had been held in low esteem, kept ignorant, used wastefully, and bought and sold as a mercenary. Armies had lived off the countryside and been the scourge of the people. Politically indoctrinated armies were a new thing in Modern China. In this as in other respects it was typical of the Kuomintang that it had modernized its military machine to the point of giving social prestige to a patriotic new officer corps and giving new arms and training to their peasant soldiers, but it had not reached the point of indoctrinating the ordinary rifleman to fraternize with the farmer and fight in his behalf, because this would have been revolutionary. For that very reason Mao and Chu from the beginning had trained their troops to regard themselves as the defenders of the populace. In practice this meant paying for supplies, helping the households on whom they were quartered, and making the Eighth Route Army the friend of the people. As the Communists put it, "the soldiers are fish and the people water" — the army depended upon popular support. This slogan is an illuminating contrast to the orthodox statement of the philosopher Hsün-tzu (ca. 300–235 B.C.) that "the people are the water and the ruler is the boat; the water can support the boat but it can also sink it." The Communists, so to speak, by being immersible among the people added a dimension to their movement.

This fraternization with the populace meant that the Communist troops could dispense with the modern paraphernalia of a central commissary. By using civilian intelligence networks they could more easily decentralize their military organization. This enabled the Eighth Route Army to operate as a scattered, mobile force, appearing and disappearing in the populated farm land behind the Japanese lines. This was something that the Central Government forces could not do unless they combined their military operations with a more popular political program.

In their political organization the Chinese Communists expanded to fill a vacuum. Local politicians had been the first to go as the Japanese advanced, and in some cases had gone over to puppetry. New leadership had arisen locally, teachers from Peiping in some cases becoming chairmen of guerrilla governments. Into these local situations where new leadership was arising came a great influx of young students from the coastal centers. Intellectuals from Yenching and the big government universities at Peiping, inheritors of the spirit of the May Fourth Movement, packed their belongings in a bundle and joined the guerrillas. Living close to nature and the common people, they emulated the adventurous heroes of Chinese folklore, daring all with loyal comrades in a righteous cause to succor the downtrodden, like the famous characters of the picaresque novel *Shui-hu-chuan* (translated by Pearl Buck as *All Men Are Brothers*).

The migration of patriots was common to both South and North, but with different effect. In the more modern centers of the unoccupied Southwest, the students became symbols of the country's future technological development and remained in the universities-in-exile. In the Border Regions and Liberated Areas of North China, on the other hand, where universities were lacking, they were recruited to be Communist cadres, in teams of political workers. The Communist area during the early united front period attracted venturesome idealists who sought action. By degrees the Communists organized these diverse individuals into a network of decentralized government.

Organization of Popular Support. In their land policy the Communists temporarily abandoned their program of land confiscation and redistribution in favor of rent reduction. This merely carried out the Kuomintang law of 1930 which limited rent to 37½ per cent of the crop. At this time landlords were very generally left in possession, guaranteed a reduced rent and also allowed to vote in local elections, so that there was no great flight of the propertied class from the Communist area. Instead of their former soviet system, the Communists announced direct elections by the so-called three-thirds system in which they would confine their own representation to one-third and seek to retain Kuomintang and independent participation in the other two-thirds of the offices. This was based on the theory that in a community unified against the Japanese the Communists would provide leadership most effectively by refraining from a monopoly of government. The system had the merit of apparent competition. Although the Communists had preponderant force in reserve, their local political representatives had to prove their administrative competence and political wisdom before the bar of public opinion. While this was a passive Chinese type of public opinion, expressed by tacit acquiescence and lack of protest rather than by speeches and editorials, it was still a determining factor in wartime politics. Like traditional contenders for the Mandate of Heaven, the Communists had to steer by the willingness of the populace to put up with their regime rather than turn against it. In practice the Communist movement and the Eighth Route Army in these years could prosper only in proportion as the populace actually supported them, for the war period was one of free political competition, in which the Japanese and their Chinese puppets as well as the Kuomintang offered feasible alternatives to the Communist regime.

The key to popular support lay in the CCP leadership of a patriotic war of resistance and, at the same time, in the Communists' economic program. In the densely populated North China plain where some fifteen hundred people try to live off each square mile of cultivated land, food was more important than civil liberties. The latter had been unknown. Chinese governments had never countenanced the active participation of the farmer in politics. Privately sponsored meetings and speeches had been seditious, elections unheard of, and freedom to publish meaningless among illiterate peasants.

Against this tradition it was comparatively easy to develop an effective economic program. This included production drives both by troops and by farmers which sought to achieve the self-sufficiency of each area in food supply and, with more difficulty, in cotton production. The Communists were not well supplied with improved seeds and farming techniques such as those developed by scientific farming in the West. But they made up for this lack by their emphasis upon cooperation in land reclamation, labor exchange among farmers, transport cooperatives, and small-scale industrial cooperatives. Since the old order had inveterately discouraged the cooperative association of peasant households in any way which might threaten authority, the immense potentialities of peasant cooperation at the village level were ready at hand for Communist exploitation. By bringing the farmers into associations for common ends and controlling these associations through leadership and propaganda, the Communists found a new road to political power.

Compared with the years of decline and disaster in the wilderness after 1927, the Yenan decade of the united front after 1936 was full of vitality, growth and innovation. While not renouncing their orthodox Communist aims, the CCP now stressed "agrarian reform," though far from being "mere agrarian reformers." When an enterprising American journalist, Edgar Snow, interviewed Mao and his colleagues after the Long March, he found a self-confident and even jovial band of veteran revolutionaries, whose homespun earthiness and evident devotion to the peasant's cause, brilliantly portrayed in *Red Star Over China,* captured the imagination of readers around the world. During World War II the electric optimism and sunny atmosphere of Yenan impressed foreign visitors, who invariably came there from the clammy fog and frustration of the capital at Chungking. Communist propaganda in this period sang a liberal tune, for "national independence, democratic liberty and the people's welfare" (paraphrasing Sun's *Three Principles*), with no further stress on soviets, bolshevization, class war, dictatorship or even the absent proletariat. This façade for outside observers, however, did not disclose the Party's inner aims and methods, nor its problem of organizing central power during its wartime growth.

3. WARTIME IDEOLOGICAL DEVELOPMENT

CCP expansion had created decentralization. Party membership grew from 40,000 (claimed by Mao in 1937) to 80,000 (claimed by Chou in 1943) to 1,200,000 (claimed by Mao in 1945). Strenuous efforts were required to keep the CCP a disciplined, centrally-controlled Leninist party. Its membership was new. It was less than ever a party of the proletariat, even though peasants were now called "rural proletarians." At the same time its activities were spread over a quarter of a million square miles where travel was mainly by foot of man or beast and communication was quick only by radio. Control could be exercised only by Communists working with proper ideological coordination in the four parallel hierarchies of party, local government, army, and mass organizations (for women, youth, labor, and the like). Veterans of the Long March usually headed these hierarchies. P'eng Te-huai, Liu Po-ch'eng, Lin Piao, and others commanded armies, Liu Shao-ch'i headed the labor federation. But to retain central direction it was essential to indoctrinate the new cadres (party workers) in Leninist assumptions and principles of organization.

For this purpose party schools processed thousands of students at Yenan and in 1942 Mao inaugurated an ideological reform movement for "correcting unorthodox tendencies" (cheng-feng) in thought, in personal relations inside and outside the party, and in speech and writing. Borrowing heavily from Russian and Comintern sources, he and his colleagues produced a body of documents for intensive study and discussion — "How to be a Communist Party Member," "In Opposition to Liberalism," "Liquidation of Menshevik Thought," "On the Intra-Party Struggle." Prolonged criticism and self-criticism in small groups, confessions of guilt and repentance in public meetings, became standard procedures. The aim was to maintain the party's militancy and dedication during all the distractions of a united front period, to keep its membership prepared for future tasks. Behind the jargon of "subjectivism, sectarianism and formalism" (the three main evils attacked), one can perceive a strenuous effort to re-educate and discipline new followers still contaminated by a liberal background, an individualistic temperament, or traditional morality.

Simultaneously the *cheng-feng* movement marked the final eclipse (though not a physical purge) of the doctrinaire "returned-student" group who had behind them more training in Moscow than work in the villages. Marxist-Leninist theory must be tested in action, applied to rural China's concrete realities: this became the basis of "Maoism." As the new CCP constitution of 1945 put it, "the ideas of Mao Tse-tung, the combined principles derived from the practical experience of the Chinese revolution" were now added to Marxism-Leninism as the party's guiding principles. While not calling for an independent national Communism like that of Tito in Jugoslavia, this growth of "Maoism" represented the final Sinification of Communism in China, in a period of wartime nationalism and minimal Russian influence. Henceforth it was no longer an alien creed. Its principal achievement had been to build a Leninist party on a peasant base, demonstrating (contrary to its own theory) that the Communist order is in fact independent of the proletariat.

This inversion of Marxism implied that a man's ideological tendencies did not come from his class affiliation, as posited by historical materialism. His class was now determined by his ideology; a bright peasant could become a "proletarian." This triumph of political power considerations over the influence of the economic mode of production — "putting the Leninist cart before the Marxist horse," as Peter S. H. Tang calls it — marked another step in the doctrinal disintegration of Marxism-Leninism.

The party line for public consumption in the Yenan period was laid down in Mao's essay *On the New Democracy* of 1940, a persuasive propaganda document which justifies the united front as a temporary phase and yet reaffirms the party's long-term mission. The Chinese revolution, Mao says, must be divided into two stages: first, a "democratic revolution" (the New Democracy), and then a "socialist revolution." The two are quite different. The New Democracy must take its first step by changing the old "semi-feudal" society into an independent "democratic" society. The Chinese people, says Mao, have been attempting this ever since the Opium War. The 1911 Revolution was a step in this direction but it was bourgeois-democratic and not proletarian-socialist. When Sun Yat-sen declared "the revolution is not yet complete, our comrades must still strive on," he was speaking of the bourgeois-democratic revolution. The New Democracy, however, is not part of that general movement but represents a Chinese phase of the world-wide proletarian-socialist revolution, in which China can win her freedom from imperialism only with the aid of international socialism represented by the Soviet Union. Thus the New Democracy aims to develop a type of "democratic" state ruled by an alliance of several revolutionary classes (unlike the "dictatorship of the proletariat" in Russia), before proceeding to a second stage of socialism.

The New Democracy in China must have bourgeois help, says Mao, for this new government cannot be a Soviet-style socialist republic ruled by the proletariat (in Chinese literally, "propertyless class"), even though that will become in time the ruling form of government in all advanced countries. Since that newest style is not suited to a semi-colonial country, China's New Democracy must be a third type, ruled neither by the bourgeoisie alone nor by the proletariat alone, a transitional form for a certain historical period.

In form the New Democracy should have a government of "democratic centralism" based on elections in which all participate, but graded through a hierarchy of people's assemblies from the village on up to a national congress. In economic life the new government should own and operate large-scale and monopoly activities including big banks, big industries, railways, and the like. This is in accord with the declaration of the first Kuomintang Congress of 1924. On the land the New Democracy will confiscate and distribute the holdings of big landlords in order to realize Sun Yat-sen's slogan, "Land to those who till it." By turning the land into the private property of the peasants, this reform will produce something quite different from a socialist agricultural system. Thus China's economy, says Mao, should follow the rule of restriction of private capitalism and equalization of land rights, in order to prevent the few capitalists and landlords from "manipulating the life of the people." This program will be, as Dr. Sun declared, according to nature's law, human reason, the world's trend and the people's needs. China cannot follow the example of European and American capitalism.

Mao subscribes to Sun's Three Principles of 1924, which included the three policies of alliance with Soviet Russia, cooperation with the Chinese Communists, and support of workers and peasants, that is, the awakening of the people in a mass revolution. Sun Yat-sen's program before 1924, while correct for the period of the 1911 Revolution, had lacked this essential new ingredient of mass mobilization. Thus Mao claims for the New Democracy direct descent from Sun Yat-sen, whose true principles he says have been abandoned by the Kuomintang and inherited by the Communists.

In the cultural revolution Mao sees the period before the May Fourth Movement of 1919 as a struggle of bourgeois culture against the old "feudal" culture. It was motivated by the bourgeois liberal ideas of the West. The May Fourth Movement, he asserts, was chiefly significant for the introduction of Communist cultural thought. For the current phase the new culture should not try to be socialist, since socialism is not yet achieved, but must be based upon the three elements of nationalism, science, and the masses of the people.

Thus in his *New Democracy*, Mao Tse-tung toward his non-Marxist audience blandly claimed to inherit the mantle of Sun Yat-sen as the democratic leader of the Chinese revolution and skillfully identified the May Fourth Movement with Communism. Meanwhile for Marxists he put himself on the level of Marx-Engels-Lenin-Stalin as an original contributor to Communist theory. In actual fact Mao's "innovations" had been in the realm of practice, not theory. All his dicta could be found in earlier literature. His real "contribution" had been the creation of a state within a state — a party, an army, and mass support in a territorial base. But this was not something to boast of in 1940. Thus, as Benjamin Schwartz puts it, "the *New Democracy* is a Marxist-Leninist scaffolding which conceals as much as it reveals." Its appeal to liberal-minded individuals was very great. The ambiguity of its terminology catered to their hopes while actually building a framework in which to control them.

"Liberation." The semi-totalitarianism of wartime in any country, when life is mobilized by the state under the sanction of a common struggle for survival, may for a time create high morale in the midst of suffering. With Japanese armies in the land, the Communists' organizational know-how, their current reasonableness and moderation, their militant and messianic faith, set the stage for a new cult of the common people. "Liberation" aimed at the awakening and activation of the Chinese peasant masses. The cultural movement stressed pictorial art in the form of the woodcut, which could be cheaply reproduced by wood-block printing for mass distribution. Choral singing was another wartime development in all parts of China. In the Communist areas it was combined with an ancient type of country dance to create a new art form in the *yang-ko* ("seedling song"), an all-talking-singing-dancing poorman's opera which used simple rhythms, folk tunes, a very simple chain dance step, propaganda stories, and the subject matter of everyday life to provide entertainment which indoctrinated as it liberated. Getting the common man to express himself in public in country dancing and choral singing was part of a process of social integration of the individual.

Popular participation in cultural, economic, and political programs created a new psychological atmosphere. Participants in this new wartime order were moved by a new creed, a humanitarian love of the peasant masses. This religion of the common man embraced the revolutionary ideal that modern technology and a new social organization could be used to remake and enrich the life of the peasant. This cult of the common people, the *lao-pai-hsing*, animated the cadres and the military forces. In order that the revolution might draw perpetual sustenance from the masses, the party worker was taught that he must live in the villages, work with the peasant, eat his food, lead his life, think his thoughts. Only thus could party cadres lead the peasant masses in their regeneration.

This almost spiritual concept of "liberation" became a dynamic element in the Communist movement, and by the inexorable logic of events became also the sanction for the new party dictatorship. The reasoning in this paradox proceeded on orthodox lines: (1) the revolution aimed to give the masses a new life, beginning with their economic betterment; (2) this betterment could be achieved only through the exercise of absolute political power, sufficient to change the old order; (3) political power could not be achieved by uncoördinated individuals but only through organization in a centralized party; (4) a party could be effective only if its members submitted to absolute party discipline — in party councils all might have a voice, but once the party decision was taken, all must obey it. By this logical progression the party took on the character of an ongoing, living entity with an historic mission, transcendent over individuals who expended themselves in its cause. With its alleged scientific foreknowledge of the historical process, it became (or rather, its leadership became) a law unto itself.

Coalition. When the CCP held its seventh congress in April–June 1945, the first since 1928, it perfected its strategy for the postwar period by adopting the flexible line of "coalition government." After the New Fourth Army incident of January 1941, when Nationalist troops had fought an 8-day battle with a CCP force as being out of bounds south of the Yangtze, the government had blockaded the CCP area more intensively (partly to prevent contact with Russia through Central Asia). Henceforth it had focused its attention as much on the Communists as on the Japanese, who in any event were plainly going to be dealt with by the United States. A general fear arose in China that World War II would be followed by civil war. Both Chungking and Yenan responded by promising to seek a "political" rather than military solution of their differences, and negotiations began early in 1943.

Building on his New Democracy line, Mao now declared that,

being still in the stage of "bourgeois-democratic revolution," China needed a "New Democratic government of a coalition nature embracing all parties and non-partisan representatives." Depending on expediency, this could mean a coalition including the KMT, as was to be proposed in 1946, or a coalition with minor parties and liberals against the KMT, as was to be achieved in 1949. Meanwhile this line appealed particularly to the modern-minded but frustrated intellectuals of Free China — professors, students, journalists, the literate and technically trained, who formed a basic resource for postwar reconstruction.

By war's end in 1945 the CCP had created a dynamic centrally-controlled movement in its own areas and exerted a great attraction upon intellectuals in Free China. Having done less of the fighting against Japan than the Nationalist Government and having avoided the burdens of city government and modern services, it was prepared to bid for power in the countryside. Only at this point did it become an immediate and inescapable problem for United States policy.

14

Our Traditional China Policy

OUR INHERITED IMPRESSION of the Chinese people, acquired during the century of the unequal treaties, had not prepared us for their succumbing to militant communism.

Before Pearl Harbor our folklore about the country, our early contact, our aspirations and even our actions in the creation of national policy, had all been a bit unrealistic — that is, we had been rather remarkably vocal about our interests in China, but they had never seemed like really vital interests. A curious gap had often emerged between the ideals we enunciated concerning China and the practices we followed there. This gap between word and deed reflected, no doubt, the gulf between American and Chinese ways and conditions.

In politics, for example, by our own revolutionary tradition we were conscientiously opposed to colonialism, suspicious of European machinations, a bit holier-than-they in our early abstention from empire and even from power-politics. Yet at the same time by demanding most-favored-nation treatment we were quick to enjoy all the semi-colonial fruits of extraterritoriality.

In daily life, even the most undistinguished American citizens — dead beats escaping their failures, remittance men sent abroad for their families' sake, stowaways and adventurers — once they disembarked at Shanghai had upper-class status thrust upon them. Like the Chinese gentry, they were set above the masses, not subject to local police coercion. Embarrassed at first to be pulled by a human horse in a ricksha, the average American soon accepted his superiority and found Oriental life and its inexpensive personal services enjoyable. Even the most egalitarian missionary had to compromise with Chinese hierarchic realities.

From this ambivalent experience, I suggest, emerged the sometimes startling contrast between the vigor of our verbal pronouncements and the limitations of our official actions. We would not abandon our ideals of national self-determination and individual freedom for the Chinese people, but somehow we could never get these values realized in fact. The ideals we treasured as part of our own culture; the facts were part of China's. They remained intractable.

1. THE AMERICAN APPROACH TO CHINA

Our folklore has included several types of images — exotic, idealized, disillusioned, sociological — which now seem in retrospect to have been less than adequate to picture Chinese realities.

The exotic approach used to emphasize cultural oddities — men's pigtails, women's bound feet, everyone's long fingernails, opium smoking, and other trappings of the pre-modern age. Reader interest in man-bites-dog items was satisfied by tidbits like "Chinese eat rats." The exotic approach also made much of all things "Chinesey" (an adjective denoting Westernized versions of things Chinese) like "Chinese chow," moon gates, and the cunning handicraft curios produced for the tourist trade. Emphasis was on dissimilarity. "Everything in China is opposite." The men wear gowns and the women trousers. They read from up to down and right to left. The soup comes last. Mourners wear white and brides red. The last name comes first. The compass points south. Left is the seat of honor, and so on. In more serious vein this school went in for literal translation of Chinese proper names, like the servant "Bald-the-third" in Nora Waln's inside view of a big family, *House of Exile.* Quips like "Confucius say" and "Damn clever, these Chinese" belong in this category, as well as the inscrutable Dr. Fu Manchu. Other sources of exoticism were the supposed Chinese indifference to suffering and the tradition of fiendish Oriental tortures, associated respectively with lower economic and lower political standards of living. The latter is echoed today in the mystery of Chinese Communist brainwashing, as though it were something we could not do, assuming we wanted to.

The idealized approach to China has had more substance. It includes our reverence for the wisdom of the East, which has been exhibited at appropriate times by characters like Charlie Chan and even more by the mellow type of Chinese gentleman whose "old roguishness" has been profitably described by Dr. Lin Yutang. In real life our penchant for idealization has been applied to such contrasting persons as Madame Chiang Kai-shek, on her famous grand tour of the United States in 1943, and the Communist guerrillas of the Eighth Route army, during the earlier stages of the anti-Japanese war — both of whom were assigned incredible virtues by the obvious predilections of the American public. Idealization of Chinese resistance against Japan, at a time when the United States was still supplying war materials to the latter, no doubt sprang from a guilty conscience; but other factors of American mass psychology have also entered into our periodic enthusiasms about China — our sympathy with the underdog, the missionary urge, the romantic escapism of *Lost Horizon,* to name but a few.

To the annoyance of Chinese officialdom, our excessive idealization has been punctuated by a recurrent mood of cynical disillusionment. The Rev. Arthur H. Smith in his *Chinese Characteristics* expressed the tolerant but sometimes acerbic frustration of nineteenth-century missionaries who found the Chinese villager impervious to progress and the gospel. Disillusionment has also stemmed from too close, and uncomprehending, a contact with a lower standard of living, especially when Americans who were not fundamentally interested in Chinese life came up against the sorry beggars and the greedy opportunists who inevitably flocked to them. Formerly this approach was epitomized in the "Shanghai mind" of the treaty port businessman, whose low view of Chinese character was summed up in the 1920's in Rodney Gilbert's *What's Wrong with China.* During World War II, this disillusionment was distilled in the GI hatred of Chinese filth and poverty ("Why can't they at least clean up this place?"), heightened by the scandalous rumors, lonely boredom, and complaints of wartime. Later the Chinese Communists' manufacture of the germ warfare charge and their treatment of American prisoners in Korea seemed to exemplify the super-evils produced by modern·totalitarianism in a backward country. The cold war has made our earlier mood of patronizing enthusiasm for a land of sturdy peasants and attractive students fade into the background.

The studious response to China has been part of our heritage ever since the publication a century ago of compendious works on

"China, her History, Commerce, Diplomacy, Laws, Institutions, Philosophy, etc.," of which the classic was S. Wells Williams' *The Middle Kingdom,* first published in 1848. This sociological approach, together with first-person narratives of field experience and the general increase of contact, became our chief avenues of understanding. With their blockage in recent years, there has developed, a bit late, a serious academic effort at interdisciplinary area study and linguistic training for research. Yet none of our ideas and attitudes about China can quite account for the facts of American policy there. Our diplomacy has had several other sources.

America in the British Empire. If we turn to the record of Sino-American relations, we will find that the milestones of our activity in China have a peculiar common element. In 1785 our trade began at Canton under the shadow of the British East India Company. In 1844 the first Sino-American treaty was peacefully negotiated, modeled on the British Treaty of Nanking for which the British had fought in 1840–1842. In 1899 we enunciated the doctrine of the Open Door for trade, which Englishmen had chiefly formulated.

Although after 1900 we stood for the territorial integrity of China, usually without any reliance upon British diplomacy, the fact remains that our traditional policy began as an inheritance from the British who, as a trading nation at a great distance, wished to preserve China as an open market. The contradictory idealistic and realistic elements in our China policy can be understood only if we remember that until the early 1920's our interests in China were junior to those of Britain, under whose leadership they had grown up. This allowed us the luxury of constantly denouncing British imperialism while steadily participating in its benefits.

The result was, I think, to encourage in our traditional policy a disconcerting split between humanitarian ideals and strategic realism. At times we have been almost preternaturally concerned about the fate of "China," meaning some cause or faction which we supported there with admirable righteousness. Yet we passed moral judgment more readily than we took action. Sometimes we seemed irresponsible. Our policy oscillated between involvement and abstention, action and inaction.

According to one eminent school of historians of American foreign policy, our "great aberration" as a people was the acquistion of the Philippines in 1898 and our increased activity in the Far East thereafter. It was followed by the successive "blunders" of the Open Door policy in 1899, Theodore Roosevelt's good offices in settling the Russo-Japanese War in 1905, and Secretary Knox's scheme for commercial "neutralization" of Manchuria in 1909.*

I do not agree that our China policy after 1898 was an aberration. I believe a closer look at the American position in China in the nineteenth century will indicate that we were already, as a people, partners with the British in our common day-to-day activities in the opening of the country. This is not apparent in the American archives. To a student of the American end of the record, American policy in China before John Hay is poorly documented and seems dull as dishwater. The scanty correspondence of our diplomats was chiefly enlivened by the anti-British fulminations of doughty and oratorical amateurs like Humphrey Marshall, American Commissioner in 1853. Mr. Marshall has been often quoted by students of the American record because he asserted our duty to support the Chinese Empire against British machinations. But he was there so briefly, knew so little of the facts, and had such inadequate assistance that his dispatches express an attitude rather than a policy. British imperialism in its commercial phase on the China coast was not particularly selfish or exclusive. British consuls and gunboats set up law and order in the treaty ports. We benefited accordingly. The real American policy in this early period was usually to acquiesce, sometimes querulously, in British policy.

Thus the British and French fought for the treaties which completed the opening of China in 1858 and 1860. We and the Russians got identical treaties without fighting. The underlying reality was manifest in 1859 when the British mission to exchange ratifications of the 1858 treaty was disastrously repulsed outside Tientsin: as soon as Commodore Tatnall of the American frigate *Powhatan,* bearing our peacefully inclined envoy, saw half the British gun-

---

* As Professor Bemis eloquently puts it: "If the expansionists of 1898 could have read the future as we can read the past, or if they had even taken the pains to study a few statistics of trade and investment demonstrative of the small stake which the United States had in the Far East compared with other parts of the world, or the problems of strategy involved, we are constrained to believe that they would not have embarked so precipitately upon the conspicuous but unprofitable and foolhardy venture into the world politics of Asia, so alien to American continental traditions and interests, so dangerous to the welfare of the United States." S. F. Bemis, *A Diplomatic History of the United States* (New York: 1942), pp. 501–502.

boats and landing force put out of action, he uttered his famous statement, "Blood is thicker than water!" and moved in to rescue some of his British cousins.

When Robert Hart, in building up the Chinese Imperial Maritime Customs Service, enlisted E. B. Drew of Cambridge, Massachusetts, and Drew in turn enlisted four members of the Harvard class of 1874 to go to China and superintend the foreign trade of the treaty ports, it had nothing to do with American policy. But it was private American participation in British policy, mediated through Manchu policy at Peking. American citizens became aberrant earlier than our diplomatic record indicates. If the year 1898 was our coming of age as an active power in the Far East, our youth had been spent there as a cousin of England.

The American Motive. The American concern about the Open Door in 1899 was the latest expression of a long-continued interest which had been manifest in commercial, missionary, diplomatic, and other channels for more than a century. Our interest in China was not confined to any one of these channels and it was not, fundamentally, a calculated interest. Our traditional China policy resulted partly from attitudes of mind created in us by our westward expansion across the open spaces of the American continent. Long before the continent had been crossed, Americans had begun to move into the open spaces of the Pacific. In the whaling industry, in the fur trade on the Northwest coast, and in the trade of New England clipper ships with Canton, Manila, Singapore, Batavia, and other Far Eastern emporia we found continued scope for American enterprise in the first half of the nineteenth century. In the 1890's after the passing of the frontier at home, we established a new theoretical frontier in the Open Door doctrine in China; we were continuing the same process.

The American frontier in Asia was very different from that of the Great Plains: instead of open spaces and natural resources, we found Cathay. This new and strange type of human society aroused our curiosity and eventually our sympathy quite as much as our greed or avarice. Toward it we proceeded to apply attitudes developed at home. These were expansive, adventurous, and acquisitive. They included conceptions of progress, growth, and improvement as the law of life. The American merchant in Shanghai spoke of the beneficent and civilizing role of commerce, the missionary of saving the heathen from their state of sin, and the politician of manifest destiny. All these different formulations, in the words of various professional groups, reflected a single though complex social phenomenon, an expansion of the American people which was not solely economic, religious, or nationalist, but a combination of all of them.

Since our own great-grandfathers participated in this expansion, these points need not be labored. The thing to note is that American activity in Asia from the very first followed an American pattern of individualism. Instead of the joint-stock trading companies with their armed fleets and semi-official merchant-administrators who had conducted the European expansion in the age of mercantilism, the early New Englanders went as commercial adventurers, a few boys and men in one tiny ship at a time. They took with them the peculiar philosophy of the young American nation — an eye for profit, innovation, and invention; concern for the moral worth and salvation of the individual; energy and self-confidence.

Beginning with Peter Parker's celebrated eye-hospital in Canton in the 1830's, American missionaries soon rivalled the British in numbers and in resources, decades before the American merchant caught up with his British counterpart. Missionary constituencies have been the seed bed of our humanitarianism toward China, a sentiment that has always affected and sometimes almost dominated our policy.

Fluctuations of Policy. Allied to this generosity has been our egalitarian, and sometimes patronizing, concern for the underdog. In 1894 when China was still a vast archaic empire and Japan an up-and-coming pupil of the West, American opinion favored Japan in her war against China. (Needless to say, the Peking propaganda today that "American capitalist imperialism instigated Japan's attack" is quite untrue.) American opinion, on the same underdog principle, also favored Japan against Russia in 1904. It began to turn against Japan after 1905 only when Japan gave promise of being top dog in the Far East. In the present generation American opinion has supported the valiant but ill-equipped efforts of Chinese patriots to withstand Japanese aggression. This sentiment was particularly evident in the American support of Chiang Kai-shek during the early war years. Yet the same sentiment operated in favor of the Chinese Communists when they represented a minority cause among the peasantry, struggling against the weight of Chiang's legions. Our concern for the underdog has led us to shift our emotional support from one contestant to another depending on the apparent justice of their cause and the circumstances of their relative strength. It may be doubted whether the Japanese or Chiang Kai-shek or the Chinese Communists have changed as greatly as American opinion concerning them has changed.

The moral righteousness which for so long has distinguished American Far Eastern policy was remarkable for its omission of any idea that war is a practical tool of policy. We were ready to pronounce vigorous moral judgments condemning Japanese aggression at the same time that we refused absolutely to contemplate going to war in support of our moral and diplomatic position. This resulted in anomalous situations, as when the Stimson doctrine of 1931 upheld our honor by refusing to recognize "Manchukuo," while we still sold war supplies to Japan. Perhaps this gap between ethical judgment and practical action came from our feeling of isolation from Europe. Having no major powers on our borders, we did not live under the threat of war nor frame our foreign policy to include war as one of its alternatives. Consequently our policy statements, which from other powers would be fighting words, were often for the moral and legal record only.

This tradition that peace is our policy in Asia and that war cannot serve it, was confirmed during the nineteenth century by the fact already noted, that Britain did our fighting for us. It was this British leadership in setting up and maintaining a commercial empire open to all traders in Asia which allowed American policy to develop ideally rather than realistically. We seldom acknowledged that our first century or more of access to China rested in part upon American enterprise and philanthropy and in part upon the harsher facts of British imperial control and exploitation, which we considered an evil thing.

The long-term fluctuations in our interest in Asia have been a function of many complex factors in American life, including the fact that we were never as dependent as Britain upon our overseas trade. We were late-comers at Canton and even later in California. Both the Spanish and for a time the Russians were on the Pacific coast ahead of us. (One incentive to the Monroe Doctrine of 1823 was the Russian ukase of 1821 which declared the Pacific coast from 51 degrees northward to be a Russian preserve.)

After our efforts in the period 1818–1824 had given us a continental position stretching to the Pacific, our diplomats remained profoundly uninterested in transpacific expansion. Repeated plans and proposals by Americans in the Orient left the American home government unmoved. In Formosa, Americans from Canton explored the island, built a port, raised the American flag, loaded some 78 vessels with cargoes worth half a million dollars, and got the American commissioner to China to advocate annexation. The American government did not even reply to the proposal.

Even after the Mexican War, the California gold rush, and Perry's opening of Japan, the American westward expansion of the forties and fifties was followed by another period of apathy. When the Russians in the 1860's decided to sell Alaska as indefensible in war and unprofitable in peace, Secretary Seward had great difficulty in getting Congressional approval. The area for which he was paying about two cents an acre was denounced as "an inhospitable, wretched and God-forsaken region worth nothing." The House of Representatives passed the appropriation bill only after nine months' delay and after the Russian Minister had paid out thousands of dollars in bribes.

2. THE EVOLUTION OF THE OPEN DOOR DOCTRINE

In the circumstances of 1899 John Hay's notes take on a significance quite different from the tradition of benevolence toward China which later became associated with them. The Open Door must be viewed in connection both with our expansion in 1898 and 1899 in Hawaii, Samoa, and the Philippines and with the contemporary British predicament in China.

In July 1898 Congress annexed Hawaii. In December the treaty with Spain gave us Puerto Rico, Guam, and the Philippines. In December 1899 a tripartite treaty awarded us part of Samoa. These acquisitions in the few months preceding and following the Open Door notes of September 1899 outstripped those of the other powers in the Pacific. While the Germans were securing a naval base at Kiaochow in Shantung and the Russians at Port Arthur, we got potential bases in Hawaii, Samoa, and the Philippines. Similarly while the European powers were seeking spheres of interest for commercial exploitation in China, we annexed an Asian archipelago. This American expansion is all the more significant because it was so largely unpremeditated in the public mind.

Britain's original interest in the Open Door is clearly visible in the trade statistics. In 1898 British shipping carried two-thirds of the tonnage in China's ports and paid two-thirds of the customs revenue. To defend this commercial empire against imperialist encroachment by other powers Britain followed at first a policy of taking compensation. In the great-power rivalry which set in after China's disastrous defeat by Japan in 1895, Britain got in on two of the three big foreign loans and secured two leased territories (Weihaiwei and Kowloon) and by far the greatest mileage of railroad concessions. But no amount of success in a partition of China could benefit British interests when they already dominated the trade of the whole country. Concessions and spheres could only reduce her area of trade.

By early 1898 the Russians had given no promise that they would not establish preferential rates for their trade in Manchuria, and the British had failed to secure all that they desired in the Yangtze valley. They therefore considered again the traditional idea of preserving an Open Door for trade in China by the "collective influence of the trading nations." This idea was broached in the House of Commons early in 1898. The Foreign Secretary proposed it to John Hay, then our Minister in London. But the British after March 1898 reverted to their more concrete program of building up a Yangtze sphere and generally keeping up with imperialism.

Hay as Secretary of State asked W. W. Rockhill, in August 1899, to draft a memorandum on the Open Door. Rockhill had studied Chinese affairs and had definite views of his own. He also got the advice of a British Commissioner of Chinese Maritime Customs, Alfred E. Hippisley, a friend who had recently come from China on leave and had a first-hand acquaintance with the problem. Hippisley had been one of the closest co-workers and assistants of Robert Hart — so much so that when Hart thought of retiring from the Inspector Generalship of the Customs in 1896, Hippisley was then his probable successor. Robert Hart's amazing career has not yet been thoroughly studied. He was at this time the chief proponent of equal taxation of, and commercial opportunity for, the trade of all nations in China. His policy differed from that of the British Foreign Office.

Following Hart's general views, the Open Door notes of September 1899 made no reference to the integrity of China and interposed no bar to the extension of spheres of influence. The notes were primarily concerned with the customs problem. After proposing, first, that each power not interfere with the vested interests of other powers within its sphere, the notes then proposed, second, that only the Chinese government should collect customs duties, and only according to the Chinese treaty tariff, and, third, that no preferential harbor dues or railroad charges should benefit the subjects of a power having a sphere. It was not until Russia had begun to occupy Manchuria as a consequence of the Boxer Rebellion that Hay's supplementary notes of July 1900 raised the question of the integrity of China. In its origin the Open Door was intended to preserve foreign trade in China, not the Chinese state. In 1898 it was called for specifically by American business groups, but very soon it began to represent a good deal more than an economic interest.

The Integrity of China. The Open Door began as a political, not a legal, doctrine. It was expressed in the form of policy statements and in bilateral treaties on many occasions after 1900, but it was not until 1922 that it was stated in a legal form binding on all parties. The doctrine itself underwent growth and expansion. The second set of notes of July 1900 was much more positive, and supported Chinese "territorial and administrative entity," a phrase later supplanted by "territorial and administrative integrity." This reflected the fact that Russia had moved very rapidly into Manchuria, contrary to the interest of most of the powers. Here we can see clearly an interest, on the part of the United States as a humanitarian and a trading power, in keeping Chinese people and territory out of Russian hands. This is a long-term motive which still contributes to our China policy. It is a consideration arising from a good deal more than economic motives — from great power rivalry as much as from ideological conflict, also from a friendly and philanthropic sympathy.

Thus by 1900 Hay had developed his doctrine actually to the point of attacking any extension of spheres of influence. The Anglo-Japanese alliance of 1902 introduced the phrase "equal opportunity." This was entirely in keeping with the British conception of the Open Door for trade. In later statements, however, "equal opportunity" was applied to "cultural" activities as well as commercial, and was also made to embrace the idea of freedom of "movement."

By 1938 American policy statements were regularly including the phrases "free competition" and "fair treatment."

In this way the Open Door doctrine developed two main tenets: the integrity of China, and the equal treatment of all foreigners there. The latter tenet suited Chinese tradition. The Emperor had always sought to demonstrate his universal superiority and benevolence by granting favors to all barbarians equally. In twentieth-century diplomacy, however, China having become only one nation among others, the Chinese have tended to stress the idea of integrity, while the barbarians have stressed the idea of equal treatment.

Viewed cynically, the doctrine of China's integrity was a device to prevent other powers, for example, Russia, from taking over areas of China and excluding us from them. But the independence of China has also appealed to Americans as a matter of political justice. Until recently it fitted the doctrine of the self-determination and sovereignty of weaker nations, which constitutes one of our major political sentiments.

The nonrecognition doctrine of Bryan in 1915 and Stimson in 1931, by which we refused to recognize any Japanese impairment of China's integrity, was a corollary of the integrity idea itself. As a doctrine, nonrecognition proved as unavailing as our other invocations of righteousness. In the later stages of Japan's aggression during the 1930's, Secretary Hull emphasized another aspect of the same idea, nonintervention. This became one of the chief moral thunderbolts he hurled so unavailingly at the Japanese. Today the Open Door and its attendant doctrines have chiefly historical interest, yet a certain residue from them remains in our policy.

Collective Action. After World War I the United States sought to carry out its policy toward China through collective action. This was in marked contrast to our Latin-American policy, in which we interpreted the Monroe Doctrine in such a way as to forbid a collective approach by the United States and European powers. It also contrasted with our European policy, in which we stayed out of the League and so in effect left Europe's problems to the British and French. Only in the Far East did we take the lead in action through the concert of powers.

The legal basis for our collective action in the Far East was established by the Washington Conference of 1921–22, particularly in the Nine Power Treaty concerning China. This was a codification of the Open Door doctrine in expanded form. In 1928 collective action was buttressed on paper by the Kellogg-Briand Pact. The United States also joined collective action against Japan, to no avail, by associating an American representative with the League of Nations (Lytton) commission which fruitlessly investigated Japan's seizure of Manchuria in 1931. During the 1930's the foreign policy of Stimson and Hull generally followed the line of collective or at least parallel action as the best hope of mobilizing diplomatic pressure to stop Japan. This approach was a second-best and ineffective alternative at a time of isolationism, when it seemed impossible to mobilize unilateral American economic or military activity.

After World War II the United Nations became another vehicle for collective action against aggression and we joined with it actively to repel the North Korean attack on the Republic of Korea in June 1950 and the Chinese intervention which followed. A similar UN basis for the defense of Formosa has, however, not as yet been achieved.

Our Economic Interest. It is a truism that the American commercial interest in China has had a large admixture of imagination and hope. Actually our financial investments in China and Japan in the 1930's were about equal. American investments in China, chiefly direct investments, were less than a quarter of a billion United States dollars, while our investments in Japan, chiefly in Japanese bonds, were also something less than a quarter of a billion. In fact, our entire investment in the Far East was only about three-quarters of a billion. Our Far Eastern investments all together were only 5 or 6 per cent of the total American investment abroad.

Moreover, our financial investment in China was a very small part indeed of the total foreign stake in China, a good deal less than one-tenth. British and Japanese investments were each over a billion dollars, while ours were barely one-fifth of the British. Two-thirds of our financial interest was concentrated in Shanghai.

If we turn to foreign trade the figures are no more encouraging to the theory of economic determinism as the sole source of our policy. In the 1930's Japan took between 8 and 9 percent of our total foreign trade, while China accounted for less than half that amount (this was counting Manchuria as still part of China). It is true, however, that our trade with China, although it was less than half our trade with Japan, was carried to a greater degree in American vessels and was steadily increasing, until by 1936 the United States had begun to take the largest single share of China's foreign trade. While Japan's trade with Manchuria naturally expanded, her trade with China proper declined during the 1930's. In this way we seemed to be getting ahead of Japan commercially in China. But this minor factor in the general situation must be bracketed with the fact that Japan's large foreign trade was conducted one-third with the United States, while of all our Far Eastern trade two-fifths was with Japan and only about one-fifth was with China.

Our missionary investment in China represented about 40 million dollars in terms of money but obviously a great deal more in terms of sentiment. However we approach the problem, dollars and cents, even in the minds of businessmen, have not been an all-compelling factor in our China policy.

Recognition of Nanking. The operation of sentiment rather than dollar diplomacy in the State Department has been documented by Dr. Dorothy Borg's study of the period 1925–1928. She makes it plain that Secretary Kellogg based his China policy on a "simple almost instinctive reaction" typical of the general American attitude toward China in the 1920's. He wished to get rid of the unequal treaties and make China fully independent as soon as possible. He wanted to remain neutral among factions within China and refused to be obsessed by the Bolshevik menace there. He steadfastly refused to apply sanctions after the incident in which Americans were attacked at Nanking in 1927. On the other hand he was equally determined to deal only with a Chinese government that represented a unified country. He did not want to facilitate in any way a division of China into two parts.

The historical record brings out many incidents and attitudes of thirty years ago which are worth pondering. The vigor of the anti-foreign feeling in China in 1925 was sudden and unexpected. It caught the treaty powers as well as the missionaries by surprise. The Shanghai business community became convinced very soon that this Chinese anti-foreignism was a Moscow plot. Many voices were raised advocating intervention to save China from Soviet domination. Secretary Kellogg and his chief assistant, Nelson Johnson, refused to be stampeded by this hysteria.

Chiang Kai-shek's turn to the right in 1927 was not a price that he had to pay for American recognition. There is no evidence of a deliberate American effort to back the right wing of the Kuomintang against the left wing and the Communists. Chinese politics did not seem quite so simple. During the latter part of 1927, when Chiang was in retirement, the continued existence of the Nanking Government was by no means assured. Its effort to suppress the Communists was at its height. Presumably this would have been the time for an active American effort to support reaction in the interest of trade. But the American diplomats were chiefly concerned with settlement of the Nanking incident (which was not settled until March 1928, a year after its occurence). Meanwhile Secretary Kellogg's offer to revise the unequal treaties had been made in January 1927, in order to catch up with the British Christmas Day offer of 1926. This gesture was, of course, *before* the Communist-Kuomintang split; the new Sino-American tariff treaty, which carried out Kellogg's offer and recognized Chiang's government, was not signed until July 1928, a year *after* the Communist-Kuomintang split.

American Aid. Aid to China was for long a private matter for the attention of the missionary profession, the public organs concerned with famine or flood relief, agencies like the Rockefeller Foundation interested in educational and medical development, and other groups and individuals. By the remission of part of the Boxer indemnity in 1908, the remainder in 1924, and similar gestures, the United States Government began to take a hand in the process of helping China remake herself.

In 1934 Washington inaugurated, primarily for domestic reasons, a silver purchase program which soon began to dislocate and depress the Chinese economy. It led to vast amounts of silver being smuggled out of China, which had to leave the silver standard and adopt a managed paper currency in 1935. Subsequently, however, the Treasury under Secretary Morgenthau was able to make the silver purchase program of direct though unpublicized aid to the Nationalist Government by paying it gold or US dollars for 500 million ounces of silver. In 1937–1939, for example, we paid 184 million dollars on this account.

With World War II official aid to China became the dominant form of American assistance. Beginning with loans in the months before Pearl Harbor and the clandestine development of Col. C. L. Chennault's "Flying Tigers" (American Volunteer Group) as an air force in Burma and Yunnan, we embarked in 1942 upon a continuing government program of financial, material, and technical aid.

This was a milestone, if not indeed a grave-marker, in our relations with the Chinese people. Before this, American aid had been from person to person, group to group, small-scale but persistent, maintaining institutions or helping movements but never supporting governments. Now our aid was official as well as massive. It could go only to the recognized government of the country, which was well aware of its right to be the sole channel. Unfortunately our ally the Nationalist Government was by 1942 already well advanced in that process of decline noted in a previous chapter. Our aid could not remake its inner nature but served merely to make it less dependent on domestic opinion and more inclined eventually to rely upon its new armaments made in USA. In fighting Japan we had no recourse, in conscience or in reality, but to support the government of Chiang Kai-shek. Not the intent of our aid but the method seems imperfect, in the light of another fifteen years' experience in aiding foreign allies. Our half-billion-dollar morale-booster of early 1942, for example, was given with no strings attached. We never learned exactly who used it, for what purposes. No country program was set up by treaty, calling for bilateral actions in planned phases. From the beginning of our wartime alliance, American officials found themselves dealing with an ineffective administration, too debilitated by its domestic problems to respond to foreign stimuli. Trying to aid it, we became entangled in its decline and fall.

The United States Government finally found itself, almost involuntarily, playing a major role in China's domestic politics. This had never been part of our traditional policy.

15

United States Policy
and the Nationalist Collapse

MY VIEW OF THIS controversial question is that the
American capacity to influence the Chinese scene in the 1940's
has been exaggerated. I do not believe that a sub-continent of half
a billion or more people, still largely imbedded in their own immemorial culture, inaccessible for the most part except by footpath
or sampan, can be controlled from outside. It is noteworthy that
the Chinese Communist Party, created expressly as a tool for foreign influence, followed the guidance of the Comintern in the
1920's only to disaster. It began its rise to power only after its alien
creed had been adapted and Sinicized under Mao Tse-tung.

The outcome in 1949 showed, not that Soviet aid had been
greater than American, but that the Chinese Communists had been
able to mobilize and utilize the potentialities of revolution while
the Nationalists had not. The Communist victory also showed that
over a period of thirty years the American influence on China had
not contributed to the organization of political power in an American fashion as effectively as the Soviet influence had contributed to
its organization in a Soviet fashion. We had no Comintern. Behind
our lack of a conspiratorial revolutionary apparatus lay the more
general lack of any philosophy or method for forced-draft economic
development and political collectivism. Considering the suffering
that rapid modernization of any sort was bound to bring upon the
Chinese people, we need not entirely regret our inability to be
China's model for the brutal task of remaking and industrializing
her ancient society in the shortest possible time.

My answer to the imponderable question, Could we have saved
China from Communism? is: Not without an utterly different

approach prior to 1944; not at all thereafter. By the time we began to try, it was already too late.

Now historians have a weakness for accepting what happened as inevitable in the context of "social trends and forces" alleged and abstracted after the fact. This annoys men of action, who are conscious of the random elements of chance and personality in history. The only way to appraise the American role in the Fall (or Liberation) of China is to study the official record in the State Department archives, as Herbert Feis has done so ably in his book, *The China Tangle,* and to try to relate it, as no one yet can do, to the experience of the Chinese people in the same period.

War's Frustrations. Japan's Pacific War after December 7, 1941, soon intensified Chunking's frustration: Chiang Kai-shek failed to get a coordinated allied strategy centered around himself. Britain failed to hold Singapore or the Burma Road. General Stilwell had hardly arrived to be Chiang's chief of staff when he was given the hopeless task of defending Burma. Burma fell, with much Anglo-Chinese-American recrimination, and he then set himself the grueling three-year task of reopening a land route to China across the North Burma jungle. Yet even after it and its accompanying pipeline were opened in early 1945, the incredible Hump airlift still carried more tonnage. Again, our 20th Bomber Command got five big airfields built near Chengtu in Szechwan, of rock crushed by Chinese corvée labor. Supplying their B-29s took more Hump tonnage in 1944 than was allocated to the Chinese armies. But they had hardly begun to bomb Japan before their base was shifted to the Marianas, supplied by sea and nearer Tokyo. Entering the war as the prospective allied base for defeating Japan, Free China found that job done by naval-air-power at sea and herself cut off, a low-priority sideshow. The American aim became merely to keep Free China in the war. The result was not defeat but neither was it victory.

These frustrations of warfare should not surprise us, in an era when we have bloodily extirpated Fascism only to be confronted by Communism. But many felt that the frustration rate in the China-Burma-India Theater was preternaturally high.

Chinese nationalism continued to suffer frustration after Japan's defeat. Well before Pearl Harbor, in May 1941, we had offered to abandon extraterritoriality as soon as peace should come in China.

In October 1942 we offered to negotiate immediately, and a new Sino-American treaty on equal terms was signed January 11, 1943. But within five months another agreement was made, freeing American troops in China from Chinese criminal jurisdiction. American bases, supply and transport services, radio networks, air-lines and army post offices were soon operating on Chinese soil in greater volume and with greater license than Southwest China had ever seen under the unequal treaties. At war's end Shanghai streets for many months were filled with GI's and roistering sailors far beyond the memory of treaty-port days. This ill suited China's new great-power status. China's new-found sovereignty took on a quizzi-cal character. Right-wing chauvinists, Communists, and patriotic liberals could unite in inveighing against GI incidents connected with wine, women, and jeeps.

1. AMERICAN AID AND MEDIATION

Our Wartime China Policy. From late 1943 American diplomats began to glimpse the inherent danger in KMT-CCP rivalry — "civil war at some undetermined future date," which might hamstring the war effort and eventually let Russia back the Communists. The Americans aimed therefore (1) to avert civil war by encouraging a political settlement, which Chiang Kai-shek advocated as early as September 1943, and (2) to strengthen the Nationalist Government position, partly by building up its armies, partly by getting it to reform itself. Armies were built up but reform proved impossible, for reasons already indicated. The idea of a political settlement, however, was accepted by all parties at least verbally. KMT-CCP negotiations had been resumed early in 1943. American policy pro-ceeded on three levels.

First, on the international stage we tried to make China a great power in form if not in substance. She was permanently excluded from the high command of the war at the Anglo-American con-ference at Quebec in August 1943, but was included along with the Soviet Union in the Moscow Declaration of great-power princi-ples in October. The Anglo-American-Chinese Cairo Declaration of December 1943 promised to return to China all territories lost to Japan, and Roosevelt at the Teheran conference stood firm for China's great-power status on the future UN Security Council. But this conferring of great-power status on the Nationalist Government was an American accomplishment, not Chinese or, least of all, British or Soviet. It was seen at the time as a fine and friendly gesture toward a great and deserving people. History, however, may view it with disillusion as a doctrinaire effort at trans-pacific master-minding of Chinese history, trying with words from abroad to strengthen a regime already in decline at home. (Peking of course now calls it simply an imperialist plot.)

Second, our idealistic support of Chungking's international prestige accompanied a realistic military effort, which produced a modern-ized Nationalist army and airforce. Stilwell's successor, General Albert C. Wedemeyer, with a thousand American instructors and advisors, carried on the training and equipping of 39 divisions.

Third, we tried to heal the KMT-CCP breach. The U. S. Army's single-minded concern for defeating Japan led it to question the efficacy of having 200 to 400 thousand Nationalist troops blockade the Communist area. In June 1944 Vice-President Wallace visited Chungking to suggest that Nationalist and Communist forces both fight Japan rather than watch each other. He got Chiang to let an American Military Observer Mission stay in Yenan, whither West-ern journalists had already been admitted in May. This opened an interesting window on the Communist scene but it remained ap-parent that Chungking and Yenan were each more concerned about the other than about Japan. Japanese forces meanwhile by late 1944 had pushed south through the Hunan rice-bowl and west from Canton to seize the major Sino-American base at Kweilin. During this crisis Chiang had held out against Stilwell's appointment to over-all command in China, and forced his recall in October; he also held out against the projected arming and use of Communist forces in a unified Chinese war effort. Unity and reform both remained remote hopes, but Ambassador Patrick J. Hurley, with more bravado than finesse, continued to encourage a Nationalist-Communist *rapprochement*.

At Yalta in February 1945 Roosevelt tried to secure Stalin's future support of the Nationalist Government as the price of Rus-sia's recovery of the Tsarist position in northeast Asia. This was made known to Chiang, whose concurrence we had promised to obtain, only in June; and ratified in a Sino-Soviet treaty only as Japan surrendered, on August 14. By that date Russia was already in possession of Manchuria.

Behind all the infinitely detailed complexities of this story looms a basic fact: the Soviet Union and the Chinese Communists had the military capability to expand into Manchuria and parts of North China, respectively, and they could hardly have been controlled merely by a token show of force. Soon the Communists were further strengthened with surrendered Japanese arms which they got through Soviet connivance in Manchuria.

With peace came a great American air-and-sea lift of half a million Nationalist forces back to the coastal centers, a Communist race overland to expand by taking Japanese surrenders in North China, and American repatriation of 1,200,000 enemy troops to Japan. Even as the United States began to relax and demobilize, the long foreseen civil war began in the rivalry over the occupied areas. This was a moment when the American people were least prepared, emotionally and intellectually, to face a Chinese crisis. We had no intention in the winter of 1945–46 of fighting another war in East Asia.

General Marshall's Mediation. It was against this background that George C. Marshall went to Chungking in December 1945. His first months there were a hopeful chapter of American diplomacy. His aim was a political settlement of the burgeoning civil war. The only statesmanlike alternative to internecine warfare was to get the Chinese Communists into the political and military framework of a constitutional regime, in a position similar to that of Communist parties in Western Europe. The two contending parties would both be represented in a reorganized coalition government under Chiang; their armies would be merged and reduced, whereupon American aid would be forthcoming. In January 1946 the Political Consultative Conference in Chungking reached a political agreement. A cease-fire order was issued by both armies. In February a military merger was agreed to. Meanwhile an unprecedented tripartite agency, the Executive Headquarters, was set up in the modern halls of the Rockefeller hospital in Peiping to superintend the quelling of a subcontinental civil war. American planes took jeeps, radios, supplies, and truce teams, composed usually of an American colonel with Nationalist and Communist generals, to far-flung inaccessible spots where fighting was in progress. Fighting practically stopped.

This breath-taking achievement was a personal tribute to General Marshall. It involved a strenuous effort to remain neutral in China's internal political process, and simultaneously to uphold the supremacy of the recognized government without being used by it. The truce collapsed principally in Manchuria, which still remained beyond the effective cease-fire limits. Behind the renewal of civil war in 1946 lay an intransigent Nationalist confidence in their superior armament, a shrewd Communist calculation of the Nationalists' actual vulnerability, and also, I think, the Russians' determination to embark upon a cold war of force and fraud against their erstwhile allies. While Stalin showed little confidence in the Chinese Communists' being soon victorious over the Nationalists, his cold war with the West gave them stimulus and opportunity to bid for power.

Stated conversely, one main background factor was the aversion of the American people in 1945-46 to use their armed power in continued warfare if necessary to secure and maintain a satisfactory peace settlement. On the contrary, we had only a vague idea of the kind of peace we wanted in East Asia. Like any postwar democracy, we were intent on demobilization and normalcy. Our China policy-makers were confined within this sincere but disastrously inhibiting framework of assumptions.

Might the American mediation, after all, have been successful? In the unfolding of history it is hard to prove a might-have-been: neither Chinese party trusted the other, nor was ready to give up its hope of eventual country-wide control. They had rival armies and organizations, and bitter memories of two decades of killing and being killed. In its historical context, a more irrepressible conflict can hardly be imagined. In the long view it is easy to conclude that Marshall's effort was a forlorn hope.

Yet the Chinese people wanted peace, the United States had enormous prestige and power to bring to bear upon the scene, the Communists stood to gain from the agreements, the Kuomintang was heavily dependent upon us. Not the least of our problems was how to get a party dictatorship to pursue democratic reforms in order to head off a revolution. Actually we had a divided objective: to press the Kuomintang leaders into reform which would diminish their autocratic power and facilitate internal peace; at the same time to strengthen the Kuomintang-controlled regime as a step toward political stability in East Asia. We became involved in continuing to build the Kuomintang dictatorship up materially at the same time that we tried to get it to tear itself down politically. But we could not control Chiang and his generals, who preferred to do things their way. They relied on their new arms.

After General Marshall became secretary of state in 1947 and we checked Communist expansion with the Greek-Turkish aid program, some felt that we should have saved China in the same way. China was roughly 45 times bigger than Greece in territory and 85 times in population. To treat China like Greece might have required millions of American troops and billions of dollars and even so would probably have been a failure. General Marshall, of all people, best knew the magnitude of such a task. We had no alternative after 1947 but to abstain from intervention in the Chinese civil war. Whether we should have given greater aid to the Nationalists in this period has been much disputed. Responsible American generals say there was no lack of arms. Many disputants have overlooked the severe limitations of our capacity to affect the outcome by means of material aid from outside.

2. THE NATIONALIST DEBACLE

From 1946 to 1949 China saw one of the big wars of modern times. Nationalist forces totaled at the beginning about three million men, the Communists about one million. United States aid to China between V-J Day and early 1948 cost over two billion dollars, in addition to some billion and a half committed during World War II. By sheer weight of arms Nationalist forces spread out to major cities and, when eventually permitted by Russia, into Manchuria. An infinitude of factors undid them: the military under Chiang were out of civilian control, their postwar reorganization heightened the confusion, the sessile Whampoa clique discriminated against provincial commanders and armies, particularly those of Kwangsi. Their strategic doctrine was to hold strong positions defensively, their instinct was to hoard supplies and wait for others to move first, their field tactics were sometimes masterminded by the Generalissimo from a great distance. Corruption, demoralization, and desertion steadily depleted the Nationalist armies. The Communists pursued opposite tactics, maneuvering in the countryside, recruiting among the populace, destroying railroads, avoiding unfavorable terms of battle. They grew in numbers and armament, both from the Japanese Manchurian stocks already noted and from Nationalist defections, sales, and surrenders. By June 1948 they were roughly equal in numbers of men, rifles, and cannon. Late in 1947 they had cut off the Manchurian garrisons. In October 1948 they forced their surrender — a third of a million men. This set the stage for a showdown.

The balance of power had not shifted only at the front, where the Communists steadily built up their stock of American guns and supplies. The Nationalist cause had also been degutted in the rear, in its city bases, by an economic collapse indexed by inflation.

Bombing by an enemy, like flood, fire, earthquake, or other disasters of nature, though destructive, tends to increase public morale and community effort in the face of a common danger. Hyperinflation, on the other hand, impoverishes and demoralizes each salaried individual as it gradually destroys the regime's fiscal capacity and public confidence in it. Life under hyperinflation is a slow strangulation. Salaries and wages never keep up. Furniture, books, and clothing go for food. Gradual malnutrition produces skin diseases, stomach ailments, tuberculosis. The whole society sickens, and the responsibility is put on those in power. Nationalist military collapse when it came was headlined in America, the ten-year hyperinflation which preceded it was not.

Free China's price level had risen only moderately in 1937-1939. The Nationalist currency still circulated over the whole country; Japanese-puppet note issues began at Peking only in 1938 and at Nanking only in 1939. Thereafter the Japanese mounted a campaign to undermine Free China's price stability, and meanwhile Chungking steadily increased its expenditures, with income lagging far behind outlay. In 1941, when revenues provided only 15 per cent of expenditures, the Central Government finally took over the land tax in kind. Income from it and from government monopolies and indirect taxes still provided, temporarily, only 30 per cent of the budget. Government taxes, domestic loans, gold sales and bond drives proved ineffective in mopping up the public's excess purchasing power. The situation steadily deteriorated, prices doubling every few months or weeks. In September 1945 the volume of note issue was 465 times that of July 1937.

The end of World War II gave a brief respite as the Nationalist currency spread back over all China, but large government expenditures continued, to say nothing of the buying spree by civilians returning to the coastal cities. Hyperinflation was resumed. Prices doubled 67 times in the two and one-half years from January 1946 to August 1948. Counting on its military superiority to end the civil war quickly, Nanking let its foreign exchange reserve be gradually reduced to pay for consumer imports and industrial raw materials. Foreign exchange was at first not seriously rationed nor imports restricted, and so capital fled the country. Meanwhile the domestic currency began to be replaced by foreign dollars and gold.

In order to break the vicious circle a "currency reform" in August 1948 demonetized the old currency and replaced it by the "gold yuan." At the same time price ceilings were set and enforced by police methods, and private holdings of specie and foreign currencies were forcibly converted to the new currency, while new note issue still continued to finance the civil war. Thus the few resources remaining to the most anti-Communist element, the urban upper middle class, were tied to the "gold yuan"; when it collapsed in late 1948 (prices finally rose 85,000 times in six months), the last remnant of civilian support for the Nationalist cause went with it.

The great two-month-long battle of the Huai-Hai was fought in the old Nien area of the Huai River basin, south of the Lunghai Railway, 100 miles or so north of Nanking. Generalissimo Chiang against the best advice of his staff committed some 50 divisions, out of 200 still remaining, to form a strongpoint on the plains around Hsuchow. He himself from Nanking directed their tactical movements down to the division level in battle. The Communists, however, not only controlled the villages but by reactivating the railways as they advanced were able to deploy large forces. By mid-November four Nationalist army groups, about 340,000 men, had been quickly cut off and encircled on the plain around Hsuchow. A relief force of 120,000 troops, including the best American-trained divisions, was similarly blocked and encircled south of there. When the Hsuchow armies broke out to effect a junction, taking along their American trucks and cannon and the armored corps of tanks, this "mobile fortress" was blocked in turn by deep trenches and soon ripped by American-made Nationalist-surrendered heavy artillery. By late December the 130,000 surviving Nationalist forces, out of 66 divisions committed, were squeezed into six square miles, surrounded by 300,000 Reds. They learned that Nanking proposed to destroy their treasured heavy equipment "by air bombardment — *in situ,*" as Edmund Clubb (our last consul-general in Peiping) puts it; they surrendered on January 10, 1949. Of 550,000 Nationalists lost, the Communists claimed 327,000 surrendered.*

Typical of the entire Nationalist fiasco were Chiang Kai-shek's unwise decision to fight on the Hsuchow plain instead of the Huai River and his refusal to give command to the Kwangsi general, Pai Ch'ung-hsi, an able tactician who knew the terrain. Jealous non-cooperation among the Whampoa commanders, nonuse of Nanking's monopoly of the air, inability to bring their American-made firepower to bear upon the enemy, every aspect of this great defeat underlines the old adage that armament alone cannot bring victory. Tientsin and Peking surrendered in January 1949. In April the Communists crossed the Yangtze, in May they entered Shanghai, in October Canton, in November Chungking.

The Nationalist debacle had been not only military but also economic, political, and moral. The chaos, disorders and dangers of 1948–49 turned city dwellers irrevocably against the Nationalist Government and therefore against American aid to it. Having backed that government increasingly since 1937, we could not in the Chinese view divest ourselves of responsibility for its evils even though our aid had been well-intended, often critical of those selfsame evils and consequently limited in scope and amount. Our top generals opposed Chiang's strategy, to no avail.

Our worst disaster, however, came from the widening gulf between Chinese and American public feeling — in the postwar years when ineptitude and corruption were thoroughly discrediting the Kuomintang in China, we were experiencing intensified alarm over Soviet expansionist aims and methods, particularly over the cynical duplicity and ruthless ambition of the Communist movement. As the experience and circumstances of daily life continued to diverge in China and America, Communism seemed increasingly to be the only way out for one people and the mortal enemy of the other.

* *Pacific Historical Review* (November, 1956).

3. THE FALL OF CHINA IN AMERICA

For a decade the American public had idealized Free China; increasingly the combination of the atomic age and the cold war had intensified their fear of Communism. To have Free China become Communist seemed a national disaster. Like the Great Depression, it became political ammunition against the party in office. Governor Dewey used it in the 1948 campaign. Soon the Hiss case, the Fuchs case, the fear of spies and conspiracies, capped by a major war against Communist China in Korea, among other complex factors, took the lid off the McCarthy era.

The open season on China specialists in 1951–52 was facilitated by several circumstances. The American corps of China specialists both in and outside the government had been a small group in the 1930's. Most of them knew one another professionally as Foreign Service officers, scholars, or journalists. They had nearly all been "associated" with one another, if only at social or professional gatherings. If one assumed that American aid was a determining factor in China's domestic affairs, that the Nationalists could have lost their military superiority only through treachery, that American policy-makers had been anti-Chiang and therefore pro-Communist, and that Communist conspiracy could be detected through a man's associations (a series of untrue non sequiturs accepted by many during the McCarthy era) — then it became a public duty (and a rich opportunity) to investigate.

The motives for pursuing investigations were quite various. They ranged from the conscientious concern of officers responsible for our security to the shrewd calculations of political opportunists. In the background was a mood of anti-intellectualism and insecurity in a nation of whodunit readers suddenly fascinated by the morbid thought that almost anybody who seemed innocent of conspiracy might therefore be guilty of it. Along with the Congressional investigations of the time came intensified security screenings in the executive branch and industry which still continue, in a defensive imitation of totalitarianism. (This defensiveness fits the overly-pessimistic thesis that the American liberal tradition has lost its creative capacity at home, in addition to being non-exportable to Asia.)

Among China specialists the opportunity to find guilt by association was enhanced by fortuitous circumstance. The Institute of Pacific Relations since 1925 had pursued a program of research and publication punctuated by private conferences of scholars, diplomats, and businessmen representing research bodies, like the Royal Institute of International Affairs in London, in eleven countries concerned with the Pacific area. The IPR had produced some 1200 publications — books, pamphlets, reports — many of high scholarly value. While avoiding expressions of opinion itself, it had also sought contact with persons of many views and its records had been preserved. The files of the American IPR were replete with references to China specialists high and low, as well as some Communists, pro-Communists, and numerous foreigners. By seizing and exploiting these files a senatorial sub-committee was able to make frequent headlines for almost a year, up to the eve of the Republican convention of 1952.

The committee's report claimed in sweeping terms to show an IPR conspiracy to influence State Department policy-makers under Democratic administrations in favor of the Chinese Communists. The 14 volumes of hearings disregarded almost entirely the IPR's conferences and publications and concentrated on dubious contacts and questionable or pro-Communist utterances, whether or not actually connected with the IPR. My personal view is that the investigation got the truth of the matter thoroughly mixed up with hearsay, evidence out of context and guilt by association.* If this had been combined with executive powers and police measures, it might have resembled a totalitarian purge trial. It was based on the necessary legislators' right of investigation, but exploited the great American tradition of playing cops-and-robbers and dirty politics.

This personal impression is not the verdict of history, which has yet to be worked out by research. The only action resulting from the IPR hearings was the indictment of one of Senator McCarthy's numerous targets, Owen Lattimore, for perjury allegedly committed during a record-breaking 12 days of public questioning. A federal court threw out this indictment in 1955.

* I have been a trustee of the American Institute of Pacific Relations since 1946. In Washington I was "identified" as a communist (by L. Budenz) and as part of a "hard inner core" of an alleged pro-communist conspiracy. In Peking I have been cited as an "imperialist spy" and "the number-one cultural secret-agent of American imperialism," et cetera.

These hearings and those on General MacArthur's recall were only the visible top of the iceberg. They were paralleled by secret security investigations of Foreign Service officers and other government employees on a wide and continuing scale. The China specialists were generally transferred to other areas, some were dismissed and some resigned. John S. Service was cleared six times in succession by the State Department Loyalty Board but was eventually dismissed at the request of the Loyalty Review Board. In June 1957 as a result of a Supreme Court order he was reinstated.

To an observer outside the government, the chief results of all these China policy investigations seem to have been security-consciousness and conformity. Very little if any Communism, espionage, or treachery was uncovered but everyone was intimidated. Fearfulness has handicapped our officials ever since. The peoples abroad whom we seek as allies cannot be cleared for security; our representatives who seek friends there may endanger their own careers.

Matters so recent as our China policy and the conduct of our China specialists are hard to judge. One's personal picture of the scene is too narrow. In addition each observer must strike his own balance between cognate but frequently conflicting interests. How reconcile the demands of national security, on which our freedom depends, with the free functioning and freedom of contact of the individual, for whom the nation exists? How evaluate the threat of totalitarian subversion from abroad as against the danger of totalitarian tendencies at home? Each citizen must work on these questions for himself.

My own impression is that the American people responded to the cold war and the Chinese Communist victory more fearfully than creatively. The chief significance of McCarthy was that he was tolerated for so long by those Americans who approved his stated aims but not his methods and yet out of fear were willing to countenance his methods.

Fear was compounded by ignorance. After 1949 the score or more of American press correspondents formerly in China were excluded. The gigantic upheavals among the Chinese people, the metamorphosis of Chinese society, remained almost unknown in America.

Fear and ignorance lead only toward disaster. We need instead a great effort to find out about Communist China in every way and to compete creatively with the totalitarian approach to Chinese problems, at least in our thinking and when possible in action. Constructive action on a frontier of modernization suits us better than a conservative, security-conscious defensiveness.

4. OUR ALLY TAIWAN

Our frontier of contact with the Chinese people after 1949 was Formosa, as the Europeans named it, or Taiwan, as it is called in both Chinese and Japanese. It is about 250 miles long and 60 to 80 miles wide, with a good many peaks over 10,000 feet in the mountain spine on the east and only about a quarter of the area cultivable, mainly on the west. Chinese immigration became important only in the Ming period. The Dutch and Spanish both maintained trading settlements in the 17th century, and the island was the last Ming refuge against the Manchu conquerors. Nineteenth-century Western trade never became important, but four treaty ports were opened after 1860 and some modernization had begun before the Japanese take-over in 1895. Japanese colonialism established order, created some material progress and eventually became less harsh. No real political life was encouraged, although by the 1930's the regime had moved toward local self-government with a limited franchise. The Japanese land policy checked absentee landlordism and encouraged farmers' associations for agricultural improvement, as well as public health services. With a single-minded interest in increasing production, the Japanese regime got about half the children into elementary schools and established a fairly high level of literacy, although less than a hundred students a year reached the university level.

The very small top class of modern-trained Formosan leaders of Chinese background which had been permitted to develop under the Japanese was decimated by the Nationalist massacres of March 1947, carried out to suppress complaints against the corruption of the Nationalist postwar take-over. Several thousand leading Taiwanese were killed. The American attitude until 1950 was to refuse responsibility for the island, although continuing economic aid without military aid, as part of our attempted disengagement from China. The North Korean aggression of 1950 led to our Seventh Fleet patrolling the Formosa Strait, to keep the island out of the war and protected from mainland attack. Thereafter an American military mission assisted in the application of our aid program, and the Nationalist forces of half a million or so eventually combatted superannuation by conscripting Taiwanese. Meanwhile the Nationalist Government in exile remained superimposed upon the Taiwan provincial government which it dominated, but native-born personnel were taken increasingly into the latter. Kuomintang reform efforts were accompanied by continued control measures, including a ban on contact with the mainland.

Economically, the island's earlier reliance on sugar and rice production for the Japanese market had to be followed by a considerable reorientation to achieve greater self-sufficiency and to push industrialization in the face of rapid population increase. The three million population of 1905 had approached seven million by 1940; with an influx of two million or more from the mainland, the total by 1958 was about eleven million, and rapidly increasing. Compared with the mainland, however, Taiwan had a higher living standard with moderately good prospects for economic growth. Development proceeded within a general framework of government domination or monopolies in industry. American assistance fostered industrialization but created a dependence on foreign aid. Inflation steadily continued as one of the many evils inherited from the mainland past, and the military burden of the Nationalist forces could be maintained only with a continued American subsidy of the economy.

One creative instance of Sino-American collaboration was the Joint Commission on Rural Reconstruction, set up by our China Aid Act of 1948. When it began operations on the mainland in October 1948, the JCRR aimed to increase the food supply and raise the farmers' standard of living mainly through technological assistance, following the recommendations of an expert Sino-American commission. Agricultural specialists had often argued that since land redistribution could not increase acreage, it bore little promise of increasing productivity as compared with the many improvements possible in seeds, breeding, tools, farming techniques, elimination of plant and animal diseases, and the like. As the program got started in South China and on Taiwan, it stressed development of irrigation through dike-building, but left unsolved the problem of farmer organization, as a necessary means of mobilizing local resources and securing credit to finance improvements. This led the Joint Commission in turn to the actual problem of land tenure reform, specifically the reduction of rent to the statutory 37.5 per cent of the crop and at the same time the extension of contracts to more than one year as a safeguard against landlord extortion. Thus an American type of farm-extension approach, beginning with technology, soon found in practice that landlord-tenant relations were an essential aspect of a rural reform program in Asia.

Once confined to operations on Taiwan, the JCRR secured the backing of the provincial government and was able to build on the Japanese structure of farmers' associations. It carried through a general rent reduction and eventually a program for each farmer to own his own land. All this was combined with practical demonstrations, publications, producers' and credit cooperatives, and rural handicraft development. As an institution the JCRR also avoided the problems of official relations between two governments by having a single administrative echelon and by using established agencies rather than building up its own apparatus. Like our own Tennessee Valley Authority, the JCRR on Taiwan has set an example of great interest to Asia.

Since the American people in their history have created 48 states at home, dealt with 21 others in Latin America, fostered the Philippine Republic and seen the postwar emergence of numerous republics in Asia, it is quite natural for us to suggest that the eleven million people on Taiwan might also form a new state, independent of the mainland. This would be a concrete application of our own traditional principles. It would preserve an alternative, though small, center of modern Chinese political, economic, and cultural development, outside the totalitarian monopoly of all forms of Chinese life on the mainland.

However, Chinese politics for two thousand years has been focussed on the unity of all Chinese under one rule. The Anglo-Saxon concept of "two Chinas" has been denounced by practically everyone from Chou En-lai to Chiang Kai-shek. The real issue is not that of "two Chinas" but of an independent Taiwan, which remains the chief fruit of our China policy since 1949.

16

Communist China

THIS CHAPTER concerns contemporary and disputed events perceived dimly from a distance. China is very big and changing very fast. Even Mao Tse-tung must often wonder what is actually going on.

Studies of Communist China from the outside easily fall into that ancient trap — finding the evidence one seeks. From Peking press sources one can paint a picture in which China today looks remarkably like Russia. Alternatively the historian can discern in the Communist regime many features of the old Chinese empire. Each approach, by way of the Russian model or by way of Chinese tradition, has much to offer. Neither can be disregarded, as some would like to do. The beginning of wisdom is certainly to accept both, but only as ways of approach. For in Communist China a new power-state is struggling to create a collectivized society, in which certain influences of the past and from abroad are inextricably fused. But the totalitarian product will be something new and distinctive.

Below we look first at the measures and mechanisms by which the Chinese Communist Party built up its control over the Chinese society, state, and people, and secondly at its effort to remake them. Though the two processes went hand in hand, remaking depended on first controlling.

1. POLITICAL CONTROL

The military take-over occupied a year and a half, from the fall of Mukden on November 1, 1948, and of Peking and Tientsin in January 1949, until the occupation of all the mainland and Hainan Island by May 1950. The Chinese Peoples Republic was proclaimed in the midst of this process on October 1, 1949. The take-over left in office most local administrators. On the surface the Communist cadres gave it a festive air, dancing the *yang-ko* in the streets, proclaiming peace and liberation. The troops generally behaved scrupulously. It was a hopeful honeymoon period, devoted to military mopping-up, economic recovery, and political organization.

Coalition Government. The policy for this period, laid down by Mao in January and confirmed by the CCP Central Committee in March 1949, amounted to a platform of getting rid of the Kuomintang, supplanting it with a coalition government, and reforming China's armies, foreign relations, and economic system. In order to mobilize a broad basis of support, the coalition government should be organized by a new People's Political Consultative Conference, reminiscent in name but not in membership of the multi-party conference at the time of General Marshall's mediation.

This line was developed in Mao's statement of July 1, 1949, "On the people's democratic dictatorship." Echoing Lenin's theory of a "democratic dictatorship of workers and peasants," Mao propounded the thesis that the new government should be a democratic coalition under Communist leadership at the same time that it was a dictatorship directed against the reactionary classes or "enemies of the people." Thus the "people's democratic dictatorship" would attempt to line up the broadest possible support for the regime and at the same time eliminate its foes within the Chinese world. The "people" were defined as composed of four classes: proletariat, peasantry, petty bourgeoisie, national bourgeoisie. For the peasantry there was a prospect of maintaining, at least temporarily, private property in land, and for the bourgeoisie, a sector of privately owned industry. This carried out the original idea of the New Democracy.

Since any individual could be transferred by a stroke of the pen to the category of reactionaries or enemies of the people, this framework was completely flexible as a basis for sifting out dissident members of the population. The power of class imputation remained with the Communist Party, and a reformed "reactionary" could be declared by it to be a member of the "people." Leaving this mechanism at first in the background, Mao Tse-tung called upon his countrymen, in this moment of hope and general relief, to take the first step on a 10,000 mile march, to wipe out domestic and repulse foreign enemies and to remake Chinese society, without help from abroad except that of the Soviet Union, using the means at hand but learning from all quarters.

After several months' preparation, the Preparatory Committee of the People's Political Consultative Conference was set up at Peking in June 1949, nominally representing 23 parties or groups. The PPCC itself was convened in September for 10 days, with 662 delegates. It passed the *Common Program,* a general statement of aims of the new coalition government, and the *Organic Law* of the Central People's Government, which made the working class the leader of the republic. Since the CCP was the vanguard which represents the working class, this meant that the government was to be its administrative arm. The new administration was given complete executive, legislative, and judicial powers on a centralist basis, with no strings attached. Four committees and 30 ministries were set up, 15 of them connected with economic affairs. In the top committee, 31 out of 56 seats were occupied by Communists.

This powerful autocratic administration by Communist desire left the minor parties in existence, though without much following, and gave posts of prominence to non-Communists in order to carry out the idea of coalition government, that the talents of all the people must be used in building the new society. It was essential for Communist China to use the training and ability of that major part of the upper class which had never been Communist. These people, like the peasantry in the preceding 20 years, now formed a social group not susceptible to complete remaking into Communists but nevertheless essential for the time being as part of the Communist structure and program. Liberal intellectuals were therefore catered to, given scope for their talents and placed in high position, interlarded in the new ministries with party members who lacked their abilities but were more disciplined. (One is reminded of barbarian dynasties' use of Chinese administrators.) The larger part of the Western-returned scholars, including those educated in the United States, appear to have been in this category.

As patriots, they were devoted to their country's future. Long since estranged from the Kuomintang, they saw no alternative. The Communist Party also had long since developed its methods for manipulating and utilizing liberal intellectuals.

The constitution adopted in 1954 did not appreciably remake the governmental structure except for the further concentration of authority in Peking. The Communists, in short, like the Kuomintang, set up a tripod of power — party, government, and army, each forming a separate echelon but all three tied together by the Communist leadership. The Party grew to twelve million in 1957.

Communist organization went far, far beyond the Kuomintang, however. On a territorial basis, People's Representative Congresses, modeled on the Russian soviets, were set up in a hierarchy from the village level on up to the People's Congress at the top, which was first convened in 1954. These congresses have quasi-legislative functions and are used mainly as sounding boards and transmission belts, to maintain a façade of democratic procedure and an arena for popular participation but without final power.

The Mass Organizations. Cutting across the structure of congresses, there were set up the new nation-wide mass organizations on a functional basis. The All-China Federation of Trade Unions had been founded in 1922 and by 1956 claimed a membership of over 13 million. In 1949 there was created a full panoply of parallel bodies: an All-China Federation of Democratic Women (76 million members in 1953), of Democratic Youth (34 million in 1957), of Cooperative Workers, i.e., peasants in cooperatives (162 million in 1956), and of Literature and Art, under the prolific writer Kuo Mo-jo, to mobilize intellectuals. In addition there were an All-China Students Federation (4 million in 1955), a Children's Pioneer Corps (30 million in 1957) and many comparable bodies more specialized in nature, dealing with science, art and learning, welfare activities, or international relations — for example, the Sino-Soviet Friendship Association (68 million members in 1953) and similar associations for Sino-Indian and Sino-Burmese friendship. Finally in 1953 was established the All-China Association of Industry and Commerce, for the national bourgeoisie, who at that time still existed. (Three years later they had ceased to exist, as we shall note.)

These mass organizations, as studied by Dr. K. C. Chao, reach the individual in his professional or social role, among his peers, in ways that the government cannot. Each is controlled from the top by "democratic centralism" though authority is nominally vested in a national congress meeting at long intervals. Party members of course predominate in key posts but through them reach out to mobilize the general public. Each organization has broadly defined purposes and programs and an extensive administrative apparatus. Something like half the adult Chinese population are thus brought into one or another action group and involved in its program of meetings, study, and agitation.

The mass organizations have developed big training programs with schools and indoctrination centers, and serve as recruiting agencies for talented and activist personnel. Their welfare and cultural work has included such things as labor insurance, leave and pension systems, literacy classes, maternity hospitals and midwife training, or recreational activities, accompanied by a large output of books, magazines, and pamphlets circulated through libraries. Their members can also be used in the security system or in nation-wide campaigns like that against reactionaries. Their representatives can participate in the similar international bodies of the Communist world.

The mass organizations stand out as institutions of a new type in China, fulfilling primarily political functions as quasi-governmental agencies that bridge the immemorial gap between populace and officialdom. They receive government aid and even representation in the structure of People's Congresses. Their function is mainly to indoctrinate, working closely among the populace with meetings, demonstrations, and protests on demand as well as propaganda through mass media. The result is to mold and manipulate the climate of opinion. The mass organizations have a comprehensive coverage of the population and recruit its more able members. They can work also through the local street committees, which have the duty of promoting welfare measures, mutual surveillance and denunciation among neighbors and within families in every street. The mass organizations, when coordinated in each locality, can thus bring to bear upon every individual a completely pervasive and overwhelming public pressure.

The control mechanism for the application of this pressure is the campaign or drive. Campaigns may seem to start spontaneously once the Party has decided upon them. They are led generally by enthusiasts in each locality. Several may go on at the same time. Campaigns, in short, can quickly set in motion the enormous new apparatus of party, state, and mass organizations and direct its hammer blows against one target after another among the various classes and their institutions.

Standing behind this apparatus are well-paid security forces. In the forefront is the hierarchy of courts, also an arm of the central administration. Western jurist observers have found the kind of justice administered in open court less objectionable than the fact that cases normally come to trial only after the accused has fully confessed and denounced any others concerned in the crime with which he has been charged.

2. ECONOMIC RECONSTRUCTION

The intensive program of political organization sketched above was carried on concomitantly with a vigorous economic effort. Early in 1949 Mao announced a "shift to the cities" as the focus of effort, reaffirming the primacy of the urban proletariat in a party which was now about 90 per cent of peasant origin.

The first industrial objective set in 1949 was to get production back to its prewar level within about three years. Japan's industrial build-up in Manchuria had been reduced in 1945 by Russian removal of more than half the capital equipment, with an estimated replacement value of at least two billion American dollars. In China proper, railroads had been torn up by civil war, urban labor demoralized by hyperinflation. After the Communist victory it took some time to convince the city worker that Liberation had brought him first of all the opportunity to work harder. Wartime blockades between city and country had increased rural self-sufficiency; market crops like cotton had to be revived. Meanwhile inflation was still a major problem. With military operations still continuing in 1949–50 and some 9 million persons on government rations or payrolls (including minor Nationalist administrative and military personnel who had been taken over), the substitution of a new "people's currency" for Nationalist banknotes, even at favorable rates, left the regime still obliged to expand its note issue steadily to meet a budget deficit of perhaps 75 per cent. Shanghai prices rose 70 times in nine months, from May 1949 to February 1950. All this demanded strenuous measures.

The first move toward quelling the inflation was to get the budget more or less balanced by increasing revenue, first in the countryside by collecting agricultural taxes in kind, then in the cities through devices like a sales tax on each major commodity and business taxes set by "democratic appraisal" of trade associations to meet quotas previously set by government. The result of the latter was to squeeze money out of the more monetized sector of the economy. Secondly, the entire fiscal administration was reorganized and rationalized to give the central government control over formerly local taxes, to eliminate private banks' handling of official funds and generally to reduce expenditures, licit and illicit. The regime gradually made the collection process more efficient, got control of money and credit, and set up six government trading corporations to dominate prices in major consumer commodities.

One device for restoring confidence was to express wages, salaries, bank deposits, some government payments and bond issues in terms of commodity units, linked to quantities of goods of daily use rather than to monetary prices. A typical unit might be composed of 6 catties (8 lbs.) of rice, 1½ catties of flour, 16 catties of coal, and 4 feet of white shirting. As prices rose, the commodity-based unit would rise accordingly in money terms. Paid in this unit, one could save by making bank deposits or buying bonds in similar units; either way, one was protected against further inflation. Thus by a variety of methods designed to achieve a balance between the supply of goods and the flow of money income, the inflation was conquered by mid-1950.

Another achievement of the first year was an extensive reopening of railway track, to get most of China's 13,500 miles into operation. Economic recovery was aided by three good harvests in 1950–51–52. By 1952, the pre-1949 peaks of production had been equalled or surpassed in pig iron, cement, steel and oil (all very modest in China), and in coal, electric power, flour, and cotton cloth, but production was still short of the pre-1949 peak in some consumer goods such as sugar. Most important, by 1952 the national economy had been given greater unity than it had ever had before. Railway track had expanded to 15,000 and highways to 75,000 miles. A centralized banking system and single uniform currency now covered the country. Budgeting could be attempted realistically for the first time.

Peking's long-term economic aim was to mobilize China's resources and reallocate them for purposes of industrialization. This required a gradual extension of government control over all segments of the economy. Private enterprise was permitted to continue in form but in fact it was brought increasingly under state control through numerous devices — taxation and capital levies, rationing of credit, competition by state enterprise, demands of labor unions — so that businessmen practically became bureaucrats. By controlling credit and raw materials and monopolizing key commodities, the state could now dominate production and commerce, in addition to its outright control of most heavy industry, railways and foreign trade. The other requirement was a traditional one brought up-to-date — control of the surplus product of the land.

Land Reform. In the history of Chinese Communism there had been several shifts of land policy, exemplified by the severity of the Kiangsi period, when many landlords were exterminated, and the moderation of the Yenan period, when they were guaranteed a reasonable rent. As Communist power expanded after 1946, land reform had proceeded on a piecemeal and often violent basis, sometimes with more peasant violence than the Party claims to have desired.

The nation-wide land reform, begun in mid-1950 and completed by late 1952 or early 1953, was not merely economic but also social and political in aim. A work team of cadres coming to a village first identified out-and-out enemies, if necessary got them out of the way, and then explained the desirability of land reform to the poor peasantry in particular, who would theoretically be the main beneficiaries. By this means active elements were selected who had the motivation and the capacity to lead the forthcoming movement. After this preparation a period of "class struggle" was inaugurated. In a series of "struggle meetings" the accumulated grievances of the populace could be brought forth in "speaking bitterness" or "settling accounts." Hatred could be fanned into mob violence in public "trials." Unpopular landlords or "local despots" chosen for public denunciation were either killed, expelled, or brought to confess and reform, while the entire community by taking violent measures committed themselves to the new order.

The next phase was to create the peasants association, which by a process of community assent could work out the definition of class status for each individual as landlord, rich peasant, middle peasant, poor peasant or farm laborer and could carry on the classification, confiscation, and redistribution of landholdings. The resulting "equalization of land tenure" was in the old tradition of peasant rebellions. Through Communist direction of this process, the activists were usually favored, the well-to-do reduced, and the remnants of the landlord gentry wiped out either in person or in status, while the Party representatives established their authority over the village. The tiller now had title to his land, at least for the moment.

While this New Democracy phase of private ownership had been advertised in 1950 to last for a "rather long time," in fact it lasted no longer for the farmer than it had for the capitalist. To supplant the old order the Communist regime moved without delay toward the construction of the new collectivist agrarian system beginning with a first stage of cooperatives.

Cooperation could achieve greater efficiency of production: six donkeys could go to market with one donkey-driver, not six. One housewife at a time could cook for several families. Since there were fewer draft animals than households, their use could be shared. Joint savings could buy a pump or a tool no individual could afford. In particular, handicraft cooperatives could use scattered local materials and unemployed farm labor in the off season to increase the production of consumer goods with rather little state investment. As larger units of operation, they could create a division of labor, with specialization. With organization might come literacy, health, technology, and higher productivity. Rural supply and marketing cooperatives meanwhile promoted exchange between farm and factory, handling state purchases and making available a wider variety of manufactures than the villages had seen before.

In agriculture the reform program for increased production, as it was termed, moved gradually from north to south through a series of planned phases, first setting up temporary, usually seasonal, small-scale mutual-aid teams, then larger permanent ones, and then agricultural producers' cooperatives. In the latter the peasants began to cultivate in common and share a common product in proportion to their pooled contributions of land, equipment, and labor.

The drive for agricultural producers' cooperatives which got under way in 1953 was still posited on private ownership of land and voluntary cooperation for mutual benefit. However, the goal began to shift. The regime had heretofore argued that land redistribution in itself, by eliminating landlordism (though without much increase of acreage), would release the peasantry's "productive energy." Now it was admitted that only eventual collectivisation could effect the increase in agricultural product necessary to pay for industrialization. The effort was to lead the inveterately property-conscious peasant, through propaganda, practice, and steady pressure, to become (as the French agronomist, René Dumont, records it) "a socialist without knowing it."

Soviet Aid. In most of their changes the CCP followed the Soviet example, which was plainly their greatest inspiration both in theory and in practice. Mao Tse-tung spent nine weeks in Moscow (December 1949–February 1950) and signed a Sino-Soviet Treaty of Friendship, Alliance, and Mutual Assistance, valid until 1980, against aggression by Japan or any power joined with Japan. Russia gradually gave up her position in Manchuria, turning Dairen back to China in 1950, ending her joint control of the main railways at the end of 1952, and withdrawing from the Port Arthur naval base in May 1955. By a 1950 agreement she loaned China $60 million a year in economic aid for five years, all to be repaid — a meager sum compared to our largesse to the Nationalists. Russian engineers, by the thousands, have been a greater help. Later agreements called for Soviet credits and technical aid in building or renovating some 211 old and new projects, as the chief centers of the industrial program.*

Although the exact total of such economic aid remains unknown to us, Russian blueprints and technicians have evidently been a priceless ingredient in Communist China's performance. In addition, very extensive Soviet military assistance made it possible to build up the Chinese army without burdening the economy unbearably. But much of the Soviet industrial aid has been paid for by Chinese exports of agricultural and mineral products.

Whether or not Peking expected to participate in the Russian-armed North Korean aggression of June 1950, rather than seizing

---

* Note: 141 such projects were announced in September 1953; 15 more in October 1954; and 55 in April 1956.

Taiwan and expanding her influence southward, she undoubtedly gained military strength from the Korean war. In her intervention from October 1950 a million or so Chinese "volunteers" benefited from the use of Russian tanks, planes, and artillery. By the time of the truce in July 1951 the battle-hardened Chinese army was boasting of "glorious victories" over the superior armament of the greatest "imperialist" power. Military modernization with Russian help continued thereafter. In 1955 compulsory military service began to draw upon the five million young men who reach the age of 20 each year to create history's largest reservoir of military man power.

3. SOCIAL REORGANIZATION

Terror and Enthusiasm. The Korean War provided a useful sanction for heightened anti-Americanism, extirpation of irreconcilables, and popular mobilization. Two major campaigns were mounted, to "Resist America, Aid Korea" and to "Suppress Counter-revolutionaries." They called for patriotic spying on neighbors and relatives, public denunciation of parents by their children, and consignment of enemies of the people, reactionaries, and counter-revolutionaries to "reform through labor." Together with the results of "people's courts" in the land reform, executions in 1951–52 evidently ran into the hundreds of thousands (some say millions). The regime benefited by extensive confiscations of property. It showed its claws and teeth, and the effect was not lost upon the populace, who became more amenable to discipline and direction.

In this context of terror on the one hand and patriotism on the other, foreign missionaries were denounced as spies and jailed or expelled. A "three-self" movement was set going, for "self-government, self-support, and self-propagation" of the Christian church in China, free of the missionaries' alleged "cultural imperialism." Uncooperative church leaders were gradually eliminated from positions of leadership and "national churches" free of foreign ties were finally set up to give Chinese Christians a religion subservient to the Communist state.

Minor campaigns were also pursued to secure a more effective payment of taxes and greater regularity in economic life. Victory bond and war donation drives mopped up public funds in order to counteract inflation. Another program was designed to raise the social status of the soldier, another to increase output and labor efficiency through the Stakhanovite system of work quotas and team competition.

The pressures and dangers of a war with the United States, whose power had bulked so large in the Chinese mind, were thus turned to purposes of totalitarian social reorganization and industrial efficiency. The germ warfare hoax was also elaborately fabricated and publicized, with the approval of an international board of left-wing scientists and a mass of circumstantial evidence, to blacken the American name. Yet even here a subsidiary aim was also realized, since the germ warfare theme stimulated public health measures all over the country.

The mechanisms for mobilizing public pressure against designated types of individuals were used more and more plainly for refashioning China's social structure. A new height in this effort came with the Three-anti and Five-anti movements of 1951–52. These were organized very thoroughly and proceeded through well defined phases with standardized methods.

The Three-anti campaign was directed against officialdom, in the government, in state industries, and in the party. The movement was anti-corruption, anti-waste, and anti-bureaucratism — plainly an attempt to weed out and invigorate the vast administrative apparatus inherited from the Kuomintang and rapidly added to since 1949. The Three-anti movement permitted replacement of administrative personnel by new blood, as fast as it could be developed for the purpose, and brought the enlarged bureaucracy more thoroughly under central control by keeping the bureaucrat insecure in his new power. Like many major drives, it began in Manchuria, the most advanced area under the new regime. Special committees and an apparatus were soon formed to promote the movement countrywide with spectacular denunciations, public "trials," and great publicity.

The Five-anti movement was a similarly well organized and concerted attack on merchants and manufacturers, the bourgeoisie or middle class in general. Nominally it was against bribery, tax evasion, theft of state assets, cheating in labor or materials, and stealing of state economic intelligence. Employees were inspired to accuse employers, customers accused shopowners, and there was a general screening of all persons in urban trade and industry. As in all campaigns, the public were mobilized, committees established, and appearances created of great popular initiative, righteous anger, and enthusiasm for the triumph of virtue. Confessions, apologies, and the reform or elimination of culprits by suicide, execution, or labor camp followed. But it is evident that one immediate aim in this anti-middle-class program was financial. Large sums were squeezed out of the business class, probably somewhere between one and two billion United States dollars. From this time the national bourgeoisie existed on sufferance; those who remained in business were thereafter thoroughly amenable to the continued pressure for socialization of private enterprise. (Eventually they were all expropriated and in January 1956 dutifully celebrated, with firecrackers and dancing, their own demise as a social class.)

All these manipulations of the body politic squeezed out great numbers of enemies of the regime. Forced labor camps were the natural result, built both on the Soviet model and on the ancient *corvée* or labor-service tradition of China. Muscle-power has always been the country's chief natural resource. The modern use of labor armies of 4 million persons on one project of public works, like the much-publicized Huai River dikes and dams, was no great innovation except for its increased scope and the edifying moral exhortation which accompanied it. Whether the millions of Chinese who now perform forced labor on short rations are more numerous than the millions who have normally starved and still starve while farming every year, no one can say. The difference is that the grinding down and slow extinction of life through prolonged and ill-equipped labor, always a part of the Chinese scene whether planned or purely circumstantial, is now well organized.

Another imponderable to the outsider is the degree to which the revolutionary ardor which inspired the tremendous exertions of the early years of "liberation" still continues to burn. The Communist attempt is to institutionalize ardor and self-sacrifice, as well as terror and compulsion, so that hope and fear together may build a new order. Since the youth of China are an inexhaustible resource, the inspired example of selected young people, the principles of emulation and competition, the leadership of party cadres may keep the new order operating on a partially voluntary basis. It is impossible, at any rate, to understand Communist China by either extreme approach. It seems to be neither a vast prison nor a new Jerusalem but some kind of mixture, depending on who you are and where you function in the new order. This viability of totalitarianism is what makes it so ominous.

Pre-Communist China was pre-modern and particularistic in many ways — in the neglect of punctuality, the lack of civic-consciousness and public neatness, in putting family before community and personal interests before national, in all those attitudes and habits that the futile New Life Movement had condemned in 1935. The Confucian order having been eroded away, China was truly "a sheet of loose sand" as Dr. Sun complained, a country that our G.I.'s felt "ought to be cleaned up." In the old days, everyone haggled over prices, took note of manners, and treated every situation *ad hoc* and every person according to the circumstances if not on his merits. All this was quite contrary to the efficent impersonality of modern, universalistic market relations. This pre-modern character of Chinese society, its "medieval" traits, had fascinated foreigners and humiliated patriots for a century. The Confucian scholars who sought a panacea in gunboats, then technology, and finally in the reform of institutions have now been succeeded by revolutionists who condemn old ways as "feudal" and seek to remake their cosmos by applying the allegedly universal, abstract principles of a new Marxist-Leninist "science" of society. With reforming zeal their Leninist party, once thoroughly in control, has applied itself to remaking not only the economy and social order but also the individual.

4. THOUGHT REFORM

The Communist achievement in organization, among a people so recently famous for their lack of it, has depended upon the inspiring, coercing, or manipulating of individual personalities. Building upon methods used in Yenan to Leninize the party (as well as to convert Japanese war prisoners), Liu Shao-ch'i and other organizers developed empirical procedures to deal with every type of enemy or supporter. When American P.O.W.s in Korea "confessed" to germ warfare and collaborated with their Chinese captors, they were responding to techniques developed through use with Chinese of all sorts, including Party members. As a result of these methods capitalists and rich peasants smilingly gave their property to the state, professors scathingly denounced their Western bourgeois education, middle school students devotedly gave their lives to Party work.

These diverse phenomena represent the real Communist effort at revolution, to change Chinese thinking and behavior. This is far more significant than the material efforts in technology and industry and at the same time is a prerequisite for their material success. Though very diverse, thought reform generally has had certain common features: control of the environment, both of the person physically and of the information available to him (this is now true of the whole country); the stimuli both of idealism and of terror, intermixed; and a grim psychological experience, undergone with guidance through successive phases and intensified by the manipulation of one's sense of guilt and shame. The Chinese slang term "brainwashing" imparts perhaps too much mystery to a process faintly visible elsewhere in religious crusades of the past, only now more thoroughly organized. Modern psychologists can explain how privation, prolonged insecurity and tension, combined with exhausting fatigue and repetitive indoctrination can shatter the individual's sense of inner identity and create pressures from which the only escape for many is submission to authority and acceptance at least temporarily of new attitudes and concepts. This coercing of the human mind, quite different in degree from the mild voluntary form of American advertising methods, is still only partially understood and exploited. Spread over the world it would create the ultimate crisis of individualism. Perhaps it is not surprising that in China, where the practical art of human relations has been more fully developed than anywhere else, these psychological methods should be most advanced.

For the Chinese student class, from whom the CCP must get its cadres, this intellectual-emotional reconditioning was carried out in the big revolutionary colleges set up through the reorganization and expansion of the educational system. Thousands of trainees went through indoctrination courses of several months duration. A center of this type containing 4,000 students might be subdivided into classes of one or two hundred and then into study groups of six to ten persons. A psychiatrist who has analyzed the procedure, Dr. Robert Lifton, divides a typical six-months course of thought reform into three stages — first, group identification, a period of togetherness and considerable freedom and enthusiasm. During this stage major Marxist-Leninist-Maoist concepts are studied and systematic rational indoctrination is delivered, partly in lectures but mainly in small group discussions. A free exchange of views, with a high *esprit de corps* and feeling of common effort, leads the trainee to expose himself freely and engage wholeheartedly in a "thought mobilization."

The second phase is one of induced emotional conflict within each individual. The daily schedule continues to be physically exhausting. The milieu, which is carefully controlled behind the scenes, now seems to close in. The individual submits his first summary of his own life and thought. He begins to feel under pressure as criticism and self-criticism intensify and the dangers of being rejected become apparent. The evils within the old individual are now attacked, not merely the old society in the abstract, and the student strives to dig up his failings and correct them. Group pressures are focussed by experienced leaders so that each individual becomes heavily involved emotionally, under assault. His failings may be labelled with any one of dozens of terms. He may struggle with himself and be "struggled with" by his group-mates over an excess of subjectivism or objectivism, of opportunism or dogmatism, bureaucratism or individual-heroism, and so forth. The individual who attempts to hold back and resist the process cannot win and suffers a psychological beating. Each participant, whether or not he resists, is completely alone, isolated within himself like all his fellows. Under this pressure, which is similar to that used against prisoners, the individual soon feels guilt — he has sinned and should be punished — and also a sense of shame — he has lost face and self-esteem, which creates intense humiliation. In attacking himself, he is thus prepared to achieve through confession and self-condemnation a psychological catharsis, feeling as though he were mentally ill and needed a cure.

The third phase is that of submission and rebirth. When his final thought summary or confession has been gone over from every angle and is accepted by the group and the authorities, the individual is likely to feel exhilarated, cleansed, a new person. This months-long process constitutes on a larger scale a sort of induced religious conversion, like those of our own revival meetings, but with added elements of pressure and psychotherapy. The individual has been manipulated so that the wellsprings of his own nature have put him under intense emotional pressure and the relief from this self-induced tension is associated with the external authority of the group and the Party, on whom he should henceforth be dependent. For the Party's aim is not only to secure control over disciplined activists but also to raise the quality of their performance by changing their idea of themselves, their goals and values. They renounce family and father, and accept the Party and the revolution in their place.

In the case of older intellectuals, particularly returned students from the West, criticism, self-criticism, and confession cannot take place in a malleable young mind but only as an overlay of the formative experience of a now mature person. The statements put out by Peking professors seem to be somewhat *pro forma*. They denounce the corrupting influence of the bourgeois West and their former subjection to it, possibly with some sense of guilt at having been seduced or alienated from their native culture. But the net effect of their self-criticism is probably less to change these individuals than to align them properly in the public eye as supporters of the new order. Thus the one class who might represent a Western non-Communist influence neutralize themselves and present no model for youth.

Communism and Confucianism. Few who have lived in China will assume that a revolution, however irresistible, can quickly alter the immovable Middle Kingdom. The new marriage law of 1950, which attacked the family by proclaiming equal rights between the sexes, seems not to have been vigorously pushed. Substitution of the ancient ideographic script by an alphabet — the greatest literary project in all history — has been held up and modified from time to time. Our schematic account of thought reform should not imply that Communism has as yet remade the Chinese personality. However, the strategy is long-term, to maintain a controlled environment of lip-service if not love for the regime until the new socialist generation can take over.

Out of the Chinese inheritance, moreover, authoritarian traditions can be invoked for modern purposes. Thus Confucianism in one of its aspects has a certain resonance with Marxism. This is not an identity, only a partial overlap; nor is it surprising, for Confucianism is almost as broad and various as Christianity.

One point of resonance is in the important concept of the unity of theory and practice. The Bolshevik emphasis on putting theory into revolutionary practice contended that theory was no good in itself but must be applied in activity, as part of an effort not only to understand the world but to change it. Marxism as a "science of history" when put into practice must become an ethic, a personal philosophy animating one's entire thought and conduct. Self-criticism is a necessary part of discipline for this purpose. It is also a Communist doctrine that Marxist-Leninist theory should be applied according to the content of each national background, blending Communist ideas with the local tradition. As Mao says, "We must unify appropriately the general truth of Marxism with the concrete practice of the Chinese revolution."

Now it happens that Communist self-criticism is in some degree reminiscent of the Confucian doctrine of self-cultivation in the form which is associated particularly with the sixteenth century philosopher, Wang Yang-ming (1472–1529). Wang attacked the dualism of knowledge and action. In Wang's view, as David Nivison puts it, "To know is to know how and to know that one ought." The completely sincere man must express his moral perceptions in equally moral conduct. Wang and others therefore urged self-cultivation as a process by which the true philosopher can bring his thought and conduct into consonance, so that knowledge is realized in action and action contributes to knowledge. This idea was echoed in Sun Yat-sen's "Knowledge is difficult, action is easy" and later by Chiang Kai-shek.

While Confucian self-cultivation was not a group affair, it stressed the moral improvability of human nature, the ancient Chinese belief that through proper ethical instruction and exhortation, man can be made into a more social being. The gap between individual self-cultivation and group self-criticism is a very broad one in fact but the two have something in common. Thought reform at Yenan and since has made use of traditional Chinese terminology and invoked Confucian sanctions. The good Communist, according to Liu Shao-ch'i, must discipline himself through self-cultivation, through "watching himself when alone," so as to become flexibly and resourcefully obedient to the Party's leadership. Through greater consciousness of the historical influences playing upon him, it is argued, he may indeed achieve a certain feeling of freedom within the confines of the historical process. Thus where Confucian-

ism instilled loyalty to father and Emperor, Maoism now diverts it
to the party and the people. The classics are quoted for this totalitarian purpose. This makes Marxism-Leninism seem less outlandish.

Criticism, literary and political. In the process of thought reform,
the Chinese intellectual and literary world has been agitated by
ideological struggles, in which Mao Tse-tung's dictum on literature
and art of 1942, that literature is a political tool in the class
struggle and thoroughly subordinate to politics, has provided a
major premise. The full force of meetings, denunciations, and
special publications was assembled to attack Hu Shih as the symbol
of decadent bourgeois pragmatism. One campaign was against
his interpretation of the famous eighteenth century novel, *The
Dream of the Red Chamber,* as an autobiographical work. Communists preferred to see in it the inner collapse of China's feudal
society, thus salvaging this fascinating book from China's heritage
as belonging to "the people," like other selected heroes, poets, and
cultural inheritances. The campaign simultaneously discredited
Western-type literary criticism based on historical research, as part
of the effort to stamp out the "worship America" tendency and
the intellectual freedom associated with the West — in short, as part
of the attack upon Chinese liberalism and its foreign allies.

It is a neat trick to foster intellectual vitality within a framework
of uncritical loyalty to the Communist leadership. Creative ideas
are still needed from the 10,000 or so higher-level non-Communist
intellectuals. In the aftermath of Russia's blood bath in Hungary,
which coincided with student and peasant discontent in China, Mao
announced in 1957 his latest doctrine of contradictions — some "an-
tagonistic" as between the regime and its enemies abroad or at
home, and some "non-antagonistic," normal and arguable, as between the bureaucracy and the people. Here was a framework
within which it was evidently hoped that a continuing struggle over
policy could be healthily pursued and yet contained. As in the
cheng-feng movement of the Yenan period, this dialectical process
would call for criticism and then would meet it, letting extreme
views emerge to be dealt with through open argument, in order to
discover faults and correct them and also to discover fault-finders.

The campaign of 1956–57 for freer criticism of the bureaucracy
under the classical slogan "Let a hundred flowers bloom together,

let the hundred schools of thought contend" was not a clarion call for free speech except within the carefully enunciated limits of complete devotion to the Party's final authority. It was designed to resolve "non-antagonistic" contradictions between populace and government and stimulate a public catharsis through a degree of criticism. (This would be in the imperial censor's tradition of "loyal remonstrance," pointing out the ruler's errors on the basis of the ruler's assumptions, not like a "loyal opposition" which in the West would be free to attack the regime's aims and policies on a basis of continued loyalty to the state.)

Repeated invitations eventually released a surprising torrent of publicly expressed dissatisfaction with the CCP's totalitarian political system, its ideas, aims, and methods. This torrent simultaneously disclosed the minor-party and Western-educated critics of the regime, who were soon brought under attack as "rightists." Many observers felt that in the beginning Mao had honestly wanted some liberalization of thought and expression. But the widespread and basic criticism which had resulted required harsh suppression. The recent critics were soon publicly accusing themselves and condemning one another. The regime put pressure on the non-Communist press and the minor-party leaders to make the so-called coalition more closely subservient to the dominant party, and also no doubt to destroy the position of non-Communists with a Western background.

The campaign method of revolutionary development is undoubtedly dynamic. The enormous apparatus which encourages activists to attack certain heterodox ideas or undesired activities develops a high momentum and easily overshoots the mark, achieving "excesses." One campaign therefore gives rise to another, to check, redirect, or supersede the previous one. No doubt this comparatively non-violent but total manipulation of political life is particularly feasible when the peasant masses are still just moving into literate public activity. In time, the tempo may slacken or more concrete coercion may have to supplement the publicity and "persuasion."

Behind the Party decisions, its campaigns and shifts of line, one may discern some faint echo of the bureaucratic politics of the imperial era. Parties as organized factions (*tang*) were anathema to the imperial ideal of harmony (a bit like the minor parties today) and were generally proscribed as treason, yet it is evident that official cliques or personal groupings have been an immemorial pattern among Chinese officialdom. Indeed, if policies are to be reasoned out in party councils, such groupings seem inevitable, even if the traditional concern for personal loyalty is now lacking. Observers have often, if too hopefully, seen the potentialities of rivalry between the theoretician and disciplinarian Liu Shao-ch'i, who studied in Moscow and is listed as second to Mao, and Chou En-lai, who studied in Paris and has had vastly more contact with the outer world.

5. COLLECTIVIZATION AND INDUSTRIAL GROWTH

The practical completion of land reform by the end of 1952, together with the tightening of controls over the urban and industrial sector of the economy, meant that by 1953 Peking was in a position to inaugurate joint programs for industrialization and for the collectivization of agriculture. Catching up with the West militarily had been commenced in Korea. The effort to catch up industrially would require a harsh regimentation of economic effort over a prolonged period. The process would lead to urbanization (Shanghai, instead of withering away as first proposed, was already approaching seven million). The swelling cities would increase their demand for agricultural products. Industrialization would also necessitate foreign imports, which could be paid for only by exporting, again, agricultural products. To extract more from the farm economy, a squeezing mechanism must be created in the form of true collectives. While these might lower incentives among agricultural workers, they were the only sure way to enforce saving, and also incidentally the most efficient means for agronomic technical development. Collectivization was therefore inaugurated along with the first five-year plan.

The 1953 grain output did not rise as hoped and a state grain trade monopoly was instituted in November, with a beginning of collection quotas and rationing of supplies. Heavy floods in 1954 and continued stringency led in August 1955 to setting tax quotas for each grain-producing household as well as purchase quotas for grain-deficit households. Collectivization was the logical next step. It required what Alexander Eckstein has called "high-

pressure gradualism," using coercion short of violence and manifold forms of persuasion on the farming populace.

The initial decision to move toward collectivization announced
in December 1953 got results much faster than anticipated. Fifteen
per cent of the farm land and farming families were in agricultural
producers' cooperatives by mid-1955, with many reports of 10 per
cent or even higher increases in production. Mao Tse-tung spent
several weeks touring the major provinces, testing local sentiment.
In October, encouraged by a bumper harvest, the CCP Central
Committee, though apparently not without misgivings and ob-
jections, accepted his startling proposal for accelerated collectivization, with the final elimination of the rich peasant, the merchant-
speculator, land rent, and all capitalistic tendencies in rural life.
Mao called for 2 million agricultural producers' cooperatives of 50
families each (among the 200,000 administrative communities and
their million or so villages) by 1958. This bold plan again went faster
than expected — within less than a year, by May 1956, nine-tenths
of the peasantry were reported to have joined agricultural producers'
cooperatives, which were quickly asked to move on to the higher
level of socialized agriculture by turning themselves into full collective farms. How had this been accomplished?

The experienced French agronomist René Dumont, who visited
43 villages in 14 provinces in late 1955, pointed to a number of
factors. Unlike the disastrous Soviet collectivization of 1929–1932,
the process in China did not lead directly to state ownership of the
land but to ownership by the individual cooperatives, which formally bought out the peasant proprietors. The process was gradual
— from temporary mutual aid teams by successive stages to permanent full-scale cooperatives, from small groups to large ones (the
two million agricultural producers' cooperatives would be reduced
to one million or less, each larger). Most important, the program
at its successive stages had evidently produced results enough to
obviate resistance — at least very little was reported. A sufficient
proportion of China's peasantry seem to have seen no alternative
but to have faith in Chairman Mao and the Party, the celebrated
burning of landlords' title deeds being still fresh in memory even
though the New Democracy had now run its course in only five
years. Unlike Lenin, Mao had begun with the villages.

The proof of this farm program would lie in its capacity to increase production. In the new structure, at least for the moment, state farms (3300 at the end of 1955) served only as pilot operations to lead local development, meeting technical problems of the region, setting an example, absorbing technical graduates of some 26 agricultural colleges. Mechanized agriculture, except on the new plains of Manchuria, remained for the distant future. Instead of the Machine Tractor Stations of the Soviet Union, the center of gravity in the Chinese rural program remained the cooperatives, which would develop forthwith into fully collective farms. They now served as the new focus of village life, undertaking the local public works and welfare activities which under the empire had been the province of gentry leadership. Where the local Confucian degree-holders of the big families had traditionally taken the initiative to repair temples and bridges or maintain schools and charities, it was now the local cooperative or collective farm chairman, probably an enthusiastic Maoist-minded Party appointee, who initiated projects for reforestation, combatting erosion, care of the aged, or improving the local dispensary. While the directives came down from above, the actual measures must be worked out at this level — introduction of pumps or new plows, literacy classes, campaign meetings.

At this level also the ambitious twelve-year rural plan for 1956–1967 set forth bright promises — to see cultural amenities introduced (radios, libraries, cinemas, et cetera), the multitude of diseases and all flood and drought eliminated, forests widely planted, labor fully employed. Mainly by full employment (never yet achieved) the plan hopefully envisioned 400 man-days of work applied annually to every hectare of land, doubling production in South China, increasing it by half nationally. Equally ambitious was the long-term plan to control the Yellow River by a "staircase" of 46 dams on the main stream, plus hydropower and multi-purpose projects, so as to irrigate much of North China.

For the farm boy just learning to read, this confident vision was undoubtedly inspiring. For doubters and dissenters there was plainly announced "reform through labor." Meantime food rationing was institutionalized and quotas set for compulsory delivery of commercial crops. How to resolve the competing investment demands of agriculture and industry was not indicated. Significantly, the farmer's new day was scheduled to dawn only by the end of twelve years, not five.

Industrialization. Preparation for a Soviet-type forced-draft industrial development had gone forward with the nationalization of banking, industry, and trade, with the state buying shares in enterprises to make them joint state-private concerns and with campaigns to exhaust the entrepreneur and make him in effect a state employee. The first five-year plan for 1953–1957 was not published until two and a half years had elapsed for testing it, training technicians and building up statistical services. It was heralded as the "transition to socialism," which now superseded the New Democracy. Among some 1600 major projects in all fields, half would be in industry (including the 156 announced in 1953–54 to be commenced with Soviet aid). The new plants would make tractors, trucks, automobiles, generators, ships, and all the materials and equipment for heavy industry. University graduates would be one-third engineers, produced at the rate of 20,000 a year.

The conflict between the development of agriculture and industry, and the consequent subordination of the former, was apparent in the first five-year plan targets announced in 1955: steel to be quadrupled, power and cement doubled, machine tools more than tripled but cotton piece goods to be increased by less than one-half and food grains by less than one-fifth. In other words, industry could grow only as the farmer kept his consumption down. Collectivization had put him in a box: through price manipulation in favor of industry, his product could be taken from him indirectly as well as by outright collection of crops and taxes. Textile goods would be manufactured to exchange for rural products. But just as men had been cheaper than armament in Chinese warfare, so in her agricultural development China would have to stress capital-cheap, labor-intensive projects like flood control dikes and irrigation ditches, while capital investment was concentrated in industry. Pigs could be multiplied but artificial fertilizer manufacture, for example, was likely to be limited.

This forced-draft industrialization was soon able to channel something like 30 per cent of the gross national product through the government, which used it approximately one-fourth on defense, one-fourth on administration and social services, and one-half for investment. Any growth rate depends on complex definitions and can be endlessly disputed. Communist China's industrial growth, in any case, was rapid, impressive and formidable — the fastest of any underdeveloped Asian country.

Communist China's capacity to follow the Russian industrial model seems likely to be increasingly inhibited as certain specific conditions, which by nature limit China's economic potential, begin to have effect. While China has extensive coal and iron ore reserves, and mineral resources undoubtedly greater than we now know, their utilization requires as a prerequisite a very costly investment in power and transport. China at her level of industrial development in the early 1950's was actually closer to Russia in 1900 than to the Soviet Union of 1928. As Eckstein has pointed out, Russia *in 1900* had only one-quarter China's present rural population pressure and already had a higher per capita production of pig iron, steel, and cotton goods, and more railroad track per square mile, than China had in 1952. By 1928, Russia had a much more extensive rail network and in per capita terms her production of coal, iron, steel, power, textile products, and the like was far greater than China's in 1952. In brief, when the Soviet industrial program began, Russia's over-all per capita product was four times that of present-day China and her land and mineral resources potentially much greater. Only in her coastal and internal water-transport network would China appear to be relatively better off.

When this is viewed against the background of population increase in the two countries and their respective balances between population and food resources, China's prospects of emulating Russia grew perceptibly dimmer. The superabundance of people, estimated at well over 600 million and increasing 1 to 2 per cent yearly, combined with the comparative lack of new land for cultivation, means that China's population must press upon the food supply as Russia's has not. The standard of living therefore cannot be modernized very far, in the sense of raising it from the bamboo-and-rice or -millet level, within the foreseeable future, even though the centralized Chinese state may build up a superstructure of heavy industry and military power — a colossus weak in the stomach.

China's economic dependence on Russia has been marked by the reversal of her foreign trade pattern. Formerly Japan and the West took her soybeans, tung oil, and other farm products and the present Communist-bloc area took hardly 2 per cent of the total. Now China's trade is mainly with the latter. It stresses capital goods imports, which provide something like 15 to 20 per cent of the investment needed for industrialization.

Meanwhile the railroad network has been extended to the northwest, to Outer Mongolia so as to connect with the trans-Siberian (done in 1956), and over the desert road to Turkestan to reach Russian Central Asia by 1960. These lines, accompanied by migration, have opened up the arid northwest frontier for mineral exploitation and also have political-strategic importance, strengthening the revived Chinese grip on Inner Mongolia and Sinkiang even as they permit closer collaboration with Russia in Asia.

Peking's motive in industrializing is to create national power. If the aim were popular welfare, more than a mere seventh or eighth of investment could go into light industry as opposed to heavy, less could go into the armies and strategic railroads. The tribulations of the Chinese people as they come into modern industrial life via the forced-draft totalitarian route will be thus, in a curious way, an index of the national pride of their leaders. Consciously or not, they are the heirs of the imperial tradition of the Middle Kingdom — they refuse to be a second-rate nation. Any estimate of their future course must take account of their view of themselves.

6. IDEOLOGY AND HISTORY

How far Mao Tse-tung has shown originality in applying Marxism-Leninism to the "concrete realities" of China is perhaps a rather academic question. Every translator of ideas from one culture to another must be to some extent an innovator, in the mere act of translation; in transplanting a mode of action, he must be all the more creative, in practice if not in theory.

On the verbal level Mao's homely exhortations are studded with Chinese proverb and metaphor, both classical and colloquial. He castigates neutralists who would "sit on top of a mountain to watch the tigers fight," as well as supercilious cadres who think arguing with peasants is like "playing music to a cow." No one who has skirted a pit of nightsoil covered with maggots can fail to understand Mao's abhorrence of what he calls "the deep, stinking cesspool of Chinese reaction." To quote Confucius' sage advice, "Think twice," does not necessarily promote Confucianism but it helps to fit Communism into the Chinese landscape.

On the level of theory, Mao has continued to warp and bend Communist doctrine to adjust it to local needs. We have noted in

Chapter 13 how Chinese circumstances early made the "rural proletariat" substitute for a genuine urban labor-class in the Maoist modification of Leninism. Again, Stalin had asserted that the Soviet experience, which reached socialism by passing through the stage of "dictatorship of the proletariat," offered the only path to socialism, and this path must be followed by the "people's democracies" of Eastern Europe and presumably by all others. But the Chinese Communists after 1949 quietly denied the necessity of such a dictatorship, maintaining that a mere "hegemony of the proletariat" at the head of a united front and coalition government could lead China to socialism, and moreover could do it by a gradual, persuasive, non-violent transformation, quite unlike the abrupt and violent change postulated by Lenin and Stalin. The doctrine of "many paths to socialism" accepted at the Soviet Twentieth Party Congress in 1956 gave ground to the Maoist as well as the Titoist modifications of Marxism-Leninism, and also confirmed Peking's proud claim to be the model for Asia to follow. Thus Sino-Russian ideological solidarity has been preserved only at the price of concessions which tend to hasten the disintegration of Marxist-Leninist doctrine.

The alignment with international Communism and the remaking of society have also required the rewriting of China's modern history. The new order has stimulated the documenting of new themes, as well as notable achievements in archaeology. Many volumes of valuable historical documents and dubious historical essays have emerged from Peking, mainly on topics prominent in Marxist-Leninist ideology — peasant risings, the early sprouting of capitalism, periodization, the aggressions of imperialism. Meanwhile history is reinterpreted on a vigorous doctrinaire basis for purposes of propaganda, much of it aimed at blackening the American record: our piratical traders trafficked in opium, we joined in plotting the Anglo-French "Second Opium War," we helped the alien and reactionary Manchus suppress the people's revolution led by the Taipings. Thereafter we supported the Manchu rulers and Chinese landlord class, who toadied to us ignominiously, against the Chinese masses struggling to free themselves of oppression. We let our commercial exploitation of the Chinese people be taxed through the Maritime Customs just enough to give financial support to the Ch'ing dynasty which kept them in subjection. China was humiliatingly dragged into what the writer Hu Sheng calls "the imperialist world order (international law)." Our missionaries got their Christian converts privileged status, which however did not always protect them from the people's righteous indignation. Thus the Western powers sustained the Chinese "feudal" order which in turn helped them suck the blood of the Chinese people.

"Tseng Kuo-fan may be considered the first pro-American official in China's political history," says Hu Sheng, for he sent students to study in the United States. But this ignominious "learning from foreigners" only paved the way for their aggressions. The West "never intended to allow China to become a country which could stand on its own feet." Britain and the United States encouraged Japanese imperialism to offset Russian expansion. Our Open Door policy was merely a demand to share equally in the rape of China. A similar use of half-truths and sense of grievance and moral outrage permeates the historical reinterpretation of the reform movement, the Boxer episode, Yuan Shih-k'ai, warlordism, and last but not least, Chiang Kai-shek.

The fault in such interpretations is not so much their inaccuracy — some seem accurate, some not — as their animus. Modern historians can work out a considerable list of valid Chinese grievances against the West, including some that Western residents in their sheltered extraterritorialized existence were hardly aware of at the time. But the story is not all black nor one-sided in fact, and if we are to have Sino-American peace this must be recognized in principle.

Since capitalist-imperialist aggression is an essential element in Peking's view of history, we should be less surprised at the role assigned us. Japan's being the national enemy helped the Chinese Communists' rise to power. Once our military force displaced that of Japan, we inherited her role. Stalin's strategy called for it. Korea confirmed it. One wonders whether Peking could have got along without having the United States as national enemy number-one. In any case, this posture facilitates the destruction of the vestiges of American influence in Chinese life, including the returned-student class of educators, Chrstian leaders, and professional workers formerly trained in the United States. It also undoubtedly reflects the narrow world-view of the Chinese Communists, whose foreign contact has been limited almost entirely to the Soviet bloc. This in turn gives American policy-makers less room for diplomatic maneuver — cast in the role of national enemy of the Chinese revolution, we can hardly respond with uncritical friendliness. A settlement of differences, including mutual diplomatic recognition, has to be a two-way street; its achievement does not depend entirely on us.

The systematic inculcation of invidious historical half-truths in the minds of 600 million people is disquieting, especially when we are labeled the long-time enemy. Another fact is equally disquieting, however: in the present state of their knowledge of Chinese history the American public are often in no position to distinguish truth from half-truth. We have home-work to do before we can criticize constructively, or defend ourselves against the Communist interpretation of China's modern history.

17

Perspectives on
China and Ourselves

THE FIRST CENTURY of contact between America and
China had great significance for both peoples. But it ended in the
final dissolution of the old order — both of traditional Chinese
civilization and of the unequal treaty system which had ushered
it into the modern world. Our traditional China policy and the
attitudes which underlay it are similarly bankrupt. No longer can
we support the Open Door. Quite the contrary, since 1949 we have
embargoed strategic goods for the mainland. No longer can we
defend China's administrative and territorial integrity. On the
contrary, since 1949 we have impaired that of the mainland by our
steadfast defense of Taiwan. The second century of Sino-American
relations has begun with bloody warfare and bitter suspicion.
Plainly a stock-taking is overdue. Now, if ever, we should seek
perspective, both on the Chinese revolution and on American
policy.

1. CHINA TODAY IN THE LIGHT OF HER PAST

This can be approached both from within and from without, in
terms of Chinese domestic political processes (usually subsumed
under the term "dynastic cycle") and in terms of foreign influence
and native response (which we may call a process of "modernization"). Both approaches are attempted below. Neither is fully adequate. The problem is how to synthesize and get beyond them to a
view of China's new totalitarianism.

Echoes of the Dynastic Cycle. The decline and fall of the Ch'ing
Empire and the rebellions of the nineteenth century had many
classic features, which we have noted above and need not recapitu-
late. In the interregnum which followed 1911, Yuan Shih-k'ai, Sun

Yat-sen, Chiang Kai-shek, and Mao Tse-tung with increasing success strove to reunify the Middle Kingdom. The Kuomintang was the precursor of the Chinese Communist Party in seeking to train a new type of scholar-bureaucrat in a new ideology, so as to revive the functions once performed by the Confucian literati and the classics.

Generalissimo Chiang sought to quell the warlords by his personal rectitude as well as by bigger armies and smarter politics. Like Emperors of the T'ang and Sung, he traveled widely over the provinces on tours of inspection and performed ritual acts, climbed T'ai Shan, the sacred mountain, conducted sacrifices at the tombs of the Han Emperors near the Yellow River north of Loyang. Beginning his rule by the military conquest of his rivals, he proceeded in the 1930's to draw scholars into his civil administration while himself setting a moral example as the paternal head of the state. His strength lay in these traditional qualifications: courage and determination to retain power, ethical fervor and austerity that gave him personal prestige, loyalty to those who were loyal to him, ruthlessness and subtlety in balancing his rivals against one another. It was entirely in keeping with this ancient pattern that Chiang Kai-shek, a prisoner of the past, should seek to progress from the status of Hero to that of Sage, a transformation symbolized in 1943 when he became head of the National Central University at Chungking and published *China's Destiny* as a textbook.

Mao in his turn unified the country as a hero risen from the people, like the founders of the Han and Ming. (He went them one better in 1956 and swam the Yangtze, it is said.) Mao's armies in the 1940's were not a scourge upon the peasantry but avenged their wrongs. He "won the hearts of the people" sufficiently to secure food and soldiers from territorial bases. He attracted college students to staff his administration. His ideology claimed the Mandate of History, if not of Heaven. Once in power, his regime surveyed, classified and redistributed both the land and the populace. His example mightily affected the peripheral states. Rising to power with barbarian help, he yet patronized Chinese culture and employed scholars to document the record of the previous regime and point the lesson of its fall. In Peking he built a great Red Square, whither came delegations from Southeast Asia and the Western Regions to watch the great processions.

The reader can continue for himself to recognize echoes of the past in China today. C. P. Fitzgerald, for example, has summarized the traditional Chinese social concepts as embracing (1) a single authority coterminous with civilization, (2) a balanced economy basically managed by the state, (3) an orthodox doctrine which harmonizes and guides all forms of human activity, including the selection of intellectuals for state service. As of 1952, he suggests that these concepts, destroyed during modern times in their traditional form of expression, have found expression again under Communism. Yet at the time of writing he foresaw the New Democracy persisting for some time and collectivization remaining afar off. Events have now outstripped the historian's precedents. Institutional changes have broken the cadence, and the differences between past and present are as great as the similarities. The old patterns cannot even begin to encompass the full sweep of the totalitarian prospect.

Values have changed as well as institutions. The K'ang-hsi Emperor never watched the calisthenics of ten thousand selected maidens wearing shorts, nor commended sons for denouncing their fathers. He did no physical jerks to the noon radio. His succession was provided for in the bedchamber where he begat 35 sons, and was fought out among them, within a family, not a party. K'ang-hsi wooed the scholars, who had nowhere else to turn, but they had only to criticize the classics textually, not themselves in every act and thought. He paid no honors to peasants who exceeded norms nor to the idea of progress or the dialectic, though he would have acknowledged the sequence of *yang* and *yin*.

Since the patterns of the past cannot be entirely expunged, they remain curiously intertwined with new motifs. Peking today has a Marxist-Leninist-Maoist ideological orthodoxy as vigorous as Confucianism used to be; but it believes in progress toward a future millennium, not cyclical repetition descending from a golden age. Dynastic absolutism has been replaced by party dictatorship, the imperial family-clan council by the central executive committee, the scholar-elite by a party elite, tax-gatherers by cadres in the countryside, Confucian classics by Communist classics, written examination by group discussion, scholarly self-cultivation by guilt-ridden self-criticism. Merchants continue to be disesteemed, being undoubtedly bourgeois, but soldiers are now glorified. The sages are class-angled and reevaluated. Labor heroes are the new models to emulate. Women do not aspire to lily feet but approach their romantic nadir, functional interchangeability with men. Responsibility for good conduct is still mutually shared among family and neighborhood groups, but now this ancient automatic check on deviance is extended to include the neighbors' thoughts. The *paochia* is replaced by the street committee. Villages still are mobilized for public works, but the state philosophy of seeking harmony with nature has given way to the industrial urge to conquer nature. Government used to be thinly spread out and superficial and the peasant passive, a sub-political animal. Today the government penetrates every hut, and peasants are people, unless they misbehave.

Modernization. In explaining China's modern history, the chief alternative to the traditional Chinese pattern is, of course, a traditional Western one. Where the Chinese pattern was cyclical, the Western view of history is based on the idea of linear progress (the two can be combined in a spiral). The expansion of the Atlantic community underlies this Western pattern. (Since the Marxist-Leninist scheme was drawn up mainly with the expansion of Europe in mind, much of China's modern history, seen as a product of this expansion, can be fitted into the categories of the Communist interpretation.) When we apply the Western view, certain phases may be distinguished, even though they overlap in time.

In *Phase One,* the traditional Chinese state, being incompatible with and weaker than the modern world, is attacked and mortally wounded by it. Over a period of a century, from the 1840's to the 1940's, the old order is progressively destroyed as a result of contact with the West. The imperial military system is discredited by Western firepower. The agrarian economy and the imperial fiscal system, based on rural tax-gathering, are disrupted by the influx of Western trade and the eventual rise of modern industry. The Emperor's prestige is dimmed by successful foreign aggression against the peripheral vassal states and eventually within spheres of influence in China proper. Efforts at self-defense on the part of the Confucian scholar-administrators — such as by adoption of Western arms, technology, and industry — prove unavailing because the agrarian-bureaucratic society of China cannot modernize as rapidly as the Western nations are modernizing.

China's old order is out of date, maladjusted, and unable to respond adequately and in time. Efforts to reform the administration while retaining its Confucian values are attempted, but they are fore-doomed to failure.

Phase Two begins during this process of decline. New dynamic elements of modernization are absorbed into the traditional Chinese society and begin to work their transformation. One of these is the Western type of nationalism — loyalty to state and country as sovereign symbols in an international order of similar nations. This undermines the old faith in the Confucian relationships under the Emperor. Naturally, the new nationalism has behind it a large backlog of ethnocentrism and xenophobia, suspicion of foreigners and devotion to things Chinese. The transformation from a Sino-centric culturalism to a more modern nationalism implies the destruction of the alien Manchu dynasty.

Another new element injected into the Chinese scene is the idea of economic development, particularly under official supervision and leadership. Economic growth has, of course, been a fact since the early foreign trade began to disrupt the traditional economy. China's great increase in population since the eighteenth century has been a permanent and not a cyclical change. The ingress of foreign transport in the form of coastal and river steamships, followed by railroads, mines, and textile mills, all demonstrate the growth capacities of modern industrialization based on science and technology. The early reformers themselves attempt to achieve economic development under the banner of the traditional idea of strengthening the state. In the process, a new type of scholar, the scientific technician, emerges, and more specialized administrators are required to guide the multiform types of industrial effort.

By the 1930's there develops the concept of rural reconstruction, the application of modern technology to the agrarian economy, a forerunner of part of our contemporary doctrine of economic development. While the Nanking Government achieves relatively little in this regard, during its period of rule the concept takes firm shape among Chinese patriots. As in so many other lines of mod-ernization, the Western missionaries' interest in village reconstruc-tion points the way to a new China in which missionaries will have no part.

Other new elements from abroad which revolutionize the Chinese

social order in the early part of this century are Christianity and
Western liberalism — a body of concepts and practices from which
China has made a rather fastidious but nonetheless important selection. For example, the freedom of the individual from family
controls has gone hand in hand with the denial of the authority
of the sages in intellectual matters and of the Son of Heaven in
politics. In some degree we may speak of the influx of the ideals
of the French Revolution, flowing into China a century afterward
and undermining the old order before the subsequent wave of
Marxism. Startling upsets and reversals of values now occur, often
the result of Christian missionary teachings. Youth is honored over
age, or at least youth is able to acquire the prestige of scholarship
which age formerly monopolized. Egalitarianism likewise extols the
common man, and the modern leader is able to convert the paternalistic Confucian concern for the populace into the Marxist cult of
the people. In this welter of changes, women as individuals are
freed from the severe inequalities of their former status. Under
the general banner of liberalism, democracy, laissez-faire, and
humanitarianism, there emerge new values and new social groups,
which have yet to be integrated into a new order.

Phase Three sees the putting together of some of these elements,
in a new revolutionary dispensation. Looking back over the last
century, one can see in retrospect the emergence of those new forces,
methods, ideals, and social classes which served as raw material for
the Nationalist and the Communist organizers in turn. Patriotic
youth are ready to sacrifice themselves to wipe out China's past
humiliations and build a new nation. New classes of factory workers and treaty-port merchant capitalists have been created by economic growth. New social groups — emancipated women, soldiers
possessed of a new social status, peasants ready to participate in
political life, students ready to join a party — are now in being. The
very multiplicity of these new elements creates a great need for a
new unity under the banner of nationalism and industrialism.

If one follows this Western-type pattern of unilinear social change
in modern China, one may imperceptibly work one's historical
interpretation around to the entirely false conclusion that Chinese
Communism represents the inevitable current phase of China's
modernization.

This would be just as simple-minded as to conclude that it is merely another in a long succession of dynasties. Neither view seems to me adequate.

In actual fact, of course, historical trends seldom develop in straight lines and Mao Tse-tung's being in power today depends on at least two particular circumstances among others: first, that Japan attacked and destroyed the more modern area of Kuomintang China; second, that Chiang Kai-shek, indomitable and uninstructable, developed in his long years on the mainland no rural reconstruction program such as has now been achieved on Taiwan. Peking naturally contends that historical necessity made Japan aggressive and Chiang blind to agrarian reform, but this hindsight overlooks the fact that historical trends are no one's monopoly and may be ridden by alternative power groups.

In some ways (but not others) the Kuomintang period may now be viewed, at the peril of distortion, as a part-way stage toward the present regime. At least in respect of party government, the creation of a party army, the mobilization of youth, and the modernization of the economy, the Kuomintang took faltering steps down the road which the Communists have since traveled. Yet there is another element of the Kuomintang period which it would be a distortion to overlook — namely, the influx of Western ways and values under a government oriented primarily toward the Western democratic world, which I have tried to characterize above under the general term of liberalism. Thus if China under the Kuomintang seemed sometimes to move down the totalitarian road in politics, its cultural activity remained on the whole far different. It is worth noting that the Marxist-Leninist dispensation in China as elsewhere has seemed under pressure to pay lip service to certain liberal goals, even while trying to pervert them in its own interest of state power.

The New Order. Chinese Communism derives its vigor from the clash of cultures, the century of revolutionary change from which it has emerged. In its new order may be seen elements of the imperial tradition, elements of the Western impact. As a fusion of such elements no doubt it may be called the latest phase of China's response to the West, the latest phase of the modernization process. Note, however, that the mixture of old and new, native and foreign, is a selection, made at the level of the lowest common denominator, in the interests of a power state; thus Leninist centralism revives the imperial despotism at the top but gives it a new grip on the masses; five-year plans for industrialization echo the bureaucratic tradition of monopoly over large-scale economic activity but inject a new demand for forced-draft increase of production. Meanwhile the Western checks on state power are rejected in favor of totalitarian "elections," false-front coalitions, "free" criticism in the shadow of "reform through labor." China's past and the Western example are both rich store-houses, but the selections made from them add up to a totalitarianism which is something quite new in China's experience.

Communism in underdeveloped areas offers a rapid shortcut to industrialization, as many observers have noted. In China it is also a shortcut to modern nationalism, to the forced-draft participation of the masses in political life, even against their will as individuals. They no longer have the freedom of silence. Thus the potentialities of modern technology and organization, both economic and political, are used to create national power.

No single formula can describe, much less explain, China's metamorphosis. A number of sequences of terms can be put forward, each from a certain angle. The native political tradition offers unity-decline-rebellion-reunification. The Communist sequence is feudalism–capitalism(imperialism)–socialism. One approach is from oriental despotism to modern totalitarianism, another from Western impact to Chinese response, another by way of industrialism-nationalism. The reader can make his own mixture in appraising the confluence of inner and outer, tradition and innovation.

One feature seems essential to any picture. I refer to the unusually wide gap between pre-modern and modern, the extraordinary contrast between traditional and present-day China. Because of the long isolation of the Chinese culture and social order and their great inertia in their own channels, the past century has precipitated more drastic changes than any other major people has ever experienced. It included among other things, 5 major rebellions and 5 wars involving every world power within the seventy years *before* World War I. The Chinese have had a prouder and more distinctive tradition, have responded more slowly to its collapse, have suffered the humiliations of backwardness longer, than any other people. We in America have moved fast in our material culture, from the horse, buggy, and kerosene lamp to television, jet planes, and missiles, but we have not scrapped and rebuilt in the same short period our system of government and foreign relations, our language and the content of our learning, our whole society. We have not felt the same proud urge to catch up.

This speed of change makes it impossible to prophesy whether Mao Tse-tung is to go down in history as another First Emperor of the Ch'in, who creates a new order by violence during a brief span of tyranny, or as a Khubilai Khan who injects powerful alien elements into the tradition of the Middle Kingdom, or as an Asian Lenin quite outside the bounds of China's previous ken.

Past and Future. Three considerations seem to me primary in any effort to gauge China's future from an historical perspective.

The first is that ancient evils of bureaucratism lie in wait for Peking's mammoth administration at any time its morale declines. Past bureaucracies in China have been peculiarly susceptible to long-term changes of attitude affecting the prestige of the regime in power, partly because administration was so largely personal, according to the character and sense of responsibility of the administrators. Once a regime was contemptible in the public view, the personal relations in the governmental process lent themselves to collusion and corruption, which could be organized the more thoroughly because the old society was less dependent for its survival on the vitality of its legal institutions. Officials and commoners could still remain moral family pillars while they connived at defrauding the Emperor. The latter's only ultimate safeguard was to ensure that they retained a correct attitude toward his regime. Mao Tse-tung is still in this position: bureaucrats with the wrong attitude can defeat his ends and destroy his power.

Secondly, Communist China's methods for ensuring universal conformity in attitude, which seem to be regarded as essential partly to stave off the evils of bureaucratism, are far more complete and intensive than anything the old China ever devised. The organized assault upon the individual personality, neighbor denouncing neighbor, child watching parent, friend "struggling" with friend, and everyone isolated, is the experiential essence of a new totalitarian situation. This is the more threatening to Western values of individual integrity because it seems so thoroughly facilitated, even sanctioned in many Chinese minds for the foreseeable future, by feats of material construction, public welfare and hygiene, technical training and patriotic devotion, which loom on every side in a period of rapid national growth. The French correspondent, Robert Guillain, who had reported the Communist take-over in 1949 not unsympathetically, was appalled in 1955 by the degree of intellectual conformity and critical vacuity. After six years he found a people dressed all alike, sober, quiet, and drably self-effacing in their blue suits, a nation of orderly, industrious "blue ants," trained to have only correct ideas: "thought must come from the anthill and not from the ant." His conclusion: "material achievement, remarkable; spiritual achievement, terrifying."

A third and conclusive consideration, which seems to lock the Chinese people irrevocably into their struggle to increase production through conformity and at the expense of personal freedom, is the rate of population increase. Pressure of numbers has influenced their way of life from early times. It is still the most grievous part of China's inheritance. Every year, famine waits around the corner. Like it or not, the Chinese populace will have to put up with some kind of centralized and dictatorial (whether or not Communist) planning and controls for the foreseeable future simply because there is no alternative in prospect by which to feed them, employ the youth, and satisfy the national pride.

Tradition in Foreign Relations. Historical perspective can give us little reassurance as to the future compatibility of the American and Chinese ways of life. In international politics, however, the strength of China's modern nationalism seems likely in time to reinforce the deeply ingrained attitude which views foreign relations as a problem in the balancing of foreign powers against each other to China's advantage. The ancient dictum, "use barbarians to control barbarians," was followed by dynasty after dynasty in dealing with militarily stronger alien powers. The Han dynasty sought the help of the Yüeh-chih people against the Hsiung-nu. Fifteen hundred years later the Ming used the western Mongols to crush the eastern Mongols and also used the eastern Mongols to crush the western Mongols. The chief recourse of Modern China has been to play off one imperialist against another, the Americans against the British, the British against the Russians, or more recently the League of Nations and the United States against Japan. This principle of Chinese diplomacy crops up in the writings of every official of consequence in century after century. It is no surprise that the Kuomintang right wing looked to the United States to take care of its Soviet problem or that Peking relies upon Russia today.

Using one barbarian against another had its counterpart within China in the occasional use of aliens by one Chinese group against another. The Manchus first entered Peking at the invitation of loyal Ming supporters who sought their help against Chinese rebels. Ward and Gordon were hired by the Chinese government to help suppress the Taipings. The tradition of foreign mercenaries and advisors goes far back. Borodin and Chennault had their predecessors. Marco Polo and Robert Hart have had their successors in the American technicians, professors and press agents of the last decade and the Russian engineers of the present one.

All this suggests the elementary thought that our tactics in power politics toward the Moscow-Peking axis should be divisive, that the Sino-Soviet partnership is not psychologically indissoluble nor indispensable on grounds of Chinese sentiment. Unfortunately for the free world, however, the same factors within the Chinese scene which facilitated the rise of Communism continue thus far to reinforce the tie to Moscow.

2. OUR CHINA POLICY IN THE LIGHT OF ITS FAILURE

The American attitude toward China during the century of the unequal treaties was consciously acquisitive but also benevolent, seeking to give as well as get. We have been proud of our record, indeed a bit patronizing toward the imperialist powers, of lesser virtue.

Inevitably, however, the Chinese experience of Sino-American relations was different from the American experience. We found our contact with China adventurous, exhilarating, rewarding in material or spiritual terms. Americans who didn't like it could avoid it. China, on the other hand, found this contact forced upon her. It was a foreign invasion, humiliating, disruptive, and in the end catastrophic. There can be little doubt that the Western menace to the traditional Chinese way of life often seemed, in the nineteenth century, every bit as dire, as evil and ominous, as the totalitarian Nazi and Soviet threats have seemed for the American way in recent decades. The Chinese, behind their polite exterior, did not fully share our national enthusiasm for Sino-American friendship.

We were also misled by an historical circumstance. We discovered China in an era of dynastic decline and social demoralization, not realizing that it was an interregnum between periods of unity and central power. We lumped together two different phenomena — technological backwardness and social disorder. No doubt the two are somewhat interdependent. But we now know that a new social order can be built up without waiting for technological progress to be achieved. Morale and social cohesion, in other words, do not depend on gadgetry as much as Madison Avenue would like to think. Communists still dusty from the caves of Yenan took over metropolitan Shanghai and the modern economy and made them work.

As a result, where China formerly seemed condemned by fate to a quaint if sometimes exasperating backwardness in all things economic, political, and social, we now face a strong government in a still backward country. Nationalism, though long retarded, has achieved maturity; industrialism must follow.

Our thinking, in conservative America, has not kept pace with China's revolution. The first reaction of many Americans, suddenly confronted by a China strong, chauvinist, and anti-Western (instead of weak and pro-American) was to seize upon international Communism as the explanation and attribute our reverse to Kremlin plots and State Department treachery. Some held that the Communist take-over was not a "real" revolution but a contrived one. Senators agreed that we should never have "permitted" it. A few still speak of our "loss" of China.

This loss, I suggest, has been chiefly in our heads. For this latest phase of China's long history (unprecedented in our brief experience but not quite so much so in that of the Chinese people) has called into question our own view of ourselves and our place in the world process. The tables have turned. A totalitarian China seems to threaten the future of our way of life. Must the densely populated, underdeveloped peasant-bureaucratic societies of the East all go Communist? Is there no chance of genuine, individualist democracy in the crowded paddy-fields of monsoon Asia?

This emotional question, I submit, has put some of us in a mild state of shock, demoralized and disinclined to use our heads in serious study. Possibly it calls up a more general fear, that the day of individualism is waning. At all events, we have had a prolonged national distaste for the topic of Communist China. For example, we have supinely acquiesced in a blockade of elementary news reporting, as though we could put our faith in a combination of our mighty Seventh Fleet and our even greater ignorance.

If it be true, as I am suggesting, that our emotional reaction to the rise of Chinese Communism has been an attempted rejection of reality, the reasons for this escapism are not far to seek. Insofar as the missionary conversion and general uplift of the Chinese people expressed our conviction that we led the march of human progress, our self-confidence has been dealt a grievous blow. One fourth of mankind in China have spurned not only Christianity but also town-meeting democracy, the supremacy of law, the ideals of individualism, the multi-party election process, civil liberties and the self-determination of peoples, indeed, our entire political order and its concepts of freedom and security through due process. How can we not feel our basic values directly menaced? The dirty face of the police state was, to our view, clearly visible behind the promises of Communism in China as elsewhere. *If* the Chinese people willingly chose it, it can be concluded that a majority of mankind are not going our way — at least, not for the present.

One consolation in this crisis, therefore, is to think that the Chinese Communist dictatorship does not represent the interests of a large enough proportion of the Chinese people, that it maintains itself only by force and manipulation, that, in fine, it is too evil to last. This can be endlessly debated. Some will argue that the new order is not viable.

Such, I fear, is not the case. Peking's collapse is always a possibility but at present (in 1958) we have little reason to think it probable. What we see in mainland China today is a new all-powerful bureaucracy coercing the populace but drawn from it for the purpose; a new elite urging on their labors, organizing their lives. This new totalitarian system has profound evils built into it but it has remained viable in Russia. A less thorough and more superficial autocracy proved viable under one Chinese dynasty after another. We cannot conclude that Chinese Communism's obvious evils are likely to be sufficient to destroy it. Clutching at this straw will not help us.

In short, we have to face it.

Once this psychological adjustment has been made, we can set to work to live in the same world with the new China. Intellectual recognition of its existence, however, does not necessarily mean diplomatic recognition, which is a matter of expediency, something to bargain over — preferably before our bargaining power declines. Realism about the mainland may bring realism about Taiwan, which cannot be one of "two Chinas" but should be guaranteed independence as a separate state if the people there desire it, which seems likely to be the case.

Living in the same world with a nationalistic, overpopulated, poverty-stricken Communist-managed China may become a challenge that will make or break us. The new phase of our relations will demand hard study, emotional maturity, skilled personnel. These call for effort by American citizens, not merely the United States Government.

The first edition of this book in 1948 concluded as follows:

"If we consider the United States and the Soviet Union as competing centers of a new world order, it is plain that the disintegration of the old order in China leaves that country open to reorganization under the dominant influence of one or the other of these two competing world powers. But this is not primarily a military issue. It is fundamentally a social issue in the broad sense, a question of the formation and sustenance of new patterns of life, the use of new skills and knowledge, the creation of a new social structure and new sources of political authority, among the Chinese people. The outside power which can contribute most to this process can thereby gain the greatest influence in China. Our task is therefore how to contribute to solving China's problems more effectively than the Russians can contribute."

As of 1958 we have fallen behind in this competition. Some say we have lost it. History does not warrant our taking any estimate as final. But the challenge is plain: the century during which the Chinese had to learn to live in our Western world is past. Now we both have to learn to live on the same planet.

Suggested Reading

China used to be a journalist's dream and a statistician's nightmare, with more human drama and fewer verifiable facts per square mile than anywhere else in the world. Today Peking pumps out production data as if to make up for lost time, yet even the current flood of figures cannot quite drown out the national personality. For the American reader it is more than ever necessary to penetrate the past and get a long-run view of China's recent transformation. As successful revolutionaries the Chinese Communists see evil in the past and good in the present, and want to rewrite history accordingly, to a greater degree than historians are likely to do. Yet the historical perspective of non-Communist foreign observers is also constantly menaced by the subjective hopes and fears of both the historians and their readers.

Research in libraries and observation in the field are both indispensable in the study of another society, but I believe the latter has a special value in the case of China. The present volume probably owes as much to seven years spent in various parts of China as it does to twenty years devoted to study of China in the West. This is because the ways of an alien land have to be experienced to be understood or even believed. Western man since Marco Polo has not stopped trying to comprehend Chinese ways. Yet the writers of each generation, whether philosophers of the eighteenth-century Enlightenment or exemplars of the treaty-port mind, have viewed Chinese civilization with a large degree of subjectivity. I doubt that social scientists can avoid doing so today, for the final portrait that one makes of an entire culture or society is a work of art, not of measurement.

The only recourse in this situation is for the reader to become in part a student, comparing one book with another, and in part a statesman, remembering that life is never quite encompassed in print, least of all Chinese life.

Sections 1 and 2 below indicate major studies or recent works on various aspects of China — traditional, and modern. On the problem of maintaining an informed and critical view of American policy and Chinese Communism, see Sections 3 and 4.

The post-war world has seen multiple explosions — demographic as well as nuclear — along with the accelerated growth of science and technology. In the midst of this frenetic expansion of numbers, knowledge and problems, Chinese studies have not been left behind. So voluminous has been the outpouring of research in this field that this bibliography has greatly increased in length, even though I have omitted many works cited in the first edition.

1. STUDIES OF CHINA'S TRADITIONAL CIVILIZATION

In the following suggestions I have stressed the work of the new generation of American specialists on China, not because their research is innately superior to that of the older European Sinology, by which they have benefited, but because it is sometimes more recent and up-to-date, as well as accessible to the American reader. Works not in English are omitted.

General. For a summary of the facts known about China the most reliable general source is still Kenneth Scott Latourette, *The Chinese: Their History and Culture* (Macmillan,* third edition, revised, 2 volumes, 1946), which has chapters on Chinese history and society from nearly all angles, with useful bibliographical sections. It is not exciting reading, however. Facts about the land and the people's use of it are attractively presented in George B. Cressey, *China's Geographic Foundations: A Survey of the Land and its People* (McGraw-Hill, 1934), some of which is summarized in his *Asia's Lands and Peoples* (McGraw-Hill, 1944). The same author's *Land of the 500 Million* (McGraw-Hill, 1955) is an interesting re-do of the subject, up-dated bibliographically. Herold J. Wiens, *China's March toward the Tropics: a discussion of the southward penetration of China's culture, peoples and political control . . .* (Hamden, Conn.: Shoe String Press, 1954) is one of the few works in historical geography. The most complete historical atlas is A. A. L. Herrmann, *Historical and Commercial Atlas of China* (Harvard University Press, 1936). Theodore Shabad, *China's Changing Map: A Political and Economic Geography of the Chinese People's Republic* (Praeger, 1956) is a systematic survey based on Moscow and Peking data.

Of general works on Chinese history, in addition to Latourette, two of the most readable are C. P. Fitzgerald, *China: A Short Cultural History* (4th revised edition, Praeger, 1954 [1935]) and Wolfram Eberhard, *A History of China* (Berkeley and Los Angeles, University of California Press, 1950). They are not, however, very comprehensive (nor undisputed on all points of scholarship). A more detailed scholarly

* If not otherwise noted, publishers are in New York.

survey is by Professor L. Carrington Goodrich of Columbia, *A Short History of the Chinese People* (Harper and Brothers, 1943), which is most concerned with the origins and development of China's material civilization and her early contacts with foreign peoples. A readable but rather superficial survey is a translation from the French, René Grousset, *The Rise and Splendour of the Chinese Empire* (Berkeley and Los Angeles, University of California Press, 1953). All these works deal with the traditional or imperial era down *to* modern times.

The symposium edited by the late Harley F. MacNair of the University of Chicago, *China* (Berkeley and Los Angeles: University of California Press, The United Nations Series, 1946), in its various chapters by some thirty contributors deals mainly with Chinese history, philosophy, religion, and literature rather than with the social sciences. A useful bibliography of books and articles on Sinological studies and the history of Chinese civilization is L. C. Goodrich and H. C. Fenn, *A Syllabus of the History of Chinese Civilization and Culture* (China Society of America, fifth edition, revised, 1950). The most useful chronology, really an historical epitome, is in W. L. Langer, *An Encyclopaedia of World History* (Boston: Houghton Mifflin, revised edition 1948 [1940]); the China sections are mainly by Charles S. Gardner. My colleague Professor Edwin O. Reischauer has prepared a useful *Chronological Chart of Far Eastern History* (Cambridge: Harvard University Press, 1947).

Origins. The most authoritative brief survey of archaeological origins, with a bibliography, is by the distinguished leader of the Academia Sinica at Taipei, Dr. Li Chi, *The Beginnings of Chinese Civilization: Three Lectures Illustrated with Finds at Anyang* (Seattle: University of Washington Press, 1957). While very extensive diggings and further discoveries have been reported from the mainland, comprehensive scholarly studies are not yet available in English. The early Anyang finds and the cultural evidences of the oracle bones are described in a popular style by Herrlee G. Creel, *The Birth of China* (London: J. Cape, 1936). Professor Creel, who can be either popular or scholarly, has written among other things an interesting little pamphlet on *Chinese Writing* (Washington, D. C.: American Council on Education, 1943). Bernhard Karlgren, *The Chinese Language* (Ronald Press, 1949) is a brief exposition by a leading Sinologist.

Society. Chinese society has been described for centuries but seldom analyzed. On Chinese social structure one creative modern worker is Professor Hsiao-t'ung Fei, whose writings in English include *Peasant Life in China: A Field Study of Country Life in the Yangtze Valley* (Dutton, 1939); with Chih-i Chang, *Earthbound China, A Study of*

Rural Economy in Yunnan (Chicago: University of Chicago Press, 1945); and "Peasantry and Gentry, an Interpretation of Chinese Social Structure and its Changes," an article in *The American Journal of Sociology* (volume LII, number 1, July 1946). A volume of Fei's essays, *China's Gentry* (Chicago: University of Chicago Press, 1953), was published after his absorption into the new order in Peking. The most thorough statistical research on the gentry class, in the sense of degree-holders, is Chung-li Chang, *The Chinese Gentry, Studies on their Role in Nineteenth-Century Chinese Society* (Seattle: University of Washington Press, 1955). Work in this field has been stimulated by the systematic writings early in this century of Max Weber, recently made available in English — for example, *The Religion of China: Confucianism and Taoism,* translated by H. H. Gerth (Glencoe, Illinois: The Free Press, 1951).

On the family system Olga Lang, *Chinese Family and Society* (New Haven: Yale University Press, 1946), makes use of field studies and Chinese popular literature as well as the work of earlier writers. The family system at work in a village may be seen in Martin Yang, *A Chinese Village: Taitou, Shantung Province* (Columbia University Press, 1945); Lin, Yüeh-hua, *The Golden Wing: A Sociological Study of Chinese Familism* (London: Kegan Paul, Trench, Trubner, 1948); and Francis L. K. Hsu, *Under the Ancestors' Shadow: Chinese Culture and Personality* (Columbia University Press, 1948). The most recent field study is by Morton H. Fried, *Fabric of Chinese Society: A Study of the Social Life of a Chinese County Seat* (Praeger, 1953). The chief theoretical work is by Marion J. Levy, *The Family Revolution in Modern China* (Cambridge: Harvard University Press, 1949).

On China as an "Oriental" society the most fertile ideas have been put forth over three decades by Karl August Wittfogel, who has directed a large-scale analysis of social and economic data from the twenty-four standard histories. The first volume of this project is *History of Chinese Society: Liao (907–1125)* by Wittfogel and Feng, Chia-sheng (Philadelphia: American Philosophical Society, 1949). Dr. Wittfogel's massive and long-awaited theoretical exposition is *Oriental Despotism: A Comparative Study of Total Power* (New Haven: Yale University Press, 1957). The problem of China's early social structure is dealt with by Derk Bodde in a chapter, "Feudalism in China," in pages 49–92 of Rushton Coulborn, ed., *Feudalism in History* (Princeton: Princeton University Press, 1956).

The Classical Period. The Chinese classics have long been available in standard translations, principally by James Legge, *The Chinese Classics* (Oxford: At the Clarendon Press, second edition, 7 volumes, 1893–1895).

Among others, Arthur Waley has contributed a number of very attractive versions — *The Analects of Confucius* (London: G. Allen and Unwin, 1938); *The Book of Songs* (London: G. Allen and Unwin, 1937); *The Way and Its Power* (London: G. Allen and Unwin, 1934), which is a Taoist classic. See also his *Three Ways of Thought in Ancient China* (London: G. Allen and Unwin, 1939; Doubleday Anchor Books, 1956) for a study of the early philosophies. A collection of passages from the classics is by Lin Yutang, *The Wisdom of China and India* (Random House, 1942).

On Chinese philosophy the leading general work is the translation by Derk Bodde of Fung, Yu-lan, *A History of Chinese Philosophy* (volume I, Peiping: H. Vetch, 1937; reissued together with the publication of volume II, Princeton: Princeton University Press, 1952). Fung, Yu-lan, *A Short History of Chinese Philosophy* (Macmillan, 1948), though edited by Professor Bodde, is a separate study. The greatest of the sages is restudied in detail by H. G. Creel, *Confucius: The Man and the Myth* (John Day, 1949). Professor Creel has also done a readable nontechnical survey, *Chinese Thought from Confucius to Mao Tse-tung* (Chicago: University of Chicago Press, 1953). James R. Ware has published a new translation, *The Sayings of Confucius* (Mentor Books, 1955). A fascinating, fresh account of Taoism is presented in Holmes Welch, *The Parting of the Way: Lao Tzu and the Taoist Movement* (Boston: Beacon Press, 1957).

The political institutions of the Warring States period are analyzed in Richard L. Walker, *The Multi-state System of Ancient China* (Hamden, Conn.: Shoe String Press, 1953). The unification of China by the Ch'in dynasty is pictured by Derk Bodde in two works, *China's First Unifier* (Leiden: E. J. Brill, 1938); and *Statesman, Patriot, and General in Ancient China* (New Haven: American Oriental Society, 1940). On the Han, Homer Dubs has translated the annals section of the official history, *The History of the Former Han Dynasty by Pan Ku* (Baltimore: Waverly Press, volume 1, 1938; volume 2, 1944; volume 3, 1955). C. Martin Wilbur, *Slavery in China during the Former Han Dynasty 206 B.C.–A.D. 25* (Chicago: Field Museum of Natural History, 1943) includes a brilliant analysis of Han society. Key economic sections from the Former Han history by Pan Ku have been translated by Nancy Lee Swann, *Food and Money in Ancient China* (Princeton: Princeton University Press, 1950).

The Middle Period. So strong was the hold of the Chinese classical tradition that up until a decade ago relatively few monographic studies had as yet appeared on the long period from 220 to 1644 A.D. One of the few such studies is by Woodbridge Bingham, *The Founding of the T'ang Dynasty* (Baltimore: Waverly Press, 1941). In recent years a number of important works have appeared. Edwin O. Reischauer, *Ennin's Diary: The Record of a Pilgrimage to China in Search of the Law* (Ronald Press, 1955) translates a unique first-person account of T'ang China. The companion volume, *Ennin's Travels in T'ang China* (Ronald Press, 1955) is an absorbing summary and commentary, rounding out this ninth-century Marco Polo's picture of China at the apex of world civilization. Other recent monographs on successive periods include Edwin G. Pulleyblank, *The Background of the Rebellion of An Lu-shan* (Oxford University Press, 1955); E. A. Kracke, Jr., *Civil Service in Early Sung China, 960–1067* (Cambridge: Harvard University Press, 1953); and Herbert Franz Schurmann, *Economic Structure of the Yuan Dynasty* (Cambridge: Harvard University Press, 1956, Harvard-Yenching Institute Studies XVI).

Among topical surveys the largest is Joseph Needham's seven-volume *Science and Civilization in China* (Volume I, *Introductory Orientations,* Cambridge University Press, 1954; Volume II, *History of Scientific Thought,* 1956). Volume 7 on *The Social Background* will contain unified bibliographies and indexes. Lien-sheng Yang, *Money and Credit in China, A Short History* (Cambridge: Harvard University Press, 1952) describes these important institutions over two millennia. James Robert Hightower, *Topics in Chinese Literature: Outlines and Bibliographies* (Cambridge: Harvard University Press, 1950) provides a guide to this undeveloped field. Another important topical monograph is T. F. Carter, *The Invention of Printing in China and Its Spread Westward,* as revised and up-dated by Professor L. C. Goodrich (second edition, Ronald Press, 1955 [1925]).

Although adequate reference to European Sinological studies is impossible and perhaps inappropriate here, note may be taken of a comprehensive bibliography in German, Herbert Franke, *Sinologie* (Bern: A. Francke, 1953) which refers to the work of Etienne Balazs (Paris), Wolfgang Franke (Hamburg) and other leading scholars on the Continent.

Chinese intellectual history, including Buddhism and Neo-Confucianism, may be pursued in volume 2 of Bodde's translation of Fung, already noted, and in two symposia representing a score of authors — Arthur F. Wright, ed., *Studies in Chinese Thought* (American Anthropological Association, Memoir No. 75, and Chicago: University of Chicago Press, 1953) and John K. Fairbank, ed., *Chinese Thought and Institutions* (Chicago: University of Chicago Press, 1957). W. T. de Bary with others has edited an important volume of general readings for use in course instruction, *Sources of the Chinese Tradition,* including new translations (Columbia University Press, for publication in 1959). One of Arthur Waley's recent volumes is *The Real*

Tripitaka and Other Pieces (London: Allen and Unwin, 1952), mainly on the Chinese Buddhist pilgrim Hsuan-tsang who went to India in 629–645. Whether or not the parochial discipline of philosophy in the Western tradition survives as a discipline, the new study of intellectual history may be expected eventually to take fuller account of the Chinese philosophical experience.

Chinese art, as something to look at as well as read about, is beautifully and critically represented in a popular volume, Laurence Sickman and Alexander Soper, *The Art and Architecture of China* (Baltimore: Penguin Books, 1956) with excellent plates and references also to the larger works of Osvald Siren and others.

The Barbarians of Inner Asia. Study of Chinese border relations with Manchuria, Mongolia, and Sinkiang have been illumined and greatly stimulated by Owen Lattimore, *Inner Asian Frontiers of China* (American Geographical Society, second edition, 1951 [1940]), which builds on the same author's earlier publications and field experience — for example, his *Manchuria, Cradle of Conflict* (Macmillan, 1932). Wolfram Eberhard, *Conquerors and Rulers, Social Forces in Medieval China* (Leiden: Brill, 1952) pursues some of the same themes historically, differing with certain views of K. A. Wittfogel. Conceptions of Chinese-nomad relations have been fruitfully developed in a case study by Franz Michael, *The Origin of Manchu Rule in China, Frontier and Bureaucracy as Interacting Forces in the Chinese Empire* (Baltimore: Johns Hopkins Press, 1942).

The most thorough work on the Mongols in history has been done in Europe, particularly in France. A detailed study of their trans-Asian imperial structure is given in George Vernadsky, *The Mongols and Russia* (New Haven: Yale University Press, 1953). Although many studies have since appeared, one of the briefest, readable scholarly summaries in English is still that of B. Y. Vladimirtsov, *The Life of Chingis-Khan* (London: 1930).

Marco Polo is a field in himself. One of the most available of many editions is the translation of William Marsden in the Everyman's Library (Dutton). His description of the world has been summarized in a most interesting fashion in Aldo Ricci, *The Travels of Marco Polo* (London: G. Routledge and Sons, 1931), based on the Italian of L. F. Benedetto; and by Henry H. Hart, *Venetian Adventurer* (Palo Alto: Stanford University Press, 1942), among others.

Political Institutions. The political institutions of the old China, although they endured longer than any others recorded in history, as of 1948 had not yet come to the attention of American political scientists. As of 1958 interest has been expressed but still no leading political scientist has succeeded in leaving his general field long enough to study

Chinese and interpret Confucianism in modern political terms. For pioneer studies by James T. C. Liu and others, see the symposia on Chinese thought noted above.

On Chinese law, A. F. P. Hulsewé has published *Remnants of Han Law,* volume I (Leiden: Brill, 1955). Other able Dutch studies are by Marinus J. Meijer, *The Introduction of Modern Criminal Law in China* (Batavia: De Unie, 1950), and M. H. van der Valk, *Conservatism in Modern Chinese Family Law* (Leiden: Brill, 1956). A few other works on modern Chinese law have also appeared, but no one has ventured far into the voluminous records of China's recent dynasties. The Ming remains mysterious, and the functioning of the Manchu dynasty can best be understood, on the whole, through the compendious accounts of eyewitnesses like the American missionary, S. Wells Williams, *The Middle Kingdom: A Survey of the Geography, Government, Literature, Social Life, Arts, and History of the Chinese Empire* (Wiley and Halsted, 1848; revised edition, 1883).

The chief milestone in our knowledge of early modern China is A. W. Hummel, editor, *Eminent Chinese of the Ch'ing Period (1644–1912)* (2 volumes, Washington, D. C.: Government Printing Office, 1943–44), a biographical dictionary recounting the official careers and achievements of some 800 Chinese of note. This is the main reference work for serious students of the Ch'ing period. A similar work is needed for the Ming. The Sung is being studied by an international project led by E. Balazs at Paris.

2. MODERN CHINA

Early Western Relations. The old Chinese system of international relations and the Western countries' position in it are described in a heavily bibliographical article by J. K. Fairbank and S. Y. Teng, "On the Ch'ing Tributary System," *Harvard Journal of Asiatic Studies* (volume 6, number 2, June 1941), which attempted to explore a new field for research rather than to give the final word on it.

The factual outlines of China's foreign relations down to 1931 are summarized in H. B. Morse and H. F. MacNair, *Far Eastern International Relations* (Boston: Houghton Mifflin, 1931) which builds upon earlier standard works by Dr. Morse. For details of the amazing Ming expeditions through the Indian Ocean, however, one must still go to the files of the Sinological journal, *T'oung pao* (Leiden: 1890–), for articles by P. Pelliot (volume 30, 1933; volume 31, 1935) and J. J. L. Duyvendak (volume 34, 1939).

On the Jesuits at Peking, one of many studies is Arnold H. Rowbotham, *Missionary and Mandarin: the Jesuits at the Court of China*

(Berkeley: University of California Press, 1942). The Jesuit pioneers, like Marco Polo, form an entire field of study. Father Louis J. Gallagher has translated a basic work, *China in the Sixteenth Century: The Journals of Matthew Ricci: 1583–1610* (Random House, 1953). A popularly written and interesting general account of Ricci is Vincent Cronin, *The Wise Man from the West* (London: Rupert Hart-Davis, 1955). The Portuguese pioneers in China and Japan have been illumined in a series of notable studies by C. R. Boxer, including, on Macao, *Fidalgos in the Far East 1550–1770* (The Hague: Nijhoff, 1948). The broad outlines of the early European contact with China are discussed in the early sections of G. B. Sansom, *The Western World and Japan, A Study in the Interaction of European and Asiatic Cultures* (Knopf, 1950). The discovery of China by the philosophers of the European Enlightenment has also been studied in many monographs: the most general is still A. Reichwein, *China and Europe* (Knopf, 1925); an interesting recent study is W. W. Appleton, *A Cycle of Cathay. The Chinese Vogue in England* . . . (Columbia University Press, 1951).

The Western Impact and China's Response. Western imperialism in China is most vividly summarized in W. L. Langer, *The Diplomacy of Imperialism* (2 volumes, Knopf, second edition, 1950 [1935]), while Christian missionary efforts are recorded in detail in K. S. Latourette, *A History of Christian Missions in China* (Macmillan, 1929). The latter have been surveyed also in the same author's monumental *A History of the Expansion of Christianity,* volume 6 (Harper, 1944). These works, however, are based on the published record; missionary archives are as yet unstudied.

A volume of some 65 translated documents with narrative summaries, *China's Response to the West. A Documentary Survey 1839–1923* by Ssu-yü Teng and John K. Fairbank with E-tu Zen Sun and Chaoying Fang (Cambridge: Harvard University Press, 1954) was accompanied by an 84-page *Research Guide for China's Response to the West,* separately published without fanfare, which attempted to indicate what had been done and not done in this field as of 1953. Since this work provides both a bibliographical list and critical discussions of sources under most of 28 chapter headings, including full references to six other bibliographical publications by the present writer, it is believed that the noting of lists of bibliographical lists of bibliographies, et cetera, on this topic may for present purposes safely cease at this point.

Survey Texts. Well-based surveys of China's modern foreign relations are given in Paul H. Clyde, *The Far East: A History of the Impact of the West on Eastern Asia* (Prentice-Hall, third revised edition, 1958 [1948]); H. F. MacNair and Donald Lach, *Modern Far Eastern International Relations* (Van Nostrand, 1950); and H. M. Vinacke, *A His-*

tory of the Far East in Modern Times (Appleton-Century-Crofts, fifth edition, 1950 [1928]), among others. These three volumes each represent an organic development from earlier works or editions. The latest text and one of the most comprehensive is *The Far East in the Modern World* by Franz H. Michael and George E. Taylor (Holt, 1956), who have directed the work of the Far Eastern and Russian Institute at the University of Washington, Seattle. Not many writers have yet attempted to narrate China's modern domestic politics. One of the few such volumes is Li Chien-nung, *The Political History of China 1840–1928,* translated by Ssu-yü Teng and Jeremy Ingalls (Van Nostrand, 1956).

Rebellion, Reform, and Revolution. This is one of the fastest-changing sectors of Chinese studies. Western monographs are steadily appearing, while the new regime in Peking is sponsoring extensive compilations of documents and drastic reinterpretations of events from the Opium War to the present. Michael Greenberg, *British Trade and the Opening of China 1800–42* (Cambridge University Press, 1951) provides a first approach through the archives of the leading British firm of Jardine, Matheson and Co. Among recent American studies are Earl Swisher, *China's Management of the American Barbarians: A Study of Sino-American Relations 1841–1861, with Documents* (New Haven, Conn.: Far Eastern Publications, 1953), which provides extensive translations of Chinese official correspondence; and John King Fairbank, *Trade and Diplomacy on the China Coast: the Opening of the Treaty Ports 1842–1854* (Cambridge: Harvard University Press, 1953, 2 volumes). The Opium War itself still awaits definitive treatment.

On the Taiping upheaval, a British consular interpreter's nineteenth-century classic, Thomas Taylor Meadows, *The Chinese and their Rebellions* (London, 1856) has been reprinted (Stanford: Academic Reprints, 1953). E. P. Boardman, *Christian Influence upon the Ideology of the Taiping Rebellion 1850–1864* (Madison: University of Wisconsin Press, 1952) analyses textually the Taiping borrowings from the Old Testament. Another brief workmanlike study, Siang-tseh Chiang, *The Nien Rebellion* (Seattle: University of Washington Press, 1954) illumines this neglected subject for almost the first time. The mid-century era of rebellion as a whole, however, also awaits the hand of a master. John F. Cady, *The Roots of French Imperialism in Eastern Asia* (Ithaca, New York: Cornell University Press, 1954, for the American Historical Association) thoroughly explores French activity in and near China during this period.

On the post-Taiping epoch Mary C. Wright, *The Last Stand of Chinese Conservatism. The T'ung-chih Restoration, 1862–1874* (Stanford: Stanford University Press, 1957) uses extensive Chinese documentation to make a major contribution to our understanding of the Confucian state and its responses to domestic and foreign crises. A similarly penetrating view of the Self-strengthening and Reform movements in later decades is still wanting. One essential source on the period, based on the now inaccessible Chinese Imperial Maritime Customs archives, is Stanley F. Wright, *Hart and the Chinese Customs* (Belfast, Ireland: Mullan, 1950), already a rare book. Nathan A. Pelcovits, *Old China Hands and the Foreign Office* (King's Crown Press for the American Institute of Pacific Relations, 1948) studies British policy formation up to 1900.

Economic developments in the late nineteenth century are dealt with in three monographs: Harold C. Hinton, *The Grain Tribute System of China (1845–1911)*, Edwin G. Beal, *The Origin of Likin*, and Ellsworth C. Carlson, *The Kaiping Mines (1877–1912)*, all distributed by the Harvard University Press (1956, 1958, and 1957). The "official-supervision and merchant-operation" mode of enterprise is analyzed by Albert Feuerwerker, *China's Early Industrialization: Sheng Hsuan-huai and Mandarin Enterprise* (Cambridge: Harvard University Press, 1958).

The setting up of government schools to deal with Western studies will be studied in a forthcoming volume by Knight Biggerstaff.

At the end of the century, one leading reformer is brilliantly interpreted by Joseph R. Levenson, *Liang Ch'i-ch'ao and the Mind of Modern China* (Cambridge: Harvard University Press, 1953). The efforts and, on the whole, success of Chinese diplomacy in 1900 are explored for the first time by Chester C. Tan, *The Boxer Catastrophe* (Columbia University Press, 1955). The process of military reform, particularly under Yuan Shih-k'ai, is traced by Ralph L. Powell, *The Rise of Chinese Military Power 1895–1912* (Princeton: Princeton University Press, 1955). Valuable studies of Li Hung-chang, Chang Chih-tung, constitutional reform, and many other leaders and issues are in process but not yet completed.

A thorough study of Sun Yat-sen's life and work is long overdue. One of the best of many superficial biographies is still Lyon Sharman, *Sun Yat-sen* (John Day, 1934). Others, more recent, but sketchy, are Bernard Martin, *Strange Vigour* (London: W. Heinemann, 1944); and Stephen Chen and Robert Payne, *Sun Yat-sen, A Portrait* (John Day, 1946). Sun's famous lectures on the Three Principles of the People have been translated by Frank W. Price in an authorized version, *San Min Chu I* (Shanghai: 1927, reprinted Chungking: Ministry of Information of the Republic of China, 1943), and also by a Jesuit father, M. D'Elia, *The Triple Demism of Sun Yat-sen* (Wuchang: Franciscan Press, 1931) with commentary. Marius B. Jansen, *The Japanese and Sun Yat-sen* (Cambridge: Harvard University Press, 1954) explores the early Japanese aspect, indeed orientation, of Sun's many-sided career.

On the warlord era several studies are in progress. Franklin W. Houn,

Central Government of China 1912-1928 (Madison: University of Wisconsin Press, 1957) studies the political institutions at Peking. On Wang Ching-wei there are some adulatory biographies, but almost nothing as yet on other early Kuomintang leaders.

The Treaty System and Modernization. This is becoming a major area for monographic contributions by Western scholars. In general, study of economic development is more advanced than is the critical analysis of the influence of Christian missions.

On foreign rights and interests under the unequal treaties, the latest and presumably last handbook is H. S. Quigley and G. H. Blakeslee, *The Far East* (Boston: World Peace Foundation, 1938). Two works reflect China's problems of modernization within the framework of the unequal treaties — S. F. Wright, *China's Struggle for Tariff Autonomy: 1843-1938* (Shanghai: Kelly and Walsh, 1938), and Chang Kia-ngau, *China's Struggle for Railway Development* (John Day, 1943). A useful monograph on railway diplomacy is E-tu Zen Sun, *Chinese Railways and British Interests 1898-1911* (King's Crown Press, Columbia University, 1954). Rhoads Murphey, *Shanghai: Key to Modern China* (Cambridge: Harvard University Press, 1953) is that rare item, an historico-geographic monograph. G. C. Allen and Audrey G. Donnithorne in *Western Enterprise in Far Eastern Economic Development: China and Japan* (Macmillan, 1954) outline the modernization of commercial and industrial processes in general. Another key study is Frank M. Tamagna, *Banking and Finance in China* (International Secretariat, Institute of Pacific Relations, 1942), which traces the growth of the money market and modern banking. A symposium of preliminary studies in a new field to be presented by Alexander Eckstein and John K. Fairbank, editors, on Chinese economic development, is in preparation. These works help to sketch the picture of the Western diplomatic and economic impact on China.

Inner Asia. The modern history of Inner Asia is surveyed in three works — a symposium by Owen Lattimore and others, *Pivot of Asia: Sinkiang and the Inner Asian Frontiers of China and Russia* (Boston: Little, Brown, 1950); Owen Lattimore, *Nationalism and Revolution in Mongolia* (Oxford University Press, 1955); and Tieh-tseng Li, *The Historical Status of Tibet* (King's Crown Press, Columbia University, 1956). Early Ch'ing relations with Tibet are also studied in interesting monographs by L. Petech, *China and Tibet in the Early 18th Century* (Leiden: Brill, 1950), and Schuyler Cammann, *Trade through the Himalayas: The Early British Attempts to Open Tibet* (Princeton: Princeton University Press, 1951).

Christian Missions. On the Christian colleges a useful series of preliminary factual narratives has been issued under the auspices of the

United Board for Christian Higher Education in Asia (formerly the United Board for Christian Colleges in China, at 150 Fifth Ave., New York 11, N. Y.): Roderick Scott, *Fukien Christian University* (1954); Charles H. Corbett, *Shantung Christian University (Cheeloo)* (1955); Mary Lamberton, *St. John's University, Shanghai, 1879–1951* (1955); Clarence B. Day, *Hangchow University* (1955); Mrs. L. Thurston and Ruth M. Chester, *Ginling College* (1955); L. E. Wallace, *Hwa Nan College, The Women's College of South China* (1956); and W. B. Nance, *Soochow University* (1956). John Leighton Stuart, *Fifty Years in China* (Random House, 1954), gives the reminiscences of a leading missionary administrator, particularly at Yenching University. The extensive literature in this field awaits further academic research.

The May Fourth Movement and the History of Chinese Communism. "May Fourth" is being built up by the Chinese Communists as a great turning point in history, at which they entered the scene. The term at least may be accepted as a useful over-all designation for the literary renaissance and *pai-hua* movement, and the ferment of ideas and politics generally, in the years around 1919. Wen-han Kiang, *The Chinese Student Movement* (King's Crown Press, 1948) gives a brief general survey with bibliography. John de Francis, *Nationalism and Language Reform in China* (Princeton: Princeton University Press, 1950) treats an important background aspect. Monlin Chiang, *Tides from the West* (New Haven: Yale University Press, 1947) presents the reminiscences of a former chancellor of Peking National University. A general study of the May Fourth Movement by Dr. Ts'e-tsung Chow will soon be published (Cambridge: Harvard University Press). A useful bibliographical survey of modern Chinese thought is by O. Brière, S. J., *Fifty Years of Chinese Philosophy 1898–1950* (London: Allen and Unwin, 1956). Modern Buddhism, inter alia, is surveyed by Professor Wing-tsit Chan, *Religious Trends in Modern China* (Columbia University Press, 1953).

On the early days of the Communist movement, Benjamin I. Schwartz, *Chinese Communism and the Rise of Mao* (Cambridge: Harvard University Press, 1951) is a major survey beginning with intellectual and ideological origins in the May Fourth period. Allen S. Whiting, *Soviet Policies in China 1917–1924* (Columbia University Press, 1954) deals with the various early Soviet approaches to China. Two invaluable collections of documents with historical narrative comments have recently appeared. Xenia J. Eudin and Robert C. North, *Soviet Russia and the East 1920–1927* (Stanford: Stanford University Press, 1957, publication no. 25 of the Hoover Library on War, Revolution and Peace) describes and documents the whole Soviet approach to Asia. Malcolm Kennedy, *A History of Communism in East Asia* (Praeger, 1957) gives a more superficial and popular account. The second recent collection is by C. Martin Wilbur and Julie Lienying Howe, who provide some 250 pages of factual narrative in addition to translated materials in *Documents on Communism, Nationalism, and Soviet Advisers in China 1918–1927* (Columbia University Press, 1956). The important early study of the KMT-CCP revolution and split of the 1920's by Harold Isaacs, *The Tragedy of the Chinese Revolution* has been reprinted, revised, by the Stanford University Press, 1951 (1938). A monograph by Conrad Brandt, *Stalin's Failure in China,* is being published for the Russian Research Center (Cambridge: Harvard University Press).

The first first-class report from the field in human terms on the Long March, guerrilla tactics, and the career of Mao Tse-tung was given in Edgar Snow's history-making volume, *Red Star over China* (Random House, 1938). His recent small volume, *Random Notes on Red China 1936–1945* (distributed by Harvard University Press, 1957) adds to the record of this period, as do two biographical works — Nym Wales (Helen Foster Snow), *Red Dust: Autobiographies of Chinese Communists* (Stanford: Stanford University Press, 1952) and R. S. Elegant, *China's Red Masters* (Twayne, 1951). A number of volumes by journalists — too many to note here — appeared in 1944 and later, after foreign contact was established with Yenan. Agnes Smedley's ardent *Battle Hymn of China* (Knopf, 1945) was based partly on experience in the field with the Communist New Fourth Army. The same author's posthumous volume, *The Great Road: The Life and Times of Chu Teh* (Monthly Review Press, 1956), is similarly ardent but is based particularly for its early chapters, on interviews with the Communist commander. An over-all survey of the growth of the Communist movement is given by Robert C. North, *Moscow and Chinese Communists* (Stanford: Stanford University Press, 1953). The same author's *Kuomintang and Chinese Communist Elites* (Stanford: Stanford University Press, 1952) is a socio-statistical study of personnel. The vicissitudes of the party line are traced and illustrated in Conrad Brandt, Benjamin Schwartz, and John K. Fairbank, *A Documentary History of Chinese Communism* (London: Allen and Unwin; Cambridge: Harvard University Press, 1952). Boyd Compton, *Mao's China: Party Reform Documents, 1942–44* (Seattle: University of Washington Press, 1952) describes the ideological rectification movement at Yenan. The official history of the CCP is provided by Hu Ch'iao-mu, *Thirty Years of the Communist Party of China* (Peking: Foreign Languages Press, 1951). A reinterpretation of Chinese modern history from the Communist viewpoint is given by Hu Sheng, *Imperialism and Chinese Politics* (Peking: Foreign Languages Press, 1955; first published in Chinese 1948).

Chiang Kai-shek and the Nationalist Government. An informed, critical survey of the Kuomintang government, its personalities, structure and functioning, is presented by Ch'ien Tuan-sheng, *The Government and Politics of China* (Cambridge: Harvard University Press, 1950) with a bibliography listing earlier studies such as those by Professor Paul M. A. Linebarger, particularly *The China of Chiang Kai-shek* (Boston: World Peace Foundation, 1941), and by L. K. Rosinger, *China's Wartime Politics 1937–1944* (Princeton: Princeton University Press, 1945) and others. A critical account by F. F. Liu, *A Military History of Modern China 1924–1949* (Princeton: Princeton University Press, 1956) opens up the whole subject of Nationalist military modernization.

Formal biographies of the Generalissimo have been mainly eulogies, like the authorized one by Hollington K. Tong, *Chiang Kai-shek, Soldier and Statesman* (2 volumes, Shanghai: China Publishing Co., 1937). Some 160 of his speeches and papers were translated in *The Collected Wartime Messages of Generalissimo Chiang Kai-shek 1937–1945* (John Day, 1946). But these public statements have less interest than his famous textbook written for Kuomintang indoctrination purposes in 1943, *China's Destiny*. Two competing English editions finally appeared in 1947, the authorized translation by Wang Chung-hui (Macmillan, 1947) and the unauthorized, with highly critical "notes and commentary," by Philip Jaffe (Roy Publishers, 1947). The two versions are equally adequate as translations; the latter adds to *China's Destiny* a shorter but illuminating work by Chiang called *Chinese Economic Theory*, not elsewhere available. One recent work is Emily Hahn, *Chiang Kai-shek: An Unauthorized Biography* (Doubleday, 1955). Chiang Chung-cheng (Chiang Kai-shek), *Soviet Russia in China: A Summing-up at Seventy* (Farrar, Straus and Cudahy, 1957) includes the Generalissimo's retrospect over 35 years.

On Japan's aggression in China, two contemporary narratives summarize the fateful decade 1931–1941 — T. A. Bisson, *Japan in China* (Macmillan, 1938) and Harold S. Quigley, *Far Eastern War, 1937–1941* (Boston: World Peace Foundation, 1942). The Sino-Japanese War has not received much Western monographic treatment. Japan's building of Manchukuo is surveyed in F. C. Jones, *Manchuria since 1931* (London: Royal Institute of International Affairs, 1949).

The national pride and plans of the Nanking Government are reflected in the *Chinese Year Book* (Shanghai: Commercial Press, 1936 *et seq.*). Its signed articles on cultural subjects do greater justice to the Chinese side of Modern China than the commercial data in the older British-edited *China Year Book* (London, Tientsin, and Shanghai: 1912 *et seq.*). For a picture of the structure and functioning of the government, see the *China Handbook: A Comprehensive Survey of Major Developments in China in Six Years of War, 1937–1943* (Macmillan,

1943). Revised editions of the *China Handbook* (published latterly by China Publishing Co., Taipei, Taiwan) continue to include a chronology and a who's who section.

Modern Economic Problems. After twenty-five years, one of the most penetrating and balanced brief surveys of the economic problems of China's peasant masses is still the work of a leading scholar of Western medieval economic history, R. H. Tawney, *Land and Labor in China* (Harcourt, Brace, 1932). After twenty years, a chief source of factual data about China's farm economy is still John Lossing Buck, *Land Utilization in China* (3 volumes, Chicago: University of Chicago Press, 1937), a pioneer survey conducted from the University of Nanking. Monographic study of Chinese agriculture is still scanty. T. H. Shen (Shen Tsung-han), *Agricultural Resources of China* (Ithaca: Cornell University Press, 1951) summarizes many of the quantitative estimates of careful research carried out under the Nationalist Government. Similarly the last pre-Communist estimate of mineral reserves was Juan, Vei Chow, "Mineral Resources of China," *Economic Geology* (volume XVI, number 4, June–July, 1946), based on wartime surveys. Sidney D. Gamble, *Ting Hsien: A North China Rural Community* (Institute of Pacific Relations, 1954) records pioneer work in rural reconstruction. Gerald F. Winfield, *China: The Land and the People* (Sloane Associates, 1948) surveys the Chinese subsistence problem, particularly from the view of a parasitologist.

The economic history of the pre-Communist era is just beginning to be studied. Yu-Kwei Cheng, *Foreign Trade and Industrial Development of China* (Wash., D. C.: University Press, 1956) surveys the republican period to 1948. Douglas Paauw has opened up the problems of Nanking Government economic policy and performance in two articles in a leading American academic journal (which was, however, unfortunately obliged to change its name in mid-career): "Chinese National Expenditures during the Nanking Period," *Far Eastern Quarterly,* vol. 12, no. 1 (November 1952), pp. 3–26; and "The Kuomintang and Economic Stagnation, 1928–37," *The Journal of Asian Studies (formerly the Far Eastern Quarterly)* vol. 16, no. 2 (February 1957), pp. 213–220.

Modern Literature. One neglected short-cut to understanding China lies in the numerous excellent translations now available. Standard translations of the famous pre-modern novels should now be in all libraries, particularly Pearl Buck, translator, *All Men Are Brothers* (John Day, 1933); Wang Chi-chen, translator, *Dream of the Red Chamber* (rev. ed., Twayne, 1958 [1929]); Clement Egerton, translator, *The Golden Lotus* (4 volumes, London: G. Routledge, 1939), or a somewhat expurgated edition with introduction by Arthur Waley, *Chin P'ing Mei* (G. P. Putnam's Sons, 1940); Wang Chi-chen, *Traditional Chinese Tales*

(Columbia University Press, 1943). Arthur Waley has recently published *Yuan Mei, Eighteenth Century Chinese Poet* (London: Allen and Unwin, 1956). A social satire of late Ch'ing times has been translated by Harold Shadick, *The Travels of Lao Ts'an* by Liu T'ieh-yün (Ithaca, New York: Cornell University Press, 1952).

On Chinese classical poetry, a timeless subject, recent additions are by the best-known of all translators, Arthur Waley, *The Life and Times of Po Chu-i, 772–846 A.D.* (Macmillan, 1949) and by William Hung, *Tu Fu, China's Greatest Poet* (Cambridge: Harvard University Press, 1952).

Readable collections of modern short stories include Edgar Snow, editor, *Living China: Modern Chinese Short Stories* (Reynal and Hitchcock, 1936); Wang Chi-chen, translator, *Ah Q and others: Selected Stories of Lusin* (Columbia University Press, 1941); the same, *Contemporary Chinese Stories* (Columbia University Press, 1944). Lau Shaw, *Rickshaw Boy* (Reynal and Hitchcock, 1945) had a deserved vogue in the United States; American readers intent on the boy-gets-girl theme were left happily unaware that the Chinese original ended in realistic tragedy. A novel of Peking under the Japanese, *The Yellow Storm* by the same author (Lao She, S. Y. Shu) has been translated by Ida Pruitt (Harcourt Brace, 1951). A commendable selection from both earlier and recent literature has been edited by George Kao under the formidable title of *Chinese Wit and Humor* (Coward-McCann, 1946).

After all the academic studies have been read and survived, the most direct approach to Modern China, for an American reader, is still through the writing of a few outstanding novelists and journalists. Pearl Buck's *The Good Earth* (John Day, 1931) and other novels and her autobiography (*My Several Worlds*, John Day, 1954) reflect the clash of new and old ways within Modern China as well as the reactions to it of a gifted American who grew up as the daughter of missionaries. Another best-seller, *Thunder Out of China* (Sloane Associates, 1946) by Theodore H. White and Annalee Jacoby, gives a vivid impression of Free China's wartime decline. Theodore H. White's best-seller novel, *The Mountain Road* (Sloane Associates, 1958) also portrays this period. *A Single Pebble* by John Hersey (Knopf, 1956) paints an unforgettable picture of life and labor in the Yangtze gorges.

3. AMERICAN POLICY

For the American citizen the chief policy problem is how to have a constructive and informed critical attitude toward our official policy as it develops from day to day. We should all no doubt be equally well informed, constructive, and critical concerning our European problems, domestic issues, missiles, atomic energy, and numerous other matters. How can we keep up with our China problem? This question must be answered, if we are not to give up democracy; and the answer plainly lies in occasional reading of background materials and a discriminating selection of current news sources.

American Relations with China. There is as yet no historical study of Sino-American relations as seen from the Chinese side. Our picture of this important subject is still largely a picture of Americans, painted by Americans, and designed for Americans.

The chief academic survey volumes are still those by Tyler Dennett, *Americans in Eastern Asia, A Critical Study of the Policy of the United States with reference to China, Japan and Korea in the 19th century* (Macmillan, 1922, reprinted: Barnes and Noble, 1941), which, although now ancient and superseded on many points, is based on a consecutive study of State Department archives up to 1900; and A. Whitney Griswold, *The Far Eastern Policy of the United States* (Harcourt, Brace, 1938), which pursues the subject from 1898 to 1938. Note that both these surveys of decades ago dealt with all the Far East. A brief readable narrative is by F. R. Dulles, *China and America: The Story of their Relations since 1784* (Princeton: Princeton University Press, 1946). The Western bibliography of Chinese foreign relations is well represented in the notes of Werner Levi, *Modern China's Foreign Policy* (Minneapolis: University of Minnesota Press, 1953). Comprehensive scholarly summaries are available in leading textbooks on American foreign relations, notably S. F. Bemis, *A Diplomatic History of the United States* (Holt, 4th edition 1955 [1936]) and T. A. Bailey, *A Diplomatic History of the American People* (Appleton-Century-Crofts, 5th edition, 1955). Harold R. Isaacs has appraised the variety of American impressions of "China" in a volume for the Center for International Studies at the Massachusetts Institute of Techonology, *Scratches on Our Minds: American Images of China and India* (John Day, 1958).

On successive phases of our China policy, a number of monographs have recently appeared, with much bibliographical detail on the American sources. W. W. Rockhill's career is briefly surveyed in P. A. Varg, *Open Door Diplomat* (Urbana: University of Illinois Press, 1952). C. S. Campbell, Jr., *Special Business Interests and the Open Door Policy* (New Haven: Yale University Press, 1951) explores one facet. Charles Vevier, *The United States and China 1906–1913: A Study of Finance and Diplomacy* (New Brunswick, N.J.: Rutgers University Press, 1955) deals only with the American side of the diplomatic story. Tien-yi Li, *Woodrow Wilson's China Policy 1913–1917* (Twayne, 1952) fits chronologically with Russell H. Fifield, *Woodrow Wilson and the Far East: The Diplomacy of the Shantung Question* (Crowell, 1952). Another useful chapter is added by John A. White, *The Siberian Intervention* (Princeton: Princeton University Press, 1950) and Betty M. Unterberger, *America's Siberian Expedition, 1918–1920* (Durham, N.C.: Duke University Press, 1956). Dorothy Borg, *American Policy and the Chinese Revolution 1925–1928* (American Institute of Pacific Relations and Macmillan, 1947) is one of the few thorough studies of the press and published documents bearing on policy formation. Sara M. Smith, *The Manchurian Crisis, 1931–1932* (Columbia University Press, 1948) studies a major turning point. Pauline Tompkins, *American-Russiun Relations in the Far East* (Macmillan, 1949) concerns both Siberia and Manchuria.

Memoirs of policy-makers include Henry L. Stimson and McGeorge Bundy, *On Active Service in Peace and War* (Harper, 1948) and Sumner Welles, *Seven Decisions that Shaped History* (Harper 1950). R. H. Ferrell, *American Diplomacy in the Great Depression. Hoover-Stimson Foreign Policy, 1929–1933* (New Haven: Yale University Press, 1957) concerns China inter alia. Allen S. Everest, *Morgenthau, the New Deal and Silver* (Columbia University, King's Crown Press, 1950), based on the Morgenthau diaries, includes a chapter on China and our silver policy, *ca.* 1934–1941.

Sino-American relations in the later 1930's are thus far little studied monographically but enter into the magistral volumes of W. L. Langer and S. E. Gleason, *The World Crisis and American Foreign Policy:* volume I, *The Challenge to Isolation 1937–1940,* volume II, *The Undeclared War 1940–41* (Harper and Brothers, 1952, 1953). Our traditional China policy is briefly but critically appraised in lectures by George F. Kennan, *American Diplomacy 1900–1950* (Chicago: University of Chicago Press, 1951; Mentor Books, 1952). W. R. Fishel summarizes one aspect of negotiations from the 1920's to 1943, *The End of Extraterritoriality in China* (Berkeley and Los Angeles: University of California Press, 1952).

On the course and content of unofficial relations there are a few books of special interest for themselves as good reading. Pearl Buck's *My Several Worlds* (John Day, 1954) has been mentioned. Carl Crow, *Four Hundred Million Customers* (Harper, 1937) gives the amusing reflections of a businessman confronting Chinese ways. The same author's *Foreign Devils in the Flowery Kingdom* (Harper, 1940) is an illuminating (not always reliable) retrospect on treaty port life. Graham Peck, *Two Kinds of Time* (Boston: Houghton Mifflin, 1950) is a reflective, sympathetic, non-ideological narrative of down-to-earth experience of Chinese life 1940–1947 — a book of literary merit which will one day be rediscovered. A more sociological study is by F. L. K. Hsü, *Americans and Chinese: Two Ways of Life* (H. Schuman, 1953).

On our relations with China in World War II the major study, from the State Department files, is by Herbert Feis, *The China Tangle: The American Effort in China from Pearl Harbor to the Marshall Mission* (Princeton: Princeton University Press, 1953). This balanced and lucid unraveling of complexities may be supplemented by the State Department's massive volume of once-secret documents, the so-called White Paper, *United States Relations with China, with Special Reference to the Period 1944–1949* (Washington, D.C.: The Department of State, 1949). A projected series of a dozen or more volumes of documents on China policy has begun with *Foreign Relations of the United States. Diplomatic Papers, 1942. China* (Washington, D.C.: United States Government Printing Office, 1956). Two volumes of official history have been ably and sympathetically produced by C. F. Romanus and R. Sunderland, *Stilwell's Mission to China* and *Stilwell's Command Problems* (Washington, D.C.: Department of the Army, 1953, 1956). To these may be added a salty diary, not intended for publication, Joseph W. Stilwell, *The Stilwell Papers,* edited by Theodore H. White (Sloane Associates, 1948) and another personal account, *Way of a Fighter: The Memoirs of Claire Lee Chennault, Major General, U.S. Army (Ret.)* (Putnam's, 1949).

The period of General Marshall's mediation in 1946–47 remains unstudied in a major volume although documentation is accumulating. An independent Chinese participant, leader of a minor party, Carsun Chang (Chang Chun-mai), has written a well-informed personal retrospect on the KMT–CCP problem, *The Third Force in China* (Bookman Associates, 1952). This period is also fitted judiciously into the general scene by H. M. Vinacke, *Far Eastern Politics in the Postwar Period* (Appleton-Century-Crofts, 1956).

On Formosa (Taiwan) there are several general works: J. W. Ballantine, *Formosa: a Problem for United States Foreign Policy* (Washington, D.C.: Brookings Institution, 1952), by a former officer of the State Department; H. M. Bate, *Report from Formosa* (London: Eyre and Spottiswoode, 1952); and F. W. Riggs, *Formosa under Chinese Nationalist Rule* (Macmillan, 1952). A special study is by George W. Barclay, *Colonial Development and Population in Taiwan* (Princeton: Princeton University Press, 1954). Among official reports the most interesting are from the Joint Commission on Rural Reconstruction. A history of its earlier work is in its *General Report* for October 1, 1948 to February 15, 1950 (Taipei, 1950).

The above references, though far from complete, are enough to make it evident that an American understanding of American-Chinese relations has not yet been worked out in serious research studies that attempt to deal with both sides, not just our side. The continued spate of learned lives of Confederate generals and similar increments to our self-knowledge does little to help us deal with the outer world, least of all in Asia. The American reading public have, so to speak, sat out the last decade of China's vast transformation, ignorant, impotent, and hence irresponsible concerning it. Meanwhile our role during a century of China's earlier modernization is maligned in Peking and unstudied in our schools.

4. COMMUNIST CHINA

Studies of the origins and rise of the Chinese Communist Party have been noted above. The extensive literature of the late 1940's, mainly based on foreign journalists' contact with Yenan from 1944, has not yet been winnowed by researchers, and is too extensive to be noted here. The latest work from this period, by Jack Belden, *China Shakes the World* (Harper, 1949) gave a vivid, idealized account of the people's revolutionary movement for "Liberation."

First-hand Impressions of Communist China. These raw materials for future historians display the full range to be expected of individual appraisals. Indeed the two extremes in this contemporary literature, works by enthusiasts for the ideals of a new day, on the one hand, and by horrified victims of revolutionary coercion, on the other, confront the reader with unresolved anomalies — no regime could be either so good or so bad, *over all,* as some observers' writings would suggest. All we can do here is select a few works which seem well based or representative of a certain type of experience or a certain period of time.

On the Communist take-over a small volume by Otto B. van der Sprenkel, Robert Guillain, and Michael Lindsay, *New China: Three Views* (London: Turnstile Press, 1950) gives the informed first-hand impressions in 1949 of a Sinologist, a journalist, and an economist, respectively. Derk Bodde, *Peking Diary. A Year of Revolution* (H. Schuman, 1950), by a leading American Sinologist who was in Peking before and after the take-over; and Lynn and Amos Landman, *Profile of Red China* (Simon and Schuster, 1951) by two American correspondents, mainly in Shanghai, reflect the initial sense of relief and the mixed impressions of the honeymoon period. Two books by Indian correspondents raise critical questions — Frank Moraes, *Report on Mao's China* (Macmillan, 1953) and Raja Hutheesing, *The Great Peace* (Harper, 1953). Liu Shaw-tong, *Out of Red China* (Duell, Sloane and Pearce, 1953) and Maria Yen, *The Umbrella Garden: A Picture of Student Life in Red China* (Macmillan, 1954), are two of the disillusioned writings by intellectuals who came out. Two other works, by a Protestant and a Catholic missionary, exemplify a large body of such writings: E. Olin Stockwell, *With God in Red China* (Harper,

1953) and Mark Tennien, *No Secret is Safe Behind the Bamboo Curtain* (Farrar, Straus and Young, 1952). A personal account by another victim, Harold W. Rigney, *Four Years in a Red Hell: the Story of Father Rigney* (Chicago: Regnery, 1956) is bitterly hostile. Allyn and Adele Rickett, *Prisoners of Liberation* (Cameron Associates, 1957) based on a similarly long incarceration, is comparatively sympathetic to the regime. All these witnesses testify sincerely and there are many more like them. They vary both in their respective experiences and in the criteria and assumptions in their own minds.

Among the more detached journalists, one of the most easy to read is a British correspondent, James Cameron, *Mandarin Red* (London: Michael Joseph, 1955); one of the most penetrating impressions is that of Robert Guillain, *600 Million Chinese* (Criterion, 1957).

Research Studies. The ardent but thus far ineffective effort of American policy, to bring Mao down by having nothing to do with him, has left us dependent for our first-hand view of Communist China, as of this writing, on the work of foreign journalists such as those noted above. Meanwhile, however, serious research studies have begun to appear in the United States. Yet researching a contemporary revolution from a distance, while no doubt safer, is subject to profound intellectual perils. It is like historical research without access to the original sources — certainty as to the real situation in men's minds is hard to attain. As a result, quantified economic studies, systematic descriptions of institutions and hopeful or dreadful general surveys are the chief products to emerge from researches outside the curtain. Each inquirer can get more or less the answer that his background or inclinations lead him to — that Communist China is the ancient empire in modern dress, or that, on the contrary, it is Soviet Russia over again; that conditions of life are on the whole promising, or on the whole menacing.

One of the most successful organized-from-a-distance general appraisals is by W. W. Rostow, with R. W. Hatch, F. A. Kierman, Jr., and A. Eckstein, *The Prospects for Communist China* (J. Wiley, 1954), which also has a 48-page bibliography of Western-language materials on Chinese Communism. A rather optimistic historian's view, *sub specie aeternitatis,* is thoughtfully presented in C. P. Fitzgerald, *Revolution in China* (Praeger, 1952), without, however, much attention to the new totalitarianism of Peking. A much more pessimistic and menacing picture-from-outside is assembled by Richard L. Walker, *China under Communism: The First Five Years* (New Haven: Yale University Press, 1955). Michael Lindsay, *China and the Cold War: A Study in International Politics* (Carlton, Victoria: Melbourne University Press, 1955) gives the criticisms of an English scholar who saw the Yenan period at first hand. The most recent surveys are by Peter S. H. Tang,

Communist China Today: Domestic and Foreign Policies (Praeger, 1957) and Ygael Gluckstein, *Mao's China* (Boston: Beacon Press, 1957). Needless to say, any attempt to characterize optimists and pessimists, critics and enthusiasts, as in the above, obliges the characterizer to try to sit precisely on that razor's edge where the truth is balanced. It is not a comfortable posture.

The Sino-Soviet relationship is appraised in a symposium by H. L. Boorman, A. Eckstein, P. E. Mosely, and B. Schwartz, *Moscow-Peking Axis: Strengths and Strains* (Harper and Brothers for the Council on Foreign Relations, 1957). Its historical background is surveyed by Aitchen K. Wu, *China and the Soviet Union* (John Day, 1950) and by Henry Wei, *China and Soviet Russia* (Van Nostrand, 1956). Both use Chinese as well as foreign sources, the former over a broader period; the latter with more bibliography. Tien-Fong Cheng, *A History of Sino-Russian Relations* (Washington, D.C.: Public Affairs Press, 1957), by a Kuomintang official, deals generally with the last four decades. A more concentrated scholarly study of Russia's postwar China policy is in Max Beloff, *Soviet Policy in the Far East, 1944–1951* (Oxford University Press, 1953).

The economy and its achievements have been treated critically by Yuan-li Wu, *An Economic Survey of Communist China* (Bookman Associates, 1956), and more optimistically by Solomon Adler, *The Chinese Economy* (Monthly Review Press, 1957). René Dumont, *Révolution dans les Campagnes Chinoises* (Paris: Editions du Seuil, 1957) gives the factual first-hand observations in 1955 of a trained agronomist who has studied Chinese and world agriculture over three decades. Another valuable professional estimate is the *Report of the Indian Delegation to China on Agricultural Planning and Techniques* (New Delhi: Government of India, Ministry of Food and Agriculture, 1956). Valuable documentation has been made available by Chao Kuo-chün, *Agrarian Policies of Mainland China: A Documentary Study (1949–1956)* and *Economic Organization and Planning in Mainland China: A Documentary Study (1949–1957)* (Cambridge: Harvard University Press, 1957 and 1958). Dr. Chao has done a considerable series of research studies on the mainland scene (see the Rostow volume, bibliography). The most careful economic estimates are in Alexander Eckstein, "Conditions and Prospects for Economic Growth in Communist China" (*World Politics,* volume 7, numbers 1–3, 1954–55) and in the same author's forthcoming study of China's national income in 1952–53. On the Chinese population, see the article by Irene B. Taeuber in the forthcoming volume edited by Eckstein and Fairbank, on Chinese economic development.

The political system has been studied by H. Arthur Steiner, S. B.

Thomas and others noted above. But, with some exceptions, Communist China, like Confucian China, remains impregnably beyond the grasp of American political science. Materials in translation come principally from the American Consulate General and others in Hong Kong.

Two scholarly articles deal with special topics, pending the publication of larger studies: Robert J. Lifton, "Thought Reform of Chinese Intellectuals: A Psychiatric Evaluation" (*Journal of Asian Studies,* volume 16, no. 1, November 1956); and David Nivison, "Communist Ethics and Chinese Tradition" (*ibid.*). The former makes a more careful scientific approach than Edward Hunter's sensational *Brainwashing. The Story of Men Who Defied It* (Farrar, Straus and Cudahy, 1956) and other works.

Chinese Communist Publications. These are numerous. The New China News Agency puts out informational fare in an English service. *People's China* and *China Reconstructs* are the principal English-language periodicals distributed from Peking for foreign consumption. An English edition of the *Selected Works of Mao Tse-tung* has been published in 4 volumes (London: Lawrence and Wishart, 1954–56), with volume 5 forthcoming to complete the set. Many official pronouncements appear in English pamphlets issued by the Foreign Languages Press in Peking.

Periodicals. The principal academic journals in the United States dealing with Chinese history are the *Journal of Asian Studies* (Donald Shively, editor, University of California at Berkeley) and the *Harvard Journal of Asiatic Studies* (Boylston Hall, Cambridge, Mass.). Asian problems receive increasing attention in many periodicals. Two which are specifically devoted to modern Asia are *Pacific Affairs* and *Far Eastern Survey,* both published by the Institute of Pacific Relations (333 Sixth Avenue, New York, N.Y.), which has led the way over three decades in fostering non-partisan research, discussion, and publication on the contemporary Far East.

INDEX

Abbreviations: CCP for Chinese Communist Party, KMT for Kuomintang

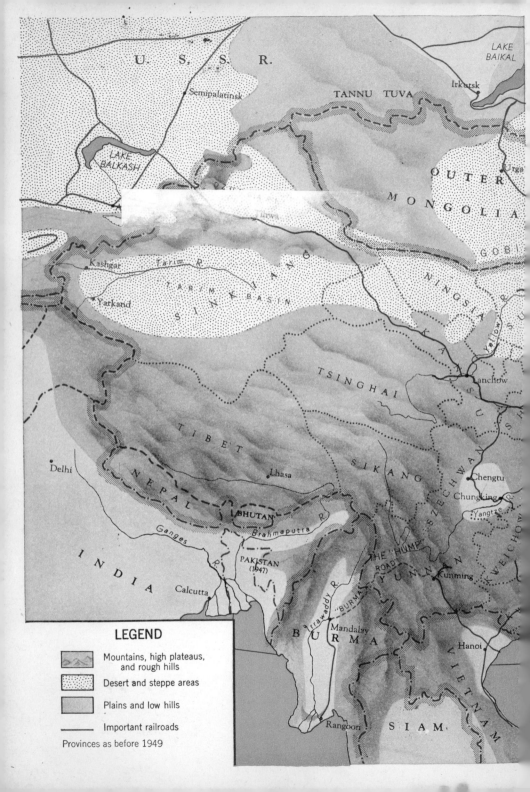

LEGEND

Mountains, high plateaus, and rough hills
Desert and steppe areas
Plains and low hills
Important railroads

Provinces as before 1949